A Defense for the Chronological Order of Luke's Gospel

Africanus Monograph Series

The *Africanus Monograph Series* is published by the Africanus Guild, based at Gordon-Conwell Theological Seminary's Boston campus, the Center for Urban Ministerial Education (CUME). Like the *Africanus Journal*, it strives to promote academic work by men and women that is globally evangelical in the historically orthodox, multiethnic, multicultural sense, with a commitment to biblical fidelity, in conversation with the realities of the world in which we live.

The journal is named in honor of Julius Africanus, a Christian scholar born around AD 200. He probably was born in Jerusalem; studied in Alexandria, Egypt; and later became bishop of Emmaus. He was considered by the ancients a man of consummate learning and sharpest judgment, a careful historian who sought to defend the truth of the Bible.

The journal may be read online at http://www.gordonconwell.edu/boston/africanusjournal.

The *Africanus Monograph Series* publishes academic dissertations and books by scholars who agree with its goals and have earned research degrees.

A Defense for the Chronological Order of Luke's Gospel

The Meaning of "Orderly" (*kathexēs*) Account in Luke 1:3

BENJAMIN WING WO FUNG

WIPF & STOCK · Eugene, Oregon

A DEFENSE FOR THE CHRONOLOGICAL ORDER OF LUKE'S GOSPEL
The Meaning of "Orderly" (*kathexēs*) Account in Luke 1:3

Africanus Monograph Series 3

Copyright © 2019 Benjamin Wing Wo Fung. All rights reserved. Except for brief quotations in critical publications or reviews, no part of this book may be reproduced in any manner without prior written permission from the publisher. Write: Permissions, Wipf and Stock Publishers, 199 W. 8th Ave., Suite 3, Eugene, OR 97401.

Wipf & Stock
An Imprint of Wipf and Stock Publishers
199 W. 8th Ave., Suite 3
Eugene, OR 97401

www.wipfandstock.com

PAPERBACK ISBN: 978-1-5326-5113-7
HARDCOVER ISBN: 978-1-5326-5114-4
EBOOK ISBN: 978-1-5326-5115-1

Manufactured in the U.S.A.

A Defense for the Chronological Order of Luke's Gospel

The Meaning of "Orderly" (*kathexēs*) Account in Luke 1:3

BENJAMIN WING WO FUNG

WIPF & STOCK · Eugene, Oregon

A DEFENSE FOR THE CHRONOLOGICAL ORDER OF LUKE'S GOSPEL
The Meaning of "Orderly" (*kathexēs*) Account in Luke 1:3

Africanus Monograph Series 3

Copyright © 2019 Benjamin Wing Wo Fung. All rights reserved. Except for brief quotations in critical publications or reviews, no part of this book may be reproduced in any manner without prior written permission from the publisher. Write: Permissions, Wipf and Stock Publishers, 199 W. 8th Ave., Suite 3, Eugene, OR 97401.

Wipf & Stock
An Imprint of Wipf and Stock Publishers
199 W. 8th Ave., Suite 3
Eugene, OR 97401

www.wipfandstock.com

PAPERBACK ISBN: 978-1-5326-5113-7
HARDCOVER ISBN: 978-1-5326-5114-4
EBOOK ISBN: 978-1-5326-5115-1

Manufactured in the U.S.A.

Abstract

Luke, in the preface of his gospel, says that he is going to write an "orderly" (καθεξῆς, Luke 1:3) account. However, scholars have no consensus on the writing order of Luke's gospel. As what kind of order Luke uses may affect the approach of study of his gospel, this thesis aims to ascertain Luke's writing order through the following objectives: (1) to analyze the different suggestions of "orderly" accounts by various scholars; (2) to conduct textual, grammatical and semantic studies of Luke's two prefaces; (3) to conduct a thorough word study for καθεξῆς, which includes a study of its etymology, its related words, and its contemporary Greek usages; (4) to analyze the narrative sequence in Luke's gospel and compare it with those of Matthew and Mark's; and (5) to analyze and evaluate the writing methodologies of Greco-Roman and Jewish historians and compared them with those in Luke's gospel.

Most scholars have reservations about the Gospel's order being strictly chronological. One of the major reasons is because when the content of the Gospel is compared with those of Matthew and Mark's, there are numerous unresolved problems regarding chronology which lead them to believe that καθεξῆς does not refer to chronological order, and some even believe that it does not mean any particular order at all. However, the findings of this thesis support the argument that Luke writes his gospel in strict chronological order. This conclusion is based on the following observations.

1. The contents of Luke's two prefaces indicate that the Gospel likely is written in such an order. Luke has probably adopted the common methodologies used by Greco-Roman and Jewish historians for writing prefaces when writing his two prefaces. Greco-Roman and Jewish historians, when writing their prefaces, usually indicate in their prefaces the writing order of their writings, and if it is not explicitly stated therein, they would write in chronological order. The word study of καθεξῆς reveals that it most likely means chronological order, but even if the research results are wrong and καθεξῆς does not indicate any writing order, according to the above-mentioned common practice that if the writing order is not explicitly stated in the preface, the writer would write in chronological order, Luke still probably writes in chronological order.

2. The narrative sequence in Luke's gospel indicates that the Gospel is likely written in strict chronological order. I have divided the Gospel into 110 narrative accounts, studied, compared them with their parallel accounts in the gospels of Matthew and Mark (if there is any) and categorized them. The investigation shows that Luke has separated his gospel into twelve sections by means of eleven summary account statements and has recorded them in overlapping chronological order, a practice commonly used by ancient historians such as the authors of the books in the Old Testament and Greco-Roman historians. Each of these statements includes a preview of the next section or an expansion of events in the current section which is not described either in the current or the next section, and the implied time frame of the preview or expansion overlaps with the time frame of the next section. However, the practice of overlapping account statements is merely a common writing technique in Luke's time and does not undermine Luke's intention to write in chronological order.

Furthermore, 99 of the 110 narrative accounts are observed to be written in chronological order. For the other 11 accounts, while Luke has not provided adequate temporal indicators to facilitate the determination of their order, and there is either no parallel account in Matthew and Mark or the information therein is inadequate to determine the writing order, there is no evidence to show that they are not written in such an order. For example, 9 out of the 11 accounts with writing order undetermined are found in section 9:52(b)-19:48, which records Jesus' last journey to Jerusalem. Because of the difficulty in ascertaining the writing order of these accounts, a chronological order for this section has been questioned by many scholars. However, my investigation results reveal that section 9:52(b)-19:48 shares similar writing style with sections 5:1–8:3 and 8:4–9:52(a), which are found to be written in chronological order. As a result, it is reasonable to believe that section 9:52(b)-19:48 is also written in chronological order. Moreover, the chronological order of 9:52(b)-19:48 seems to be supported by Jesus' route to Jerusalem in John chapters 7–12, which is believed by scholars such as Thomas and Gundry to be written in chronological order.

KEY TERMS

καθεξῆς, Luke, Acts, chronological, logical, writing order, Greco-Roman and Jewish historians, overlapping account statement

Contents

List of Tables | xvii
Preface | xix

Chapter 1: Overall Introduction | 1
    1.0 Background and Problem Statement   1
    1.1 The Aim and Objectives   22
        1.1.1 The Aim   2
        1.1.2 The Objectives   2
    1.2 Central Theoretical Argument   3
    1.3 Presuppositions and Methodology   3
        1.3.1 Presuppositions   3
        1.3.2 Methodology   5
    1.4 Outline of the Study   7

Chapter 2: Analysis of the Prefaces of Luke and Acts | 9
    2.0 Introduction   9
    2.1 Other Scholars' Opinions   12
    2.2 Thesis of this Chapter   16
    2.3 A Study of the Preface of the Gospel of Luke   17
        2.3.1 Textual Analysis   17

x   Contents

       2.3.2 Grammatical and Literary Analyses   19
       2.3.3 Analysis of the Writing Order of Greco-Roman Historians and Its Possible Impact on Luke's Writing Order   24
           2.3.3.1 Herodotus (*Persian Wars*)   25
           2.3.3.2 Thucydides (*The Peloponnesian War*)   25
           2.3.3.3 Xenophon (*Anabasis*)   25
           2.3.3.4 Polybius (*The Histories*)   26
           2.3.3.5 Pausanias (*Description of Greece*)   27
           2.3.3.6 Philostratus (*The Life of Apollonius of Tyana*)   28
           2.3.3.7 Josephus (*The Life*)   28
           2.3.3.8 Josephus (*Against Apion*)   28
           2.3.3.9 Josephus (*The Jewish War*)   29
           2.3.3.10 Eusebius (The Ecclesiastical History)   29
           2.3.3.11 Conclusion   30
       2.3.4 Preliminary Word Studies   31
       2.3.5 Summary   33
    2.4 A Study of the Preface of the Book of Acts   34
       2.4.1 Textual Analysis   35
       2.4.2 Literary Analysis   36
       2.4.3 Grammatical Analysis   43
       2.4.4 Conclusion   47
    2.5 A Study of Καθεξῆς   47
       2.5.1 A Study of the Usages of Καθεξῆς in the Bible   48
       2.5.2 A Study of the Etymology of Καθεξῆς   50
       2.5.3 A Study of the Words Related to Καθεξῆς   55
       2.5.4 A Study of the Meaning of Καθεξῆς in Contemporary Greek Usage   57
           2.5.4.1 References citied in BDAG, LSJ and pseudepigrapha   58
           2.5.4.2 Additional references cited in Thesaurus Linguae Graecae (TLG)   62
       2.5.5 Conclusion   64
    2.6 Summary of Chapter   65

Chapter 3: Analysis of Narrative Sequence in Luke's Gospel | 68
    3.0 Introduction   68
    3.1 Methodology Used   69

3.2 Other Scholars' Opinions on Luke's Writing Order 69
3.3 Narratives Study 70
    3.3.1 Luke 1:5–9:50—the Early Years of John the Baptist and Jesus, before Jesus Begins His Last Trip to Jerusalem 70
        3.3.1.1 The birth of John the Baptist foretold to Zechariah (1:5–25) 70
        3.3.1.2 Jesus' birth foretold to Mary (1:26–38) 71
        3.3.1.3 Mary's visit to Elizabeth, Elizabeth and Mary's songs (1:39–56) 71
        3.3.1.4 Birth of John the Baptist (1:57–80) 72
        3.3.1.5 Jesus' birth and the shepherds' encounter with the angels (2:1–20) 73
        3.3.1.6 Jesus' circumcision (2:21) 73
        3.3.1.7 Jesus is presented in the temple and receives the homage of Simeon and Anna, and the family returns to Nazareth (2:22–40) 74
        3.3.1.8 Jesus' Passover in Jerusalem as a child (2:41–52) 77
        3.3.1.9 The public ministry of John the Baptist (3:1–20) 78
        3.3.1.10 Jesus' baptism (3:21–23a) 79
        3.3.1.11 Jesus' ministry begins (3:23b–38) 80
        3.3.1.12 Jesus' temptation in the desert (4:1–15) 81
        3.3.1.13 Ministry and rejection at Nazareth in Galilee (4:16–30) 86
        3.3.1.14 Teaching in the synagogue of Capernaum (4:31–37) 87
        3.3.1.15 Healing of Peter's mother-in-law (4:38–39) 90
        3.3.1.16 Others healed (4:40–44) 91
        3.3.1.17 Calling of Peter (5:1–11) 94
        3.3.1.18 Cleansing a leper (5:12–16) 96
        3.3.1.19 Forgiving and healing of a paralytic (5:17–26) 97
        3.3.1.20 The calling of Matthew, the discussion of fasting and the parable about the old and the new (5:27–39) 98
        3.3.1.21 Controversy over disciples' picking grain on the Sabbath (6:1–5) 99
        3.3.1.22 Healing the man with a withered hand (6:6–11) 103
        3.3.1.23 The choosing of the twelve (6:12–16) 103
        3.3.1.24 Sermon on the plain (6:17–49) 104

- 3.3.1.25 Healing the centurion's servant (7:1–10)   105
- 3.3.1.26 Raising a widow's son at Nain of Galilee (7:11–17)   105
- 3.3.1.27 Question from John the Baptist (7:18–35)   106
- 3.3.1.28 Christ's feet anointed (7:36–50)   107
- 3.3.1.29 Jesus preaches in various cities and villages (8:1–3)   108
- 3.3.1.30 The parable of the soils (8:4–18)   109
- 3.3.1.31 Announcement of a new spiritual kinship (8:19–21)   111
- 3.3.1.32 Crossing the lake and calming the storm (8:22–25)   116
- 3.3.1.33 Healing the Gerasene demoniacs and resultant opposition (8:26–39)   117
- 3.3.1.34 Return to Galilee, healing of woman who touches Jesus' garment, and raising of Jairus' daughter (8:40–56)   118
- 3.3.1.35 Commissioning of the twelve (9:1–6)   119
- 3.3.1.36 Herod Antipas hears about Jesus (9:7–9)   119
- 3.3.1.37 Withdrawal to Bethsaida and feeding the five thousand (9:10–17)   121
- 3.3.1.38 Peter's identification of Jesus as Christ, Jesus' first explicit prediction of rejection, crucifixtion, and resurrection, and Jesus' teaching about following him, his second coming, and judgment (9:18–27)   122
- 3.3.1.39 Transfiguration of Jesus (9:28–36)   123
- 3.3.1.40 Healing of demoniac boy and unbelief rebuked (9:37–43a)   124
- 3.3.1.41 Jesus' second prediction of his death and resurrection (9:43b–45)   124
- 3.3.1.42 Rivalry over greatness in the kingdom (9:46–48)   125
- 3.3.1.43 Apostle John's question (9:49–50)   125
- 3.3.1.44 Summary of 1:5–9:50   126
- 3.3.2 Luke 9:51–19:44 – Jesus' Last Trip to Jerusalem   129
    - 3.3.2.1 Journey through Samaria (9:51–56)   136
    - 3.3.2.2 Complete commitment required of followers (9:57–62)   137

3.3.2.3 Commissioning of the seventy-two (10:1–16)   137
3.3.2.4 Return of the seventy-two (10:17–24)   138
3.3.2.5 Story of the good Samaritan (10:25–37)   138
3.3.2.6 Jesus' visit with Mary and Martha (10:38–42)   139
3.3.2.7 Lesson on how to pray and parable of the bold friend (11:1–13)   139
3.3.2.8 Blasphemous accusation and debate (11:14–36)   140
3.3.2.9 Woes against the Pharisees and teachers of law while eating with a Pharisee (11:37–54)   142
3.3.2.10 Warning the disciples about hypocrisy (12:1–12)   142
3.3.2.11 Warning about greed and trust in wealth, the coming of the Son of Man, and the coming division (12:13–59)   144
3.3.2.12 Two alternatives: repent or perish (13:1–9)   144
3.3.2.13 Opposition from a synagogue ruler for healing a woman on the Sabbath (13:10–21)   145
3.3.2.14 Question about salvation and entering the kingdom (13:22–30)   145
3.3.2.15 Anticipation of Jesus' coming death and his sorrow over Jerusalem (13:31–35)   146
3.3.2.16 Healing of a man with dropsy while Jesus is eating with a prominent Pharisee on the Sabbath, and three parables suggested by the occasion (14:1–24)   146
3.3.2.17 Cost of discipleship (14:25–35)   146
3.3.2.18 Parables in defense of association with sinners (15:1–32)   147
3.3.2.19 Parable teaching the proper use of money (16:1–13)   147
3.3.2.20 Story teaching the danger of wealth (16:14–31)   148
3.3.2.21 Four lessons on discipleship (17:1–10)   150
3.3.2.22 Jesus' healing of ten lepers while passing between Samaria and Galilee (17:11–21)   151
3.3.2.23 Instructions regarding the Son of Man's coming (17:22–37)   151
3.3.2.24 Parables on prayer: the persistent widow, and the Pharisee and the tax collector (18:1–14)   152
3.3.2.25 Example of little children in relation to the kingdom (18:15–17)   153

xiv CONTENTS

- 3.3.2.26 Riches and the kingdom (18:18–30) 153
- 3.3.2.27 Third prediction of Jesus' death and resurrection (18:31–34) 154
- 3.3.2.28 Healing of blind Bartimaeus and his companion (18:35–43) 155
- 3.3.2.29 Salvation of Zaccheus (19:1–10) 157
- 3.3.2.30 Parable to teach responsibility while the kingdom is delayed (19:11–28) 157
- 3.3.2.31 Triumphal entry into Jerusalem (19:29–44) 158
- 3.3.2.32 Cleansing of the temple (19:45–48) 159
- 3.3.2.33 Summary of 9:51–19:48 160
- 3.3.3 Luke 20:1–24:53—Jesus' Last Days in Jerusalem, His Passion and Resurrection 163
  - 3.3.3.1 Questioning of Jesus' authority by the chief priests, teachers of the law and elders (20:1–8) 164
  - 3.3.3.2 Jesus' parable of the bad tenants of a vineyard (20:9–19) 165
  - 3.3.3.3 Attempts by Pharisees and Herodians to trap Jesus with a question about paying taxes to Caesar (20:20–26) 166
  - 3.3.3.4 Sadduccees' puzzling question about the resurrection (20:27–40) 168
  - 3.3.3.5 Christ's relationship to David as Son and Lord (20:41–44) 168
  - 3.3.3.6 Beware of the teachers of the Law (20:45–47) 170
  - 3.3.3.7 A poor widow's gift of all she had (21:1–4) 170
  - 3.3.3.8 The Olivet discourse about the temple and Jesus' second coming (21:5–36) 171
  - 3.3.3.9 Jesus' last days in Jerusalem and the plot by the Sanhedrin to arrest and kill him (21:37–22:2) 172
  - 3.3.3.10 Judas' agreement to betray Jesus (22:3–6) 172
  - 3.3.3.11 Preparation for the Passover meal (22:7–13) 174
  - 3.3.3.12 The Passover meal (22:14–38) 174
  - 3.3.3.13 Jesus' three agonized prayers in Gethsemane (22:39–46) 178
  - 3.3.3.14 Jesus betrayed, arrested and forsaken (22:47–53) 178

3.3.3.15 Jesus' trial (22:54–23:25)   179
3.3.3.16 Journey to Golgotha (23:26–33a)   183
3.3.3.17 First three hours of crucifixion (23:33b–43)   183
3.3.3.18 Last three hours of crucifixion (23:44–46)   184
3.3.3.19 Witnesses of Jesus' death (23:47–49)   184
3.3.3.20 Procurement of Jesus' body (23:50–52)   185
3.3.3.21 Jesus' body placed in a tomb (23:53–54)   185
3.3.3.22 The tomb watched by the women and guarded by Soldiers (23:55–56)   185
3.3.3.23 The tomb found empty by the women (24:1–8)   186
3.3.3.24 The tomb found empty by Peter and John (24:9–12)   186
3.3.3.25 Jesus appears to the two disciples traveling to Emmaus (24:13–35)   187
3.3.3.26 Jesus appears to the assembled disciples in Jerusalem (24:36–49)   188
3.3.3.27 Christ's parting blessing and departure (24:50–53)   190
3.3.3.28 Summary of 20:1–24:53   190
3.4 Conclusion   191

Chapter 4: A Study of Overlapping Summary Statements in Greco-Roman Historian Writings | 195
4.0 Introduction   195
4.1 Methodology   196
4.2 Other Scholars' Opinions on the Writing Technique of Summary Statements   197
4.3 A Study of the Greco-Roman Historian Writings   199
   4.3.1 Thucydides—*The Peloponnesian War*   199
   4.3.2 Xenophon—*Anabasis*   200
   4.3.3 Polybius—*The Histories*   202
   4.3.4 Pausanias—*Description of Greece*   206
   4.3.5 Philostratus—*The Life of Apollonius of Tyana*   207
   4.3.6 Josephus—*The Jewish War*   209
   4.3.7 Eusebius—*The Ecclesiastical History*   210
4.4 Conclusion   213

Chapter 5: Conclusion | 218
    5.0 Summary of Findings   218
    5.1 Theological Reflection   222

Annexures
    2.1 Sentence Flow and Translation of Luke 1:1–4   225
    2.2 Analysis of the Components Used by Greco-Roman Historians in the Prefaces of their First Books   226
    2.3 Textual Analysis for the Preface of the Book of Acts   234
    2.4 Sentence Flow and Translation of Acts 1:1–5   237
    2.5 Comparison of Acts 1:1–5 with the Gospel of Luke   239
    2.6 Categorization of the Meanings of Καθεξῆς Found in the N.T., the Septuagint, and Contemporary Usages   242
    2.7 Categorization of the Meanings of Εξῆς Found in the N.T. and the Septuagint   245
    3.1 Harmony of the Narrative Accounts in the Synoptic Gospels   247

Bibliography   271
Index   281

Tables

1. First category of scholarly opinions about καθεξῆς /writing order: some literary order appropriate to the Gospel of Luke | 13
2. Second category of scholarly opinions about καθεξῆς /writing order: broadly chronological | 14
3. Third category of scholarly opinions about καθεξῆς /writing order: salvation-historical | 14
4. Fourth category of scholarly opinions about καθεξῆς /writing order: logical | 15
5. Fifth category of scholarly opinions about καθεξῆς /writing order: does not indicate order | 15
6. My translation of Luke 1:1–4 from the original Greek text | 18
7. The four elements Luke includes in the preface of his Gospel | 21
8. My translation of Acts 1:1–5 from the original Greek text | 35
9. Comparison of Matthew 9:36–10:16, Luke 9:1–6; 10:1–12 and Mark 6:7–13 | 89
10. Narrative accounts inserted between Matthew 9:9–17 and 12:1–8 | 102
11. Analysis of accounts in Matthew and Mark which Luke has and that come immediately before the parable of soils in Luke | 110

12. Comparison of the sequences of "parable of the soils" and "new spiritual kinship" in the synoptic gospels | 111

13. Estimated time of Jesus' activities in Matthew 12:15–13:52 and Mark 3:20–4:41 | 113

14. Narrative accounts inserted between Matthew 10:1–11:1 and 14:1–2 | 120

15. Comparison of the sequences of "Herod Antipas hears about Jesus," "withdrawal to Bethsaida," and "feeding the five thousand" in the synoptic gospels | 122

16. Narrative accounts inserted by Matthew and Mark between Matthew 14:31–21/Mark 6:30–44 and Matthew 16:13–28/Mark 8:27–9:1 | 123

17. Analysis of the narrative accounts in Luke 1:5–9:50 | 126

18. Comparison of the sequences of "healing of the blind man" and "triumphal entry into Jerusalem" in the synoptic gospels | 159

19. Analysis of the narrative accounts in Luke 1:5–19:48 | 160

20. Comparison of the sequences of "a small gift of all she had" and "the Olivet discourse about the temple and Jesus' second coming" in Luke and Mark | 171

21. Events during the Passover meal and before Jesus reaches Gethsemane | 175

22. Events during Jesus' trial | 179

23. Analysis of the narrative accounts in Luke 1:5–24:53 | 192

24. An overview of the study of overlapping statements in Greco-Roman historian writings | 214

Preface

I ALWAYS LOVE TO study the narrative accounts in the Bible. It has been a great privilege for me to spend a number of years in this activity; especially in studying the books which I love the most, the gospels. I would like to extend my heartfelt thanks to Dr. Francois Viljeon. He empathized with my family situation (my daughter was found to have special needs and requires constant intensive care, and my family had experienced a number of deaths when I was working on my chapters three and four) and was willing to extend my program in a significant way, without which this thesis would not be completed. His comments from time to time have inspired me and enabled me to strive for higher academic standards.

Dr. Aída Besançon Spencer and her husband, Dr. William David Spencer (Bill), are the first ones to put the thought of pursuing a doctorate degree into my mind. They enrolled me into the Africanus Guild doctoral support program which had provided me with the opportunity to teach Greek Head Start course and New Testament Survey course at Gordon-Conwell Theological seminary in the years 2008–9. Aida is more than a supervising professor to me. She and Bill have mentored me in many different ways, both academically and spiritually, when I ministered with them at Pilgrim Church between year 2003 and 2010. Their encouragement to me and their model as servants of God have greatly impacted me in various ways.

Dr. Catherine Kroeger has named my daughter Theodora and has given me a lot of insights in my study of Greco-Roman historians. I am very thankful to have learned under her in a number of couses before her passing. I am also indebted to Dr. Sean McDonough for his feedback on my chapter two. I am also grateful to Mary Riso and Kris Johnson who have carefully proofread the manuscript.

Scarlet, my beautiful wife and lifelong love who has a very different character from me, is always an inspiration. Although I have spent substantial amount of my time attending to my daughter's special needs, she is a constant delight to me and I am very thankful to have her in my life. I am eternally grateful to my late parents, who had supported me in various ways in this project. And I would like to express my sincere thanks to my dear Lord, the risen King, who has raised me up and sustained me in difficult times, and taught me how to endure and wait for Him in life.

Chapter 1

Overall Introduction

1.0 BACKGROUND AND PROBLEM STATEMENT

LUKE, IN THE PREFACE of his gospel mentions that he is writing his narrative as "an orderly account" (καθεξῆς—1:3b).[1] However, scholars have been unclear and have no consensus about the kind of order he is seeking.[2] Hence the question of order has become one of the controversial issues in the study of the Gospel of Luke. Luke's writing order is important for understanding the Gospel, as what kind of order Luke uses may affect the approach of the study of his Gospel. If the Gospel is written in chronological order, a study of the chronology therein may be important to understanding the Gospel as a whole. Moreover, in order to study a particular narrative account, attention may have to be paid also to the previous narrative accounts since these accounts may provide additional background information, particularly regarding the timing of the events. But if the Gospel is written in a logical order instead of a

---

1. All the translations in this chapter are my own translations from texts in the original languages, unless otherwise stated.

2. A brief review of the scholars' opinions on the meaning of καθεξῆς is conducted in 2.1. Out of the opinions of twenty-four scholars there are at least five different categories of view: some believe that it means some literary order appropriate to the Gospel of Luke; some think that it indicates a "broadly chronological" order; some opine that it refers to a salvation-historical order, and may also refer to a geographical order at the same time; some argue that it only means a certain logical order, and some comment that it does not indicate any order at all. Please refer 2.1 for a detailed discussion on this subject.

chronological order, a study of the logic Luke uses for the book may be the key to understanding the Gospel as a whole, and to study a particular narrative account we may have to study the reason why Luke places that account in that particular position in his Gospel and what relevance that account has in regards to Luke's overall logic. Since different beliefs in the writing order may result in different study approaches which may in turn affect the overall understanding of the Gospel and the individual narrative accounts, a study of the particular writing order Luke chose to use for his Gospel seems important. What is Luke's writing order for his gospel? In order to answer this research question, this thesis will address the following problems:

1. What scholars have suggested is the significance of an "orderly" account when referring to the prefaces of the Gospel of Luke and the Book of Acts and as they study the narrative sequences?
2. Does the textual and grammatical study of Luke's two prefaces shed light on Luke's writing order?
3. Does a study of καθεξῆς in Luke 1:3b shed light on Luke's writing order?
4. Does a study of narrative sequence in Luke's gospel shed light on his writing order?
5. Does a study of writing methodologies of Greco-Roman and Jewish historians shed light on Luke's writing order?
6. What are the academic and ecclesial implications of the study?

1.1 THE AIM AND OBJECTIVES

1.1.1 The Aim

The aim of this research is to ascertain Luke's writing order for his gospel by analyzing the writing methodologies of other ancient Greek, Roman and Jewish historians and investigate how these methodologies possibly impact Luke's technique of sequencing events.

1.1.2 The Objectives

In order to reach the aim, the following objectives will have to be attained:

1. To analyze and evaluate the different suggestions of "orderly" account by various scholars

2. To conduct textual, grammatical and semantic studies of Luke's two prefaces
3. To conduct a thorough word study for καθεξῆς in Luke 1:3
4. To analyze the narrative sequence in Luke's Gospel
5. To analyze and evaluate the writing methodologies of Greco-Roman and Jewish historians as compared and contrasted with Luke's gospel
6. To evaluate the academic and ecclesial implications of this study

1.2 CENTRAL THEORETICAL ARGUMENT

The central theoretical argument is that καθεξῆς in Luke 1:3b most likely refers to chronological order, and Luke has written his gospel in this order, though Luke also likely promotes an overall thematic purpose to strengthen Theophilus' faith based on the truthfulness of Jesus' humanity and his role as the Son of Man.

1.3 PRESUPPOSITIONS AND METHODOLOGY

1.3.1 Presuppositions

This thesis adopts the perspective of the Reformed tradition and its emphasis will be placed on the Bible as a primary source document. This research will presuppose an authoritative and historically reliable biblical text. In the past two hundred years, numerous scholars began to question the historical reliability of the Bible. For example, according to Norman Geisler (1999:86-91), Johann Christian Konrad von Hofmann opines that certain parts of the biblical history may not be literally true; Martin Dibelius (2004:5, 8) and Rudolph Bultmann (1962:20) believe that the evangelists arranged the oral tradition and created artificial contexts to serve their own purposes. Redaction critics favor a view that the biblical books are written much later than and by different authors from, what the early church tradition describes,[3] and as a result of the alleged late completion dates the information therein may be distorted during transmission and may not be historically accurate.

---

3. For example, Eusebius 3.24.6–7 describes that the synoptic gospels are completed and are distributed to all including the Apostle John, and that he has the chance to read and testify their truth; indicating that the synoptic gospels are completed at a time when many eye-witnesses of Jesus are still alive, conflicting the argument of the redaction critics that they are completed at much later dates where information therein may be distorted.

4 A Defense for the Chronological Order of Luke's Gospel

Regarding these negative views about historical reliability of the Bible, Craig Blomberg gives some key counter-arguments. When responding to the allegation that the gospels cannot be trusted because the text has been greatly corrupted, Blomberg (1992:292) counters that "textual critics have been able to reconstruct a highly reliable prototype of what the original Gospel writers undoubtedly wrote," considering the voluminous manuscripts and fragments[4] which survive from the earliest centuries of the Christian church. Geisler (1999:532) also supports this view. Concerning the debate about whether the gospels preserve Jesus' actual teachings and deeds, Blomberg (1992:294) believes that the gospels truthfully record what Jesus teaches and conducts, because "Jesus was perceived by his followers as one who proclaimed God's Word in a way which demanded careful retelling . . . the almost universal method of education in antiquity, and especially in Israel, was rote memorization, which enabled people accurately to recount quantities of material far greater than all of the Gospels put together . . . (and) the lack of teachings ascribed to Jesus about later church controversies (e.g., circumcision, speaking in tongues) suggests that the disciples did not freely invent material and read it back onto the lips of Jesus." Moreover, Donald Guthrie (1996:24–26) also concludes that "by the end of the second century it is clear from all the evidence available that our four gospels were accepted, not only as authentic, but also as Scripture on a level with the Old Testament," and he quotes extensively from various early church fathers such as Irenaeus, Tertullian, Justin Martyr and Papias to substantiate his claim. With regards to the argument that miracles and supernatural events in the gospels may not be literally true, Blomberg (1992:296–297) thinks that "for many readers the historicity of the Gospels is called into question simply because they are filled with miracle stories about the supernatural deeds of Christ . . . (but) if there is a theistic God such as the Judeo-Christian tradition has affirmed, miracles are a natural corollary of his existence. Whether or not such a God exists cannot be determined by science . . . " This thesis supports the above-mentioned views of Blomberg, Geisler and Guthrie.

Other presuppositions of this study are as follows. First, I agree with many scholars (e.g., Bock [2004, vol.1: 4–7], Marshall [1978:33–35] and Garland [2011:21–24]) that Luke, a close travel companion of the Apostle Paul, is the author of the Gospel; and his relationship with the Apostle Paul and other eye-witnesses in Jesus' time enable him to write a reliable record about Jesus. Second, I concur with scholars such as Stein (1992:26) and Nolland

---

4. J. Hernández Jr (2013:959) indicates that there are "over 5,800 Greek manuscripts of the NT currently exist (nearly 2,400 of them Gospels)."

(2002:10) that Theophilus, the recipient of the Gospel, is not a metaphorical or a fictional name, but a real person with an honorable social status at that time. I agree with scholars such as Stein (1992:26–27) who concludes that Theophilus is likely a Gentile instead of a Jew. For example, Stein comments that Luke gives explanations to some Jewish festivals in the Gospel (22:1, 7) and extends Jesus' genealogy back past Abraham to Adam (3:23–38). Luke does not need to do so if Theophilus was a Jew. Third, Luke 1:4 appears to indicate that Theophilus is a new believer or a God-fearer and Luke is writing to assure him of the certainty of what he has learnt. Moreover, Luke 1:4 likely indicates that Theophilus is a new believer or a God-fearer and Luke is writing to assure him of the certainty of what he has learnt. Fourth, similar to Spencer (2007), I support a composition date of the Gospel in the early 60's, based on the logic that the last event Luke records in the Book of Acts, Paul's unhindered preaching of the gospel at Rome, probably happens before the nationwide persecution of Christians which begins after the fire in Rome under Nero's reign in A.D. 64.

1.3.2 Methodology

To ascertain Luke's writing order and to answer the questions raised in 1.0, the following steps will be conducted in this thesis:

1. An introduction and evaluative analysis of the various scholarly opinions as to what does Luke mean when he uses καθεξῆς in the introduction of his Gospel through a study of various commentaries and articles (chapter 2).

2. A textual and grammatical analysis of Luke's prefaces will mainly follow the methodologies suggested in Gordon Fee's *New Testament Exegesis* (Fee, 2002) and A.T. Robertson's *A Grammar of the Greek New Testament in the Light of Historical Research* (Robertson, 1934): to analyze all the significant textual variants to establish the original Greek text; to conduct sentence flows to understand the structure of the pericopes; to pay particular attention to sentence order, word order, use of adverbs, verbs and participles to understand what the author's emphases are. A preliminary study of key words in the prefaces in their contexts will also be conducted (chapter 2).

3. A semantic study of καθεξῆς in Luke 1:3b will follow the methodologies suggested in Gordon Fee's *New Testament Exegesis* (Fee, 2002) and Moisés Silva's *Biblical Words and Their Meanings: An Introduction to Lexical Semantics* (Silva, 1983) which will involve a study of all the

usages of καθεξῆς in the New Testament Greek Bible,[5] the etymology of the word, all related words which share the same roots with καθεξῆς, and its contemporary Greek usages (chapter 2).

4. A study of the narrative sequence of individual story accounts in the Gospel to ascertain the time sequence of each account. The study will make reference to the chronology suggested in Robert Thomas and Stanley Gundry's *The NIV Harmony of the Gospels* (Thomas and Gundry, 1988) and will include the following steps:

   a. Divide the Gospel into separate story accounts with reference to *The NIV Harmony of the Gospels* (Thomas and Gundry, 1988) (chapter 3).

   b. Categorize the story accounts into the following categories (chapter 3).

      i. Category 1—there is (are) explicit or implicit indication(s) of time and/or writing order in Luke's narrative account which help(s) us determine the writing order of the account.

      ii. Category 2—there is no explicit or implicit indication of time and/or writing order in Luke's narrative account, but there is (are) explicit or implicit indication(s) of time and/or writing order in its parallel account(s) in other synoptic gospel(s) which help(s) us determine the writing order of the account.

      iii. Category 3—there is no explicit or implicit indication of time and/or writing order in Luke's narrative account or in its parallel account(s) in other synoptic gospel(s), or the indication(s) of time and/or writing order is (are) not sufficient for us to determine the writing order of the account, and as a result the writing order of the account cannot be ascertained.

   c. From the study of the narrative accounts in the gospel of Luke, identify the methodologies and techniques Luke employs for his writing order (chapter 3).

5. For the study of the writing methodologies of various Greco-Roman and Jewish historians, a historical-literary study of the writings of various historians such as Herodotus, Thucydides, Polybius, Philostratus, Josephus, and Eusebius will be conducted. I will focus on understanding what writing methods and techniques they have commonly used in writing histories, in particular those related to writing order (chapters 2, 3, and 4).

---

5. There is no usage of καθεξῆς in the Septuagint.

6. Based on the research finding I will evaluate academic and posit ecclesial implications of this study (chapter 5).

1.4 OUTLINE OF THE STUDY

I. Introduction

   A. Preview of study

   B. Gospel of Luke—presentation of basis for authorship of Luke and historical context of Luke

II. Prefaces of Luke and Acts as bases of understanding the order of the Gospel of Luke

   A. Presentation of various scholarly approaches to the order of the Gospel of Luke

   B. Analysis of the textual apparatus of the prefaces, especially those which may affect the interpretation

   C. Grammatical and semantic analysis of words in the preface of the Gospel of Luke that may affect understanding of Luke's methodology (two adverbs ἄνωθεν and ἀκριβῶς and the adverbial participle παρηκολουθηκότι in Luke 1:3)

   D. Grammatical and semantic analysis of words in the preface of the Book of Acts that may affect understanding of Luke's methodology in the Gospel (ἀποστόλοις in Acts 1:2 and ἐπαγγελίαν in Acts 1:4)

   E. A semantic study of καθεξῆς and its root components in the New Testament and in contemporary writings. Καθεξῆς may indicate sequences of time, space and hierarchy of significance.

III. An analysis of the narrative sequence of all individual accounts in the Gospel of Luke, especially in light of Lucian's suggestion that upon finishing the first topic, historians should introduce the second topic in a way that "the first and the second topics must not merely be neighbors but have common matter and overlap" (Lucian, 1999:67) and other historiographers' techniques. Luke's use of chronology will also be compared to Luke's thematic purposes and summary in Acts 1:1–11.

IV. A study of the writings of the Greco-Roman and Jewish historians to ascertain the methodologies used to develop the order of events in their writings (e.g. Herodotus, Thucydides, Xenophon, Polybius, Pausanias, Philostratus, Josephus and Eusebius). Their approaches will be compared to Luke's.

8 A Defense for the Chronological Order of Luke's Gospel

    V. Conclusion: some academic and ecclesial implications of the study will be suggested.

    VI. Bibliography

In the next chapter I will conduct a thorough analysis of Luke's two prefaces.

Chapter 2

Analysis of the Prefaces of Luke and Acts

2.0 INTRODUCTION

OUR OBJECTIVE OF THIS chapter is to ascertain what order Luke uses for his Gospel as indicated by the prefaces of the Gospel and Acts. The reason the two prefaces are considered a crucial element in Luke's order is threefold: (1) A comparison between Luke's prefaces and those written by Greco-Roman historians may shed light on Luke's order. Many believe that Luke writes as a historian. As there is no indexing system used in ancient writing, it is quite common for Greco-Roman historians to communicate the order of their writings to their readers through the preface so that their readers will know at the outset how the contents will be organized (see subsection 2.3.3 for the discussion of the writing order of Greco-Roman histories). Therefore, a comparison of Luke's prefaces with those written by other Greco-Roman historians may give insights into Luke's order. (2) Luke has mentioned his research and writing methodologies in the preface of his Gospel ("just as those who are from the beginning eyewitnesses and servants of the Word have delivered to us, it seemed best also to me, after having followed from the beginning in all things carefully, to write to you in an orderly account" [1:2 to 1:3a][6]); thus, a study of Luke's methodologies, particularly on the meaning of καθεξῆς ("in an orderly account") seems important for under-

---

6. This is my own translation from Greek. Please see subsection 2.3.1.

standing his writing order. (3) A substantial part of the preface of the Book of Acts refers to what Luke has written in his Gospel and serves as a summary of it. A study of the preface in the Book of Acts and a comparison of it with the prefaces for sequels written by Greco-Roman historians may give us hints for the order of the Gospel.

In this chapter, I will first discuss various scholars' opinions about the order of the Gospel; I will summarize them into several categories (section 2.1), and then I will give my own tentative view on Luke's writing order and my reasons for supporting it (section 2.2). After a brief introduction of different scholars' opinions and an introduction to my view, the research in this chapter will focus on three major parts. First, I will conduct a thorough analysis of the preface of the Gospel (1:1–4) (section 2.3). This analysis will include: (1) a study of all the textual variants (subsection 2.3.1) in order to establish the original Greek text; (2) a grammatical analysis (subsection 2.3.2) including a sentence flow (Annexure 2.1) which will study: a) the relationship between the independent clause and the three subordinate clauses and the possible meanings behind these relationships, b) the word orders in individual clauses and their possible meanings, c) the tenses of the verbs and the participles used by Luke and their possible meanings, and d) the usage of uncommon words and Luke's possible intention for using these words; (3) a literary analysis (subsection 2.3.2) which will study the structure of the preface to identify the key elements and the possible reasons for inclusion of these elements. Because the Gospel is the first book of Luke-Acts written by Luke, a comparison with the key elements included in the prefaces written by other Greco-Roman historians for their first books will be conducted to see whether there are hints for the writing order in Luke's preface; (4) a more detailed study of the prefaces written by other Greco-Roman historians and their writing orders (subsection 2.3.3) for the insight(s) regarding Luke's preface and his possible writing order; and (5) preliminary word studies for the key words ἄνωθεν, ἀκριβῶς and παρακολουθέω in Luke 1:3 to understand their possible implications for Luke's writing order (subsection 2.3.4) (a word study for καθεξῆς will be conducted in a separate section because of its importance and the length of the study).

Second, I will conduct a thorough analysis of the preface of Acts (i.e., Acts 1:1–5) (section 2.4). This analysis will be similar to the analysis of the preface of the Gospel in many ways: it will include an analysis of all the textual variants to establish the original text (subsection 2.4.1), a grammatical study (subsection 2.4.3) including a sentence flow (Annexure 2.4) to discuss the relationships between the independent clauses and subordinate clauses, a study of the structure of the preface to identify the key words and Luke's emphasis, a study of the tenses of the verbs and participles and their possible meanings, and a study of the word order in individual clauses and possible meanings. Also, a literary analysis (subsection 2.4.2) will be conducted to compare Luke's preface in Acts, which is a sequel to his Gospel, with the prefaces for the sequels written by other Greco-Roman historians.

Third, after the study of the two prefaces, I will conduct a detailed word study of καθεξῆς to ascertain its meaning (section 2.5). This will include (1) a study of all the usages of καθεξῆς in the Bible (subsection 2.5.1). I will study the meaning of the word in each occurrence and then categorize them; (2) a study of the etymology of the word (subsection 2.5.2)—including the meaning of the root words (κατὰ, ἑξῆς and ἔχω) of καθεξῆς and the impact of these root words on the meaning of καθεξῆς when they come together; (3) a study of all the related words of καθεξῆς (subsection 2.5.3) (related words here is defined as words which share the same root words with καθεξῆς, words which belong to the same word family, and words which are indicated by the lexicons as having meanings similar to καθεξῆς and which can be used interchangeably with καθεξῆς). I will study the meaning of each related word to gain insight into the meaning of καθεξῆς, I will also study the phrases in the Bible which contain the root words of καθεξῆς to see if they will shed light on the meaning of καθεξῆς; and (4) a study of the meaning of καθεξῆς in contemporary Greek usages (subsection 2.5.4)—I will cover all the usages of καθεξῆς cited by two reputable lexicons, in the Apocrypha and the Pseudepigrapha, in Josephus and Philo, in some reputable references to the papyri, and all the usages closest to the time of Luke from 1 B.C. to A.D. 1 listed in the *Thesaurus Linguae Graecae* computer data bank. I will again analyze the meaning of the word in each occurrence and categorize them. At the end I will analyze which category of meaning καθεξῆς in Luke 1:3 most likely falls into and draw an overall conclusion for the meaning of καθεξῆς.

Through this chapter I intend to establish my own view on Luke's writing order for his Gospel through a thorough analysis of his two prefaces, a comparison of his prefaces with the prefaces written by other Greco-Roman historians, and a detailed word study of καθεξῆς. I will give a summary conclusion (section 2.6) at the end of this chapter stating the findings of this chapter and the next step I will take to ascertain the writing order of Luke's gospel.

2.1 OTHER SCHOLARS' OPINIONS

A study of the writings of twenty-four scholars[7] about the preface of the Gospel of Luke and Luke's writing order reveals that only a few scholars form an opinion on Luke's order based on a word study of καθεξῆς. Most others reach their conclusions based on a study of the contents of the Gospel and Acts, while some form their opinions on both a word study and a study of the contents. I will first present those scholars' opinions on Luke's writing order based on a word study of καθεξῆς, as the word study of καθεξῆς forms one of the major parts of my research in this chapter. Then I will briefly address scholars' opinions which are based on a study of the contents, or both a word study and a study of the contents, and at the end I will give my view on Luke's writing order and the reasons for supporting my view.

Only two of the twenty-four scholars, Lockwood (1995:101–104) and Easton (1926:2), based their opinions of Luke's writing order solely on their studies of καθεξῆς. Both of them conclude that the meaning of the word should be "chronological order." The opinions about the meaning of καθεξῆς of the remaining twenty-two scholars can be divided into five basic categories.[8] (1) nine scholars (40.9%) think that καθεξῆς means some literary order appropriate to the Gospel of Luke; (2) eight (36.4%) think that καθεξῆς means broadly chronological in order; (3) four (18.2%) opine that καθεξῆς refers to a salvation-historical order, while some at the same time also opine that it also points to a geographical order; (4) two (9.1%) conclude that καθεξῆς refers to a logical order; and (5) two (9.1%) believe that καθεξῆς does not indicate any order, but should be translated simply as "as follows." Now I will briefly go through each of the five categories of opinions.

In the first category, scholars believe that καθεξῆς means some literary order appropriate to the Gospel of Luke. For example, it may simply mean "organized," "a neat arrangement of materials," "a connected whole,"

---

7. These are writings about the Gospel of Luke found in the libraries of Gordon-Conwell Theological Seminary and Gordon College in S. Hamilton, Massachusetts at the time when I first worked on this subject in Fall 2008. These writings intend to provide a wide spectrum of views between the early 20th century and the early 21st century, including both liberal and conservative ones, trying to present a comprehensive overview of scholarly opinions on the meaning of the word καθεξῆς.

8. While there is a total of 25 scholarly opinions on the meaning of καθεξῆς, only 22 scholars' writings were studied, because there is one scholar (François Bovon) who supports categories 1, 2 and 3 (i.e., gives two additional opinions), and there is another (Darrell L. Bock) who supports categories 1 and 3 (i.e., gives one additional opinion). Therefore, there are 22 opinions plus 3 additional ones which add up to 25 opinions.

"comprehensive, balanced composition" or "events told one at a time." The comments of the nine scholars in this category are as follows:

Table 1. First category of scholarly opinions about καθεξῆς /writing order: some literary order appropriate to the Gospel of Luke

Name of scholar (source)	Opinion about καθεξῆς /writing order
1. Talbert (2002:9)	"work will be organized"
2. Cadbury (1999:345–346)	"a narrative orderly and continuous in itself . . . the first part of (καθεξῆς) implies that events will be told one at a time 'in succession'"
3. Geldenhuys (1975:53)	"a narrative which would form a connected whole"
4. Bovon (2002:22)	"*comprehensive scope*, as well as to a chronologically or salvation-historically correct sequence, *and also to balanced composition*"
5. Ellis (1974:66)	"*a connected whole*, whether the sequence is chronological, logical or otherwise"
6. Moessner (1999:84–123)	the sequence of a distinctive narratological sense
7. Green (1997:44)	a "persuasive order" to win his (Luke's) audience over to his perspective on the events he recounts
8. Thompson (1972:45)	"a neat arrangement of material"
9. Nolland (1989:9)	"an ordering according to the sense of the whole"

In the second category, scholars believe that καθεξῆς means "broadly chronological" in order. Most scholars in this category, though believing that the Gospel is broadly chronological, express reservation about a strict chronological order because the narratives in the Gospel do not seem to support such an order. The comments of the eight scholars in the second category are as follows:

Table 2. Second category of scholarly opinions about
καθεξῆς/writing order: broadly chronological

Name of scholar (source)	Opinion about καθεξῆς /writing order
1. Robertson (1920:53)	"such an order would be chronological in its main features. That is true of the great turning points in the Gospel, most assuredly . . . "
2. Marshall (1978:43)	"although he (Luke) is not interested in assigning precise dates and places to the events he records he is broadly chronological in his treatment"
3. Bock (2004, vol.1:62)	"(Luke's Gospel) is broadly chronological . . . "
4. Hendriksen (1978:57)	"by and large the sequence of events as reported by Luke is chronological"
5. Creed (1960:5)	"Luke intends to give a *continuous* narrative. Chronological order was probably in his mind"
6. Plummer (1953:5)	"(Luke) probably has chronological order chiefly in view"
7. Felix (1997:61–82)	some type of chronological and historical order
8. Bovon (2002:22)	"comprehensive scope, as well as to a *chronologically* or salvation-historically correct sequence, and also to balanced composition."

In the third category, scholars believe that καθεξῆς refers to a salvation-historical order, and some opine that it also refers to a geographical order at the same time. Scholars in this category believe that "events (in Luke-Acts) are moving in a single direction toward the fulfillment of God's purpose of inclusive salvation" (Tannehill, 1986:10) and geographical order refers to "a geographical arrangement to the material (in Luke-Acts) . . . from Galilee, to Samaria, Jerusalem, Judea-Samaria, and then Rome . . . it represents the broad geographical sweep of Jesus' ministry and the church's growth" (Bock, 2004: vol.1:61). The comments of the four scholars are as follows:

Table 3. Third category of scholarly opinions about
καθεξῆς/writing order: salvation-historical

Name of scholar (source)	Opinion about καθεξῆς /writing order
1. Bock (2004, vol.1:61)	"(Luke's gospel) is broadly chronological and *geographic, and deals with sacred history*"

Name of scholar (source)	Opinion about καθεξῆς /writing order
2. Sneen (1971:40–43)	Luke's gospel is "in order of significance, because he is giving 'witness' and writes with a soteriological concern"
3. Tannehill (1986:10)	"an order which nourishes faith because it discloses a saving purpose behind events"
4. Bovon (2002:22)	"refers to comprehensive scope, as well as to a chronologically or *salvation-historically correct sequence*, and also to balanced composition."

In the fourth category, scholars believe that καθεξῆς refers to a logical order. However, they did not state to what kind of logical order they refer. The comments of the two scholars are as follows:

Table 4. Fourth category of scholarly opinions about καθεξῆς /writing order: logical

Name of scholar (source)	Opinion about καθεξῆς /writing order
1. Stein (1992:65)	"by his use of this term (καθεξῆς) Luke was stating that he had written his Gospel in a logical fashion"
2. Morris (1995:73–74)	a logical and artistic arrangement

In the final and the fifth category of opinions, scholars believe that καθεξῆς does not indicate order, but should be translated simply as "as follows." The comments of the two scholars are as follows:

Table 5. Fifth category of scholarly opinions about καθεξῆς/writing order: does not indicate order

Name of scholar (source)	Opinion about καθεξῆς /writing order
Brown (1978:107)	"if the correct translation is simply 'as follows,' then the purpose which Luke expresses in vs. 4 would be achieved not by any sort of order but simply by accuracy of what he writes"
Plessis (1974:259–271)	"as follows," following the meaning of ἑξῆς (one of the root words of καθεξῆς) which always means "the following" by Luke

16   A Defense for the Chronological Order of Luke's Gospel

2.2 THESIS OF THIS CHAPTER

A study of the meaning of the word καθεξῆς can direct one to conclude that Luke's writing order for his two books is broadly or strictly chronological (i.e., the events in Luke-Acts are recorded in the order in which they happened). One of the major reasons is that Luke uses this word again in Acts 11:4 where it likely refers to chronological order. Moreover, a study of the usages of ἑξῆς, one of the root words of καθεξῆς, indicates that ἑξῆς is used five times in the New Testament, only by Luke, and it always refers to a time sequence. These two findings are confirmed by my study of καθεξῆς in section 2.5. However, when the content of the two books are studied, the unresolved problems about chronological order in the narratives lead many to believe, in contrast, that καθεξῆς may not actually mean "chronological order," and the two books are probably written in some other order or are written without any particular order at all.

While I will address the many questions about the chronological order of the narratives of Luke's gospel in chapter 3, this chapter supports the view that the prefaces indicate that both the Gospel of Luke and the book of Acts are written in chronological order, or a time sequence. The view of this chapter is based on the following logic: Luke either has clearly indicated in the prefaces of his two books the writing order for his Gospel and Acts or he does not do so. If Luke has clearly indicated the writing order in the prefaces, a thorough study of the two prefaces will probably shed light on Luke's order in the writings. A thorough study of the two prefaces is conducted in sections 2.3 to 2.5, which includes a comparison of Luke's two prefaces with the prefaces written by other Greco-Roman historians. The research results indicate that καθεξῆς in Luke 1:3 most likely means "chronological order" and as a sequel the book of Acts very likely shares the same writing order as the Gospel.

On the other hand, even if Luke has not clearly indicated the writing order in the prefaces (i.e., in case the research results of καθεξῆς in this chapter are incorrect and the word does not indicate any particular order), based on research on the writing order of the Greco-Roman historians (subsection 2.3.3), I have found that there still seems to be an implicit understanding between the historians and the general readers that if the authors do not state the order they are going to use in their writings, they will write in chronological order. If this observation is correct, and if Luke does not mention in the prefaces what kind of writing order he uses, we can still reasonably believe that he is writing his two books in chronological order. Therefore, no matter whether Luke has clearly indicated his writing order in his prefaces or not, I will still show that he likely writes in chronological order. In the following section (2.3) of this chapter, I will conduct a study of the preface of the Gospel of Luke for the indications of its writing order.

2.3 A STUDY OF THE PREFACE OF THE GOSPEL OF LUKE

This section is designated for a thorough study of the preface (1:1–4), because such a study seems crucial to the understanding of Luke's writing order. Please refer to section 2.0 for a brief description of the objectives of the different subsections here. The main arguments of this section are: (1) Luke writes as a historian and has included in the preface of his Gospel the four components Greco-Roman historians usually used for writing their prefaces, namely, the content of the book, the reason(s) for writing, the methodologies used and the expected results from the readers; (2) Luke has placed particular emphases on the reliability of the source materials used, his research methodology and his writing order;[9] (3) Luke is able to write in chronological order because his research is done in such an order, and (4) even if Luke does not clearly indicate his writing order in the preface of his Gospel, he probably follows his contemporaries and writes in chronological order.

2.3.1 Textual Analysis

The objective of this subsection is to analyze all the significant textual variants in the preface of Luke's Gospel to establish the original Greek text. There are not many significant textual variants in the preface of Luke's Gospel. While the *Greek New Testament* (Bible, 1994) does not mention any significant variant in the preface, the one mentioned in *Novum Testamentum Graece* (Bible, 1993) is an insertion found in some manuscripts in verse 3. Some Old Latin manuscripts (it[b] and it[q]) and some Vulgate manuscripts have "et spiritui sancto" after ἔδοξε κἀμοὶ… As suggested by Metzger (2002:108), the phrase would be translated as "it seemed best to me *and to*

---

9. Keener also shares a similar view on Luke's particular emphasis on the reliability of his sources. For example, he comments (2012:183): "it also appears that Luke undertook to examine extant sources for his gospel narrative firsthand in a manner no longer available to us, by interviewing some survivors closests to the events described" and (2012:185) "Luke's use of παρηκολουθηκότι suggests that he has a thorough familiarity with reports . . . and that he is able to evaluate their accuracy."

the Holy Spirit . . . to write to you in an orderly account." All Greek manuscripts omit this phrase and it is only found in a few Old Latin manuscripts. Witnesses ℵ, A, B, C, D, L, Q, W, Ξ, Y, it[d,e,f,aur,r1,c], sy[p,h], cop[sa,bo] which support the text without the insertion are of various text-types. ℵ, B are Alexandrian text-types and are the earliest witnesses (4th century) which include verse 3. L, Ξ and cop[bo] are also Alexandrian. A, C, W, Y, sy[p] and Q are Byzantine text-types, and D, it[d,e,f,aur,r1,c], cop[sa] and sy[h] are Western. Italic b and it[q], on the other hand, are translations (Western text-types). Italic b has the same date as it[d,e] (5th century) but it[q] is dated 6th to 7th century. The text with insertion is probably composed and used in limited areas of the ancient world in view of its limited text-type (only Western). From the above analysis the witnesses without the insertion are of much higher quality, are much earlier, are circulated in a much wider region of the ancient world, and outnumber those witnesses which have the insertion. Therefore, the version without the insertion is preferable. The witnesses having the insertion are probably affected by Acts 15:28 ("For it has seemed good to the Holy Spirit and to us . . ."), and the scribes who made the insertion probably wanted to emphasize that the Gospel of Luke is inspired by the Holy Spirit.

Although this variant does not give us insight into what an "orderly account" is, it reveals that the Gospel was probably valued highly among the ancient Christians so that some even tried to add the phrase "and to the Holy Spirit" to stress that the Gospel is inspired by the Holy Spirit. The Gospel surely achieves what Luke had originally hoped for—to strengthen the Christian faith of others. Therefore, I will accept the text in the *Greek New Testament* and *Novum Testamentum Graece* as the original text, and my translation of Luke 1:1–4 is as follows.

Table 6. My translation of Luke 1:1–4 from the original Greek text

Original Greek	My translation
Part 1: verses 1–2 is an adverbial dependent clause (reason) modifying the main clause in verse 3: Ἐπειδήπερ πολλοὶ ἐπεχείρησαν ἀνατάξασθαι διήγησιν περὶ τῶν πεπληροφορημένων ἐν ἡμῖν πραγμάτων, καθὼς παρέδοσαν ἡμῖν οἱ ἀπ᾽ ἀρχῆς αὐτόπται καὶ ὑπηρέται γενόμενοι τοῦ λόγου,	Part 1: Inasmuch as many have attempted to compile a narrative concerning the things having been accomplished among us, just as those who are from the beginning eyewitnesses and servants of the Word have delivered to us,

Original Greek	My translation
Part 2: it includes the main clause (v. 3), and an adverbial dependent clause (result) in verse 4 modifying ἔδοξεν... γράψαι in the main clause: ἔδοξεν κἀμοὶ παρηκολουθηκότι ἄνωθεν πᾶσιν ἀκριβῶς καθεξῆς σοι γράψαι, κράτιστε Θεόφιλε, ἵνα ἐπιγνῷς περὶ ὧν κατηχήθης λόγων τὴν ἀσφάλειαν.	Part 2: it seemed best also to me, after having followed from the beginning in all things carefully, to write to you in an orderly account, most excellent Theophilus, in order that you may know exactly about the certainty of the words of which you have been informed.

2.3.2 Grammatical and Literary Analyses[10]

The objective of this subsection is to conduct detailed grammatical and literary analyses of the preface in Luke's Gospel to understand how the preface is structured and what Luke's emphases are.

The preface is a sentence consisting of two parts.[11] The first part, verses 1 and 2 together, is an adverbial dependent clause starting with the

---

10. Refer to Annexure 2.1 for the sentence flow. Sentence flow is a technique used to relate the individual clauses, phrases and words in a passage to each other, in order to understand the overall structure of that passage and the writer's emphases in the passage. In a sentence flow, the subject, verb and direct object in the same clause are placed from left to right on the same line. A clause, phrase or word which modifies a particular word will be placed under that word, slightly indented to the right. A clause, phrase or word which is parallel in meaning to a particular word will be placed directly under that word. The function of each clause will be identified in the sentence flow and an English translation for that passage will also be given.

11. Bock (2004, vol.1:51) sides with Blass, Debrunner and Funk (BDF) that Luke has eloquently written his preface in the form of a beautiful period (according to BDF [1961:§464], a period, an "organization of a considerable number of clauses and phrases into a well-rounded unity, is rare in the NT. Since the period belongs to a more elegant style, it is most frequently met in Hebrews, which certainly is to be regarded as artistic prose by reason of the composition of its words and sentences"), dividing the sentence into protasis (i.e., condition 'if,' verses 1 and 2) and apodosis (i.e., conclusion, verses 3 and 4) having the two parallel each other. In Bock's opinion, the parallel suggested by BDF is most likely as follows:

    a inasmuch as many have undertaken (1:1a)

      b to compile an account of the things . . . (1:1b)

        c even as those . . . delivered to us (1:2)

    a′ it seemed good also to me . . . (1:3a)

      b′ to write an orderly account for you . . . (1:3b)

        c′ that you might know certainty . . . (1:4)

conjunction ἐπειδήπερ ("Inasmuch as"). Verse 2, starting with καθὼς ("just as"), is an adverbial comparative dependent clause modifying ἐπεχείρησαν ἀνατάξασθαι ("many have attempted to compile") in verse 1. Although the adverbial dependent clause in verses 1 and 2 can function as a comparison clause, it seems more likely to be a reason clause modifying the independent clause ἔδοξε . . . γράψαι ("it seemed . . . to write") in verse 3, given that the usage of ἐπειδήπερ is usually causal[12] and the context also supports a reason clause. Through this clause in verses 1 and 2 Luke wants to inform Theophilus of the reason why he writes his Gospel—because many people have undertaken to write about Jesus. Luke does not mention in verses 1 and 2 precisely why this is his motivation. One of the possible reasons is that being a close companion to both Paul and Peter, Luke believes that he can do as able a job as others (if not more able) (1:3). In verses 1 and 2 Luke also indirectly indicates that his Gospel is comparable to the narratives other people have undertaken to write in two aspects: (a) the content—it is compiled from facts about Jesus' life that are fully established, widely known and narrated by many (verse 1: "the things having been accomplished among us") (see Plummer [1898:3], Robertson [1930:§Luke 1:1] and Marshall [1978:41–42]), and (b) the source materials used—Luke uses eyewitnesses' testimonies to ensure his information's historical accuracy. According to the context and the sentence structure, verse 1 together with verses 3 and 4 form a complete sentence which is self-contained in both meaning and structure. It is therefore likely that Luke inserted verse 2 to give particular emphasis to the reliability of the information he is about to write in his Gospel, a quality which he believes is of utmost importance.

The second part includes an independent clause (verse 3) starting with the verb ἔδοξε. ("it seemed") and an adverbial dependent clause (verse 4) starting with ἵνα ("in order that") followed by a subjunctive ἐπιγνῷς ("you may know") functioning as a result clause to ἔδοξε . . . γράψαι ("it seemed . . . to write") in verse 3. Instead of telling Theophilus right away, in verse 1, what he will write and the objective in writing it, Luke structures his preface to present his independent main clause, about what he will write, in verse 3 and his objective in writing in verse 4. At first glance it may seem a bit indirect and clumsy to modern readers, especially to those who work in the

---

Although Luke may have written his preface in the form of a period comparable to the prefaces written by other Greco-Roman historians, I have reservations as to whether Luke really intends to create a parallel when he writes his preface, as the parallel in the third unit (c and c') is not clear, a point also highlighted by Bock (2004, vol.1:51). There may be parallel only in thought but not in form.

12. According to BDAG (2000:360), the word is a "marker of cause or reason."

commercial world and are used to receiving precise and concise answers right away for every question raised, but it is likely that Luke is using Greco-Roman history preface components.

A study of the writings of the Greco-Roman historians (see Annexure 2.2) finds that their prefaces usually include the following four elements: what the historian will write (the content), why the historian writes this narrative (the reason[s]), how the narrative will be written (the methodology—it usually tells what source materials will be used and in what order the narrative will be written) and sometimes what the historian expects from the readers (the expected result[s]). It is not uncommon for Greco-Roman historians to give lengthy reasons before describing what they will write, their methodologies, and the expected results. For example, Polybius' *The Histories*, Josephus' *Antiquities* and his *Against Apion* all give lengthy reasons at the beginning (see Annexure 2.2). It is therefore understandable why Luke structures his preface this way. Moreover, writing as a historian, Luke includes all four elements above in his preface:

Table 7. The four elements Luke includes
in the preface of his Gospel

Elements included in Luke's preface	Corresponding verses (description)
1. Reason why he writes his Gospel	Verse 1 (because there are others writing narratives about Jesus)
2. What he will write	Verse 3 (another narrative about Jesus)
3. Methodology of writing	Verses 2 to 3 (carefully investigating all the eye-witness accounts to ensure correctness and writing them in an orderly manner)
4. Luke's expectation of his reader Theophilus	Verse 4 (he hopes that Theophilus' faith will be strengthened)

Out of the nine Greek words used in the main sentence of verse 3 (not considering the last two Greek words κράτιστε Θεόφιλε, which indicate the recipient of the Gospel), three are adverbs (ἄνωθεν, ἀκριβῶς and καθεξῆς). These are the only adverbs in the preface (not considering adverbial clauses or phrases). Because an adverb usually gives additional information regarding the word it modifies, these three adverbs are used by Luke to describe how he will write his Gospel. They probably indicate that Luke wants his reader Theophilus to understand in a very precise way the methodology of writing he will adopt—he will *carefully* investigate all things *from the beginning* and write them *in an orderly manner*.

Almost all the verbs and participles in the preface are in the aorist tense.[13] The only two participles in a different tense are τῶν πεπληροφορημένων (verse 1, "the things having been accomplished") and παρηκολουθηκότι (verse 3, "after having followed" or "investigated"), both in the perfect tense. In general the aorist tense is less marked and is used to provide background information for the context, while the perfect tense is the most heavily marked, even heavier than the present tense and is used to describe very specific information (see Porter [2005: 34–35, 42]). This probably means that while using the aorist tense in general to write his preface, Luke particularly uses the perfect tense for πεπληροφορημένων and παρηκολουθηκότι to emphasize to Theophilus what he is going to write and what research approach he is going to use: he is going to write about facts connected with Christ's life that are fully established and widely known, and that he has done a thorough investigation on all the eyewitness accounts for his writing.

Scholars' opinions vary regarding the positions of independent clauses and subordinate clauses. For example, Robertson (1934:418) opines that "the position of the subordinate clause varies greatly. It often comes first . . . " However, Spencer (1988:166, see table 4) finds that the independent clause tends to come first in a sentence. A study of the prefaces written by other Greco-Roman historians in Annexure 2.2 reveals that historians may start their prefaces with either a subordinate or an independent clause. Therefore, it is likely that Luke put the two subordinate clauses (in verses 1 and 2) first in the preface because he wants to emphasize to Theophilus what he is going to write in his Gospel: again, the facts about Jesus which are fully established, handed to him from reliable witnesses.

Regarding the word order in the individual clauses in the preface, Luke does not follow the normal Greek word order[14] in a number of areas. According to Robertson (1934:417), " . . . emphasis may be at the end as well as at the beginning of the sentence, or even in the middle in case of antithesis.

---

13. The following verbs or participles are in the aorist tense. In verse 1: ἐπεχείρησαν ("have attempted"), ἀνατάξασθαι ("to compile"); in verse 2: παρέδοσαν ("have delivered"), γενόμενοι ("who are"); in verse 3: ἔδοξε ("it seemed"), γράψαι ("to write"); and verse 4: ἐπιγνῷς ("you may know").

14. The normal Greek word order, according to Spencer (2001:119 and 1998:24) and Demetrius (1995:§199), is subject-verb-object (or complement) + modifying phrases and clauses.

The emphasis consists in removing a word from its usual position to an unusual one." Porter (1999:295), when discussing Greek word order and clause structure, also opines that "in analysis of a given biblical writer, it is not incumbent upon the exegete to explain the normal patterns of usage, but to explain the instances which depart from these patterns." In verse 1 the participle τῶν πεπληροφορημένων ("the things having been accomplished") and the propositional phrase ἐν ἡμῖν ("among us") are placed before πραγμάτων ("things") which is the object of the preposition in the proposition phrase starting with περὶ. Luke probably wants to emphasize the fact that his accounts are fully established and widely known. In verse 2 the verb παρέδοσαν ("have delivered") and the indirect object ἡμῖν ("to us") are placed before the subjects οἱ ... γενόμενοι ἀπ' ἀρχῆς αὐτόπται καὶ ὑπηρέται ... (those who are from the beginning eyewitnesses and servants ...), Luke likely wants to emphasize the way he receives these accounts—they are directly passed onto him from those who are from the beginning eyewitnesses and servants of the Word and do not go through a third party. This means Luke claims that the source information about Jesus used for his Gospel is highly reliable.

In verse 3 the modifying phrase παρηκολουθηκότι ἄνωθεν πᾶσιν ἀκριβῶς ("after having followed from the beginning all things carefully") is placed before the verb γράψαι. Luke probably wants to emphasize his fact-finding approach. It seems that καθεξῆς in verse 3 can be used to modify παρηκολουθηκότι ("after having followed") or γράψαι ("to write"). If it modifies παρηκολουθηκότι, it means that Luke investigates in an orderly manner; and if it modifies γράψαι, it means that Luke writes his Gospel in an orderly account. It is more likely that καθεξῆς is used to modify γράψαι emphatically because καθεξῆς is placed in a closer position to γράψαι than to παρηκολουθηκότι. Marshall (1978:43); Bock (1994:62), Plummer (1896:5) and Green (1997:44) all agree that καθεξῆς modifies γράψαι. Moreover, the study of the content of the Gospel in chapter 3 also supports such an argument.

Luke also uses some rare words in his preface. For example, ἐπειδήπερ and ἀνατάξασθαι in verse 1 each only appear once in the New Testament. It would seem likely that Luke wants to use these words to make his preface more eloquent for Theophilus,[15] who likely has an important social status as a Roman official and is well educated and affluent.

15. BDAG's comment on ἐπειδήπερ (2000:360) seems to indicate its use to address an eloquent individual: "The freq. inscriptional use of the simplex ἐπειδή, in the protasis of preambles of official documents, w. the verb δοκέω foll. (as in Lk 1:3) in the apodosis,

In summary, from the above grammatical and literary analyses there are two observations: (1) Luke writes as a historian. He includes the four components commonly used by other Greco-Roman historians in their prefaces (content, reason, methodology and expected result) when constructing his preface in the Gospel, and (2) Luke seems to place particular emphases on the reliability of the source materials he uses, his research methodology and his writing order.

2.3.3 Analysis of the Writing Order of Greco-Roman Historians and Its Possible Impact on Luke's Writing Order

If Luke writes as a historian, he might have adopted the writing order used by other Greco-Roman historians. There may exist a general understanding between the historians and their readers that if they do not state clearly in what order they will write their histories, they are going to write in a certain order. If this is the case, the historians do not need to state their writing order explicitly if they do not deviate from that custom. They will have to mention their writing order only when they intend to write in a different order. In this subsection, I will conduct a study of the writings of some of the most famous Greco-Roman historians to ascertain whether there are common rules about the order of writing which Greco-Roman historians would adopt when writing their histories. The following historians and their writings are chosen for this study[16]: Herodotus (*The Persian Wars*), Thucydides (*The Peloponnesian War*), Xenophon (*Anabasis*), Polybius (*History*), Pausanias (*Description of Greece*), Philostratus (*The Life of Apollonius of Tyana*), Josephus (*The Life, Against Apion, The Jewish War*), and Eusebius (*The History of the Church*). I will give a brief description for each author and the work(s) under study, and then conduct an analysis of the order each author uses. In this subsection I will argue that Luke likely adopts the writing methodologies of the Greco-Roman historians; and these methodologies give hints as to Luke's writing order, which is very likely chronological.

---

suggests that Luke enriches the message of his own preamble with a solemn tone."

16. These historians and writings are recommended to me for this project by classicist Dr. Catherine Kroeger at Gordon-Conwell Theological Seminary, South Hamilton, MA, U.S.A., in the fall term of the year 2007.

2.3.3.1 *Herodotus* (The Persian Wars)

Herodotus (*Pers. wars* 1:5) clearly states the order of his *Persian Wars*: "These are the stories of the Persians and the Phoenicians. For my own part, I will not say that this or that story is true, but I will name him whom I myself know to have done unprovoked wrong to the Greeks, and so go forward with my history, and speak of small and great cities alike. For many states that were once great have now become small: and those that were great in my time were small formerly. Knowing therefore that human prosperity never continues in one stay, I will make mention alike of both kinds." Herodotus's *Persian Wars*, therefore, may not be written in chronological order. It may be written in a certain logical order to describe the events that happened for each Greek city as stated by Herodotus in Book 1.

2.3.3.2 *Thucydides* (The Peloponnesian War)

Thucydides does not explain at the beginning of Book 1 in what order he is going to write. He only says he writes the history of the war "beginning at the moment that it broke out." However, the events are obviously recorded in chronological order, which is evidenced by the content itself and by Thucydides' comment in Book 2 (*Pel. war* 2:1): "The events of the war have been recorded in the order of their occurrence, summer by summer and winter by winter," and his other comment in Book 5 (*Pel. war* 5.26): "The history of these events also, has been written by the same Thucydides, an Athenian, in the chronological order of events, by summers and winters . . . " Therefore, the question is why Thucydides does not mention at the outset that he is going to write *The War* in chronological order. Considering that there is no table of contents and no indexing system in the Greco-Roman world, the readers might be disinclined to read such a long book without knowing how the book is organized. One probable explanation is that there exists an understanding in the Greco-Roman world between the historians and their readers that if an author does not mention at the outset in what order he will write his book, then the book is written in chronological order.

2.3.3.3 *Xenophon* (Anabasis)

A study of the first section of each book (from one to seven) of *Anabasis* shows that Xenophon does not mention in what order he will write. However, from the content it seems that Xenophon has recorded the events in chronological order. For example, in Book 1 Xenophon describes the background of the story in the following order: how Artaxerxes rises to power to become the emperor of the Persian Empire, how he ill-treats his younger brother Cyrus after he becomes emperor, how Cyrus then determines to overthrow him and plots against him, how Cyrus gathers his troops, how Artaxerxes and Cyrus fight against each other and how Cyrus is killed in battle. The analysis above seems to support the hypothesis that if an author does not state the writing order, then he is writing in chronological order.

2.3.3.4 *Polybius* (The Histories)

According to Paton (1979, 4:227), Polybius intends to give a summary of the events of each Olympiad starting from the 129th Olympiad. He states in each of his books the order he will use, usually at the very beginning, in the preface. For example, in Book 1 (*Hist.* 1.5) he says: "I shall adopt as the starting-point of this book the first occasion on which the Romans crossed the sea from Italy. This follows immediately on the close of Timaeus' *History* and took place in the 129th Olympiad. Thus we must first state how and when the Romans established their position in Italy, and what prompted them afterwards to cross to Sicily, the first country outside Italy where they set foot ...".

At the beginning of each book Polybius usually summarizes what he has narrated in the previous book before he states the order in which he will write the next book. For example, in Book 4 (*Hist.* 4.1) he says: "In the preceding Book ... I described the invasion of Italy by Hannibal ... I shall now give an account of the contemporary events in Greece from the 140th Olympiad onwards, after briefly recalling to the minds of my readers the sketch I gave in my second book ... Next I went on to tell how they subsequently began to reunite ...".

Sometimes Polybius gives a brief description of what he will write for the next book at the end of a particular book. If this is the case, usually there will be no preface or explanation of order at the beginning of the next book. For example, in Book 4 (*Hist.* 4.87) he says: "As to how and by what means this happened, I shall defer speaking for the present and bring this Book to a close; but in subsequent ones I shall try to give a clear account of the whole matter, Philip, after making the arrangements I mentioned, returned to Argos and there spent the remainder of the winter with his friends, dismissing his troops to Macedonia." There is no preface or explanation of order at the beginning of Book 5. Polybius' summaries at the end of his books seem to be a writing technique suggested by Lucian: a historian should structure his writing so that "the first and the second topics must not merely be neighbors but have common matter and overlap" (Lucian, 1999:67). This overlapping writing technique is frequently employed by Luke in his gospel and will be discussed in depth in chapter 3.

There is one more point worthy to note. As mentioned above, Polybius narrates the events in the *Histories* in the chronological order of the Olympiads. This is evidenced by the years of occurrence of many of these events put down by Paton in the margin alongside with the contents of the *Histories*. But, if this is true, why did Polybius have to give a preface in almost every book or to give a description at the end of a book regarding how he will write in the next book? If my hypothesis applies, that there exists an understanding among the readers that if an author does not mention the writing order then he is writing in chronological order, then apparently Polybius does not have to write the prefaces and the ending descriptions if he writes in chronological order. However, in Polybius' case, there is a change of content as compared with the previous book, and, therefore, Polybius has to give a summary of what he is about to write in each book. This reason will be addressed in greater details in subsection 2.4.2 ("literary analysis") of this chapter.

2.3.3.5 *Pausanias* (Description of Greece)

Pausanias does not explain to his readers in what order he writes his *Description of Greece*. He does not mention anything about order at the beginning or at the end of each book. However, it seems that whenever he describes an important family or the history of a city, he writes in chronological order. For example, in Book 1, when Pausanias describes Lysimachus and his family, he starts with Lysimachus (*Descr.* 1:9), then describes Lysimachus' son Demetrius (*Descr.* 1:10), then Demetrius' son Antigonus (*Descr.* 1:10). The family is described in chronological order from grandfather to father to son. Another example is Pausanias' history of a city called Orchomenus in Book 9 (*Descr.* 9:34–38). Andreus is the first king, who founds Orchomenus. He then gives the throne to Athamas. The throne then goes to Eteocles, the son of Andreus, and next to Phlegyas the son of Almus. Phlegyas is followed by Chryses, son of Chrysogeneia, because he has no son. Minyas son of Chryses then becomes king, followed by his son Orchomenus. The throne then passes to Clymenus because Orchomenus has no son. His son Erginus follows Clymenus as king, the throne then being taken by Ascalaphus and

Ialmenus, sons of Ares. It is evident that Pausanias presents the rulers in chronological order. Therefore, it seems that Pausanias' writing order confirms the hypothesis that absent any statement to the contrary, the author writes in chronological order.

2.3.3.6 Philostratus (The Life of Apollonius of Tyana)

Philostratus does not specify in what order he writes *The Life of Apollonius of Tyana*. The book describes events from the very beginning, relating to Apollonius' birth (*Life Apoll.* 1:4–6), to the very end, relating to his death (*Life Apoll.* 8:30). Afterwards it even records an incident related to Apollonius after his death (Apollonius converses with a young man) (*Life Apoll.* 8:30). The content therefore shows that it is basically written in chronological order. It seems that Philostratus' writing order also follows the above hypothesis, that if the writing order is not stated, the author writes in chronological order.

2.3.3.7 Josephus (The Life)

Josephus does not mention in what order he writes *The Life*. However, the content seems to indicate it is written in chronological order. This is also supported by the years of occurrence of the many events put down by Thackeray throughout the whole book in the margin alongside with the contents of *The Life*.[17] It seems that Josephus' *The Life* also follows the above hypothesis that the order is chronological if the author does not specify otherwise.

2.3.3.8 Josephus (Against Apion)

Although it is only an apologia, Josephus does mention in Book 1 of *Against Apion* (*Ag. Ap.* 1:58) in what order he will write: "I propose, in the first place, to reply briefly to those critics who endeavour to prove the late origin of our constitution from the alleged silence of the Greek historians concerning us. I shall then proceed to cite testimonies to our antiquity from external literature, and finally to show the utter absurdity of the calumnies of the

---

17. For example, Thackeray gives the dates of the following events alongside the text in *Life* 1.1: Matthias marries the daughter of Jonathan the high-priest (153 B.C.); Matthias has a son Matthias in the first year of the reign of Hyrcanus (135 B.C.); Joseph, son of Matthias is born (70 B.C.); Josephus, a descendant in the line, is born (A.D. 6). The dates indicate that these events are described in chronological order.

traducers of our race." Josephus is writing his *Against Apion* in a logical order to defend the antiquity of his race and to rebuke the allegations from Jewish enemies. The writing order is described explicitly in the preface as not chronological, but in a certain logical order to achieve the author's purpose.

2.3.3.9 *Josephus* (The Jewish War)

Josephus gives his readers a clear description of the order he will use at the beginning of Book 1 (*J. W.* 1:7–12): Antiochus takes over Jerusalem but is expelled by the Hasmonaeans; the Hasmonaeans are overthrown by Herod; the war begins after Herod's death, the Jews fortify their towns, the Roman General Vespasian and his son Titus penetrate Galilee, the Romans advance against Jerusalem, which eventually falls. It seems that the *Jewish War* is basically written in chronological order. This is evidenced by the date of occurrence of many events noted by Thackeray throughout the book in the margin alongside with the contents of the *Jewish War*.[18] It seems that though Josephus has mentioned explicitly a logical writing order in the preface focusing on major events from the origin to the end of the war, he also writes them chronologically. It indicates that even though a historian might have described explicitly in the preface writing in a certain logical order, he can also use chronological order together with that logical order to present the historical events he is about to write.

2.3.3.10 *Eusebius* (The Ecclesiastical History)

Eusebius in Book 1 of *Ecclesiastical History* (*Hist. eccl.* 1.1.7–8) clearly states that he will write that particular book in a certain order to discuss Jesus' divinity. Although Eusebius does not explain in the introduction sections of Books 2 to 10 of the *Ecclesiastical History* in what order he is going to write these books, the content shows that they are written in chronological order. The events are seemingly narrated according to the time of reign of each Roman Emperor. This is supported by at least two comments he gives in the *Ecclesiastical History*. The first comment is recorded in Book 1 (*Hist. eccl.* 1.1.6) where Eusebius says that he has already summarized certain materials

---

18. For example, Thackeray has added the dates of the following events in the right margin alongside the text: the death of Matthias, the father of Judas (167 B.C., I.37); Judas gains control of the upper city (165 B.C, I.39a); the death of Antiochus (164 B.C., I.39b); the death of Judas and his brother John (161 B.C., I.47). The dates indicate that these events are described in chronological order.

in his "chronological canons" (χρονικοῖς κανόσιν), but he is going to give the narrative in full detail. Therefore, there is a high probability that Eusebius extends his summarized materials based on the order of his "chronological canons" and writes his *Ecclesiastical History* in chronological order.

The second comment is recorded in Book 3 (*Hist. eccl.* 3.4.11), where Lake translates as "now as we go on our way, the 'chronological details' of the succession of the Apostles will be related" (ἀλλὰ γὰρ ὁδῷ προβαίνουσιν, τὰ τῆς κατὰ χρόνους τῶν ἀποστόλων διαδοχῆς ἡμῖν εἰρήσεται). It supports the above observation that he is writing Books 2 to 10 of the *Ecclesiastical History* in chronological order. The study of Eusebius' *Ecclesiastical History* again supports the hypothesis that if an author does not specify the writing order at the outset, he is probably writing in chronological order.

2.3.3.11 Conclusion

We have three observations regarding the writing order of Greco-Roman historians. First, Greco-Roman historians will usually state in the preface in what order they will write. This is probably because many writings tend to be quite long and there was no indexing system; therefore, the historians use this approach to communicate to their readers at a glance what their writings are about and how the contents are organized. Second, there seems to be an implicit understanding between the historians and the general readers that if an author does not state the order, he is going to write in chronological order. Third, Greco-Roman historians sometimes will state in their prefaces that they will write in a certain logical order, though their writings are basically organized in chronological order. That is, they write in both chronological order and a specific logical order. Apparently it happens when a historian wants to highlight certain important events in his book to convey a message which supports the main theme of his writing.

In conclusion, the findings of this subsection support the proposal that if Luke does not mention in the preface (Luke 1:1–4) what kind of order he is using, he is probably writing in chronological order. He may also have a logical or thematic purpose for the events, but that will not undermine the chronology.

2.3.4 Preliminary Word Studies

In 1:3 Luke uses three adverbs ἄνωθεν, ἀκριβῶς, καθεξῆς and an adverbial participle παρηκολουθηκότι to give additional information about his research methodology and how he is going to write his Gospel. Therefore, word studies will be conducted for these four words for an understanding of Luke's writing order. Since καθεξῆς ("in an orderly account") is the key word for understanding Luke's writing order, a more detailed word study will be conducted separately in section 2.5. For the other three words a preliminary word study of their usages in the New Testament and in Josephus and Philo will be conducted to see whether their meanings will shed light on Luke's writing order.[19] In this subsection I will argue (1) Luke has the ability to compile a narrative in chronological order; and (2) there is no evidence showing that he is not writing in chronological order.

Other than the usage in Luke 1:3, ἄνωθεν is used 12 times in the Greek New Testament. It means "from above" when it refers to direction (Matt 27:51; Mark 15:38; John 3:31, 19:11, 23; James 1:17, 3:15, 17), and "for a long time" when it refers to time (Acts 26:5). It can also mean "again" (John 3:3, 7; Gal 4:9). Josephus uses this word 33 times;[20] ἄνωθεν also means "from the beginning in chronological order" when it refers to a chronology or a genealogy (*Life* 1:1 and *Ag. Ap.* 1:28.)[21] Philo uses this word 41 times, 40 times referring to a direction and meaning "from above,"[22] and once, in *De Vita*

---

19. The number of usages of a word, their citations and quotations in this section is obtained through Bibleworks v. 9., unless otherwise stated.

20. "From above" when it is related to direction—*Ant.* 1:27, 3:158, 7:226, 8:66, 8:84, 8:140, 13:138, 14:423, 14:460, 15:398, 15:412, 18:285, *J.W.* 1:145, 2:48, 2:435, 3:341, 4:205, 5:12, 5:13, 5:275, 6:224, 7:189, 7:317, *Life* 1:71; "a long time" when it refers to time: *Ant.* 15:260, 16:161, 16:174, 16:242, *Ag. Ap.* 1:237, 2:125; "renew" when it refers to a relationship: *Ant.* 1:263; "from the beginning" when it refers to a chronology or genealogy: *Life* 1:1, *Ag. Ap.* 1:28.

21. *Life* 1.1: "The family from which I am derived is not an ignoble one, but has descended all along (ἄνωθεν) from the priests"—it seems that if Josephus is going to describe his descent in detail, he will begin from his earliest ancestor, and then mention his ancestors one after another in the order of their seniority. Josephus is going to describe his descent in chronological order. *Ag. Ap.* 1.28: "As to the care of writing down the records from the earliest (ἄνωθεν) antiquity among the Egyptians and Babylonians"—it seems that these events are recorded from the one which is the earliest in time and then one after another in the order of their time of happening. The events are recorded in chronological order.

22. *Opificio* 1:117, *Potiori* 1:86, *Agricultura* 1:134, *Sobrietate* 1:57, *Migratione* 1:35, *Mutatione* 1:260, *Somniis* 1:162, 2:86, 2:142, 2:198, *Abrahamo* 1:43, 1:157, *Mosis* 1:115, 1:117, 2:69, 2:118, 2:144, *Immutabilis* 1:155, *Heres* 1:64, 1:166, 1:184, 1:218, 1:274, *Congressa* 1:36, *Fuga* 1:49, 1:101, 1:138, 1:166, 1:180, 1:192, *Specialibus* 1:85, 3:2, *Virtutibus*

Mosis 2:48[23] referring to a chronology and meaning "from the beginning in chronological order." From the above observation, ἄνωθεν in Luke 1:3, since referring to a history, most likely means "from the beginning in chronological order." However, this word is used to modify παρηκολουθηκότι ("after having followed") to explain Luke's research methodology, which probably is from the beginning in chronological order, rather than γράψαι ("to write") to explain Luke's writing order is chronological. Research methodology does not necessarily indicate writing order (i.e., one can research in one order but organize one's work in another order). Therefore, the meaning of ἄνωθεν does not appear to provide concrete information about Luke's writing order. However, if Luke's research is conducted in chronological order, he likely acquires the knowledge from his research process on how to write his Gospel in such an order. Hence, it probably indicates that Luke is prepared to write his Gospel in chronological order.

Other than the usage in Luke 1:3, ἀκριβῶς appears four times in the Greek New Testament. When the word refers to studying, searching or observing something (e.g., rules), it means "carefully" (Matt 2:8 and Eph 5:15); when it refers to teaching, describing, understanding or knowing something, it means "exactly" or "accurately" (Acts 18:25 and 1 Thess 5:2). Josephus and Philo use this word 37[24] and 28[25] times respectively and the meanings of the word are the same as those described in the above categories. In Luke 1:3 it probably means "carefully" according to the context. It describes that the investigation Luke does for his Gospel is a careful one. The meaning of the word does not give any hints as to Luke's writing order.

Other than in Luke 1:3, παρακολουθέω appears three times in the Greek New Testament. It means "to closely associate with" when it refers to the miracles and signs God will perform through believers (Mark 16:17), and

---

1:42, 1:217, *Poenis* 1:73, 1:133, *Qeternitate* 1:147, *Quaestiones* 4:51, *Qgp* 2:5 (2x).

23. "... he traced back the most ancient events from the beginning (ἄνωθεν) of the world, commencing with the creation of the universe ...". It seems that the tracking is from the event earliest in time and then one after another according to the time they happened; therefore, the tracing is in chronological order.

24. *Ant.* 3:70, 3:118, 3:158, 3:164, 3:176, 3:227, 3:287, 5:6, 5:358, 6:141, 7:227, 8:29, 9:276, 12:99, 13:298, 18:104, 18:129, 18:169, 18:182, 18:355, 19:110, 20:71, 20:258, 20:262, *J.W.* 1:6, 2:106, 5:324, 7:99, *Life* 1:387, *Ag. Ap.* 1:15, 1:53, 1:230, 2:17, 2:144, 2:175, 2:227 and 2:257.

25. *Legum* 2:25, *Potiori* 1:11, *Linguarum* 1:57, 1:97, *Migratione* 1:34, 1:189, 1:195, *Heres* 1:74, 1:142, *Somniis* 1:59, 1:204, 1:228, 2:99, 2:103, 2:107, *Mosis* 1:24, 1:49, 1:68, 2:52, *Specialibus* 1:195, 4:105, *Virtutibus* 1:57, 1:165, *Flaccum* 1:77, *Gaium* 1:154, 1:208, 1:372, *Qge* 3:3.

"to follow" when it refers to adopting a doctrine, teaching or belief (1 Tim 4:6; 2 Tim 3:10.) Josephus and Philo use this word eight[26] and 19[27] times respectively and besides the two categories identified above, they also use it to signify "to investigate" when referring to acquiring an understanding of event(s) (e.g., *Life* 1:357.) In Luke 1:3 παρηκολουθηκότι probably means "to investigate" since it refers to Luke's intention of acquiring an understanding of the events about Jesus. Again, it describes the careful attitude Luke uses in investigating the source materials for his Gospel; it does not seem to give any hints about his writing order.

Of the three words, ἄνωθεν, ἀκριβῶς and παρακολουθέω, ἄνωθεν very likely indicates that Luke conducts his research in chronological order. Although this does not necessarily confirm that Luke writes his Gospel in chronological order, it implies that Luke is able to compile a narrative in such an order, because his research is done in this manner. Moreover, the other word studies above do not show that the order Luke uses for his Gospel is not chronological. These three words apparently show that Luke's research is systematic and thorough, and he has carefully investigated all the necessary details to acquire an accurate understanding of the facts for writing his history.

2.3.5 Summary

The grammatical and literary analyses indicate that Luke has placed particular emphases on his source materials, his research methodology and his writing order in the preface. We find that Luke has followed the writing methodologies of other Greco-Roman historians and has included in his preface the four components commonly used by them in their prefaces (content, reason, methodology and expected results). Regarding Luke's writing order, the study of this chapter has the following observations: (1) Luke writes as a historian and has probably followed the practice used by other Greco-Roman historians when writing his Gospel: that is, either Luke has explicitly indicated the order in his preface, or if not, according to the custom of Greco-Roman historians, the writing order is probably chronological; (2) Luke is able to write in chronological order because he likely

---

26. *Ant.* 12:259, 14:1, 14:438, *Life* 1:357, *Ag. Ap.* 1:53, 1:218, *J.W.* 1:455, 6:251.

27. *Opificio* 1:17, *Cherubim* 1:30, *Sacrificiis* 1:70, *Potiori* 1:134, 1:171, *Sobrietate* 1:37, *Migratione* 1:149, 1:175, *Fuga* 1:12, *Josepho* 1:269, *Specialibus* 2:206, 3:76, *Praemiis* 1:99, *Flaccum* 1:166, *Providentia* 2:46, 2:48, *Posteritate* 1:90, *Decalogo* 1:88, *Gaium* 1:369.

does his research in this order; and (3) there is no evidence that Luke does not write in chronological order. In the next section a study of the preface of the Book of Acts will be conducted.

2.4 A STUDY OF THE PREFACE OF THE BOOK OF ACTS

This section will focus on the study of the preface of the book of Acts and will be divided into three subsections. In the first subsection a textual analysis will be conducted to establish the original Greek text. In the second subsection a literary analysis will be conducted to compare the prefaces in the sequels written by other Greco-Roman historians with that written by Luke in the book of Acts, with a particular concern for the relationship between the structure of the preface and the possible writing order. In the third subsection a grammatical analysis including a sentence flow will be conducted to understand the relationships between independent and dependent clauses and Luke's emphases for the book of Acts. The analysis will also include a study of the tenses of the verbs and the participles and the unusual word orders.

The main arguments of this section are (1) Greco-Roman historians will write a preface for a sequel only when one or more of the four components (content, reason, methodology and expected result) will be changed from that sequel onwards, and will state the change(s) in the preface of that sequel; (2) there is an implicit understanding between the general readers and the historians that if a component is not mentioned in the preface of a sequel, then that component will remain as it is in previous books; (3) Luke writes a preface for the book of Acts, a sequel to his Gospel, because there is a change in the content: the Gospel focuses on the life of Jesus while Acts focuses on the promise of the Father, and Luke has mentioned this change in the preface of Acts; (4) as Luke does not mention the writing order in the preface of Acts, it is reasonable to believe that it has not changed as compared to that of his Gospel; and (5) therefore, if the writing order can be ascertained for either one of Luke's two books, we may declare that the other book is written in that same order.

2.4.1 Textual Analysis[28]

The objective of this subsection is to establish the original Greek text for the preface in the Book of Acts. In view of the lengthy discussion of textual variants in this section, it is put in Annexure 2.3 for reference. In summary, the text contained in the Greek New Testament (Bible, 1994) and *Novum Testamentum Graece* (Bible, 1993) is preferred and my translation for Acts 1:1–5 is as follows.

Table 8. My translation of Acts 1:1–5 from the original Greek text

Original Greek text	My translation
Part 1: verses 1–3 include one main clause (v. 1a: Τὸν μὲν . . . ὦ Θεόφιλε), 5 subordinate clauses and the important word ἀποστόλοις in verse 2:	Part 1: Indeed I have produced the first book about all things, O Theophilus, of which Jesus began to do and also to teach, until the day in which he was taken up, after commanding to the apostles through the Holy Spirit whom he had chosen; to whom also he presented himself living after he had suffered by many proofs, through forty days while appearing to them and speaking the things about the kingdom of God;
Τὸν μὲν πρῶτον λόγον ἐποιησάμην περὶ πάντων, ὦ Θεόφιλε, ὧν ἤρξατο ὁ Ἰησοῦς ποιεῖν τε καὶ διδάσκειν, ἄχρι ἧς ἡμέρας ἐντειλάμενος τοῖς ἀποστόλοις διὰ πνεύματος ἁγίου οὓς ἐξελέξατο ἀνελήμφθη. Οἷς καὶ παρέστησεν ἑαυτὸν ζῶντα μετὰ τὸ παθεῖν αὐτὸν ἐν πολλοῖς τεκμηρίοις, δι' ἡμερῶν τεσσεράκοντα ὀπτανόμενος αὐτοῖς καὶ λέγων τὰ περὶ τῆς βασιλείας τοῦ θεοῦ·	
Part 2: verses 4–5 include another main clause (v. 4a: καὶ συναλιζόμενος . . . ἐπαγγελίαν τοῦ πατρὸς), 2 subordinate clauses, and the important word ἐπαγγελίαν in verse 4:	Part 2: and while being assembled he commanded them not to depart from Jerusalem but to wait for the promise of the Father which, (he said), "you have heard me, that on one hand John baptized with water, on the other hand you in the Holy Spirit will be baptized not after many these days."
καὶ συναλιζόμενος παρήγγειλεν αὐτοῖς ἀπὸ Ἱεροσολύμων μὴ χωρίζεσθαι ἀλλὰ περιμένειν τὴν ἐπαγγελίαν τοῦ πατρὸς ἣν ἠκούσατέ μου, ὅτι Ἰωάννης μὲν ἐβάπτισεν ὕδατι, ὑμεῖς δὲ ἐν πνεύματι βαπτισθήσεσθε ἁγίῳ οὐ μετὰ πολλὰς ταύτας ἡμέρας.	

---

28. Refer to Annexure 2.3 for detailed work.

2.4.2 Literary Analysis

A literary analysis is conducted in this subsection to compare the prefaces for sequels written by other Greco-Roman historians and their writing orders with the preface in the Book of Acts, expecting that the exercise will shed light on Luke's writing order. In this subsection I will argue that Luke likely follows the approach used by other Greco-Roman historians in writing prefaces for sequels. If this is true, the writing order of Acts is probably the same as that in the Gospel of Luke.

It seems that Luke does not follow the general approach of the Greco-Roman historians in structuring the preface (Acts 1:1–5) of Acts, because this preface, unlike the preface of his Gospel, does not seem to include any of the four components (what content the historian is going to include, his reason(s) for writing, the methodology which will be used for writing and the expected result from the reader[s]) the Greco-Roman historians usually used in writing prefaces. However, a study of their writings shows that Luke's approach is similar to the approach adopted by some Greco-Roman historians in writing prefaces for sequels. When some Greco-Roman historians write prefaces for sequels, they give only a brief description of what they have written in the previous book and then go on to describe what they are going to write in the current book.

It seems that Luke is also using this approach when he writes the preface for Acts. For example, Polybius usually gives a summary at the beginning of each book of *Histories* about what he has written in the previous book, and then will explain what he will write in that particular book. For example, Polybius in *Histories* 4.1 writes: "In the preceding Book . . . I described the invasion of Italy by Hannibal . . . I shall now give an account of the contemporary events in Greece from the 140th Olympiad onwards, after briefly recalling to the minds of my readers the sketch I gave in my second book . . . Next I went on to tell how they subsequently began to reunite . . ." Also, in section 1 of Book 2 of *Against Apion,* Josephus, when writing the preface for this sequel, follows the same approach to describe briefly what he has written in the previous book and what he will write in the current book: "In the first volume of this work, my most esteemed Epaphroditus, I demonstrated the antiquity of our race . . . I shall now proceed to refute the rest of the authors who have attacked us."

However, not all Greco-Roman historical writings which have a preface for the first book have prefaces for their sequels. For example, Herodotus includes a preface only in the first book of his *Persian War* but not in the other books (i.e., Books 2 to 9); Thucydides writes prefaces only for the first and second books of his *History of the Peloponnesian War* but not for the rest (Books 3 to 8); Josephus also follows this approach for his *Jewish War* and writes a preface only for the first book but not for the others (i.e., Books 2 to 7); and Philostratus writes a long preface describing all four elements (reason, content, methodology and expected result) in the preface of the first book of his *The Life of Apollonius of Tyana* (sections 1 to 3) but does not also write a preface for the rest (Books 2 to 8). Why are prefaces written for some Greco-Roman historian sequels but not for others? Is there a common practice for writing prefaces for sequels that the Greco-Roman historians adopt only when writing under certain circumstances? If so, what are these circumstances? And does Luke, when writing a preface for Acts, a sequel to his Gospel, follow this common practice? And, if this is the case, what is the significance, if any, of this common practice for Luke's preface in the book of Acts? Is there any significance for Luke's writing order for his Gospel and Acts?

A study of Herodotus, Thucydides, Polybius, Philostratus and Josephus finds that while these historians usually write a preface at the beginning of the first book of their histories, they will write a preface for a sequel only when one or more of the four elements (content, reason, methodology and expected result) described before will be changed from that sequel onwards. In such a case a historian will usually describe in the preface of that sequel what has been written in the previous book, probably as a refresher to his reader(s) and a connector between the previous and the current book, and then he will describe the change(s) together with what he is about to write in the current book.

Sometimes a historian may reiterate in the preface of a sequel a particular element which has already been mentioned in the preface of a previous book even though it will not undergo any change, in order to emphasize its importance to the reader(s). However, in general the historians will not mention in the preface of a sequel those elements which will remain unchanged, no matter whether that element is mentioned explicitly in the preface of a previous book or is only implied in the previous content.

In Herodotus' the *Persian War* (with a total of 9 books), Philostratus' *The Life of Apollonius of Tyana* (8 books) and Josephus' *The Jewish War* (7 books), while the historians write a preface at the beginning of their first books, they do not write a preface for the sequels. A brief study of the contents of their writings seems to support the argument that because the content, the reason, the methodology and the expected result all remain unchanged throughout these writings, there is no need for a preface for the sequels.

In *History of the Peloponnesian War* (8 books), Thucydides writes prefaces only for Books 1 and 2, and, in a quite unusual manner, he also writes an introduction, which is similar in content to a preface, in the middle of Book 5 (5.26). A comparison of Books 1 and 2 reveals that the content of the two are basically different. In Book 1 Thucydides seemingly only gives background information—he only explains the relationships and the conflicts between various states but does not describe the war itself. He only begins to describe the war in Book 2. This observation is confirmed by what Thucydides writes in the preface of Book 2: "at this point in my narrative begins the account of the actual warfare between the Athenians and the Peloponnesians and their respective allies" (2:1). Moreover, in the preface of Book 2, Thucydides describes his methodology of writing, which he does not do in the preface of the first book: "the events of the war have been recorded in the order of their occurrence, summer by summer and winter by winter" (2:1).

Based on the above observations, Thucydides probably writes a preface for Book 2 because the nature of the content in Book 2 onward will be different from that in Book 1; he has to make it clear to his readers what he is going to write from Book 2 onward. Thucydides also describes the writing order he is going to use from Book 2 onward, an element which he does not mention in the preface of the first book. It either implies that Book 1 is not written in that same order (i.e., he states it in the preface of Book 2 because there will be a change in the writing order beginning with Book 2), or that he wants to emphasize this order to his readers because of its importance. Regarding the reason, Thucydides writes an introduction in 5.26 (Thucydides writes: "the history of these events, also, has been written by the same Thucydides, an Athenian, in the chronological order of events, by summers and winters, up to the time when Lacedaemonians and their allies put an end to the dominion of the Athenians and took the Long Walls and Peiraeus. Up to that event the war lasted twenty-seven years in all . . . "), I agree with T. E. Page[29] that this is written because at this point Thucydides has decided to enlarge the scope of his writing from the first ten years to the first twenty-seven years (i.e., there is a change in the scope of the content). The last sentence in 5:25 ("but at last they were forced to break the treaty which had been concluded

---

29. Page opines that "this chapter forms a kind of second introduction, and was probably written after the author enlarged his plan from a history of the first ten years to that of the whole war." (Thucydides, 1966, vol.3:48)

after the first ten years, and again engaged in open war") also supports this argument. Here Thucydides reiterates the writing order which he has already described in the preface of Book 2 ("in the chronological order of events, by summers and winters"). This is probably because Thucydides considers the writing order to be an important element and wants to emphasize it to his readers. Based on the descriptions of the writing order in the preface of Book 2 and the introduction section in Book 5 (5.26) and the content itself, Thucydides' *History of the Peloponnesian War* is clearly written in chronological order. This observation supports the argument that if an element (here the writing order) is not mentioned in the sequels, it will remain unchanged as it is in the previous books. Besides Books 2 and 5 Thucydides does not mention the writing order again, but the evidence shows that the writing order is consistent and has not been changed throughout the work, remaining the same as described in Books 2 and 5.

In the first eight books of the *Histories*,[30] Polybius writes a preface for almost every book. In the prefaces he will usually summarize what he has narrated in the previous book before stating what he will write and in what order in the current book. Sometimes Polybius will give a brief description of what he will write for the next book at the end of a particular book, and, when this is the case, usually there will be no preface at the beginning of the next book (see 2.3.3.4). The reason Polybius writes a preface for almost every book is probably that unlike Thucydides or Herodotus he is not describing a particular war or event; but as Finley (1971:441) says, the *Histories* is about a universal history: Rome's conquest of the world from 220 to 144 B.C. including the final conquest of Spain, Africa and Greece. The material Polybius is going to write is so diverse that it is impossible for him to give his reader a brief summary of all the individual events in the preface of the first book. What Polybius does there is to give his reader a general explanation of what he is going to write (according to *Hist.* 1.1.5–6, his objective is to write about how the Romans in such a short period of time have succeeded in conquering the whole world) and then to summarize the events he is going to describe in each book in its preface. The preface of a particular book is therefore a description of the new events he will describe in that book. In summary, Polybius writes a preface for each book probably because there is a difference in the content of each book as compared with the previous one.

---

30. Only fragments for most other books are available; therefore, no study is conducted for them.

In *Jewish Antiquities* (20 books), Josephus writes a preface only for Books 1 and 14. The preface at the beginning of Book 14, according to R. Marcus (see Josephus' *Jewish Antiquities*, 1926, vol. 6:3), is written probably because Josephus will begin to use Nicholas of Damascus as his chief source from Book 14 onward. Considering that in the preface of Book I section 3 Josephus states that he will use the sacred Scriptures (the Hebrew and the Greek Scriptures) as his chief source and will follow them closely to write his books, it represents a change of chief source from Book 14 onward (i.e., a change in his writing methodology). Also, in the preface of Book 14 Josephus reiterates two elements he has already mentioned in the preface of Book 1: comprehensiveness and accuracy—elements which he probably believes to be very important in this work.

In *Against Apion* (2 books), Josephus writes a preface for both Books 1 and 2. A study of the prefaces of the two books finds that the content of these two books is seemingly different in nature: in the first book Josephus focuses mainly on his demonstration of the antiquity of the Jewish race through writings from various nations, while in the second book he focuses mainly on refuting the negative statements given by enemies. (In the preface of his second book he writes: "In the first volume of this work, my most esteemed Epaphroditus, I demonstrated the antiquity of our race, corroborating my statements by the writings of Phoenicians, Chaldaeans, and Egyptians . . . I shall now proceed to refute the rest of the authors who have attacked us.") If the above observation is true, the reason why Josephus writes a preface for Book 2 is probably that the nature of the content of Book 2 is different from that of Book 1.

If Luke has followed the common practice of the Greco-Roman historians in writing a preface for the book of Acts because one or more of the four elements (content, reason, methodology and expected result) described in the preface of his Gospel has been changed in Acts, then what is changed? The preface of Acts indicates that it is the content. The Gospel focuses on ὧν ἤρξατο ὁ Ἰησοῦς ποιεῖν τε καὶ διδάσκειν (Acts 1:1b: "of which Jesus began to do and also to teach"), while the content of Acts focuses on τὴν ἐπαγγελίαν τοῦ πατρὸς (Acts 1:4b: "the promise of the Father"). While the above argument—that the focus of the Gospel of Luke is on Jesus' actions and teachings—can easily be supported by the content of the Gospel itself, the argument that the focus of the book of Acts is on the promise of the Father is supported by the way Luke structures his preface in Acts, gradually guiding his reader Theophilus to focus on this subject. The structure is analyzed as follows.

At first glance, it seems that Luke does not state in the preface what he is going to write in Acts. However a comparison of Acts 1:1–5 with the Gospel of Luke (see Annexure 2.5) reveals that Luke actually does indicate what he is going to write. In the preface, Acts 1:1–2 is a brief summary of the whole Gospel of Luke. 1:3 is a summary of chapter 24, the last chapter of Luke's Gospel. 1:4a (καὶ συναλιζόμενος παρήγγειλεν αὐτοῖς ἀπὸ Ἱεροσολύμων μὴ χωρίζεσθαι ἀλλὰ περιμένειν τὴν ἐπαγγελίαν τοῦ πατρὸς—"and while being assembled he commanded them not to depart from Jerusalem but to wait for the promise of the Father") is Luke's paraphrase of Jesus' message in Luke 24:49a, the first half of the last verse in Chapter 24 before Jesus' ascension (καὶ [ἰδοὺ] ἐγὼ ἀποστέλλω τὴν ἐπαγγελίαν τοῦ πατρός μου ἐφ' ὑμᾶς· ὑμεῖς δὲ καθίσατε ἐν τῇ πόλει—"And behold I am sending the promise of my Father to you; but you stay in the city").

Acts 1.4b (ἣν ἠκούσατέ μου—"which, (he said), 'you have heard me'"), together with 1:5 (ὅτι Ἰωάννης μὲν ἐβάπτισεν ὕδατι, ὑμεῖς δὲ ἐν πνεύματι βαπτισθήσεσθε ἁγίῳ οὐ μετὰ πολλὰς ταύτας ἡμέρας—"that on one hand John baptized with water, on the other hand you in the Holy Spirit will be baptized not after many these days.") elaborates on Luke 24:49b (ἕως οὗ ἐνδύσησθε ἐξ ὕψους δύναμιν—"until when you may be clothed with power from high"). "You may be clothed with power from high" in Luke 24:49b can now be understood as "you in the Holy Spirit will be baptized." From the above analysis it appears that while in the preface Luke is giving a brief summary of what he has written in his Gospel to Theophilus, he highlights chapter 24 from his Gospel and then from chapter 24 he highlights verse 49. Judging from Luke's usage of Acts 1:5 to elaborate the meaning of the promise of the Father in Luke 24:49b, he seemingly structures the preface in Acts to focus on this promise. Moreover, this promise of the Father is further elaborated in Acts 1:8, which describes what will happen after the apostles are baptized by the Holy Spirit: "But you will receive for yourselves power after the Holy Spirit comes upon you; and you will be my witnesses in Jerusalem and in all Judea and in Samaria and as far as the end of the earth." It is therefore reasonable to believe that in Acts, Luke wants to write to Theophilus about the promise of the Father, which is mentioned in both Luke 24:49 and Acts 1:4–5 and is further elaborated in Acts 1:8. The content of Acts also supports such an observation. The whole book actually revolves around the fulfillment of this promise: after the preface in 1:1–5, Luke elaborates on the theme of Acts (the promise of the Father) in 1:8, and then describes Jesus' ascension and what happened before the coming of the Holy Spirit in 1:6–26. Luke then goes on to narrate the fulfillment of this promise: in

2:1–47 the Holy Spirit comes; in 3:1–7:60 with the power of the Holy Spirit the apostles spread the gospel throughout Jerusalem; in 8:1–12:24 through the lead of the Holy Spirit, the disciples carry the gospel to Judea and Samaria; in 12:25–21:16 Paul, Luke and other disciples, empowered by the Holy Spirit, circulate the gospel to much of the empire on three missionary trips; and in 21:17–28:31 Paul is arrested but the Holy Spirit uses this event to finally spread the gospel to Rome. Therefore, based on the above analysis, Luke does indicate what he is going to write in Acts: the promise of the Father (i.e., with the coming of the Holy Spirit, the apostles and disciples will be empowered to spread the gospel from Jerusalem to the rest of the world, notwithstanding their limitations in financial resources and manpower.)[31]

Concerning the significance of the above study on the writing order of the Gospel of Luke, let me summarize it as follows. Luke writes his Gospel and Acts as a historian and follows the approaches commonly used by the Greco-Roman historians in writing histories. Although Luke indicates in the preface of Acts that there will be a change in content as compared with that in his Gospel (from a description of what Jesus began to do and to teach, to a description of the promise of the Father, which is about the coming of the Holy Spirit and the Spirit-filled ministries of the apostles and disciples in spreading of the gospel), Luke does not mention in the preface what other elements (i.e., reason, methodology including the writing order, and expected result) will be changed. Based on the above observation that if a Greco-Roman historian does not mention an element in the preface of

---

31. Many scholars comment on the theme of Acts, but not all of them explain the difference of contents between the Gospel of Luke and Acts. A study of the works of six scholars (Bock [2007], Bruce [1988], Barrett [2004], Peterson [2009], Schnabel [2012], and Marshall [1980]) finds that only three describe the change of contents. They all share the same view that while the Gospel describes all that Jesus begins to do and teach, Acts records the continuation of Jesus' work through the apostles and believers, empowered by the Holy Spirit. This is much like the promise of the Father we discussed here. The comments of the three scholars are as follows. Peterson (2009:102) opines that "all that Jesus began to do and to teach until the day he was taken up to heaven summarizes the contents of Luke's former book . . . The opening verses of Acts suggest that Luke is about to narrate what Jesus continued to do and to teach after his ascension, through his Spirit and the ministry of his followers," Schnabel (2012: not available) believes that "in the first volume, Luke described the beginning of Jesus' work and teaching, in the second volume, he now describes the continuing work of Jesus through the Holy Spirit in the ministry of the Twelve and other believers such as Stephen, Philip, and Paul," and Marshall is of the view that "the first book is of course the Gospel, which is summed up as an account of all that Jesus began to do and teach . . . (and Acts is about the continuation of Jesus' work) so that Luke is associating what Jesus began to do during his ministry with (implicitly) what he continued to do after his ascension; the ministry of Jesus was the beginning of Christianity."

a sequel that element will remain unchanged from the previous book, we can reasonably conclude that Luke uses the same writing order for the book of Acts as for his Gospel. If this observation is true, it means that if we can prove that Acts or the Gospel is written in a certain order (e.g., chronological order), we may declare that the other book is also written in that order.

2.4.3 Grammatical Analysis[32]

The objective of this subsection is to conduct a detailed grammatical analysis of the preface of the book of Acts to understand how the preface is structured and what Luke's emphases are. In this subsection I will argue that the main focus of Acts, as indicated in its preface, is the "promise of the Father."

Regarding the overall structure of the preface, Bock (2007:52) agrees with BDF that "unlike Luke 1:1-4, which is a sentence in periodic style, this passage is simply a collection of clauses." Bock is right that the preface is not a period;[33] however, it is beautifully and stylishly structured so as to bring two important words and one main focus to the attention of its reader Theophilus. The preface of the book is one compound sentence divided into two sections, each with its own main clause and its respective subordinate clauses. The first section is from verses 1 to 3. It includes one main clause (Τὸν μὲν πρῶτον λόγον ἐποιησάμην . . . [v. 1a: "Indeed I have produced the first book . . . "]) and five subordinate clauses (1. ὧν ἤρξατο ὁ Ἰησοῦς ποιεῖν τε καὶ διδάσκειν [v. 1b: "of which Jesus began to do and also to teach"], 2. ἄχρι ἧς ἡμέρας . . . ἀνελήμφθη [v. 2a: "until the day in which . . . he was taken up"], 3. οὓς ἐξελέξατο [v.2b: "whom he had chosen"], 4. οἷς καὶ παρέστησεν ἑαυτὸν ζῶντα . . . [v. 3a: "to whom also he presented himself living . . . "], and 5. μετὰ τὸ παθεῖν αὐτὸν [v. 3b: "after he had suffered"]). An important word in the first three verses is ἀποστόλοις ("to apostles"). This is evident in the fact that in verses 1 and 2 Luke makes use of the main clause and the first two subordinate clauses to draw his reader's attention step by step to this word. In verses 1 and 2 he first refers to his Gospel, and then explains further the content of this first book—it is about the things Jesus began to do and to teach. Luke then explains further the time frame in which Jesus acted and taught—until the day when he was taken up. He follows with details

---

32. Refer to Annexure 2.4 for the sentence flow.

33. The definition of a period given by Spencer (1998:199, 201) is as follows: "For the ancient Greek, a period is a sentence in which one to four clauses (members) or phrases are combined in such a way as to have a beginning and an end, a circular form, arranged to fit the thought to be expressed. A period is a well-rounded unity."

of Jesus' assumption: after he has commanded his apostles. Finally, Luke stresses that these apostles are the ones whom Jesus himself has chosen. In verse 3 Luke uses a long subordinate relative clause to modify the important word ἀποστόλοις, explaining to Theophilus that it is *to these apostles* Jesus has presented himself alive after his passion by many proofs, *it is to them* Jesus has presented himself in a total of forty days and *it is to them* that Jesus spoke about God's kingdom.

The second section is from verses 4 to 5. It includes another main clause (παρήγγειλεν αὐτοῖς ... μὴ χωρίζεσθαι ἀλλὰ περιμένειν τὴν ἐπαγγελίαν ... [v. 4a: "he commanded them not to depart ... but to wait for the promise ..."]), one subordinate relative adjectival clause (ἣν ἠκούσατέ μου [v. 4b—"which you heard me"]) and one subordinate adverbial clause (ὅτι Ἰωάννης μὲν ἐβάπτισεν ὕδατι ... [v. 5: "that on one hand John baptized with water ..."]). An important word in the second half of the sentence is ἐπαγγελίαν (v. 4—"promise"). This is evident from the reason stated in the main clause: the apostles cannot leave Jerusalem because they have to wait for this promise. In verses 4b and 5 Luke uses the rest of the sentence, the two subordinate clauses, to modify and elaborate on what this ἐπαγγελίαν is: it is what "you (the apostles) have heard (from) me (Jesus), 'that on one hand John baptized with water, on the other hand you in the Holy Spirit will be baptized not after many these days.'"

The reason the emphasis of the first part of the sentence in the preface is on ἀποστόλοις and the emphasis of the second half is on ἐπαγγελίαν is that Luke wants to explain to Theophilus the importance of the apostles in God's sovereign plan in the fulfillment of this promise in this book—God, through the Holy Spirit, is going to use them to do this impossible job. Perhaps this helps explain why the ancients named this second book of Luke πράξεις ἀποστόλων (Acts [or Activities] of the Apostles).[34] However, the final emphasis of the preface, and the focus of the book, is the ἐπαγγελίαν, because this is the important word Luke step by step leads his reader Theophilus to focus on—when Jesus talks about the kingdom of God to these apostles (v. 3b), what did he discuss? He told them not to depart from Jerusalem. Why? Because they have to wait for this promise of the Father (v. 4). And what is this promise? The promise of being baptized by the Holy Spirit (v. 5).

Based on the above analysis, there is a similarity in the clause sequence in sections one and two. Each section begins with a main clause; Luke then

---

34. See Bible (1994:407) and Bible (1993:320).

uses modifiers such as adverbial clauses or propositional phrases gradually to bring attention to the key concept, which is also the climax in each section. In each section Luke uses two to three subordinate clauses to elaborate on the important word, to demonstrate its importance. Moreover, the two sections form a continuous flow and overlap each other in the sense that section two is built on the content of section one, leading the reader gradually to focus on the main focus of the book which is "the promise of the Father."

Regarding the tenses of the verbs and participles in the preface, most are in the aorist tense[35] and Luke seemingly uses them to describe background information. However, there are also a number in the present tense, which Luke likely uses to emphasize the messages conveyed through these words. They may also represent actions ongoing today. In verse 1, ποιεῖν ("to do") and διδάσκειν ("to teach") are in the present tense. Luke probably wants to emphasize to Theophilus that Jesus' actions and teachings are carried on by the Holy Spirit through the obedience of believers. In verse 3, ζῶντα ("living" or "alive"), ὀπτανόμενος ("appearing"), λέγων ("speaking") are in the present tense. Luke may want to emphasize the validity of Jesus' resurrection: Jesus appears to his apostles alive as a human being for a long period of time after he has been resurrected and even teaches them about the kingdom of God. The present tense accentuates the ongoing reality of these events. In verse 4 συναλιζόμενος ("while being assembled"), χωρίζεσθαι (not "to depart") and περιμένειν ("to wait for") are in the present tense. Apparently συναλιζόμενος has to be read together with the two previous participles ζῶντα and ὀπτανόμενος in verse 3, and χωρίζεσθαι and περιμένειν are Jesus' commands that come during the three participles ζῶντα, ὀπτανόμενος and συναλιζόμενος. Luke likely wants to emphasize that during the limited time (forty days) Jesus is with his apostles, he gives them important commands while they are together. Luke probably wants to stress what Jesus has actually commanded the apostles to do in the preface; he uses a direct quote of what Jesus has said instead of a paraphrase, and therefore the two infinitives are in the present tense: "not to depart from Jerusalem but to wait for the promise of the Father."

---

35. The following verbs or participles are in the aorist tense: in verse 1: ἐποιησάμην ("I have produced"), ἤρξατο (" he began"); in verse 2: ἐντειλάμενος ("after commanding"), ἐξελέξατο ("he had chosen"), ἀνελήμφθη ("he was taken up"); in verse 3: παρέστησεν ("he presented"), παθεῖν ("to suffer"); in verse 4: παρήγγειλεν ("he commanded"), ἠκούσατέ ("you heard"); and verse 5: ἐβάπτισεν ("he baptized").

Concerning the individual clauses in the preface, there are a number of areas where Luke does not follow the normal word order. In verse 1 the direct object Τὸν ... πρῶτον λόγον ("the first book") is placed before the verb ἐποιησάμην ("I have produced"). It may be a writing style of some Greco-Roman historians to put the direct object before the verb in the first sentence of the preface if it describes what they have written in their previous books. In the beginning of Book 2 of *Against Apion* (see 2.1) Josephus writes an opening which is similar to the first part of verse 1 in the preface of the book of Acts: Διὰ μὲν οὖν τοῦ προτέρου βιβλίου ... ἐπέδειξα ... ("Accordingly on the one hand through the former book ... I have proved ... "). In this case Josephus also put the prepositional phrase (Διὰ ... τοῦ προτέρου βιβλίου) with the object of the preposition (βιβλίου) before the verb (ἐπέδειξα). The effect of this writing style seemingly is for the readers to focus on the author's earlier work. Therefore, through this word order, Luke likely wants his reader Theophilus to focus on his first book for the time being. The verb ἤρξατο ("[he] began") in the subordinate relative adjectival clause in verse 1 is placed before the subject ὁ Ἰησοῦς ("Jesus"). This is probably because Luke wants to emphasize that what he has written about Jesus' actions and teachings in his Gospel is not an end but only a beginning, because in his second book Jesus continues to act and teach through the Holy Spirit working through the obedience of his followers. In verse 2 the verb ἀνελήμφθη ("he was taken up") in the subordinate relative clause ἧς ... ἀνελήμφθη is placed at the end of the clause instead of immediately following the relative pronoun ἧς, and ἐντειλάμενος τοῖς ἀποστόλοις διὰ πνεύματος ἁγίου οὓς ἐξελέξατο ("after commanding the apostles through the Holy Spirit whom he has chosen") is placed between ἧς and ἀνελήμφθη. Luke likely wants to stress that this incident happened after Jesus has commanded his apostles whom he has chosen through the Holy Spirit– although Jesus eventually ascends to the heaven, but before he leaves Jesus has already instructed his apostles what will happen next. In verse 4 the participle συναλιζόμενος ("after being assembled") modifying the verb παρήγγειλεν ("he commanded") is placed before the verb instead of after it. Luke may want to structure a participle parallel with the earlier two participles ὀπτανόμενος ("appearing") and λέγων ("speaking") in verse 3. The prepositional phrase ἀπὸ Ἱεροσολύμων ("from Jerusalem") is placed before μὴ χωρίζεσθαι ("not to depart"), the verb structure it modifies. This would seem to stress the place the apostles must stay for the promise of the Father (i.e., baptism of the Holy Spirit) to be fulfilled. In verse 5 the first part, ἐν πνεύματι, of the propositional phrase ἐν πνεύματι ... ἁγίῳ ("in the Holy Spirit") is placed before the verb βαπτισθήσεσθε ("you will be baptized"). Jesus, as recorded by Luke, likely wants to stress that the baptism is different from that of John: it will be from the Holy Spirit.

In summary, the grammatical analysis results in several observations: (1) in the preface Luke highlights two important words—ἀποστόλοις ("apostles") and ἐπαγγελίαν ("promise"), and an overall theme for Acts—the promise of the Father. This observation affirms the results of the literary analysis: there is a change of content from Luke's Gospel to Acts; (2) Luke seems to place particular emphases on Jesus' continued actions and teachings through the Holy Spirit, his resurrection, and his final command to his apostles not to depart from Jerusalem but to wait for the promise of the Father: baptism by the Holy Spirit.

2.4.4 Conclusion

Luke seems to have followed the general approach used by Greco-Roman historians in writing a preface for his sequel. He includes a preface for Acts because there is a change in one of the four components (content, reason, methodology and expected result) in Acts as compared with his Gospel, that component being the content. As Luke does not mention the writing order in the preface of Acts, based on an understanding of the general approach used by Greco-Roman historians for writing prefaces for their sequels that if they do not mention a component in the preface that component will remain unchanged in the sequel, the writing order in Acts is probably the same as that of the Gospel of Luke. We have now completed the study of Luke's two prefaces. In the next section a detailed word study for καθεξῆς will be conducted.

2.5 A STUDY OF ΚΑΘΕΞΗΣ

Luke states in the preface of his Gospel that he writes it "in an orderly account" (καθεξῆς, 1:3). As Luke does not explain in the context what an orderly account means—whether it means chronological or other logical order—a study of the meaning of καθεξῆς is important for us in understanding what possible meanings it has, which in turn may shed light on the order Luke uses in writing his Gospel. This section will include the following subsections: In subsection one I will study all the usages of καθεξῆς in the Bible and ascertain its probable meaning in each occurrence, and will categorize them according to the categories of meaning shown in BDAG. In subsection two I will study the etymology of the word. In subsection three

48   A Defense for the Chronological Order of Luke's Gospel

I will study the words related to καθεξῆς (words which share the same root words with καθεξῆς) and also the phrases in the Bible which contain the root words of καθεξῆς. In subsection four I will study the meanings of καθεξῆς in contemporary Greek usages and then categorize them as in subsection one above. At the end of this section I will give a conclusion for the studies conducted in subsections one to four. The main arguments of this section are (1) καθεξῆς does not refer to just any logical order, it refers to a sequence with the characteristic "next down to the end," with "next" referring to the neighbor closest to the one before in the unit of measure mentioned or implied in the context (i.e., time, distance or hierarchy of importance), and sharing the same subject under discussion with the one before; (2) καθεξῆς in Luke 1:3 likely means a sequence which features the characteristic "next down to the end"; with "next" referring to the next act or teaching closest in time (the unit of measure) to the one before conducted by Jesus (the subject under discussion), and this means chronological order; and (3) καθεξῆς in Luke 1:3 refers to a time sequence. In the case of the Gospel, it most likely means "in chronological order."

2.5.1 A Study of the Usages of Καθεξῆς in the Bible[36]

According to BDAG (2007:490) καθεξῆς means "pertinent to being in sequence in (1) time, (2) space, or (3) logic." In this subsection I will study the meanings of καθεξῆς in the biblical usages and categorize them according to the three categories above and then ascertain which category καθεξῆς in Luke 1:3 most likely falls under. In this subsection we find that καθεξῆς usually is categorized as "sequence—time," and when Luke uses καθεξῆς to describe "sequence- time" in other passages, he uses it to describe chronological order.

Καθεξῆς appears only five times in the New Testament and does not appear in the Septuagint. All five occurrences are by Luke in his Gospel and Acts. Other than the usage in Luke 1:3, καθεξῆς appears in Luke 8:1, Acts 3:24, 11:4 and 18:23. Luke 8:1 describes the beginning of a new episode where Jesus travels with the twelve apostles to towns and villages to preach the gospel, after he has forgiven the sins of a woman in the Pharisee Simon's house (Luke 7:36–50). The Greek may be translated as: "and it happened in the *following* (days) also he himself went about through city and village while preaching and bringing good news (about) the kingdom of God and

---

36. Refer to Annexure 2.6 for categorization of the meanings of καθεξῆς in usages discussed in this section.

the twelve (were) with him" (Καὶ ἐγένετο ἐν τῷ καθεξῆς καὶ αὐτὸς διώδευεν κατὰ πόλιν καὶ κώμην κηρύσσων καὶ εὐαγγελιζόμενος τὴν βασιλείαν τοῦ θεοῦ καὶ οἱ δώδεκα σὺν αὐτῷ). Καθεξῆς seemingly means "following (days)" here.[37] It describes a sequence of days in which Jesus' traveling and preaching happens; it also relates the current event in 8:1 to the previous event of 7:36–50 in the sense that the current event happens right after the previous event. It is therefore categorized as "sequence—time."

Acts 3:24 is a statement Peter made in his second sermon in Acts. The Greek may be translated as: "and also all the prophets from Samuel and *the ones*[38] *that follow* as many as spoke and proclaimed these days" (καὶ πάντες δὲ οἱ προφῆται ἀπὸ Σαμουὴλ καὶ τῶν καθεξῆς ὅσοι ἐλάλησαν καὶ κατήγγειλαν τὰς ἡμέρας ταύτας). Καθεξῆς here seemingly means "that follow" or "following." It seems to describe the prophets who come after Samuel in the order of their appearances in history, which probably refers to chronological order. It is therefore categorized as "sequence—time." Acts 11:4 describes Peter when he tries to explain to the circumcised believers in Jerusalem the coming of the Holy Spirit to the Gentiles at Cornelius' house. The Greek may be translated as: "But after starting Peter explained to them *in chronological order* saying" (Ἀρξάμενος δὲ Πέτρος ἐξετίθετο αὐτοῖς καθεξῆς λέγων). Καθεξῆς appears to mean "in chronological order" here because according to the biblical content that follows, Peter describes events in the order in which they happened: he first sees a vision (11:5–10), then the Holy Spirit tells him to follow the messengers sent by Cornelius (11:11–12), Cornelius tells him that he is instructed by an angel to send for him (11:13–14), and finally he begins to preach and the Holy Spirit falls on those who listen (11:15).[39] It is categorized as "sequence—time."

---

37. For reference, ESV and NRS translate the word καθεξῆς as "soon afterwards." NET translates it as "some time afterwards." REB and NIV translate it as "after this."

38. It seems that τῶν is in genitive form because it is an article used as a pronoun and is the object of the preposition ἀπὸ, and therefore I translate τῶν as "the ones" according to the context. According to BDAG (2000:490) and LSJ (1996:852), καθεξῆς has only one form (i.e., it is fitted to modify a word in any form, including the genitive form) and Luke seems to use the word to modify τῶν. Therefore, I translate τῶν καθεξῆς as "the ones that follow." ὅσοι is in the masculine nominative plural form and it matches and parallels οἱ προφῆται in structure which is also in the same form. For reference, NRS translates τῶν καθεξῆς as "those after him." ESV translates the phrase as "those who came after him." NET translates it as "those who followed him." NIV translates it as "(from Samuel) on." REB translates it as "From Samuel onwards."

39. For reference, ESV translates the word καθεξῆς as "in order." NRS translates as "step by step." NET translates as "point by point." NIV translates as "everything . . . precisely as it had happened." REB translates as "the facts as they had happened."

Acts 18:23 describes what Paul does after he has visited Antioch (18:22) in one of his missionary trips. The Greek may be translated as "And after spending some time he went out while passing through *in order* the Galatian country and Phrygia, strengthening all the disciples" (Καὶ ποιήσας χρόνον τινὰ ἐξῆλθεν διερχόμενος καθεξῆς τὴν Γαλατικὴν χώραν καὶ Φρυγίαν, ἐπιστηρίζων πάντας τοὺς μαθητάς). Later in his journey Paul reaches Ephesus (19:1). According to the geographic locations of Antioch, Galatia, Phrygia and Ephesus, Antioch is east of Galatia, Galatia east of Phrygia, and Phrygia east of Ephesus. It seems that Paul is gradually traveling west away from Antioch and towards Ephesus. If this is true, καθεξῆς here probably means "in the order from the cities which are closer in distance west of Antioch (i.e., those cities in the Galatian country) to the ones further away west of it (i.e., those in Phrygia)," which seems to be an order of increasing geographical distance. It is therefore categorized as "sequence—spatial."

The meaning of καθεξῆς in Luke's four uses in Luke 8:1, Acts 3:24, 11:4 and 18:23 seems to fall into two categories. In Luke 8:1, Acts 3:24 and 11:4 it is categorized as "sequence—time," and in Acts 18:23 it is categorized as "sequence—spatial." The unit of measure is time or distance. Καθεξῆς in Luke 1:3 most likely falls under the "sequence—time" category, as Luke uses this word to describe a particular order for presenting the events about Jesus. If this order is the same as that in Luke 8:1, Acts 3:24 and 11:4, it means chronological order.

2.5.2 The Study of the Etymology of Καθεξῆς

We have analyzed the biblical usages of καθεξῆς and in this subsection a study of the etymology of καθεξῆς will be conducted to understand the meanings of its root words and the possible impact on the meaning of καθεξῆς when the root words come together. Silva (1994:43–51) believes that though etymology may be important in understanding the meaning of a Greek word of rare usage in the New Testament, the biblical writer has to intend the word to be taken in its etymological sense for the study of etymology to be meaningful in understanding of the meaning of that particular word in a specific context (i.e., the root words of a word may not necessarily indicate the real meaning of that word unless the biblical writer intends to use the word according to the meanings of its root words); and such an intention can be demonstrated through the notion of transparency. Silva (1994:48) further explains that "the notion of transparency is applied rather broadly to all those words that are motivated, that is, words that have some natural relation to their meaning." One of the examples Silva gives is the word 'leader,' "for someone who knows what to lead means and what the suffix -er stands for can easily arrive at the meaning of the word (Silva, 1994:48)." Silva (1994:50) also stresses the ultimate importance of the biblical context: only when the meaning of a word derived from etymology can nicely fit into the biblical context that the meaning would be meaningful in that specific context. Καθεξῆς seems to be transparent because on the surface it is a compound consisting of two components (or root words) καθ (the short form of κατά) and ἑξῆς, and ἑξῆς means "sequence" in its biblical usages (see my discussion on ἑξῆς below in this section), it seems to imply that καθεξῆς is related to some kind of sequence. The meaning of "sequence" also seems to fit perfectly in the biblical context of Luke 1:3, and it also agrees with the meanings of καθεξῆς in its four other usages in Luke 8:1, Acts 3:24, 11:4 and 18:23 (see 2.5.1), which also indicate "sequence." Accordingly the study of etymology of καθεξῆς seems important. In this subsection we find that καθεξῆς has a possible meaning "next down to the end," and when Luke writes his Gospel in this manner, he probably writes in chronological order.

"Etymology" in CCD (2003) means "the study of the origins . . . of words." There are at least two different opinions about the root words (i.e., the origins) of καθεξῆς. According to Thayer (1930:313) κατά and ἑξῆς (adverb) are the two root words that form καθεξῆς, while Kohlenberger III (1995:486) opines that κατά and ἔχω (verb) are the two root words of καθεξῆς. Thayer (1930:223) believes that ἑξῆς and ἔχω are related and ἑξῆς comes from the future form of ἔχω (ἕξω). This study will cover all the three words κατά, ἑξῆς and ἔχω.

Κατά is a preposition used extensively in the Greek Bible. There are 488 usages in the NT and 1,871 usages in the Septuagint.[40] According to BDAG (2000:511–513), κατά has quite a number of meanings. When it is put together with a genitive, it can mean "down from," "down upon," "down against," "throughout" or "into," while with an accusative, it can mean "in," "through," "during," "according to," or "for." Meanings above such as "down from," "down upon," "down against," "into" and "in" all indicate a downward motion. According to LSJ (1996:882–884), when κατά is put together with a genitive it can mean "down from," "down upon or over," "toward," or "against," while with an accusative, it can mean "of motion downwards,"

---

40. Numbers indicated by the search engine of Bibleworks, v. 7. As the usages are numerous this study will resort to two reputable lexicons, BDAG and LSJ, for the meaning of the word.

"throughout," "opposite," "in accordance with," "concerning," or "nearly, about." The meanings given by LSJ are similar to that of BDAG in the sense that many possible meanings indicate a downward motion. LSJ specifically mentions that this preposition can indicate a "downward motion" when put together with either a genitive or an accusative. Moreover, regarding κατά, Robertson (1934:605–606) also agrees that "the root-meaning of the preposition is not perfectly clear, though 'down' seems to be the idea . . . we sometimes find . . . the genitive (means) *down upon*, and the accusative (means) *down along*." Robertson also mentions that when κατά is combined with other words, "often κατά occurs with 'perfective' force." Based on the above observations it is likely that κατά, when combined with ἑξῆς to form καθεξῆς, gives a meaning of "down" (or indicates "a downward motion") and at the same time gives a "perfective" force to the word, which means "down to the end."

Another root word of καθεξῆς is the verb ἔχω. The word is frequently used in the Greek Bible and in the NT alone it is used 708 times.[41] According to LSJ (1996:749–751) ἔχω commonly means "to have" or "to hold," it can also mean "cling to," "come next to," "follow closely," "neighboring" or "next." BDAG (2000:420–422) agrees with LSJ that if ἔχω is used with a spatial aspect it can mean "to be next to something" or "neighboring," and if used with a temporal aspect it can mean "to be next" or "immediately following." These meanings are very similar to the meaning of the adverb ἑξῆς discussed below.

Contrary to κατά, the adverb ἑξῆς is not common in the Greek Bible. According to BDAG (2000:349), it means "next in a series" or "in the next place," and according to LSJ (1996:594) the more important meanings of the word are (1) "next," if used to indicate time, (2) "next to" or "next in order to," if used to indicate logical connection, and (3) "next place," if used to indicate place. It is used only five times in the NT and is solely by Luke, in Luke 7:11, 9:37, Acts 21:1, 25:17 and 27:18. It appears six times in the Septuagint, in Exodus 10:1, Deuteronomy 2:34, 3:6, Judges 20:48, 2 Maccabees 7:8 and 3 Maccabees 1:9. I will study the meaning of ἑξῆς in each of the above eleven occurrences and will categorize them according to LSJ's three major categories mentioned above.[42]

---

41. See Kohlenberger III (1995:n.2398). As the usages are numerous, this study will again resort to BDAG and LSJ for guidance.

42. Refer to Annexure 2.7 for categorization of the meanings of ἑξῆς for these eleven occurrences.

Luke 7:11 describes Jesus and his apostles going to a town called Nain. The Greek reads: Καὶ ἐγένετο ἐν τῷ ἑξῆς ἐπορεύθη εἰς πόλιν καλουμένην Ναΐν καὶ συνεπορεύοντο αὐτῷ οἱ μαθηταὶ αὐτοῦ καὶ ὄχλος πολύς. In the context ἐγένετο ἐν τῷ ἑξῆς seems to mean literally, "it happened in the *next*." As no noun comes after ἑξῆς it is not clear whether Luke wants to imply χρόνῳ ("time"—i.e., next time or soon afterwards) or ἡμέρᾳ ("day"—i.e., next day) as the noun in this phrase, and Luke mentions neither χρόνῳ nor ἡμέρᾳ earlier. BDAG (2000:349) opines that it should be "time" and read "soon afterwards," while LSJ (1995:594) suggests that it should be "day" and read "in the next day." Since τῷ is in the masculine/neuter form which matches the masculine form of χρόνῳ, and ἡμέρᾳ is in the feminine form, I prefer χρόνῳ to ἡμέρᾳ. Therefore, I would translate this verse as "And it happened *soon afterwards* he went into a city called Nain and his disciples and a great crowd went with him." Based on the context, here the word ἑξῆς means "next" and is related to time.

At the beginning of Luke 9:37 Luke uses ἑξῆς in a phrase which is very similar to the phrase in 7:11. Luke 9:37 says that in the next day, when Jesus and the apostles come down from the mountain, a great crowd meets him. The beginning of the verse reads: Ἐγένετο δὲ τῇ ἑξῆς ἡμέρᾳ, which I translate as, "and it happened in the *next* day." Again ἑξῆς ("next") is related to time. The meaning is similar to the phrase ἐγένετο ἐν τῷ ἑξῆς ("it happened in the next time" or "soon afterwards") used in 7:11 which shares the same construction. In Acts 21:1b Luke is describing one of Paul's missionary trips. It reads: τῇ δὲ ἑξῆς εἰς τὴν Ῥόδον κἀκεῖθεν εἰς Πάταρα. Again, Luke does not supply the noun for τῇ ... ἑξῆς. Similar to the logic mentioned above, I translated the phrase as "in the *next* (day) into Rhodes and into Patara" as an implied ἡμέρᾳ in the feminine matches the feminine τῇ. The phrase is similar to τῇ ἑξῆς ἡμέρᾳ used in Luke 9:37 and therefore ἑξῆς meaning "next" is likely related to time. In Acts 25:17 Governor Festus tells King Agrippa that he has dealt promptly with Paul's case after becoming governor. The Greek reads: συνελθόντων οὖν [αὐτῶν] ἐνθάδε ἀναβολὴν μηδεμίαν ποιησάμενος τῇ ἑξῆς καθίσας ἐπὶ τοῦ βήματος ἐκέλευσα ἀχθῆναι τὸν ἄνδρα, which I would translate as, "Then after they (the Jewish leaders who were against Paul) came together here, after making no delay, in the *next* (day), after sitting on the judgment seat, I ordered the man to be brought in." Here τῇ ἑξῆς is the same as in Luke 9:37 and Acts 21:1, and the context seems to support ἑξῆς being related to time and meaning "next." Acts 27:18 describes the ship Paul is on facing a big storm. It reads: σφοδρῶς δὲ χειμαζομένων ἡμῶν τῇ ἑξῆς ἐκβολὴν ἐποιοῦντο, which I translate as, "and while we were being violently tossed in the *next* (day) we were throwing cargo overboard." Again,

Luke seems to use the feminine τῇ ἑξῆς to describe time and to imply the "next" day. In summary, in all his five usages of ἑξῆς, Luke does not use the word separately but always with a dative article (either τῷ or τῇ). He always uses ἑξῆς to describe time sequence which means either "the next time" or "the next day." It seems that Luke understands ἑξῆς, when used to describe time sequence, as meaning "next," which agrees with LSJ's observation that if ἑξῆς is used to indicate time it means "next."

In the *Septuaginta* (1935) ἑξῆς is used six times. In Exodus 10:1 God tells Moses to approach Pharaoh after the seventh plague and God will harden the hearts of Pharaoh and his servants so that he can perform signs among the Egyptians. 10:1b reads: γὰρ ἐσκλήρυνα αὐτοῦ τὴν καρδίαν καὶ τῶν θεραπόντων αὐτοῦ ἵνα ἑξῆς ἐπέλθῃ τὰ σημεῖα ταῦτα ἐπ' αὐτούς. According to the context it appears that ἑξῆς . . . σημεῖα represents the remaining three plagues that will come but not those already experienced. It seems that God has decided to send the remaining plagues on Egypt and that this is the reason God asks Moses to approach Pharaoh. Therefore 10:1b may be translated as, "for I have hardened his heart and (the heart) of his servants so that these *successive* signs may come upon them." Ἑξῆς probably means successive signs which will happen in a time sequence. In both Deuteronomy 2:34 and 3:6 ἑξῆς is used to describe how the Israelites destroy the cities they have conquered in Canaan (ἐξωλεθρεύσαμεν πᾶσαν πόλιν ἑξῆς). I agree with Brenton (Bible, 1998–1999) that ἑξῆς should be translated as "in succession." Ἑξῆς seems to indicate a spatial sequence for the cities which are destroyed by the Israelites. Judges 20:48 describes how the Israelites destroy the cities and the people of the Benjaminites. Judges 20:48b may be translated literally as: "and they smote them with edge of sword from (the) *next* city to the (last) animal, to all things which were found . . . " (καὶ ἐπάταξαν αὐτοὺς ἐν στόματι ῥομφαίας ἀπὸ πόλεως ἑξῆς ἕως κτήνους ἕως παντὸς τοῦ εὑρεθέντος . . .) Again ἑξῆς is used to describe the spatial sequence of the cities of the Benjaminites which are destroyed one by one.

Ἑξῆς is used in 2 Maccabees 7:8, which describes the seven brothers killed one by one by King Antiochus as he tries to force them to give up their Jewish beliefs. It may be translated as "and he having answered in the language of his father, replied: No! For this very reason also he received the *next* torture as the first (brother)" (ὁ δὲ ἀποκριθεὶς τῇ πατρίῳ φωνῇ προσεῖπεν οὐχί διόπερ καὶ οὗτος τὴν ἑξῆς ἔλαβεν βάσανον ὡς ὁ πρῶτος). Ἑξῆς seems to describe the death of the brothers in a time sequence. In 3 Maccabees 1:9 ἑξῆς describes Ptolemy entering Jerusalem. It may be translated as: "and after (Ptolemy) arriving in Jerusalem and after sacrificing to the great God and after paying gifts and after doing something of the *next* acts in the place . . . " (διακομισθεὶς δὲ εἰς Ἱεροσόλυμα καὶ θύσας τῷ μεγίστῳ θεῷ καὶ χάριτας ἀποδοὺς καὶ τῶν ἑξῆς τι τῷ τόπῳ ποιήσας . . .) Ἑξῆς seems to describe a sequence of acts done by Ptolemy in chronological order according to their levels of importance in the Jewish custom. Sacrificing to the great God seems to be the most important act; paying gifts apparently is the next most important one, and the next acts likely are the least important ones so that the author does not even describe them. Therefore, I categorize it as a chronological sequence of events which is related to hierarchy of significance, according to Ptolemy's understanding of event of importance.

From the above study, the meanings of ἑξῆς in the Septuagint can be divided into three categories. When it indicates a time sequence (Exod 10:1; 2 Macc 7:8) it means "next." When it indicates a spatial sequence (Deut 2:34, 3:6; Judg 20:48) or a sequence which involves hierarchy of significance (3 Macc 1:9) it means "next to" or "next in order to".

In summary, considering the meanings of its root words, κατά and ἑξῆς or ἔχω, καθεξῆς possibly has a meaning of "next" or "next in order to" (from ἔχω or ἑξῆς) and "down" (from κατά). With the perfective force provided by κατά, καθεξῆς likely means "next down to the end" or "next in order to, and down to the end." This potential meaning seems to fit quite nicely in the context of Luke 1:3, indicating that Luke possibly intends to write one event after another according to their time of happening ("next" or "next in order to" and "down") for everything he has investigated (to the end). If this is true, the use of καθεξῆς suggests Luke writes his Gospel in chronological order.

2.5.3 A Study of the Words Related to Καθεξῆς

In this subsection I will explore the meanings of (a) the words related to καθεξῆς and (b) the phrases in the NT and the Septuagint which contain the root words of καθεξῆς. To understand whether a word conveys a concept (and in this case whether καθεξῆς conveys the concept of "sequence" or "chronological order"), Long (2005:146) seems to opine that it is problematic only to study the word: "in reality, a single theme may be represented by several different words or phrases, and the totality of a certain truth/theme may not be represented in one word," and Long proposes that we also have to study the word's cognates (words built from the same Greek root), synonyms (other words having similar meanings), and even antonyms (words with the opposite meaning)." Therefore, comparing the meaning of these words and phrases may yield a more accurate understanding of the meaning of καθεξῆς in Luke 1:3. For the first part of this exercise, "related" or "cognate" words are defined as follows: (1) words which have the same roots as καθεξῆς, i.e., words formed by κατά and ἑξῆς or κατά and ἔχω, (2) words in the same word family as classified by the *Greek-English Concordance to the New Testament* (GECNT), including antonyms (words opposite in meaning to καθεξῆς) and synonyms (words with meaning similar to καθεξῆς), and (3) words indicated by BDAG or LSJ as having a meaning similar to and used interchangeably with καθεξῆς. For the second part, "related phrases" are defined as follows: A related phrase should include either (1) κατά or its related form καθ and then ἑξῆς in proper sequence or (2) κατά or its related form καθ and then ἔχω or its related forms in proper sequence.

Using these guidelines, cognate words are κατέχω, κάθεξις, ἀνοχή and ἐφεξῆς. However, a detailed analysis of κατέχω, κάθεξις,[43] ἀνοχή[44] and

---

43. In the study of words related to καθεξῆς, κατέχω is identified as having the same root words (κατά and ἔχω). Κατέχω and its related forms appear 68 times in the NT and the Septuagint (from GECNT and Hatch & Redpath: Gen 22:13, 24:56, 39:20, 42:19; Exod 32:13; Josh 1:11; Judg 13: 15, 13:16, 19:4; Ruth 1:13; 2 Sam 1:9, 2:21, 4:10, 6:6 (x2); 1 Kgs 1:51, 2:28, 2:29; 2 Kgs 3:10 (as a variant towards παρερχομένους), 12:13; 1 Chr 13:9; 2 Chr 15:8; Neh 3:4; Tob 10:2; Jdt 5:19; Job 15:24, 23:9, 27:17, 34:14; Pss 68:37, 72:12, 118:53, 138:10; Prov 18:22, 19:15; Song 3:8; Wis 17:4; Sir 46:9; Isa 40:22; Jer 6:24, 13:21, 27:16, 37:6; Ezek 33:24; Dan 7:18, 22; 1 Macc 6:27; 2 Macc 1:31, 15:5; 3 Macc 5:12; Luke 4:42, 8:15, 14:9; Acts 27:40; Rom 1:18, 7:6; 1 Cor 7:30, 11:2, 15:2; 2Cor 6:10; 1 Thess 5:21; 2 Thess 2:6, 2:7; Phlm 1:13; Heb 3:6, 3:14, 10:23. However, an analysis of all these appearances finds that the meaning of the word is not relevant to καθεξῆς. This word seems only to pick up the meaning of "to have" and "to hold" from ἔχω (instead of the meaning "next") and means "hold," "hold back," "hold fast," "suppress" or "bound," etc. There is another word, κάθεξις, which according to LSJ (1996:852), is derived from κατέχω and probably shares the same roots. This word does not appear in either the NT or the Septuagint. According to LSJ it has a meaning similar to κατέχω which is also irrelevant to the meaning of καθεξῆς.

44. In the study of words that belong to the same word family as καθεξῆς, GECNT does not show any related words for καθεξῆς. It only indicates that κατά and ἔχω are the two root words for καθεξῆς (and as mentioned above, Thayer opines that κατά and ἑξῆς are the two root words). Therefore, this exercise focused on the root words ἔχω and ἑξῆς, which provide the meaning "next" to καθεξῆς. While GECNT indicates that the only related word for ἑξῆς is ἔχω, there are 48 related words for ἔχω. A detailed study of all these words (which includes καθεξῆς, κατέχω and ἑξῆς) shows that the only seemingly relevant word is ἀνοχή, which is formed by the root words ἀνα (meaning "up," the opposite of κατά meaning "down") and ἔχω. However, a study of ἀνοχή shows that it picks up the meaning of "to hold" and "to have" rather than the meaning of "next" from ἔχω and means "holding back" or "forbearance," which is irrelevant to the meaning of καθεξῆς.

related phrases⁴⁵ do not provide any helpful information as to the meaning of καθεξῆς. They pick up the meaning of "to have" from ἔχω instead of "next." LSJ (1996:852) and BDAG (2000:489) do list ἐφεξῆς, which can be used interchangeably with καθεξῆς. It means "in order," "one after another," "in a row," and "next to," "successively," "continuously." If used to describe time (e.g., τρεῖς ἡμέρας ἐπεξῆς meaning three successive days) it means "thereupon" and "immediately afterwards."⁴⁶ Middle and Liddell⁴⁷ also define this word as "in succession, without exception, of time." Its meanings of "successively", "continuously" and "in succession, without exception, of time" seem to support the idea that καθεξῆς can mean "in chronological order."

2.5.4 A Study of the Meaning of Καθεξῆς in Contemporary Greek Usage

In this subsection I will study καθεξῆς in contemporary Greek usage to ascertain its likely meaning during the time of Luke. This study will cover the following: (1) all uses of καθεξῆς cited by BDAG and LSJ, and all uses in the Apocrypha, the Pseudepigrapha, Josephus and Philo, (2) all uses in the papyri, and (3) all additional uses from 1 B.C. to A.D. 1 in the Thesaurus Linguae Graecae (TLG) electronic data bank. I will categorize the meaning of each usage according to the three categories mentioned earlier, that is, either a sequence related to (1) time, (2) distance/space, or (3) logic/hierarchy of significance. The categorizations of the meanings of καθεξῆς in this section and in the study of καθεξῆς in the Bible are summarized in Annexure 2.6 for easy reference. In this subsection I will argue that καθεξῆς does not mean just any logical order, but a sequence which means "next down to the end" referring to sequence of time or space or hierarchy of significance.

---

45. Using the search engine of Bibleworks v. 7, searches for the following related phrases were conducted for both the NT and the Septuagint. (1) κατά (or καθ) εχ* phrased together in proper sequence, and (2) κατά (or καθ) εξ* phrased together in proper sequence, and (3) κατά (or καθ) εσ* phrased together in proper sequence, (4) κατά (or καθ) ἑξῆς phrased together in proper sequence. Nothing relevant to the meaning of καθεξῆς is found. Another search was conducted for any of the above four combinations not phrased together but appearing as close neighbors in the same verse. Again, nothing relevant to the meaning of καθεξῆς was found.

46. See LSJ (1996:742).

47. This is the Middle Liddell lexicon found in the TLG database on the internet (there is no website information for this lexicon.)

2.5.4.1. References Cited in BDAG, LSJ and Pseudepigrapha

No usage of καθεξῆς was found in Josephus, Philo or the Apocrypha, but eight usages of καθεξῆς appear in BDAG, LSJ and the Pseudepigrapha. I will study each of these, from Plutarch's *Moralia*, Aelian's *Historical Miscellany*, *Inscriptiones Graecae ad res Romanas Pertinentes*, Oppianus Apamensis Epicus' *Cynegetica*, *Testament of Judah*, *Apocalypsis Moses*, *Martyrdom of Polycarp* and *1 Clement*. For those which have an English translation, I will quote the paragraph where καθεξῆς is used to understand the context, and if necessary, I will provide my own translation of the sentence to understand more specifically what the word means. For those usages without an English translation, I will conduct my own translation to ascertain the correct meaning of καθεξῆς in context.

a. Plutarch's *Moralia* (1969, vol.8:§615b) (A.D. 1–2)[48] describes a group singing and the use of a myrtle branch in the group. The sentence may be translated as follows: "but others say the myrtle branch is not to proceed *in the order from one to one's neighbor in the same couch*, but is to pass across according to each (position) from couch to couch" (ἄλλοι δέ φασι τὴν μυρσίνην οὐ καθεξῆς βαδίζειν, ἀλλὰ καθ᾽ ἕκαστον ἀπὸ κλίνης ἐπὶ κλίνην διαφέρεσθαι). Paul A. Clement translates καθεξῆς as "from each guest to his neighbor in orderly sequence." The way the myrtle branch proceeds is described later in more detail by Plutarch in the same paragraph. Clement translates it as follows: "that the first man to sing sent it over to the first man on the second couch, and the latter to the first man on the third couch, then the second man to the second on the neighboring couch, and so on; so, they say, it seems that the song was named *scolium* because of the intricate and twisted character of its path." It is worthwhile to note that Plutarch does not treat the way the branch is actually passed along as καθεξῆς, though it is also a logical order. Καθεξῆς, in Plutarch's understanding, seems to mean a spatial sequence which features the characteristic "next down to the end" (literal meaning of καθεξῆς found in its etymology); while "next" refers to the neighbor closest to its predecessor in the unit of measure (in a time sequence, unit of measure refers to "time;" in a spatial sequence, unit of measure refers to "distance;" in a sequence of hierarchy of importance, unit of measure refers to "level of importance") explicitly mentioned or implied, and shares the same subject

---

48. The dates of these books are extracted from the TLG online database. The Greek of Plutarch's *Moralia* is translated by Paul A. Clement.

under discussion[49] with its predecessor. In this case, "next" refers to the next person sitting on the same couch—the one who is the closest in distance (unit of measure) to the predecessor and they share the same couch (subject under discussion). The branch is passed from the first person on a couch to the second (next) person on the same couch and then to the third (again, next) and all the way (down) until it reaches the last person on the couch (to the end). Therefore, καθεξῆς does not mean just any logical order, it refers to a spatial sequence which has the characteristic "next down to the end" as mentioned above.

b. Aelian's *Historical Miscellany* (1997, book 8:§7) (A.D. 2–3) describes a large wedding conducted during the time of Alexander the Great. N. G. Wilson has rightly translated the passage as follows: "When Alexander captured Darius he celebrated his own marriage and that of his friends. The number of people marrying was ninety ... For five days *in succession* he celebrated the weddings (πέντε δὲ ἡμέρας καθεξῆς τοὺς γάμους ἔθυεν) ... " Aelian used καθεξῆς to describe how these five days are organized: it is five days in a row from the first day of the wedding to the second (next) day and all the way (down) to the fifth day (to the end). Καθεξῆς here also features the characteristic of "next down to the end," with "next" referring to the next day, the one closest in time (the unit of measure) to the previous day in the same wedding (subject under discussion). Καθεξῆς refers to a sequence which describes time.

c. *Inscriptiones Graecae ad res Romanas Pertinentes* ("Greek Inscriptions Relating to Roman Affairs" IGR IV) (1927, 1432:§9) describes the names of contest winners engraved in an inscription. The Greek may be translated: "the contests after having written under an inscription: Smyrna, Olympia in the sixth and tenth, Hadrian Rome second, Puteoli second, Neapolis third, Actia second, the body of men-at arms from Argos, Nemea third, all (winners) *in their winning order*" (τοὺς ὑπογεγραμμένους ἀγωνας· Σμύρναν Ὀλυμπία τῇ ἕκτῃ καὶ δεκάτῃ, Ἀδριανία Ῥώμην β', Ποτιόλους β', Νέαν πόλιν γ', Ἄκτια β', τὴν ἐξ Ἄργους ἀσπίδα, Νέμεα γ', πάντας καθεξῆς). Καθεξῆς here refers to the order of winning contestants (i.e., champion, first runner up, etc.). Καθεξῆς describes a hierarchy of significance of the success of the performance of the cities in the contests, beginning with the cities which won first prize, then the cities which won second prize (next), and so on (down) until all the winners are described (to the end). "Next" here

---

49. "Same subject under discussion" refers to the same background shared by the two. For example, "acts by the same person" where "person" is the common background shared by the acts.

refers to the next award of importance (unit of measure) in the same contest (subject under discussion).

d. Oppianus Apamensis Epicus' *Cynegetica* 3.59 (A.D. 2–3)[50] describes the several pregnancies of a lioness. A. W. Mair translates the related passage as follows: "Five times doth the lioness loose her zone in birth, and idle truly is the report that she bears but one. Five she bears the first time, but next she travails with four cubs; then *next in order* from her third labor spring three (κατά θ' ἐξείης ὑπένερθε νηδύος ἐκ τριτάτης τρεῖς ἔκθορον); from her fourth spring twin young; and last from her womb of noble progeny the mother brings forth the glorious Lion King." Κατά θ' ἐξείης, which includes the two root words κατά and ἐξείης, may be translated as "down next" or "next down."[51] Similar to καθεξῆς, this phrase describes a sequence meaning "next down to the end." It describes the number of cubs born each time—the first time five are born, then the second (next) time four, and so on (down) until the fifth time (to the end) only one is born. "Next" here refers to pregnancy of next time (unit of measure) by the same lioness (subject under discussion). Again, this phrase refers to a time sequence.

e. In the *Testament of Judah* 25:1 (2 B.C./A.D. 3)[52] Judah describes what will happen after all twelve sons of Jacob have been resurrected. R. H. Charles (1913, vol.2:324) translated this chapter as follows: "And after these things shall Abraham and Isaac and Jacob arise unto life, and I and my brethren shall be chief of the tribes of Israel: Levi first, I the second, Joseph third, Benjamin fourth, Simeon fifth, Issachar sixth, and so all *in order*" (πέμπτος Συμεών, ἕκτος Ἰσσαχάρ, καί οὕτως πάντες καθεξῆς). The order here is not time because it does not follow the birth order of the patriarchs in the Bible. It seems that καθεξῆς here describes the order of the twelve patriarchs according to how blessed (by God) they are. The most blessed one is described first, and then the second in order (next) is described, and so on until the least blessed is described (down to the end). "Next" here refers to the patriarch who is next most important (unit of measure) in the view of God (subject of discussion). The order is a sequence of hierarchy of significance indicating the priority of importance of the patriarchs.

---

50. See Oppianus (1928:116–117).

51. θ' is not translated, following the practice as in Psalm 119:65, where the alphabet θ' is also not translated.

52. For the Greek sentence with καθεξῆς see Charles (1966:103).

f. In *Apocalypsis Moses* 8:2 (1 B.C./A.D. 1)[53] God tells Adam, after he has eaten from the forbidden tree in the Garden of Eden, that God will bring seventy-two strokes upon his body. The author then describes the first (about the eye) and the second (about the ear) strokes and then writes "and likewise *in turn* all the strokes shall befall thee" (καὶ οὕτως καθεξῆς πᾶσαι αἱ πληγαὶ παρακολουθήσουσίν σοι.) I would translate καθεξῆς as "successively." The context seems to indicate that God will impose the strokes one by one upon Adam's body, and if so, καθεξῆς indicates time sequence or chronological order.

g. The Martyrdom of Polycarp 22:4 (A.D. 2)[54] includes a final comment by the author, which Roberts and Donaldson (1885–96:n.p.) translate as follows: "And I again, Pionius, wrote them from the previously written copy, having carefully searched into them ... even as I shall show in *what follows* ... " (καθὼς δηλώσω ἐν τῷ καθεξῆς). Holmes (1999:245) translates the Greek phrase as, "as I will explain in the sequel." Καθεξῆς here is used as a noun to describe another book, probably the sequel to the current book. "Next" here likely refers to the next book (unit of measure) in a spatial sequence written by the same writer (subject under discussion). Καθεξῆς refers to a spatial sequence concerning the next book the author will write.

h. In 1 Clement 37:3 (A.D. 1), Clement (Lake, 1912–13:n.p.) encourages fellow Christians to follow the command of the Lord. Roberts and Donaldson (1885–96:n.p.) translate it as follows: "Let us then, men and brethren, with all energy act the part of soldiers, in accordance with His holy commandments. Let us consider those who serve under our generals, with what order, obedience, and submissiveness they perform the things which are commanded them. All are not prefects, nor commanders of a thousand, nor of a hundred, nor of fifty, nor *the like* (οὐ πάντες εἰσὶν ἔπαρχοι οὐδὲ χιλίαρχοι οὐδὲ ἑκατόνταρχαι οὐδὲ πεντηκόνταρχοι οὐδὲ τὸ καθεξῆς), but each one in his own rank performs the things commanded by the king and the generals." Holmes (1999:71) translates the phrase in Greek as "Not all are prefects or tribunes or centurions or captains of fifty and so forth." My own translation is: "not all are commanders, nor captains over a thousand, nor centurions, nor leaders of a company of fifty, nor those *in (the) order commanding fewer people*." Here I treat τὸ as a collective noun and καθεξῆς as an adjective modifying it. The context describes an order

---

53. For the Greek sentence with καθεξῆς see Tischendorf (1866:4); for the English translation of the passage see Charles (1913, vol.2:n.p.).

54. The Greek text is from Lake (1912–13:n.p.).

beginning from the commander who commands the greatest number of soldiers down to the leaders who commands the smallest number. Καθεξῆς is used to describe those who command even fewer soldiers but are not explicitly mentioned by Clement. It seems that if they are mentioned, they will be mentioned in the order of decreasing number of soldiers commanded. Καθεξῆς's meaning "next down to the end" also fits here where "next" refers to the leader who commands the next smaller number of soldiers (unit of measure) in the same army (subject under discussion). In this regard καθεξῆς seems to describe a sequence of hierarchy of significance of decreasing number of people commanded.

2.5.4.2 Additional References Cited in Thesaurus Linguae Graecae (TLG)[55]

A search of TLG finds four usages of καθεξῆς between 1 B.C. and A.D. 1. As many usages in the TLG have no English translation, I will translate these passages to understand the meaning of καθεξῆς therein.

i. In Antiochus Astrol., *Fragmenta (e cod. Monac. 7)* (volume 7, page 114, lines 4 to 14) (1 B.C./A.D. 1), the context seems to describe an ancient chronological system. The passage may be translated as follows: "And the investigation of the one who acts and who turns about is this: whenever the appointed time of Cronus (Father of Zeus) may become the day, we say; it turns about the whole day and acts the first hour and while it is turning about and acting, it gives the second hour to Zeus and we say the second hour of Cronus . . . Likewise we say the 4th hour of the Sun, the 5th of the Aphrodite, the 6th of the Hermes and the 7th of the Moon, we say when Cronus is turning about, after appointed time of the day also becomes the one who acts. Then again the 8th hour turns about and acts, and the sequence of the future is thus *in order*, indeed the sun turns about the first day and acts the first hour, and the moon the second (hour) likewise . . . ". Καθεξῆς is used here to describe time. Although in the passage the way time proceeds is seemingly described in chronological order, this does not necessarily imply that the sequence of the future is also in chronological order, as the sequence of the future is not clearly explained in the context. But

---

55. No usage of καθεξῆς is found in several reputable additional references. These references include: (1) Moulton and Milligan (1930:§2517); (2) Horsely (1981–1989); (3) Deissmann (1995); and (4) Grenfell & Hunt (1898–1994) (all 18 volumes, except volume 4, which cannot be located, are checked).

if the sequence of the future is the same sequence as described earlier, καθεξῆς probably refers to chronological order.

j. In Onasander Tact., *Strategicus* (A.D. 1) (chapter 30, section T), the context seems to describe how to choose a commander for an army. The passage may be translated as follows: "As it is necessary to conclude by way of syllogism the commander before the battle, why ought he to meet during the encounter with the certain one and why with the other and thus *one after the other* to examine closely his own captains towards the ones of the opponents?" In this passage καθεξῆς is used to describe the method of how to interview people (i.e., "one after the other" or "one by one"). It seems to indicate a kind of logical sequence, though the context does not explain in detail what this sequence is. Καθεξῆς's meaning "next down to the end" also fits here—if the interview is done, the eligible ones will be interviewed according to a logical order until the last one is interviewed. It likely implies a sequential hierarchy of significance.

k. In Vitae Aesopi, *Vita Aesopi Westermanniana* (A.D. 1) (section 40, lines 7 to 8), the context describes a conversation between a master and a subordinate. The passage may be translated as follows: "You have commanded me to hear everything, and to do those things. You did not say: Throw water into the pot and wash my feet and place the sandals and everything *in their appropriate place*." Καθεξῆς is used to describe "the appropriate locations for the subjects which should be placed." It indicates some kind of spatial sequence. Καθεξῆς's meaning "next down to the end" fits here—the items will be placed one by one according to a spatial order until the last one is placed, though the type of spatial order is not specified.

l. In Heron's *Geodaesia* [Sp.] (A.D. 1?)[56] (chapter 6, section 2, lines 1 to 5), the context describes sowing. The passage may be translated as follows:

> "But it is necessary to know, that a peck measure fit for sowing contains 40 litra, and every one litra sows a land of 5 fathoms. For width and length of 5 fathoms while doing 1 litre, also *in (the following) order*:
>
> Width and length of 10 fathoms while doing 2 litres
>
> Width and length of 15 fathoms while doing 3 litres

---

56. TLG indicates that the date of this reference is uncertain.

Width and length of 20 fathoms while doing 4 litres . . . "

Καθεξῆς is used to describe a logical sequence of the area of land which can be sown with the increasing number of litres used. Καθεξῆς's meaning "next down to the end" is appropriate here—the description continues through the maximum number of litres that can be used. "Next" here refers to the next additional litre (unit of measure) used for the extra area of land sown (subject of discussion). Καθεξῆς here is categorized as a spatial sequence.

In summary, the study of καθεξῆς in contemporary Greek usages indicates that it does not usually refer to just any logical order. Plutarch's *Moralia* shows that the way the myrtle branch passes along is not considered as καθεξῆς. Καθεξῆς has a meaning "next down to the end" with "next" being the neighbor closest to the one before in the unit of measure explicitly mentioned or implied, and it shares the same subject under discussion with the one before. Of the 16 references of καθεξῆς studied (see Annexure 2.6), 7 (43.8%) refer to time sequence, 5 (31.2%) spatial sequence, and 4 (25%) hierarchy of significance. Time sequence is the most common meaning of καθεξῆς, and when it refers to time sequence it always refers to chronological order.

2.5.5 Conclusion

There are several observations about the meaning of καθεξῆς in this last section which seem to support the conclusion that καθεξῆς in Luke 1:3 most likely refers to "chronological order." They are as follows:

1. Based on a study of the etymology of καθεξῆς, the word possibly has a meaning "next down to the end" or "next in order to, down to the end." If this is applied to Luke 1:3, καθεξῆς likely means that Luke writes one event after another according to their time of happening ("next in order to") for everything he has investigated ("down to the end")—signifying that Luke probably writes in chronological order.

2. Based on a study of contemporary Greek usages of καθεξῆς, καθεξῆς does not refer to just any logical order. Καθεξῆς refers to a sequence and the "next" in its "next down to the end" definition refers to the neighbor closest to the predecessor in the unit of measure explicitly mentioned or implied in the context, and it shares the same subject under discussion with the predecessor. Most references are to time and space. The references to logic are references to hierarchy of significance.

3. If Luke's understanding of the meaning of καθεξῆς is the same as that of his contemporaries, καθεξῆς likely refers to a sequence which has the meaning "next down to the end," with "next" referring to the next act or teaching closest in time (the unit of measure) to the one previously conducted by Jesus (subject under discussion), implying chronological order.

Besides Luke 1:3, καθεξῆς occurs four times only in Luke and Acts in the N.T., and the usages in Luke 8:1, Acts 3:24 and Acts 11:4 (i.e., 75%) refer to time sequence. Root components of καθεξῆς also seem to be helpful in understanding the word. The roots κατά and ἑξῆς have to do with "next down to the end" or "next in order to, and down to the end." A sequence or order seems to be the basic idea of the root ἑξῆς. In my research I find sequencing that is organized by time, space or hierarchy of importance (see Annexure 2.7). Nevertheless, Luke always uses ἑξῆς to describe time sequence, whether referring generally to time or specifically to hour. In the Septuagint, ἑξῆς is used for time, space and hierarchy of significance. Καθεξῆς does occur outside the Bible in contemporary Greek examples, where it is used to describe sequence of time, space (physical proximity) and hierarchy of significance. Thus, any of these possibilities can occur in the Gospel. Nevertheless, Luke himself used ἑξῆς only with time. In addition, since καθεξῆς is used of a whole gospel, space or physical proximity seems not to be a relevant category. The biblical references would argue more for chronology, while the contemporary Greek references would allow time or hierarchy of significance. Some scholars (see scholarly opinions in the third category in 2.1) have suggested that καθεξῆς has to do with thematic logic. However, in our evidence, thematic sequencing does not appear to be an aspect of καθεξῆς. The study (see Annexure 2.6) shows that BDAG (2007:490) is correct in referring καθεξῆς first to time; καθεξῆς also refers to space or logic (i.e., hierarchy of significance), but those are less important.

2.6 SUMMARY OF CHAPTER

Luke's writing order for his Gospel will affect the approach of our study for Luke's Gospel; therefore, it is important to clarify what this writing order is. More comprehensive research on this subject will include a study of the contents of the Gospel, which follows in chapter 3. Due to limitation of space, study of the book of Acts is not included in this thesis. Chapter 2 has focused on the study of Luke's prefaces in his Gospel and Acts. A study of the prefaces written by other Greco-Roman historians yields the following observations:

66   A Defense for the Chronological Order of Luke's Gospel

   a. Greco-Roman historians, when writing prefaces for the first book in a series, usually include most of the following four components: what the historian will write (content), why the historian writes this narrative (reason), how the narrative will be written (methodology) and what the historian expect from the reader (expected result) (see section 2.3);

   b. there appears to be an understanding between Greco-Roman historians and their readers that the historian will state in the preface of the first book in what order he will write—which is part of the methodology. If the writing order is not stated, he will write in chronological order (see section 2.3);

   c. Greco-Roman historians write a preface for a sequel only when one or more of the four components (content, reason, methodology and expected result) will be changed from that sequel onward. In such a case, the historian will usually describe the change(s) in the preface of that sequel (see section 2.4); and

   d. there also seems to be a general understanding that if a component is not mentioned in the preface of a sequel, it will remain unchanged from the previous books, no matter whether that element is mentioned explicitly in the preface of a previous book or is only implied in the previous content (see section 2.4).

A study of Luke's two prefaces indicates that Luke likely follows the above approaches used by Greco-Roman historians when writing his prefaces. This is evident from two points:

   1. The preface of Luke's Gospel includes all four components commonly included by Greco-Roman historians in their prefaces: (a) reason: Luke gives the reason he writes his Gospel in verse 1—because there are others writing narratives about Jesus, (b) content: Luke states in verse 3 what he will write—a narrative about Jesus, (c) methodology—he describes his methodology of writing in verses 2 and 3 –he has carefully investigated all the eyewitness accounts to ensure correctness and he will write them in an orderly manner, and (d) expected result—Luke states his expectation for his reader Theophilus in verse 4—that Theophilus' faith will be strengthened.

   2. The reason Luke writes a preface for the book of Acts, a sequel, then, is that there is a change in content (one of the four components) from his first book, the Gospel. The change is mentioned in the preface of Acts—the Gospel describes what Jesus begins to do and also to teach

(Acts 1:1), while Acts describes the promise of the Father (Acts 1:4) (see section 2.4).

If the above observations are correct that Luke has followed the general approaches used by Greco-Roman historians in writing his prefaces, then it is reasonable to conclude that even if Luke were not to mention any particular writing order in the preface of his Gospel (i.e., καθεξῆς does not indicate any particular writing order), he would likely write his Gospel in chronological order, as other Greco-Roman historians did in the past (see section 2.3). Moreover, because Luke does not mention the writing order in the preface of Acts, according to the above observation that if any of the four components is not mentioned in the preface of a sequel then that element will remain unchanged as it is in the previous book, it means that Acts probably shares the same writing order as the Gospel (see section 2.4).

But if καθεξῆς does indicate a particular order, our study of καθεξῆς and its root components would possibly reveal to what order it refers. The root components of καθεξῆς are κατά and ἑξῆς (section 2.5), giving the meaning "next down to the end." Further study of contemporary Greek usages of καθεξῆς indicates that καθεξῆς does not refer to just any logical order but to a sequence, and in its definition, "next down to the end," "next" refers to the neighbor closest to its predecessor in the unit of measure explicitly mentioned or implied in the context, and shares the same subject under discussion with the predecessor. Καθεξῆς in Luke 1:3, therefore, likely refers to a sequence which means "next down to the end," with "next" referring to the next act or teaching closest in time (the unit of measure) to the preceding act or teaching conducted by Jesus (subject under discussion). Moreover, καθεξῆς in Luke 1:3 refers either to a time sequence or a sequence of hierarchy of significance. However, based on the biblical usages of καθεξῆς and ἑξῆς, it most likely refers to a time sequence, indicating that Luke's writing order for the Gospel is a chronological order.

This study shows that whether καθεξῆς refers to a particular writing order or not, Luke still likely writes his Gospel in chronological order. This study, therefore, suggests that a study of the chronology in the Gospel is crucial for the understanding of the individual story accounts therein and the Gospel as a whole. However, to test our findings, a more comprehensive study will be conducted in chapter 3 to see if the contents of the Gospel are written in chronological order.

Chapter 3

Analysis of Narrative Sequence in Luke's Gospel

3.0 INTRODUCTION

BASED ON THE FINDINGS from my study of the Greek word καθεξῆς (Luke 1:3b) in chapter 2, I have come to the conclusion that καθεξῆς can be used to describe sequence of time, space (physical proximity) and hierarchy of significance. Καθεξῆς (1) has a meaning "next down to the end" or "next in order to, down to the end," (2) refers to a sequence, and the "next" in its "next down to the end" definition refers to the neighbor closest to the predecessor in the unit of measure explicitly mentioned or implied in the context, and it shares the same subject under discussion with the predecessor, and (3) based on the biblical context in Luke 1:3, most likely refers to chronological order. In this chapter I will conduct a thorough study of the narratives in the Gospel of Luke, comparing them with their parallel accounts in the other synoptic gospels, Matthew and Mark, to see whether the findings support the above-mentioned conclusion. I will try to ascertain the writing order of the Gospel of Luke from a study of the time sequence of each narrative account. This study is based on the logic that if the evidence shows that each narrative account in the Gospel comes after its immediately preceding narrative account in time, then the Gospel must be written in chronological order. Otherwise, I will suggest in what kind of order the Gospel is written.

3.1 METHODOLOGY USED

The following methodology is adopted for the systematic analysis of the narrative accounts. First, I will divide the Gospel of Luke into separate narrative accounts with reference to *The NIV Harmony of the Gospels* by Robert L. Thomas and Stanley N. Gundry (1988) and second, categorize the narrative accounts into the following three categories:

1. Category 1—there is (are) explicit or implicit indication(s) of time and/or writing order in Luke's narrative account which help(s) us determine the writing order of the account.

2. Category 2—there is no explicit or implicit indication of time and/or writing order in Luke's narrative account, but there is (are) explicit or implicit indication(s) of time and/or writing order in its parallel account(s) in other synoptic gospel(s) which help(s) us determine the writing order of the account.

3. Category 3—there is no explicit or implicit indication of time and/or writing order in Luke's narrative account or in its parallel account(s) in other synoptic gospel(s), or the indication(s) of time and/or writing order is (are) not sufficient for us to determine the writing order of the account, and as a result the writing order of the account cannot be ascertained.

For each narrative account, I will document the explicit or implicit indication(s) of time and/or writing order (if any), the category to which it belongs, and the writing order identified (if possible). I will also check to see whether there is evidence to show that it comes after its immediately preceding narrative account in time. Furthermore, the written sequence of each narrative account in the Gospel of Luke will be compared with the written sequence of its parallel account(s) (if any) in other synoptic gospels and any apparent discord will be investigated. A table comparing the proposed time sequence of the narrative accounts in each synoptic gospel is attached as Annexure 3.1 for easy reference.

3.2 OTHER SCHOLARS' OPINIONS ON LUKE'S WRITING ORDER

From my study on this subject in 2.1 and 2.2, I find that scholars such as Easton (1926:2) and Lockwood (1995:101–104), who have based their opinions of Luke's writing order solely on their studies of the meaning of the word καθεξῆς, conclude that Luke's writing order is chronological. However, many scholars think otherwise because of the many unresolved issues regarding chronology in Luke's narratives when they compare these narratives with other synoptic gospels. I will now conduct a thorough study in 3.3 to address these unresolved issues about chronology in Luke's narratives.

3.3 NARRATIVES STUDY

The objective of this section is to ascertain the type of writing order Luke uses for his gospel through a determination of its appropriate category, a study of the time indicated in the text, and observations made on the basis of grammar, literary style and other indications of sequence identified in each narrative account in his gospel. I will also compare each narrative account in Luke to its parallel account(s), if available, in Matthew and Mark.

3.3.1 Luke 1:5–9:50—the Early Years of John the Baptist and Jesus, before Jesus Begins His Last Trip to Jerusalem

1:5–9:50 includes John the Baptist and Jesus' birth accounts, a childhood event of Jesus, the ministries of John the Baptist and Jesus before Jesus heads to Jerusalem for his passion. Important scholarly opinions related to writing order for an individual narrative account, if any, will be discussed in the respective section below.

3.3.1.1 *The birth of John the Baptist foretold to Zechariah (1:5–25) (Thomas and Gundry, 1988:32)*[57]

Category: 1

Time: "It was in the days of Herod King of Judea" (1:5—Ἐγένετο ἐν ταῖς ἡμέραις Ἡρῴδου βασιλέως τῆς Ἰουδαίας), between 37 and 4 B.C. (Schürer, 2007, vol.1:400).

Observations: It happens before the narrative account that follows (Jesus' birth foretold to Mary in 1:26–38). The angel Gabriel mentions Elizabeth's pregnancy to Mary in that narrative account (1:36), which means that Elizabeth is already pregnant

---

[57] Luke 1:1–4 is the preface of the book and is not a narrative account. Therefore, it is not studied in this chapter. For a thorough analysis of the preface in Luke 1:1–4 please refer to chapter 2 of this thesis.

at that time. Therefore the pregnancy of Elizabeth comes before the events in 1:26–38, and the foretelling of John's birth logically comes before Elizabeth's pregnancy.

Writing order identified: chronological.

3.3.1.2 Jesus' birth foretold to Mary (1:26–38) (Thomas and Gundry, 1988:33)

Category: 1

Time: The sixth month of Elizabeth's pregnancy (1:26, 36).

Observations: From 1:36 we understand that Elizabeth is already pregnant with John when the angel Gabriel appears to Mary. Therefore, this narrative account comes after the "John's birth foretold to Zechariah" account in time.

Writing order identified: chronological.

3.3.1.3 Mary's visit to Elizabeth, Elizabeth and Mary's songs (1:39–56) (Thomas and Gundry, 1988:33–34)

Category: 1

Time: After Jesus' birth is foretold to Mary by the angel Gabriel (1:42).

Observations: According to Elizabeth's conversation with Mary, "and blessed (is) the fruit of your womb"[58] (καὶ εὐλογημένος ὁ καρπὸς τῆς κοιλίας σου) in 1:42, Mary has already conceived Jesus at that time. Moreover, when Elizabeth acknowledges that Mary is the mother of the Lord (1:42–43), Mary does not seem surprised or afraid; instead, she praises the Lord (1:46ff). Elizabeth's acknowledgement of Mary as the mother of the Lord confirms to Mary what Gabriel has already told her: her baby is the Son of the Most High (1:31). Also, Mary's trip to visit Elizabeth is very likely triggered by the angel Gabriel's saying that the once barren Elizabeth is now in her sixth month of pregnancy (1:36). Therefore, this account most likely happens after Mary's encounter with the angel Gabriel in 1:26–38.

---

58. All the English translations in this chapter are my translations from the original Greek text of *Novum Testamentum Graece* (Bible, 1993), unless otherwise indicated.

Writing order identified: chronological.

3.3.1.4 Birth of John the Baptist (1:57–80)
(Thomas and Gundry, 1988:34)

Category: 1

Time: The birth of Elizabeth's baby (1:57).

Observations: 1:57 comes after 1:39–56 in time because in 1:39–56 John is still in Elizabeth's womb, while in 1:57 John is born. 1:80 describes him: "and the child (John) was growing and was becoming strong in spirit, and he was in the wilderness until the day of his public appearance to Israel" (τὸ δὲ παιδίον ηὔξανεν καὶ ἐκραταιοῦτο πνεύματι, καὶ ἦν ἐν ταῖς ἐρήμοις ἕως ἡμέρας ἀναδείξεως αὐτοῦ πρὸς τὸν Ἰσραήλ). This verse serves as a brief summary of John's early life from the time immediately after he is born until his ministry debut in Luke 3. The time frame indicated in this verse seems to overlap the time frame of the narrative accounts mentioned in Luke 2 (Jesus' birth and circumcision, Joseph and Mary's presentation of baby Jesus at the temple, and Jesus' childhood trip to Jerusalem) because the narrative accounts in Luke 2 seem to happen after John's birth but before his ministry debut. It may seem that 1:80 is not recorded in chronological order as its implied time frame overlaps the time frame of the narrative accounts in Luke 2. However, the overlapping of time frames appears to be a writing technique suggested by Lucian, a contemporary writer of Luke's time: when a historian has finished the first topic and begins to introduce the second topic, he should structure his writing so that "the first and the second topics must not merely be neighbors but have common matter and overlap" (Lucian, 1999:67). The common matter described in the narrative accounts in Luke 1 (the first topic) and Luke 2 (the second topic) seems to be the fulfillment of God's messianic promise. This fulfillment is introduced by the arrival of an Elijah-like prophet, John the Baptist (Matt 11:14), in Luke 1 to prepare the way for the coming Messiah (Isa 40:3 and Mal 4:5–6), and followed by the birth of Jesus the Messiah in Luke 2. Because it is likely a writing technique Luke has adopted, even though the implied time frame of 1:80 seems to overlap that of the narrative accounts of chapter 2, it does not necessarily indicate that Luke intends not to write in chronological order.

Writing order identified: The narrative account is recorded chronologically, and overlapping chronology is noted in Luke 1:80.

3.3.1.5 Jesus' birth and the shepherds' encounter with the angels (2:1–20) (Thomas and Gundry, 1988:36–37)

Category: 1

Time: The reign of Caesar Augustus, from 30 B.C. to 19th August A.D. 14 (Schürer, 2007, vol.1:345), and during the first census that takes place while Quirinius is governor of Syria[59] (2:1–2).

Observations: Jesus' birth comes after John's birth because his conception is about six months later than that of John (1:26, 36). Therefore, this account comes after the previous account (1:57–80) in time. The shepherds encounter the angels after Christ is born (2:11–12); therefore, it comes after Jesus' birth account (2:1–7) in time.

Writing order identified: chronological.

3.3.1.6 Jesus' circumcision (2:21) (Thomas and Gundry, 1988:37)

Category: 1

Time: The eighth day after Jesus is born (2:21).

Observations: The information regarding time in this verse indicates that this event comes after Jesus' birth account (2:1–20).

Writing order identified: chronological.

---

59. Schürer (2007, vol.2:80) believes that this census is the one mentioned in Josephus' *Antiquities* 18.1.1 §§1–10 which is conducted around A.D. 6 or 7. However, if this is the case, the timing of the census seems to contradict Matt 2:1 where it says that Jesus is born in the days of King Herod, which is likely from 37 B.C. to A.D. 4 (Schürer, 2007, vol.1:400). This is a much disputed matter and there are various explanations given by different scholars. But since it does not seem to affect our conclusion on whether this narrative account comes after its previous account in time, and in view of the insufficient historical information about this census that, as a result, no decisive conclusion can be reached, I will not go into further details of this matter. For additional information on this subject please refer to Darrell L. Bock's commentary (2004, vol.1:903–909) for a thorough discussion on the various explanations of the timing of this census.

3.3.1.7 Jesus is presented in the temple and receives the homage of Simeon and Anna, and the family returns to Nazareth (2:22–40) (Thomas and Gundry, 1988:37–40)

Category: 1

Time: About thirty-three days after Jesus' circumcision (Lev 12:1–8).

Observations: (a) Leviticus 12:1–8 requires a forty-day period of purification for the mother after giving birth to a son: seven days before her son's circumcision and thirty-three days afterwards. After the period of purification, the mother must bring sacrifices to the tabernacle for burnt and sin offerings. Therefore, the presentation of Jesus would have happened after his circumcision. The account of Anna happens at the same time as the account of Simeon. Luke 2:38 says "and in the same hour" or "and in that very hour" (καὶ αὐτῇ τῇ ὥρᾳ), indicating that the two accounts happen at the same time, while Jesus is being presented in the temple.

Luke 2:39 mentions that Joseph's family returns to Nazareth after they have performed everything according to the law of the Lord. This verse seemingly follows 2:22–38 in time. Matthew 2:19–23 also mentions that Joseph's family returned to Nazareth after King Herod's death. They are likely two separate incidents, with Luke 2:39 occurring first and Matthew 2:19–23 much later. Matthew 2:1–23 is unique and not found in other synoptic gospels. The passage is about the visit of the magi from the East, the escape of Joseph's family to Egypt, Herod's killing of the boys in Bethlehem and its vicinity (vv. 1–18), and the return of Joseph's family to Israel after Herod's death (vv. 19–23). Many scholars do not discuss about whether Luke 2:39 and Matthew 2:19–23 is a single or two separate incidents (e.g., Bock [2004, vol.1:253], Green [1997:152], Fitzmyer [2008:432], Nolland [2002:123], Garland [2012:138], Craddock [1990:40], Reiling and Swellengrebel [1993:144] all do not discuss this matter when they comment on Luke 2:39). For the few who discuss about it, Robertson and Plummer (quoted by Thomas and Gundry, 1988:38) believe that Matthew 2:1–18 comes after Luke 2:22–38 (the presentation of Jesus in the temple and the homage paid by Simeon and Anna) but before 2:39b, "they returned to Galilee to their city Nazareth" (ἐπέστρεψαν εἰς τὴν Γαλιλαίαν εἰς πόλιν ἑαυτῶν Ναζαρέθ), and Matthew 2:19–23, which describes the return of Joseph's family from Egypt and their settlement in

Nazareth, is another description of the same narrative account of Luke 2:39b. Marshall (1978:125) and Stein (1992:118) also seem to agree with this view. Robertson and Plummer also believe that Joseph and his family continue to live in Bethlehem after Jesus is presented in the temple and do not return to Nazareth right away, and that their return to Nazareth in Luke 2:39b happens after they return from Egypt after King Herod's death. Therefore, Luke 2:39b is portraying the same event described in Matthew 2:19–23. Thomas and Gundry, however, believe that Matthew 2:1–23 comes after Luke 2:39b and they are two separate incidents, arguing that after Jesus is presented in the temple, Joseph's family goes back to Nazareth right away to bring their personal belongings to Bethlehem and live there before the events of Matthew 2:1–23. Arndt (see Blight, 2008:107) also holds the same opinion as Thomas and Gundry.

I am inclined to agree with Thomas and Gundry that Matthew 2:1–23 comes after Luke 2:39b, because 2:39 says, "and as they had done all the things according to the law of the Lord, they returned to Galilee to their city Nazareth" (καὶ ὡς ἐτέλεσαν πάντα τὰ κατὰ τὸν νόμον κυρίου, ἐπέστρεψαν εἰς τὴν Γαλιλαίαν εἰς πόλιν ἑαυτῶν Ναζαρέθ). It seems that the most natural interpretation of this verse is that Joseph's family returns to Nazareth after they have circumcised Jesus and presented him in the temple. It seems more likely to me that Joseph's family then lives in Nazareth afterwards and never returns to Bethlehem, because there is no concrete evidence in Luke or Matthew to support the argument that Joseph and his family ever live in Bethlehem in this period of time.

It may seem that the star leads the magi to where Jesus lives in Bethlehem (Matt 2:9)[60], but it is also possible that the star leads the magi to Nazareth in Galilee. One may argue that Herod's order to kill the boys in Bethlehem and its vicinity (Matt 2:16) is an indication that Joseph and his family must have lived in

---

60. The works of nine scholars are consulted on whether Jesus's family lives in Bethlehem at the time when the magi visit them. Six of them believe that Jesus' family is in Bethlehem (see Carson, 1984:94; Davies, 1988, vol.1:248; France, 2007:89; Turner, 2009:85; Nolland, 2005:116; and Blomberg, 1992:65) but do not give any reason to support their claim; three (Hagner, 1998:30; Morris, 1992:40; and Luz, 2007:114) do not discuss it when they comment on Matt 2:9. Some believe that Jesus' family first plans to settle in Bethlehem after they have returned from Egypt (see Turner, 2008:97; Davies, 1988, vol.1:273; and France, 2007:74). However, they also do not give reasons or evidence to support their views. The scenarios below are based on what seem to me logical deductions from the related biblical passages.

that area, but Herod's order is based on the answer of the chief priests and the scribes (Matt 2:4) and not on where Jesus actually lives.

Still, some may posit that the angel's instruction for Joseph's family to flee to Egypt is an indication that they live in Bethlehem or in its vicinity and they are in danger at that time, but this instruction may be given because God knows Herod will keep looking for Jesus in his kingdom to kill him, and this may explain why the angel instructs Joseph to come back after Herod's death but not after Herod's killing of the boys in Bethlehem and its vicinity (Matt 2:19). And some may believe that Joseph and his family are living in Bethlehem before they flee to Egypt because they want to go to Judea when they return from Egypt (Matt 2:22), but this only indicates that Joseph's family might have wanted to live in Judea after returning from Egypt, and does not necessarily mean that they have lived in Judea before they take refuge in Egypt.

(b) Luke 2:40, "and the child was growing and was becoming strong while being filled with wisdom, and the grace of God was upon him" (τὸ δὲ παιδίον ηὔξανεν καὶ ἐκραταιοῦτο πληρούμενον σοφίᾳ, καὶ χάρις θεοῦ ἦν ἐπ' αὐτό), likely serves as the ending to the narrative account(s) from Luke 2:1 to 2:39; from the usage of the word "infant, child" (παιδίον), Luke apparently uses verse 40 to give a brief description of Jesus' childhood to come. And if this is true, its time frame overlaps the next narrative account, Luke 2:41–52, which describes Joseph's family paying annual visits to Jerusalem for the Passover festival and what happens in one of these visits when Jesus is twelve. Verse 41, "and his parents were going every year to Jerusalem for the feast of the Passover" (καὶ ἐπορεύοντο οἱ γονεῖς αὐτοῦ κατ' ἔτος εἰς Ἰερουσαλὴμ τῇ ἑορτῇ τοῦ πάσχα), likely implies that Jesus' parents bring him along to Jerusalem every year for Passover when he is a child. Therefore, the time frame of this yearly activity overlaps that of Luke 2:40. In 2:40 Luke seemingly uses the same writing technique suggested by Lucian that he has employed in Luke 1:80. The common subject of the two narrative accounts, 2:1–40 and 2:41–52, is likely Jesus' miraculous and extraordinary childhood experiences. It is unlikely that the usage of this writing technique would affect Luke's intended writing order, though the time frame of the ending or the summary statement at the end of an account will overlap that of the next narrative account (please refer to the discussion of this writing technique in narrative account 3.3.1.4 above).

Writing order identified: The narrative account is recorded chronologically, and overlapping chronology is noted in Luke 2:40.

3.3.1.8 Jesus' Passover in Jerusalem as a child (2:41–52) (Thomas and Gundry, 1988:40–41)

Category: 1

Time: Jesus is twelve (2:42).

Observations: This happens after the previous narrative account, 2:21–39, because verse 42, "and when he was twelve years old" (καὶ ὅτε ἐγένετο ἐτῶν δώδεκα) indicates that Jesus is already twelve at that time. The festival of Passover appears to be combined with the festival of Unleavened Bread during Jesus' time (see Luke 22:1, 7). According to Deuteronomy 16:1, the festival of Passover is on the fourteenth day of the first month (the month of Abib) of a Jewish year, and the festival of Unleavened Bread begins on the fifteenth day of the same month and lasts for 7 days (Lev 23:6). Therefore, the length of stay of Joseph's family at Jerusalem for the festival of Passover is about 8 days in total.

Verse 52 is a note about Jesus' growth which Luke uses to conclude this narrative account, just as he has used 2:40 to conclude the narrative accounts from 2:1 to 2:39. As Luke appears to use 2:52 to cover the time period from where he has left off at 2:51 and up to the point where Jesus begins his ministry at 3:21, then the time frame of 2:52 would overlap the next narrative account, which is about John the Baptist's ministry near the Jordan (3:1–20.) John begins his ministry earlier than that of Jesus (compare 3:3 and 3:21). Luke likely uses the same writing technique in 2:52 as he has used in 1:80 and 2:40, and if so, the common subject of 2:41–52 and 3:1–20 is seemingly the continued fulfillment of God's messianic promise. I would agree with Plummer (1896:78) that Luke has progressively described Jesus' growth from a baby to a man in chapter 2 through his usages of words: "the new born baby" (τὸ βρέφος in v. 16), "the infant, the child" (τὸ παιδίον in v. 40), "Jesus the boy" or "Jesus the youth" (Ἰησοῦς ὁ παῖς in v. 43), and finally "Jesus" (Ἰησοῦς in

v. 52, a proper name which is usually used to describe an adult). It indicates Luke's careful handling of time in a chronological manner in Luke 2.

Writing order identified: the narrative account is recorded chronologically, and overlapping chronology is noted in Luke 2:52.

3.3.1.9 The public ministry of John the Baptist (3:1-20) (Thomas and Gundry, 1988:42-44, 52)

Category: 1

Time: The fifteenth year of the reign of Tiberius Caesar (3.1). Tiberius reigned from 19th August A.D. 14 to 16th March A.D. 37 (Schürer, 2007, vol.1:358); making the fifteenth year of his reign around A.D. 28-29.

Observations: This narrative account takes up where 1:80 has left off about John's story. 1:80 says that John is in the wilderness until the day of his public appearance to Israel, but now 3:2b-3 says, "the word of God came to John the son of Zechariah in the wilderness, and he came to all the region of the Jordan while preaching a baptism of repentance for the forgiveness of sins" (ἐγένετο ῥῆμα θεοῦ ἐπὶ Ἰωάννην τὸν Ζαχαρίου υἱὸν ἐν τῇ ἐρήμῳ. καὶ ἦλθεν εἰς πᾶσαν [τὴν] περίχωρον τοῦ Ἰορδάνου κηρύσσων βάπτισμα μετανοίας εἰς ἄφεσιν ἁμαρτιῶν). The time has come: God calls John to leave the wilderness and preach in the area of the Jordan to prepare the peoples' hearts for Jesus. This account happens after 2:41-51 because at that time Jesus is only twelve (2:42); according to 1:26, John is about half a year older than Jesus, and therefore is about twelve and a half at that time, but in this account John is already an adult answering God's calling.

Thomas and Gundry (1988:43-44) believe that Luke 3:7-18, Matthew 3:7-12 and Mark 1:7-8 are describing the same narrative, and what John said to the crowds in Luke 3:7-9 is very similar to Matthew 3:7-10. The crowds mentioned in Luke 3:7, according to Matthew 3:7, include many Pharisees and Sadducees who Jesus later describes as hypocrites (Matt 23:13ff), telling his disciples to beware of their teachings (Matt 16:11). This may be the reason why John describes them as "offspring of vipers" (γεννήματα ἐχιδνῶν) in Luke 3:7 and gives them a clear warning in Luke 3:7-9. John then responds to the questions raised by others in the crowd (3:10–14). On the whole, 3:1–18 describes the ministry of John in the region of the Jordan, which comes later than the previous narrative account, 2:41- 51.

Verses 19–20 describe the conflict between John and Herod the tetrarch and John's eventual imprisonment. John's imprisonment happens later than Jesus' baptism (vv. 21–22), as it is John who baptizes Jesus (Matt 3:13–15; Mark 1:9–11). According to the gospel of John, John's imprisonment likely happens after Jesus' temptation in the wilderness (Luke 4:1–14).[61] Verses 19–20 likely serve as an endnote to John's ministry to indicate that his role in the fulfillment of God's messianic promise is completed. Luke apparently uses the same writing technique here as he has used in 1:80, 2:40 and 2:52. The overlapping of the time frame of verses 19–20 with those of the narrative accounts 3:21–23a and 4:1–14 is one of the characteristics of this technique, and as mentioned in narrative accounts 3.3.1.4 and 3.3.1.7, it serves as a tool enabling Luke to end his narrative accounts in his desired style and does not necessarily mean that Luke intends not to write in a time-sequential order. The common subject between 3:1–20 and 3:21–23a/ 4:1–14 seemingly is the continued fulfillment of God's messianic promise: with the ending of the ministry of the Messiah's vanguard, John the Baptist, comes the beginning of the ministry of the Messiah Jesus himself.

Writing order identified: the narrative account is recorded chronologically, and overlapping chronology is noted in Luke 3:19–20.

3.3.1.10 Jesus' baptism (3:21–23a)
(Thomas and Gundry, 1988:45)

Category: 1

Time: Jesus is about thirty years old (v. 23a).

---

61. Gundry and Thomas believe that a number of events happen between Jesus' wilderness experience and John's imprisonment (1988:47–52): Jesus does not go back to Galilee immediately after he has returned from the wilderness but stays near Bethany for a few days (John 1:28), and then leaves for Galilee (John 1:43). He then goes to Cana in Galilee to attend a wedding with his mother and his disciples (John 2:1), goes down to Capernaum for a few days afterwards (John 2:12), and goes to Jerusalem for the Passover festival that year (John 2:13–22). He subsequently goes into the Judean countryside to baptize, where John the Baptist is baptizing at a different location (Aenon near Salim) at the same time (John 3:22–23), and it is not until after all the above events that John is imprisoned by Herod (3:24).

Observations: Luke 3:21 says that Jesus' baptism happens "when all the people were baptized" (ἐν τῷ βαπτισθῆναι ἅπαντα τὸν λαὸν). It seems reasonable to believe that John baptizes the people after he has explained what is required of them and that he is not the Messiah they are looking for (Luke 3:7–18). And if this is so, this account happens after 3:7–18. Like Luke, Matthew and Mark place this account (Matt 3:13–17; Mark 1:9–11) after John's exhortation to the people and his explanation that he is not the Messiah (Matt 3:7–12; Mark 1:7–8).

Writing order identified: chronological.

3.3.1.11 Jesus' ministry begins (3:23b-38)
(Thomas and Gundry, 1988:30–31)

Category: not applicable

Observations: In contrast to Matthew, who records Jesus' genealogy at the very beginning of his gospel, Luke chooses to record the genealogy after Jesus' baptism. This may be due to the background difference of their readers. Eusebius believes that Matthew's readers are Hebrews (2007:99), while Luke's reader, Theophilus (Luke 1:3; Acts 1:1), is likely a Gentile.[62] If this is so, the reason why Matthew places Jesus' genealogy at the beginning of his gospel may be due to the Jewish convictions that the messianic king can come only from the line of king David (1 Sam 7:14–16) and the one who can bring blessings to all nations of the world must be a descendant of Abraham (Gen 22:18). To convince his Jewish readers that Jesus is the eligible candidate, a thorough description of Jesus' genealogy at the beginning seems necessary to substantiate these claims.

Luke, on the other hand, writes to Theophilus, a Gentile who may not have much understanding of Jewish traditions. Luke likely uses Jesus' and his forerunner John's miraculous birth accounts, which apparently are more convincing proofs to a Gentile, to show Theophilus that Jesus is no ordinary person but is the Son of God. Luke probably places Jesus' genealogy after his baptism because it symbolizes the beginning of Jesus' ministry as the Son of God. Luke's genealogy also traces back to Adam instead of Abraham, apparently because Adam is the ancestor of

---

62. For example, Luke gives explanations of some Jewish festivals in the Gospel (22:1, 7); he does not need to do so if Theophilus is a Jew. Theophilus is a Gentile is one of the presuppositions of this thesis (see chapter 1).

all human beings and therefore someone Theophilus can more easily relate to himself.[63]

As Jesus' genealogy is not related to my study of narrative sequence, no further work is conducted on this subject.

Writing order identified: thematic.

3.3.1.12 Jesus' temptation in the desert (4:1-15) (Thomas and Gundry, 1988:46, 55)

Category: 1

Time: After Jesus' baptism (4:1).

Observations: It seems that the most reasonable explanation for Luke to include "and Jesus, full of the Holy Spirit, returned from the Jordan" (Ἰησοῦς δὲ πλήρης πνεύματος ἁγίου ὑπέστρεψεν ἀπὸ τοῦ Ἰορδάνου) in 4:1 is that Luke wants to inform his reader Theophilus that this happens right after Jesus' baptism in the Jordan (3:21-22), where the Holy Spirit descends on him. Therefore, this very likely happens after 3:1-22. The observation that 4:1-15 follows 3:21-22 in time is apparently confirmed by the gospel of Mark: after Jesus' baptism in 1:9-11, Mark 1:12 says, "and immediately the Spirit casts him out into the wilderness" (καὶ εὐθὺς τὸ πνεῦμα αὐτὸν ἐκβάλλει εἰς τὴν ἔρημον). Mark indicates that Jesus goes to the wilderness immediately after his baptism. Matthew also places this event (Matt 4:1-11) immediately after Jesus' baptism (Matt 3:13-17).

Out of the three temptations Jesus experienced in the wilderness, Luke's order of Jesus' second and third temptations (Luke 4:5-12) is different from that of Matthew's (Matt 4:5-10). In Luke the second temptation is the temptation on the high mountain and the third is the temptation in the temple, while in Matthew it is the other way round. Among the nine scholars consulted, five of

---

63. Both Bock and Marshall hold similar views on this matter. Bock (2004, vol.1:348) opines that "(for Luke's gospel) the (genealogy) account concludes with ... Adam ... indicates Jesus' relationship to all humankind as their representative ... Matthew, who goes back only as far as Abraham ... focuses on the national promise of a king to Israel." Marshall (1978:160-161) believes that "Matthew shows that ... Jesus (is) the offspring of David and *a fortiori* of Abraham. He thus appears as the Davidic Messiah, and also as the heir of the promises made to Abraham ... (Luke) carr(ies) back ... the genealogy to Adam ... to stress the universal significance of Jesus for the whole of the human race, and not merely for the seed of Abraham."

them believe that Matthew records the original order of the temptations, three (Green [1997:190–196], Garland [2012:177–178], Carroll [2012:102–103]) do not comment on the sequence, and one refuses to give a stand. Marshall (1978:167) thinks that "it is more probable that Luke wished to lay stress on the conclusion of the temptations in the temple, and that he is responsible for the change in order;" Fitzmyer (2008:507–508) opines that:

> (Luke has) reversed the order of the last two scenes because of his geographical perspective—the climactic scene takes place in Jerusalem, ... Other considerations reveal that the Matthean order is the more original. There is not only the progression from desert-floor, to pinnacle, to high mountain, but the quotations of Deuteronomy used by Jesus to rebuff Satan appear in Matthew in a simple reverse of their OT occurrence: Deut 8:3 in Matt 4:4; Deut 6:16 in Matt 4:7; and Deut 6:13 in Matt 4:10. Again, in Matthew the first two temptations challenge Jesus precisely as "Son of God" (which may point to the use of an original pair, to which a third was eventually added). Coupled with the geographical consideration, these seem to argue in favor of the Lucan reordering of the sequence of "Q".

Bock (2004, vol.1:365–366) and Nolland (2002:177) seem to agree with Fitzmyer's view, and Bock (2004, vol.1:366) adds "the clearest temporal adverbs occur only in Matthew (e.g., πάλιν in 4:8, τότε in 4:10, and the summary dismissal of Satan—details that Luke lacks"; Bovon (2002:139) also shares the same view:

> Matthew has probably preserved the original sequence. Luke makes the transposition so that, first, Jesus' last temptation takes place in the temple, which will achieve salvation-historical significance in the course of the last stage of his life; second, the issue of political authority, awkward for Luke, does not take the final, that is, most important, position.

Plummer (1922:110, 114), although he insists the temptation is "an historical fact," believes that "the reasons given for preferring one order to the other are subjective and unconvincing. Perhaps neither Evangelist professes to give any chronological order. Temptations may be intermingled."

Although Marshall, Fitzmyer, Bock, Nolland and Bovon may be right, I have reservations about Matthew recording the correct order; because Matthew relocates and combines traditions quite frequently in his Gospel (see 3.3.1.14), but Luke does not seem to have this practice (see 3.4). Furthermore, I found that temporal adverbs in Matthew such as τότε do not inevitably indicate time (see 3.3.2.8). In contrast, we have seen that Luke intends to follow chronological order. One can also use subjective reasoning to posit Matthew's order having theological perspectives. For example, according to a lecture by Dr. David Matthewson (2007), Matthew 1:1 likely conveys two important themes of the Gospel: Jesus is (1) the son of David (υἱοῦ Δαυὶδ), and also (2) the son of Abraham (υἱοῦ Ἀβραάμ). The son of David indicates the messianic kingship of Jesus; and the son of Abraham refers to God's promise to Abraham in Genesis 22:18 and indicates that Jesus is the designated offspring of Abraham and through him all the nations of the earth will be blessed. Building on top of Matthewson's theory, the placement of the son of Abraham at the end in Matthew 1:1 very likely indicates that Matthew thought the role of Jesus as the son of Abraham is relatively more important than his role as the son of David, and this is supported by the great commission (Matt 28:18–20) recorded at the end of Matthew, where the message "through Jesus all nations will be blessed" is again stressed. The order of the second and the third temptations seem to follow the sequence of the two themes in Matthew 1:1. The second temptation is the temptation in the temple in Jerusalem, and if Jesus could successfully jump down from the pinnacle of the temple without any harm, the Jews who see it happen would likely regard Jesus as the messianic king for whom they have long waited. Therefore, the second temptation in Matthew likely refers to the test on Jesus' capacity as the son of David. The third temptation is about the kingdoms of the world and their splendor (Matt 4:8), the temptation is probably related to God's promise to Abraham in Genesis 22:18 regarding the blessing for the whole world, and is a test on Jesus' capacity as the son of Abraham. If the above observation is true, then apparently Matthew might have relocated the temptation on the high mountain to follow the sequence of the two themes shown in Matthew 1:1 to emphasize the importance of Jesus' capacity as the son of Abraham.

Theologian William David Spencer (2016) suggests that the temptation was an arduous experience. Luke uses the present participle ("he was being tempted for forty days by the devil", 4:2) to indicate an onging event. When "those days" "were completed" (Luke 4:2) or "afterwards" (Matt 4:2), Jesus is hungry and weak. For many days the devil continued tempting and tempting and tempting, trying to wear Jesus down. Thus, the three questions may have been asked many times in many different sequences, as they barraged Jesus over and over again. Luke and Matthew then chose in what order to place the last two temptations.

Another point worthy to note is the descriptions of Jesus' temptations in Luke and Matthew that involve the spiritual realm. Satan appears and has a number of dialogues with Jesus. The locations of the temptations change rapidly from wilderness to high mountain and Jerusalem to wilderness. Since the spiritual realm is an area beyond our knowledge, and because we do not know whether time and sequence in the spiritual realm have the same significance as we know in this world, it is possible that living in an earthly dimension limits us from understanding the time and space in a spiritual dimentsion.

Like 3:18–20, 4:14–15 likely is a summary statement Luke designs for this narrative account. On one hand, 4:14 describes the result of Jesus' victory over the temptations he experiences in the wilderness: he is now "in the power of the Spirit" (ἐν τῇ δυνάμει τοῦ πνεύματος). After Jesus' baptism in the Jordan and his time spent in the wilderness, Jesus now returns to his home town of Nazareth in Galilee (2:51). On the other hand, 4:15 apparently gives a brief summary of Jesus' ensuing teaching ministries in the synagogues of Galilee, in which Luke particularly highlights Jesus' ministries in Nazareth and Capernaum (4:16–44). Luke again seems to employ Lucian's writing technique which he has used in 1:80, 2:40, 2:52 and 3:19–20. The time frame of verse 15 probably overlaps that of 4:16–44. The common subject of 4:1–15 and 4:16–44 is Jesus the Messiah, now full of the power of the Holy Spirit, continuing his ministry.

Gundry and Thomas believe that Matthew 4:12, Mark 1:14a and Luke 4:14a are describing the same account (1988:52), but this may not be the case. Matthew and Mark clearly say that Jesus goes to Galilee after John is put in prison, but Luke seems to describe Jesus returning to Galilee right after his victory in the wilderness, not after John is put in prison. The most natural way to explain why Jesus is in the power of the Spirit seems to be the fact that Jesus has just experienced a spiritual victory in the wilderness. Therefore, Matthew 4:12, Mark 1:14 and Luke 4:14a likely describe two different trips of Jesus to Galilee. And if this is the case, Matthew 4:12 and Mark 1:14a seem to happen after Luke 4:14a, because according to the gospel of John the imprisonment of John happens much longer after Jesus' victory in the wilderness (see footnote 61 above). According to Matthew 4:12–17, Jesus begins to preach after John the Baptist is imprisoned; therefore, it is likely that Jesus' preaching at Nazareth (Luke 4:16–30) and Capernaum (4:31–44) also happens after the imprisonment of John the Baptist. And if this is true, there is a time gap between Luke 4:14 and 4:15, if 4:15's time frame overlaps that of 4:16–44. A considerable amount of time may have passed in between, which Luke chooses not to mention here. It seems that the use of a time gap is a not uncommon writing technique of Luke. For example, Acts 9:25–26 seems to show that after Paul has escaped from the Jews in Damascus he goes to Jerusalem immediately, but according to Galatians 1:18, Paul actually waits for three years before he goes to Jerusalem, producing a time gap of about three years between the events of Acts 9:25 and 9:26.

Both Matthew and Mark mention the calling of four disciples, Peter, Andrew, John, and James, after Jesus has returned to Galilee (Matt 4:18–22, Mark 1:16–20), which according to Carson (1984:119), Morris (1988:132), Gundry and Thomas (1988:57, see note f), is a different account from Jesus' calling of Peter in Luke 5:1–11 and is not mentioned anywhere in Luke (see discussion in narrative account 3.3.1.17 below). If this is so, how would the calling of the four disciples in Matthew and Mark best fit into Luke's sequence? Mark 1:29–31, a parallel account of Luke 4:38–39 (Jesus' healing of Simon's mother-in-law), states that Jesus is with James and John as they go to the home of Simon and Andrew; the most natural explanation for Mark to include the names of these four persons is that Jesus has already called them to follow him. And if this is true, then Mark 1:16–20 (the calling of Simon, Andrew, James and John) must have happened earlier than Mark 1:29–31 and Luke 4:38–39, very likely after Luke 4:14 but before 4:31–44, since all the events in 4:31–44 happen in a very short period of time—two consecutive days in Capernaum (see 4:31, 38, 40 and 42). Moreover, as Jesus seems to be alone in Nazareth in 4:16–30, without any disciples following him (also see footnote 64), it is very likely that the calling of the four disciples happens after Luke 4:16–30 but before 4:31–44.

Writing order identified: the narrative account is recorded chronologically, and overlapping chronology is noted in Luke 4:15.

3.3.1.13 Ministry and rejection at Nazareth in Galilee[64] (4:16–30)

64. Bock believes that Luke does not write his gospel in strict chronological order. One of the arguments he gives is that Jesus' preaching at his home town, Nazareth, is described much earlier in Luke (4:16–30) than in the Gospel of Mark (6:1–6a) (2004, vol.1: 62). However, there is no conclusive evidence that these accounts are describing the same event. Thomas and Gundry believe that Mark 6:1–6a and Matt 13:54–58 describe the same incident (1988:97, also see note s of that page), which is different from Luke's account, and Mark 6:1–6a/Matt 13:54–58 happens about one year after Luke 4:29. I would agree with Thomas and Gundry that Luke 4:16–30 and Mark 6:1–6a/Matt 13:54–58 are different accounts for the following reasons: First, in Matthew and Mark's accounts Jesus is accompanied by his disciples when he comes to Nazareth (Mark 6:1), but Luke's account does not mention the companionship of the disciples and gives readers the impression that Jesus is traveling alone. Second, in Matthew and Mark's accounts Jesus performs miracles (Matt 13:54, 58; Mark 6:2, 5) and healings (Mark 6:5), but none are mentioned in Luke's account. It is also difficult to imagine that Jesus would have time to perform miracles and healings as the angry crowd tries to cast him out of the city and kill him immediately after his sermon in the synagogue (Luke 4:28–29). Third, there is a difference between the comments given by the people of Nazareth after Jesus has finished his sermon in the synagogue: in 4:22 Luke says that they are amazed by his gracious words and say, "Is not this Joseph's son," but in Mark 6:2–3 and Matt 13:54–56 the people do not just question whether Jesus used to be one of them, but also question where Jesus gets his wisdom and the power to perform miracles. Fourth, Matthew and Mark do not mention the name of Jesus' father Joseph (Matt 13:55; Mark 6:3) as Luke does in 4:22 but only mention the name of Jesus' mother Mary. It is possible that Joseph is still alive in Luke 4:22 but has already passed away in Matt 13:55 and Mark 6:3, since it is quite common for the Jews to describe a man as the son of his father if the father is still alive. For example, when King Saul asks David for his name in 1 Sam 17:58, David answers that he is the son of his father Jesse; and earlier 1 Sam 17:17 describes Jesse as still alive at that time. And, on the other hand, it is not uncommon for the Jews to describe a man as the son of his mother if his father has already passed away. For example, in 2 Sam 16:10 and 19:22 David describes Abishai as the son of his mother Zeruiah, most likely because Abishai's father is already dead; earlier, 2 Sam 2:32 indicates that Abishai's father has a grave. Fifth, when Matt 13:54–58 and Mark 6:1–6a are compared with Luke 4:16–30, almost all the content of Jesus' conversation in Luke (4:18–21, 23–27) is not mentioned in Matthew and Mark. Luke 4:24 seems to resemble Matt 13:57 and Mark 6:4. However, Luke 4:24 mentions the lack of acceptance for a prophet in his hometown, while Matt 13:57 and Mark 6:4 mention the lack of honor for a prophet in his hometown. In view of the many differences, I conclude that the accounts in Luke and Matthew/Mark likely describe two separate trips made by Jesus at different times. Moreover, one may argue that Jesus' conversation in Luke 4:23, which he gives in Nazareth, indicates that he has already been to Capernaum, and that as Luke records Jesus' trip to Capernaum (4:31–44) after his trip to Nazareth, it seems that Luke does not write in chronological order. However, if Luke 4:16–30 happens after the imprisonment of John (see 3.3.1.12), it likely happens after Jesus' visit to Capernaum in John 2:12 (see footnote 61), and Luke 4:23 probably refers to what Jesus has done during his trip to Capernaum in John 2:12. Another possible solution is that Luke 4:23 is a prophecy made by Jesus about what the people of Nazareth will actually say to him in the future (i.e., not necessarily in this visit but in a future visit to Nazareth). If this is the case, it is possible that Jesus will have made a visit to Capernaum before that future visit to Nazareth.

(Thomas and Gundry, 1988:56)

Category: 1

Time: After Jesus' temptation in the desert (4:14–15).

Observations: As mentioned in narrative account 3.3.1.12, 4:15 seems to be a preview of Jesus' teaching ministries in the synagogues of Galilee, including those in Nazareth (4:16–30) and Capernaum (4:31–44) after "Jesus returned in the power of the Spirit into Galilee" (ὁ Ἰησοῦς ἐν τῇ δυνάμει τοῦ πνεύματος εἰς τὴν Γαλιλαίαν) in 4:14. With this power he returns to Galilee to begin his ministry, with Nazareth (4:16–30) as his first stop. If the above is true, Jesus' ministry in Nazareth most probably happens after his victory in the wilderness (4:1–14). Moreover, according to Matthew 4:12–17, Jesus begins to preach after John the Baptist is imprisoned. Therefore, it is likely that 4:16–30 happens after the imprisonment of John the Baptist. If this is true, it would confirm our above observation that 4:16–30 very likely happens after 4:1–14, as the imprisonment of John the Baptist seems to happen much later than Jesus' wilderness experience in 4:1–14 (please see footnote 61 under narrative account 3.3.1.9).

Writing order identified: chronological order is possible.

3.3.1.14 Teaching in the synagogue of Capernaum (4:31–37) *(Thomas and Gundry, 1988:58–59)*

Category: 1

Time: After Jesus' ministry at Nazareth (4:31).

Observations: It is very likely that this happens immediately after the previous account in 4:16–30, because Luke uses "came down" (κατῆλθεν) in verse 31 to describe how Jesus travels to Capernaum. Verse 29 in the previous account clearly says that Nazareth is built on the top of a hill, and that Capernaum is a fishing village on the northwestern shore of the Sea of Galilee, which has a much lower altitude.[65] Therefore, Luke probably uses the word "came down" (κατῆλθεν) in verse 31 to indicate the change of elevation from Nazareth to Capernaum. The sequence of Jesus first going to Nazareth (4:16–30) and then settling in Capernaum (4:31–44) is also confirmed by Matthew

---

65. Strauss (2002:364) says that "the Sea of Galilee lies almost seven hundred feet below sea level."

4:12–13, which says that, after Jesus hears of the imprisonment of John the Baptist, he returns to Galilee ("and after he left Nazareth . . . he settled in Capernaum" [καὶ καταλιπὼν τὴν Ναζαρὰ . . . κατῴκησεν εἰς Καφαρναοὺμ]), which seemingly is the condensed version of Luke 4:16–44.

The narrative sequence of Jesus' ministry in Luke 4:31–6:16 almost perfectly matches Mark 1:21–3:19: Jesus preaches at Capernaum and casts out an unclean spirit (Luke 4:31–37; Mark 1:21–28); heals Simon Peter's mother-in-law (Luke 4:38–39; Mark 1:29–31); continues to conduct healing and exorcism and stays overnight at Capernaum (Luke 4:40–41; Mark 1:32–34); leaves for other cities in Galilee on the next day (Luke 4:42–44, Mark 1:35–39); calls Simon Peter again (only in Luke: 5:1–11, see discussion in 3.3.1.17); heals a leper (Luke 5:12–16; Mark 1:40–45); heals a paralyzed man (Luke 5:17–26; Mark 2:1–12); calls Matthew (Luke 5:27–32; Mark 2:13–17); gives a discussion on fasting and on the old and the new (Luke 5:33–39; Mark 2:18–22); passes through the grain field on a Sabbath day (Luke 6:1–5; Mark 2:23–28); heals a man with a withered hand on a Sabbath day (Luke 6:6–11; Mark 3:1–6); has a significant ministry impact in Galilee (only in Mark: 3:7–12); and chooses the twelve apostles (Luke 6:12–16; Mark 3:13–19).

However, Matthew has quite a number of sequence differences compared to Luke and Mark's after Jesus has returned to Galilee from the wilderness (Matt 4:12–17; Luke 4:14–15; Mark 1:14–15). Besides the Sermon on the Mount (Matt chs. 5–7, see discussion in 3.3.1.24) which seems to be unique to Matthew, one example is Matthew describing the cleansing of a leper (Matt 8:2–4) before the healing of Simon Peter's mother-in-law (Matt 8:14–15), whereas Luke and Mark describe them the other way round (the healing of Peter's mother-in-law is recorded in Luke 4:38–39 and Mark 1:29–31; the cleansing of the leper is recorded later in Luke 5:12–16 and Mark 1:40–45). In another example, Matthew describes the healing of a centurion's servant (8:5–13) right after the cleansing of the leper (Matt 8:2–4) but Luke records the cleansing of the leper (Luke 5:12–15) before the healing of the centurion's servant (7:1–10)[66].

Carson (1984:196–198) and Bock (2004, vol.1:466–469) believe that Matthew chapters 8–9 are written in topical order instead of chronological order to reflect Matthew's thematic concerns.

---

66. Mark does not have a parallel account for the "healing of the centurion's servant" found in Matthew and Luke.

McKnight (1992:530) also opines that Matthew at times rearranges and relocates traditions found in Mark and Luke and in Jesus' discourses for thematic purposes. One example McKnight gives (1992:530) is that Matthew apparently combines two different missions in Luke (Luke 9:1–6 [cf. Mark 6:7–13], 10:1–12) into one mission (Matt 9:36–11:1) [67] to "thematically group(ed) material around 'missionary instructions' rather than paying strict attention to chronology." McKnight also believes (1992:530) that Jesus' discourse in Matthew 9:36–11:1 likely incorporates a number of Jesus' sayings at different times (compare Matt 10:17–25 with Mark 13:9–13; Matt 10:26–33 with Luke

---

67. McKnight does not give evidence as to why he believes Matthew combines the two missions in Luke 9:1–6 (cf. Mark 6:7–13) and Luke 10:1–12 into one in Matt 9:36–11:1. An analysis of all the above four passages in the synoptic gospels finds that McKnight very likely is correct about Matthew combining the above two missions, as 11 out of 19 verses (i.e., 58%) in Matt 9:36–10:16 find parallels in the two mission accounts in Luke and Mark, and 9.5 out of 13.5 verses (i.e., 70%) of Jesus' discourse in Matthew find parallels in Luke and Mark. 58% of Luke 9:1–6 (3.5 verses out of 6), 50% of Luke 10:1–12 (6 out of 12 verses) and 71% of Mark 6:7–13 (5 verses out of 7) resemble Matt 9:36–10:16:

Table 9. Comparison of Matthew 9:36–10:16, Luke 9:1–6; 10:1–12 and Mark 6:7–13

Matthew	Parallel in Luke	Parallel in Mark
9:36	-	-
9:37–38 (discourse)	10:2	-
10:1	9:1	6:7
10:2–4	-	-
10:5a	9:2a	-
10:5b-8 (discourse)	-	-
10:9–10 (discourse)	9:3, 10:4	6:8–9
10:11 (discourse)	-	6:10
10:12–13 (discourse)	10:5–6	-
10:14 (discourse)	9:5	6:11
10:15 (discourse)	10:12	-
10:16a (discourse)	10:3	-
10:16b (discourse)	-	-

The above analysis shows that Matt 9:36–10:16 apparently follows the flow of Luke 9:1–6 and Mark 6:7–13 and incorporates the essential parts of Luke 10:1–12.

12:2–9; Matt 10:34–36 with Luke 12:51–53; and Matt 10:37–39 with Luke 14:26–27 and 17:33.) Kaiser *et al.* (1996:458–459) also observe that when Matthew describes Jesus' healing of the servant of a centurion (8:5–13), he condenses the story and leaves out details which are not significant to his Jewish readers. And as a result, unlike Luke who gives the full drama of the story, Matthew leaves out two sets of intermediaries (the Jewish elders in Luke 7:3 and the centurion's friends in Luke 7:6) who are sent by the centurion to plead with Jesus.

I would agree with Carson, Bock, McKnight and Kaiser *et al.* that Matthew seems to relocate, combine and condense traditions at certain times for thematic purposes, and I agree particularly with McKnight's observation concerning Jesus' discourse in Matthew 9:36–11:1. Matthew's more thematic organization might explain why certain subjects do not seem to relate at times to the context. For example, Matthew 10:17–25 describes Jesus' teaching on how disciples should face severe persecution (even death, see Matt 10:21), but apparently persecution is not imminent when Jesus gives this discourse during his Galilean ministries. It would make more sense if this saying is, as Mark describes in 13:9–13, given by Jesus to his disciples during his last days in Jerusalem, where he is about to face persecution and death, and Matthew includes it here to advance the theme of mission and discipleship. If McKnight's observation on Matthew's tendency to combine traditions is true, then it would explain why in Matthew the healing of the servant of a centurion (Matt 8:5–13) is described adjacent to the healing of Peter's mother-in-law (Matt 8:14–15) and they are described as events happening in a single visit to Capernaum; where in Luke the healing of Peter's mother-in-law (4:38–39) and the healing of the centurion's servant (7:1–10) are described as events that happened in two different visits to Capernaum. It is likely that Matthew has rearranged and combined these events for thematic purposes instead of recording them chronologically.

Writing order identified: chronological.

3.3.1.15 *Healing of Peter's mother-in-law (4:38–39)* (Thomas and Gundry, 1988:59–60)

Category: 1

Time: After Jesus' teaching at the Capernaum synagogue (4:38).

Observations: It is very likely that this event happens right after the previous account in 4:31–37, because Luke uses "and after having arisen from the synagogue" (ἀναστὰς δὲ ἀπὸ τῆς συναγωγῆς) in verse 38. If this event does not happen after Jesus' teaching in the synagogue, then it is hard to understand why Luke puts this phrase here. Therefore, the most reasonable explanation is that this happens right after the events of 4:31–37. Luke and Mark share the same order and record this healing (Luke 4:38–39; Mark 1:29–31) after Jesus' teaching in the synagogue of Capernaum (Luke 4:31–37; Mark 1:21–28). Matthew, however, records it (Matt 8:14–15) after Jesus' healing of a leper (Matt 8:2–4) and the servant of a centurion (Matt 8:5–13), where the latter two healing accounts are recorded after this event in Luke and Mark (the leper: Luke 5:12–16, Mark 1:40–45; the centurion's servant: Luke 7:1–10). The difference in sequence between Matthew and Luke/Mark is likely caused by Matthew's rearrangement of narrative accounts to advance his thematic concerns. Please refer to narrative account 3.3.1.14 for a more detailed discussion on this matter.

Writing order identified: chronological.

3.3.1.16 Others healed (4:40–44)
(Thomas and Gundry, 1988:59–60)

Category: 1

Time: When the sun is setting (4:40), probably on the same day as Jesus has healed Peter's mother-in-law in 4:38–39.

Observations: "and while the sun is setting" (δύνοντος δὲ τοῦ ἡλίου) in 4:40 suggests that Luke intends to have it read together with the previous two accounts in 4:31–37 and verses 38–39. These accounts likely happen on the same day: verses 31–37 happen during the morning of a Sabbath day, verses 38–39 happen right after verses 31–37 (see v. 38), and verses 40–44 happen when the sun is setting. Strauss notes (2002:367) that the sunset "marks the end of the Sabbath, when people could carry their sick (to Jesus) without violating the Sabbath commandment." Matthew and Mark agree with Luke and record this narrative account (Matt 8:16–17; Mark 1:32–39) right after Jesus' healing of Peter's mother-in-law (Matt 8:14–15; Mark 1:29–31).

"And it was day" (Γενομένης δὲ ἡμέρας) in verse 42 very likely means the next day, or else this phrase would be meaningless here. Mark 1:35 uses "early in the morning (while still) at night" (πρωῒ ἔννυχα), which likely corresponds to "and evening comes" (ὀψίας δὲ γενομένης) in Mark 1:32 and refers to the next morning. If this is the case, it would confirm our understanding of Γενομένης δὲ ἡμέρας in Luke 4:42. Accordingly, Jesus' departure to a desolate place in 4:42 happens after 4:40-41.

Verse 44 says, "and he was preaching in the synagogues of Judea" (καὶ ἦν κηρύσσων εἰς τὰς συναγωγὰς τῆς Ἰουδαίας). At first sight it seems contradictory to the context, as in the following chapters 5 to 7 Jesus seems to be in Galilee instead of Judea (Luke 5:1, 17-26 [cf. Mark 2:1-12, particularly Mark 2:1], 7:1 and 7:11). Matthew 4:23 and Mark 1:39 also indicate that Jesus ministers throughout Galilee instead of Judea at that time. Both the *Greek New Testament* (Bible, 1994) and the *Novum Testamentum Graece* (Bible, 1993) record a textual variant in this verse: quite a number of manuscripts have "of Galilee" (τῆς Γαλιλαίας) instead of "of Judea" (τῆς Ἰουδαίας) at the end, which seems to be a more appropriate ending according to the context. However, an evaluation of the different manuscripts which supports the two variants finds that the variant "of Judea" has much stronger support and is preferable.[68] If the ending "of Judea" is preferable, then the question is how to explain its seeming contradiction with the immediate context. Plummer (1896:141) and Bock (2004, vol.1:441) opine that Judea here refers to the entire land inhabited by the Jews at that time, which includes Galilee and is not an uncommon usage by Luke (e.g. Luke 1:5, 7:17, 23:5; Acts 10:37). Matthew and Mark also mention some of Jesus' ministries outside Galilee not recorded by Luke (e.g.,

---

68. The Greek New Testament mentions that p75, ℵ, B, C, L, Q^vid, f¹, 157, 205, 579, 892, 1241, majority of the lectionaries together with the lectionary text of the Greek Church, syr^s, h, and cop^sa support "of Judea," while A, D, Δ, Θ, Ψ, f¹³, 28, 33, 180, 565, 597, 700, 1006, 1010, 1071, 1243, 1292, 1342, 1505, most of the Byzantine witnesses, l 211, l^AD, it^a, aur, b, c, d, e, f, ff2, l, q, rl, vg, syr^p, hmg, cop^boPt, arm, eth, geo and slav support "of Galilee." As "of Judea" is supported by the earliest and the highest quality primary Alexandrian text type manuscripts (p75- 2nd/3th century, ℵ—4th century, B—4th century, L—8th century) as well as a number of different text type manuscripts (e.g., Western: syr^s, Caesarean: f¹, 157, Byzantine: 1241), it is superior to "of Galilee," supported by a number of different text type manuscripts of relatively later dates and inferior quality (besides 33 which is a secondary Alexandrian text type manuscript of the 9th century, and D which is a Western text type manuscripts of the 5th century, most manuscripts are either Byzantine or Caesarean text types of a much later date). The variant "of Galilee" is likely an adjustment by later scribes to align the text with Matt 4:23 and Mark 1:39.

Matt 15:21-28/Mark 7:24-30: Tyre and Sidon; Matt 15:29-38/ Mark 7:31-8:9: Decapolis) before Jesus begins his final journey towards Jerusalem (Matt 18:1/Mark 10:1). Thomas and Gundry (1988:64-67, evident from their ordering of events) also believe that Jesus has made at least one trip to Jerusalem (John 5:1-47) between Luke 5:39 and 6:1 which is not mentioned by Luke. Therefore, it is likely that Plummer and Bock's interpretation of "of Judea" is correct as Jesus apparently has ministered to regions inhabited by the Jews other than Galilee at that time, though Galilee, according to the context, seems to be the major area of concern in Jesus' ministry and is specifically mentioned by Luke later in the gospel (e.g. 5:1; 7:1, 11).

Verses 42-43 seem to give a summary statement of Jesus' first visit to Capernaum: he is very well received and the people want him to stay, but he chooses to follow God's will to preach at other towns also. Apparently verse 44 gives a preview of what is going to happen next: Jesus will continue to teach and preach in the land of the Jews, particularly in Galilee. This is supported by Luke's descriptions of Jesus' teaching and preaching (5:1, 3, 15, 17; 6:6, 17, 20-49; 7:1, 22) and also his conversations, which usually are also a form of teaching (e.g., 5:20-25), from Luke 5 to Luke 7. Again, Luke has likely employed the Lucian writing technique here as he does in 1:80, 2:40, 2:52, 3:19-20, and 4:14-15. If this is the case, the time frame in verse 44 likely overlaps the coming chapters, but if so, up to which chapter? Very likely the time frame of verse 44 overlaps that of 5:1 to 7:50, just before 8:1-3 where Luke's next summary statement comes into place. As in the previous chapters when Luke employs this writing technique, the time frame of the summary statement usually overlaps the following narrative account(s) up to where the next summary statement by Luke appears. For example, the time frame of the summary statement in 1:80 seemingly overlaps 2:1-52 where 2:52 is the next summary statement; and the time frame of 2:52 apparently overlaps 3:1-20 where 3:19-20 is an ending with overlapping time frame; 3:19-20 overlaps 3:21-4:14 where 4:15 is the next summary statement, and 4:15 overlaps 4:16-43, where the next summary statement appears in 4:44.

4:16-44 and 5:1-7:50 seem to represent two different phases of Jesus fulfilling his messianic mission of inaugurating the kingdom of God in this world, with 4:16-44 being the first phase—Jesus ministers in Galilee mainly on his own, and at the same time tries to find a base for his ministry; and 5:1-7:50 being the second phase, where he has established a base in Capernaum and now, step by step, builds up his core ministry team (calling of Peter: 5:1–11, calling of Matthew: 5:27–31, choosing the twelve apostles: 6:12–16). Although he mainly ministers in Galilee, he also begins to minister in other Jewish regions (Luke 4:44).

If the above observation is true, then it may at least partly explain how καθεξῆς in Luke 1:3 is applied in Luke's gospel. In chapter 2 of this thesis I have already conducted a thorough investigation on the meaning of καθεξῆς, and I have reiterated the results in the introduction of this chapter. So far my study of the narrative accounts seems to reveal two findings: (a) the narrative accounts from Luke 1 to 4 are likely recorded in chronological order, and apparently the "next" meaning of καθεξῆς (see 3.0) could apply to each event, and (b) Luke seems to separate his gospel into different sections by the use of overlapping summary statements or endings. Because each section follows the previous section chronologically, "next" could also refer to each section. The summary statement at the end of each section usually includes a preview of the following section, where the implied time frame of the statement overlaps the next section up to where the next summary statement occurs. Each section shares common matter with its predecessor (for example, as mentioned above, the common matter of the two adjacent sections 4:16–44 and 5:1–7:50 likely are the different phases in which Jesus begins to inaugurate the kingdom of God.)

Writing order identified: the narrative account is recorded chronologically, and overlapping chronology is noted in Luke 4:44.

3.3.1.17 Calling of Peter (5:1–11)
(Thomas and Gundry, 1988:57–58, 61)

Category: 1

Time: This call happens by the lake of Gennesaret after Jesus has become famous (5:1), very likely after his visit to Capernaum in 4:31–43.

Observations: Although there is no obvious description of time in this account, the call occurs after Jesus becomes popular and many want to hear him (5:1—"And it came to pass when the crowd pressed on him and heard the word of God..." [ἐγένετο δὲ ἐν τῷ τὸν ὄχλον ἐπικεῖσθαι αὐτῷ καὶ ἀκούειν τὸν λόγον τοῦ θεου ...]). Luke explicitly mentions that Jesus becomes known in the surrounding region of Capernaum after his teaching and casting out of a demon there (4:37). It is therefore reasonable to believe that this event happens after Jesus' trip to Capernaum (i.e., 4:31–44).

Thomas and Gundry opine that this account is unique in Luke and is not mentioned in Matthew and Mark. Robertson, however, believes (quoted by Thomas and Gundry, 1988:57) that this account is parallel to Matthew 4:18–22 and Mark 1:16–20, but to me this seems unlikely. Fitzmyer (quoted by Bock, 2004, vol.1:450) observes that there are three key differences between Luke 5:1–11 and Matthew 4:18–22/Mark 1:16–20: (1) Jesus teaches in Luke (5:1–2) but in Matthew and Mark he is walking beside the sea (Matt 4:18, Mark 1:16); (2) in Luke Jesus issues the call after he has performed a miracle (5:4–7) but in Matthew and Mark there is no miracle and the call occurs while Peter and Andrew are casting a net into the lake, and (3) in Luke Jesus calls only Simon (5:10), but in Matthew and Mark, Jesus calls Peter, Andrew, James and John (Matt 4:19, 21; Mark 1:17, 20). Bock (2004, vol.1:456–457) notes that different kinds of net are used in Luke and Matthew/Mark—Luke uses δίκτυα (5:4, 5, 6), which refers to nets used for evening fishing, in contrast to ἀμφιβάλλοντας in Mark 1:16 and ἀμφίβληστρον in Matthew 4:18 which are nets used for shallow-water, day fishing.

Marshall (1978:202) also observes that in Luke "the men have just completed a nocturnal task with a seine or drag net in deep water, ... (but in Mark) they are using a casting net, which was operated during the daytime from the shore or by a person standing in shallow water." Moreover, the call of Peter in Luke is more intensive as compared with that of Matthew/Mark—only Luke mentions that Peter falls down at Jesus' knees and confesses that he is a sinner (Luke 5:8). Based on the above, I agree with Thomas and Gundry (1988:57) that subsequent to Jesus' first call in Matthew 4:18–22/Mark 1:16–20, the four fishermen, including Peter, follow Jesus temporarily and then return to their original vocation of fishing, and after some time Jesus calls Peter again in Luke 5:1–11.

Writing order identified: likely chronological.

3.3.1.18 Cleansing a leper (5:12–16)
(Thomas and Gundry, 1988:61)

Category: 2

Time: Shortly after the Sermon of the Mount in Matthew chapters 5 to 7, see Matthew 8:1–2.[69]

Observations: Luke's usage of "and more news about him was spreading" (διήρχετο δὲ μᾶλλον ὁ λόγος περὶ αὐτοῦ) in 5:15 seems to suggest that this event happens after Jesus' trip to Capernaum in 4:31–44, because after Jesus casts out a demon in Capernaum, Luke says "and the news about him was going out" (καὶ ἐξεπορεύετο ἦχος περὶ αὐτοῦ) in 4:37. Now, after cleansing the leper, there is more news about Jesus going out. However, even if it is true that this event comes after 4:31–44, we still have to decide whether it comes before or after the call of Peter in 5:1–11. Luke seemingly does not provide further information about time in the context. A study of similar passages in other gospels will now be conducted.

Thomas and Gundry believe that Luke 5:12–16, Matthew 8:2–4 and Mark 1:40–45 are describing the same event. According to Matthew 8:1–2, it is very likely that Jesus' healing of the leper happens shortly after the Sermon of the Mount in Matthew

---

69. Matthew uses "and behold" (καὶ ἰδοὺ) in Matt 8:2. The phrase is used 28 times in the Gospel of Matthew. A study of the 28 usages indicates that it adds emphasis to the current event under description and describes time connecting the previous event with the current one. In 21 out of 28 usages it indicates that the current event happens while the previous event is still happening (i.e., both events happen simultaneously), and can be translated as "at that time" or "and now." For example, Matt 2:9 (Bible, 1971) says "(w)hen they had heard the king they went their way; and (behold), the star which they had seen in the East went before them." A natural way to interpret this verse is that while the wise men are still on their way (the previous event) the star goes before them (the current event). For other examples, see Matt 3:16, 17; 7:4; 8:29; 9:3, 10, 20; 12:10, 41, 42; 15:22; 17:3, 5; 20:30; 26:51; 27:51; 28:2, 7, 9 and 20. In 7 out of 28 usages it indicates that the current event happens shortly after the previous event and can be translated as "shortly afterwards." For example, Matt 4:11 (Bible, 1971) says "Then the devil left him, and behold, angels came and ministered to him." A natural way to understand this verse is that soon after the devil leaves Jesus, angels come to serve him. Matt 8:2 likely falls into this category. That is, Jesus' healing of a leper (current event) happens shortly after he has come down from the mountain (previous event). It does not necessarily mean that the healing of a leper happens immediately after the Sermon of the Mount. According to Luke 5:12 Jesus is in one of the towns when he heals the leper, which means that after Jesus comes down from the mountain he has to take some time to enter a town for this event to happen. For other examples, see Matt 8:24, 32, 34; 9:2 and 19:16.

chapters 5 to 7 (see footnote 69). Matthew 5:1 says "his disciples came to him" (προσῆλθαν αὐτῷ οἱ μαθηταὶ αὐτοῦ) to hear Jesus' sermon. Nolland (2005:191), France (2007:156), Wilkins (2004:192), Davies and Allison (1988:425) all agree that "his disciples" (οἱ μαθηταὶ αὐτοῦ) corresponds to Matthew 4:18-22 (Jesus' calling of the four disciples) and therefore includes the four disciples Peter, Andrew, James and John. If this is the case, the healing of the leper likely happens after Jesus' calling of Peter (5:1-11). Since we understand from narrative account 3.3.1.17 that the four disciples very likely follow Jesus only temporarily after Jesus' first calling in Matthew 4:18-22 and Mark 1:16-20, it is not until Jesus calls Peter again in Luke 5:1-11 they become more committed to their teacher and remain with him permanently. The usage of "disciples" in Matthew 5:1, which seems to denote an in-depth commitment to the teacher, likely is used by Matthew after a lasting commitment to Jesus is established in Luke 5:1-11.

Writing order identified: likely chronological.

3.3.1.19 Forgiving and healing of a paralytic (5:17-26) (Thomas and Gundry, 1988:62-63)

Category: 2

Time: Some days after Jesus has cleansed the leper in Luke 5:12-16 (see Mark 2:1).

Observations: Verse 17 (Bible, 1971) says "there were Pharisees and teachers of the law sitting by, who had come from every village of Galilee and Judea and from Jerusalem." This indicates that it has been a while since Jesus has became known to the public, because the news about him has spread not only to the towns and villages of Galilee, but also to Judea and Jerusalem and has attracted attention even from the Pharisees and the teachers of the law.

Thomas and Gundry believe that Matthew 9:1-8, Mark 2:1-12 and Luke 5:17-26 portray the same incident. I would agree, as the key features in all three gospels match: some men bring to Jesus a paralytic on a mat; Jesus forgives the paralytic's sins because of their faith; teachers of the law (and the Pharisees in Mark and Luke) think that what Jesus says is blasphemy; Jesus heals the paralytic to prove that he has the authority to forgive sin, the paralytic walks home; and the crowd is in awe after seeing what happens.

Mark 2:1 explicitly says, "and after (Jesus) entered again into Capernaum after some days" (καὶ εἰσελθὼν πάλιν εἰς Καφαρναοὺμ δι' ἡμερῶν). Based on the context it likely means that some days after the healing of the leper in the previous account in Mark 1:40–45, the healing of the paralytic (Mark 2:1–12) occurs. Therefore, it is reasonable to believe that this event also follows Luke 5:12–16.

Moreover, in Luke, Matthew and Mark the healing of the paralytic comes after the cleansing of the leper, the immediate preceding account in Luke.

Writing order identified: chronological.

3.3.1.20 The calling of Matthew, the discussion of fasting and the parables about the old and the new (5:27–39) (Thomas and Gundry, 1988:63–65)

Category: 1

Time: After the healing of the paralytic (v. 27).

Observations: Verse 27 begins with "and after these (things)" (καὶ μετὰ ταῦτα). This phrase is used 7 times in the New Testament (Luke 5:27, 12:4, 17:8; John 7:1; Acts 7:7, 13:20; and Rev 15:5). A study of all the usages indicates that it likely means "and after the immediately preceding event(s)." For example, Luke 12:4 (Bible, 1971) says "do not fear those who kill the body, and after that have no more that they can do." According to this context, "and after that" naturally means after killing the body (the immediate previous event). In another example, Luke 17:8 (Bible, 1971) says "prepare supper for me, and gird yourself and serve me, till I eat and drink; and afterward you shall eat and drink." The most natural meaning of "and afterwards" is after the master eats and drinks (the immediate previous event). Accordingly, it is reasonable to conclude that this event happens after the healing of the paralytic in 5:17–26.

In Matthew, Mark and Luke, the discussion of feasting and fasting and the parables about the old and the new come immediately after the calling of Matthew. This very likely indicates that the discussion of fasting and the parable about old and new are recorded chronologically after the calling of Matthew.

Writing order identified: chronological.

3.3.1.21 Controversy over disciples' picking grain on the Sabbath (6:1–5) (Thomas and Gundry, 1988:67–68)

Category: 2

Time: On a Sabbath day, at about the time when Jesus carries out a mission in Galilee (Matt 11:1; 12:1).

Observations: There is no explicit or implicit indication of time and/or writing order in the context of Luke to facilitate our determination of the writing order of this narrative account. A study of the parallel accounts in Matthew and Mark is necessary.

Like Luke, Mark (2:23–28) does not provide any indication of time or writing order. However, Matthew (12:1–8) uses a temporal phrase "at that time" (ἐν ἐκείνῳ τῷ καιρῷ) when he begins to describe the narrative account in 12:1. This phrase literally means either "exactly at that time" or "at about that time." This phrase is used three times in the Greek New Testament and only by Matthew. Besides 12:1, the other two usages are in 11:25 and 14:1. 14:1 describes Herod the tetrarch hearing about the fame of Jesus at the time when Jesus experiences rejection in Nazareth (13:53–58) and it seems that "at that time" can either mean "at about that time" or "exactly at that time."

However, this phrase likely means "at about that time," as another usage in 11:25 describes Jesus rejoicing and giving thanks to God at the time when he comments on the non-repentant citizens of Chorazin, Bethsaida and Capernaum (11:20–24), and it is quite unlikely that Jesus would give thanks to God and condemn the non-repentant towns at exactly the same time. Therefore, it seems that Luke 6:1–5 happens at about the time when Jesus gives a comment on the non-repentant towns Chorazin, Bethsaida, and Capernaum, as the immediate preceding account of Matthew 12:1 is about Jesus condemning these cities (see Matt 11:20–30). If this is the case, then Matthew's sequence seems to contradict with that of Luke, because in Matthew Jesus' remark about the non-repentant towns and his thanksgiving prayer (11:20–30) are placed immediately before the disciples' picking grain on the Sabbath account (12:1–8), but in Luke it is the other way round—Jesus' comments on the non-repentant towns (Luke 10:13–15) and his thanksgiving prayer (Luke 10:21–22) occur during the mission of the seventy-two (Luke 10:1–24), long after the disciples' picking grain on the Sabbath (Luke 6:1–5). (Mark does not mention Jesus' comment on the non-repentant towns Chorazin, Bethsaida and Capernaum in his gospel.)

The obvious question, then, is whether Luke records the disciples' picking grain on the Sabbath account, Jesus' comment on the non-repentant towns and his thanksgiving prayer in chronological order. One possible resolution to this apparent contradiction is that possibly Jesus' comment on the non-repentant towns and his thanksgiving prayer (Matt 11:20–30) correlate with his mission described in Matthew 11:1b, "... he departed from there to preach and teach in their cities" (μετέβη ἐκεῖθεν τοῦ διδάσκειν καὶ κηρύσσειν ἐν ταῖς πόλεσιν αὐτῶν), a mission not mentioned in Luke and Mark.

"At that time" in Matthew 12:1 refers to the approximate time of Jesus' mission in Matthew 11:1b instead of the approximate time when Jesus makes his comments on the non-repentant Galilean towns and gives his thanksgiving prayer in Matthew 11:20–30. It is plausible that Jesus' mission in Matthew 11:1b actually occurs at about the time of the disciples' picking grain on the Sabbath, while Jesus gives his comments on the non-repentant Galilean towns and his prayer much later, during the mission of the seventy-two in Luke 10:1–12. This resolution is supported by two observations. First, as discussed in narrative account 3.3.1.14 and footnote 67 above, Matthew apparently combines two different missions (Luke 9:1–6 and Luke 10:1–12) into one in Matthew 9:36–11:1 for thematic purposes. If this is the case, Matthew very likely would also include Jesus' mission, which may have happened much earlier, at about the time of the disciples' picking grain on the Sabbath account, in Matthew 11:1b, and would relocate to Matthew 11:20–30 Jesus' comments on the non-repentant towns and his prayer, which actually happens much later, during the mission of the seventy-two, to advance his theme on mission. The context of Matthew also seems to support such a relocation: Luke 10:21 describes Jesus rejoicing when he gives the thanksgiving prayer, most likely because the mission of the seventy-two is successful (Luke 10:17), but Matthew omits the phrase "Jesus rejoices," likely because otherwise it would look awkward, as Jesus' prayer is now relocated to follow his unsuccessful mission in Matthew 11:1b and the doubt from John the Baptist in Matthew 11:2–3. Moreover, Luke's sequence of placing Jesus' comments and prayer at about the time of the mission of the seventy-two seems to make more sense: Jesus gives the condemnation and final judgment of the non-repentant Galilean towns after he has completed his Galilean mission and is heading towards Jerusalem for his death and resurrection (Luke 9:51), at a time when he will not return to Galilee and these towns will not have another chance to repent before him. Second, both Matthew and Luke seem to support a time gap between Jesus' Galilean mission and his comments on the non-repentant towns/ his thanksgiving prayer. After Matthew has described Jesus' Galilean mission in 11:1 he records the question raised by John the Baptist and Jesus' response in 11:2–19 before he continues to describe Jesus' comments on the results of his Galilean mission and his prayer (11:20–30). Also, Luke records Jesus' comments on the results of his Galilean mission and his prayer during the mission of the seventy-two, indicating that his Galilean mission must have been completed sometime earlier than the mission of the seventy-two. These observations seem to support the proposal that Jesus' mission to the cities he condemned likely happens much earlier than when he gives comments on those cities: his mission possibly happens at around the time of the disciples' picking grain on the Sabbath account, while his comments are given when he sends out the seventy-two.

Matthew 11:1 begins with "and it was when Jesus finished instructing his twelve disciples" (καὶ ἐγένετο ὅτε ἐτέλεσεν ὁ Ἰησοῦς διατάσσων τοῖς δώδεκα μαθηταῖς αὐτοῦ). It seems to imply that Jesus' Galilean mission is carried out at about the time of the mission of the twelve apostles (Matt 10:1–5a), which contradicts the proposed resolution above that Jesus' Galilean mission likely happens at about the time of the disciples' picking grain on the Sabbath. The phrase "and it was when" (καὶ ἐγένετο ὅτε) is used five times in the Greek New Testament and only in Matthew (7:28, 11:1, 13:53, 19:1 and 26:1). According to Carson (1984:195) it is a "formulaic conclusion that terminates the discourse in this Gospel" and "a self-conscious stylistic device that establishes a structural turning point . . . in each case the conclusion is transitional and prepares for the next section." If this is a stylistic device used by Matthew to promote his theological themes, it may not necessarily be used to indicate the time of an event but only to serve as a transitional connector between two sections.

Moreover, in Matthew[70], Mark and Luke, the picking of grain on the Sabbath comes after the calling of Matthew, the discussion of fasting and parables about the old and the new (the immediately previous account in Luke). Therefore, the picking of grain likely happens after the calling of Matthew.

Writing order identified: likely/reasonably chronological.

---

70. Matthew inserts the following narrative accounts between the "calling of Matthew, discussion of fasting and parables about old and new" account (9:9–17) and the "picking grain on Sabbath" account (12:1–8):

Table 10. Narrative accounts inserted between Matthew 9:9–17 and 12:1–8

Matthew	Description	Narrative account #
9:18–26	Healing of woman who touches Jesus' garment, and raising of Jairus' daughter	3.3.1.34
9:27–34	Three miracles of healing and another blasphemous accusation	*
9:35–38	Shortage of workers	**
10:1–11:1	Commissioning of the Twelve	3.3.1.35
11:2–19	Question from John the Baptist	3.3.1.27
11:20–30	Jesus' comments on the non-repentant towns and his thanksgiving prayer	3.3.2.3, 3.3.2.4

* : This event is recorded only in Matthew.

**: This event is recorded in Matthew and Mark but not in Luke.

The sequence of Matthew in this section is very different from that of Luke and Mark. Although both Mark and Luke have a number of accounts which are recorded only in each of them but not the other (for example, see the footnote under narrative account 3.3.1.38 for some accounts recorded by Mark but not by Luke, and refer to events such as 3.3.1.24, 3.3.1.26, 3.3.1.28, and 3.3.1.29 which are recorded by Luke but not Mark), Mark's narrative sequence basically matches that of Luke from narrative account 3.3.1.21 (the account under discussion) up to 3.3.2.4 (the last account shown in the above table). The difference between Matthew and Luke/Mark likely occurs because Matthew has rearranged traditions for thematic purposes (please see narrative account 3.3.1.14).

3.3.1.22 Healing the man with a withered hand (6:6–11)
(Thomas and Gundry, 1988:68–69)

Category: 2

Time: On a Sabbath day, after the "picking grain on the Sabbath" account (Luke 6:1; Matt 12:9—see below).

Observations: Luke 6:6 mentions only that this event happens "in another Sabbath day" (ἐν ἑτέρῳ σαββάτῳ), but does not specify which Sabbath day and whether this Sabbath day comes before or after the Sabbath day of Luke 6:1.

An analysis of the parallel accounts in Matthew and Mark finds that, like Luke, Mark 3:1–6 does not give a clear indication of time/ writing order of this incident. However, in Matthew 12:9–14, verse 9 says, "and after he departed from that place, he came into their synagogue" (καὶ μεταβὰς ἐκεῖθεν ἦλθεν εἰς τὴν συναγωγὴν αὐτῶν). According to the context, it seems that "from that place" (ἐκεῖθεν) refers to the grainfields in the earlier account of "picking grains on the Sabbath" (Matt 12:1–8). And, if this is the case, then Matthew seems to indicate that this happens after "picking grains on the Sabbath" in Matthew 12:9–14 and Luke 6:1–5.

Moreover, in Matthew and Mark as well as Luke, the healing of the man with a withered hand comes after the picking of grain on the Sabbath. Thus, the healing of the man with a withered hand likely happens after the picking of grain on the Sabbath.

Writing order identified: likely/reasonably chronological.

3.3.1.23 The choosing of the twelve (6:12–16)
(Thomas and Gundry, 1988:70)

Category: 2

Time: According to Luke 6:12, the event seems to happen around the time when Jesus heals the man with a withered hand.

Observations: "And it happened in these days" (ἐγένετο δὲ ἐν ταῖς ἡμέραις ταύταις) in Luke 6:12 seems to indicate that this incident happens around the time when Jesus heals the man with a withered hand in the immediately preceding account. Apparently Luke gives more details of this narrative account than does Mark. Luke mentions that Jesus prays all night on the mountain before he chooses the apostles (6:12a), but this is not mentioned in Mark.

Only Mark[71] and Luke record this event and in both cases it comes after the healing of the man with a withered hand. It is therefore likely that the choosing of the twelve happens after the healing of the man with a withered hand.

Writing order identified: likely/reasonably chronological.

3.3.1.24 Sermon on the plain (6:17-49) (Thomas and Gundry, 1988:70-77)

Category: 1

Time: After Jesus has chosen the twelve apostles and after Jesus comes down from a mountain (Luke 6:12-13, 6:17).

Observations: According to the context, "And after he came down with them (the apostles), he stood on a level place" (καὶ καταβὰς μετ' αὐτῶν ἔστη ἐπὶ τόπου πεδινοῦ) in Luke 6:17 seems to mean that the sermon is given after Jesus has chosen the twelve apostles, and at the time when Jesus and his apostles come down from a mountain and stand on a level place.

Thomas and Gundry (1988:70-71) believe that the "Sermon on the Mount" in Matthew chapters 5-7 is the same incident as the sermon in Luke 6:17-49. However, the settings of the two sermons are different. Matthew clearly says that after Jesus has seen the crowds, he goes up on the mountain to preach to them (Matt 5:1). Luke says Jesus comes down from a mountain and is standing on a level place when he preaches, after he has prayed overnight and has chosen his disciples. In Matthew 5:1 Jesus goes up a mountain because he wants to preach to the crowds. In Luke 6:12 Jesus goes up a mountain because he wants to pray. In Matthew Jesus preaches after he has gone up the mountain, whereas in Luke Jesus preaches after he has come down from a mountain and stands at a level place. It is likely that these two accounts are referring to separate occasions.

I would agree with Carson (1984:123-124), who opines that as an itinerant preacher Jesus "preach(es) the same thing

---

71. Between "healing the man with the withered hand" (3:1-6) and "choosing the twelve" (3:13-19), Mark inserts a description about the impact of Jesus' ministry in Galilee (3:7-12) which is unique in Mark.

repeatedly" and it is likely that Matthew chapters 5-7 and Luke 6:20b-49 are similar messages that Jesus preaches on different occasions. Plummer (1896:177) and Garland (2011:266) also conclude that the Sermon on the Mount and the Sermon on the Plain are two sermons given on different occasions. Moreover, Matthew may have conflated various sayings of Jesus at various times with Jesus' original "Sermon of the Mount" (for Matthew's possible conflation of materials see narrative account 3.3.1.14 above).

Writing order identified: chronological.

3.3.1.25 Healing the centurion's servant (7:1–10) (Thomas and Gundry, 1988:78–79)

Category: 1

Time: After the sermon in 6:17–49 and when Jesus is in Capernaum (Luke 7:1).

Observation: "After he had finished all his sayings to the hearing of the people, he entered into Capernaum" (ἐπειδὴ ἐπλήρωσεν πάντα τὰ ῥήματα αὐτοῦ εἰς τὰς ἀκοὰς τοῦ λαοῦ, εἰσῆλθεν εἰς Καφαρναούμ) in Luke 7:1; this seems to indicate that this event happens after the "sermon on the plain" in 6:17–49 and after Jesus has entered Capernaum.

Matthew gives the parallel account of this incident in 8:5–13. Please see narrative account 3.3.1.14 above for the discussion of why there is an apparent contradiction between Luke's and Matthew's sequences for this account.

Writing order identified: chronological.

3.3.1.26 Raising a widow's son at Nain of Galilee (7:11–17) (Thomas and Gundry, 1988:79)

Category: 1

Time: After healing the centurion's servant (Luke 7:11).

Observation: Luke 7:11 says "And it happened in the next" (Καὶ ἐγένετο ἐν τῷ ἑξῆς). A study of this phrase has been conducted in chapter 2 of this thesis and it is found that the most preferable meaning should be "soon afterwards." If this is true, this incident happens soon after Jesus has healed the centurion's servant in Luke 7:1–10. This account is unique to Luke, having no parallel in Matthew and Mark.

Writing order identified: chronological.

3.3.1.27 Question from John the Baptist (7:18–35) (Thomas and Gundry, 1988:79–81)

Category: 1

Time: After Jesus has raised the widow's son at Nain (Luke 7:18).

Observations: According to the context the most natural meaning of "all these things" (πάντων τούτων) in Luke 7:18 includes the immediately preceding incident of Luke 7:11–17. If this is the case, this incident likely happens after Jesus has raised the son of the widow in Nain.

Matthew records the same incident in Matthew 11:2–19. He mentions that John is in prison at that time (Matt 11:2). Matthew 11:2 indicates that this incident must have happened after Luke 3:20; and according to the observation in narrative account 3.3.1.9 if the time frame of 3:19–20 overlaps that of 3:21–23a and 4:1–14, this incident would have happened after Luke 3:21–23a and 4:1–14 in time. Moreover, while Matthew does not contain the account of the raising of the widow's son at Nain (the immediately previous account in Luke), and both Matthew and Luke put the healing of the centurion's servant (the account immediately preceding the raising of the widow's son at Nain in Luke) before the question from John the Baptist;[72] the question from John the Baptist likely comes after the healing of the centurion's servant in time. Matthew records this incident after the mission of the twelve (Matt 9:36–11:1a) and Jesus' mission (Matt 11:1b, not described in Mark and Luke—see narrative account 3.3.1.21), whereas Luke records the mission of the twelve much later in Luke 9:1–6. The apparent contradiction between Luke's and Matthew's sequences is discussed in narrative accounts 3.3.1.14 and 3.3.1.21 above. This account has no parallel account in Mark.

Writing order identified: chronological.

---

72. Matthew records the healing of the centurion's servant in 8:5–13 and the question from John the Baptist in 11:2–19.

3.3.1.28 Christ's feet anointed (7:36–50)
(Thomas and Gundry, 1988:81–82)

Category: 3

Time: Before Jesus travels around to preach the gospel in Galilee with the twelve apostles and with some women who financially provide for Jesus (Luke 8:1–3).

Observations: There is no clear indication or even a hint of time/ writing order in the context of Luke. The only indication about time is in Luke 8:1: "and it happened in the following (days) also he himself went about through city and village while preaching and bringing good news (about) the kingdom of God and the twelve (were) with him" (καὶ ἐγένετο ἐν τῷ καθεξῆς καὶ αὐτὸς διώδευεν κατὰ πόλιν καὶ κώμην κηρύσσων καὶ εὐαγγελιζόμενος τὴν βασιλείαν τοῦ θεοῦ καὶ οἱ δώδεκα σὺν αὐτῷ). "And it happened in the following days" (καὶ ἐγένετο ἐν τῷ καθεξῆς) indicates that the previous event (i.e., the anointing of Christ's feet in Luke 7:36-50) happens before Jesus begins to travel around cities and villages in Galilee with the twelve apostles to preach the gospel, as mentioned in Luke 8:1. However, there is not enough information to tell whether the anointing of Christ's feet (Luke 7:36-50) occurs after the question from John the Baptist (Luke 7:18-35).

Luke is the only one who records this incident. There is no additional information for this account in other gospels. Aland (2001: §114) places this account alongside Matthew 26:6–13, Mark 14:3–9, and John 12:1–8 but in fact the setting of Luke 7:36-50 is very different from these passages. Bock says (1994:689–690) that Matthew 26:6–13, Mark 14:3–9 and John 12:1–8 "occurs in the final week of Jesus' life and takes place in the house of a leper named Simon (Matt 26:6, Mark 14:3), where Pharisees would never dine . . . Luke's version occurs in the earlier Galilean portion of Jesus' ministry and takes place in a Pharisee's house, who also happens to be named Simon . . . In fact, Simon the Pharisee could not be the same as Simon the leper, since a leper could not be a Pharisee."[73] Therefore, it is likely that they are different incidents.[74]

Writing order identified: cannot be ascertained

3.3.1.29 Jesus preaches in various cities and villages (8:1–3) (Thomas and Gundry, 1988:82)

Category: 1

Time: After the anointing of Jesus' feet in 7:36–50 (Luke 8:1).

Observations: As mentioned in narrative account 3.3.1.28, this event likely comes after Christ's feet are anointed in 7:36–50. 8:1–3 seems to be another summary statement in which Luke employs the overlapping writing technique he used in 1:80, 2:40, 2:52, 3:19–20, 4:14–15 and 4:42–44. As discussed in narrative account 3.3.1.16, Luke seems to divide Jesus' ministry before he sets out for Jerusalem into several phases. 4:16–44 is the first phase: Jesus ministers while at the same time trying to find a base. 5:1–7:50 is the second phase: after Jesus has found a base in Capernaum, he begins to build a core ministry team and train

---

73. Hagner (2009:845) also comments that "a (Pharisee) candidate must first agree to take upon himself obedience to all the detailed legislation of the Pharisaic tradition, involving tithing and especially ceremonial and dietary purity." And section 1:1 in Kelim of the Mishnah says that a leper in the days of his counting is one of the fathers of uncleannesses. In view of the above it seems impossible that a leper could have become a Pharisee.

74. Matt 26:6–13/Mark 14:3–9 may also be a different event from John 12:1–8 (i.e., Matthew/Mark, Luke and John are describing three different events). Since Matt 26:2 and Mark 14:1 indicate that Matt 26:6–13/Mark 14:3–9 happens two days before the Passover, but John 12:1 seems to indicate that John 12:1–8 happens 6 days before the same Passover. Moreover, Matt 26:7/Mark 14:3 say that Jesus' head is anointed, while John 12:3 mentions that Jesus' feet are anointed. Also, Matt 26:6/Mark 14:3 say that the incident happens in the house of Simon the leper, but John 12:1–3 indicates that the incident likely happens in the house of Lazarus, Martha and Mary. Furthermore, Matt 26:8/Mark 14:4–5 say that the disciples complain, while in John 12:4 only Judas Iscariot complains. Thomas and Gundry (1988:168) argue that the accounts in Matthew, Mark and John are the same event and Matt 26:6–13 and Mark 14:3–9 are flashbacks of the synoptic gospel authors. Bock (2004, vol.1:692) and Köstenberger (2004:358) also agree that Matthew, Mark and John are describing the same event, but they do not give information on how to reconcile 1) the difference in time between Matt 26:2/Mark 14:1 and John 12:1; 2) the different body parts anointed in Matthew/Mark and John; 3) the potential difference in the place where the incident happens; and 4) the difference in the number of people who make(s) complaint(s). Since whether Matt 26:6–13/Mark 14:3–9 and John 12:1–8 are the same account does not affect our study of Luke's writing order, no further work is conducted.

them while continuing his ministry. And now 8:1–9:50 seems to describe the final phase of Jesus' ministry: his core team (the twelve apostles in 8:1) and his support group (a group of women in 8:2–3) have already been well established. Jesus continues to train his team while he ministers, up to the point when they are ready to minister independently (9:1–6, 9:10). While Luke 4:44 seems to describe Jesus ministering alone when the second phase begins, now, in 8:1–3 when the final phase begins, Jesus ministers with a full team.

If 4:44 is a summary of Jesus' ministry after he has set up a base in Capernaum but before his core team and support group are fully established, then its time frame likely overlaps that of 5:1–7:50. This may be the reason why Luke records 7:37–50 (Christ's feet anointed by a sinful woman) and 7:11–17 (raising a widow's son at Nain), accounts which have no parallels in Matthew and Mark. The women in these two accounts may be among those who later financially support Jesus in 8:2–3, and the time frame of 8:1–3 apparently overlaps that of 8:4–9:50, which describes Jesus' last phase of ministry before he sets out for Jerusalem in 9:51 (the next summary statement).

Writing order identified: the narrative account is recorded chronologically, and overlapping chronology is noted in Luke 8:1–3.

3.3.1.30 The parable of the soils (8:4–18)
(Thomas and Gundry, 1988:85–88)

Category: 1

Time: If Luke 8:1–3 is a summary statement which gives a preview of the following section, Luke 8:4–9:50 (see narrative account 3.3.1.29 above), then this account likely happens when Jesus preaches in various cities and villages with his core team and support group as mentioned in 8:1–3, and comes after Christ's feet are anointed in Luke 7:36–50 (the account immediately before the parable of the soils in Luke.[75])

Observations: This account has parallels in Matthew (Matt 13:1–23) and Mark (Mark 4:1–25). Matthew and Mark do not have a parallel account of Christ's feet being anointed. The

---

75. As Luke 8:1–3 is taken as one of Luke's summary statements which gives a preview of the following section (8:4 to 9:50), it is not treated as the account immediately preceding the parable of the soils.

common account shared by Luke and Matthew, which comes immediately before the parable of the soils in Luke, is the question from John the Baptist.[76] And the common account shared by Luke and Mark, which comes immediately before the parable of the soils in Luke, is the choosing of the twelve apostles. Since the question from John the Baptist comes before the parable of the soils but not after it in Matthew, and the choosing of the twelve apostles come before the parable of soils but not after it in Mark; Matthew and Mark agree with Luke that the choosing of the twelve apostles and the question from John the Baptist come before the parable of the soils account. Therefore, it is reasonable to conclude that the parable of the soils actually happens after the question from John the Baptist and the choosing of the twelve apostles. There is no indication from Matthew and Mark that the parable of soils account is not recorded in time sequence in Luke.

76. An analysis of the account common to Luke and Matthew which comes immediately before the parable of the soils in Luke, and the account common to Luke and Mark which comes immediately before the parable of the soils in Luke:

Table 11. Analysis of accounts in Matthew and Mark which Luke has and that come immediately before the parable of soils in Luke

Description	Luke (in descending sequence)	Matthew	Mark
The parable of the soils	8:4–18	13:1–23	4:1–25
Jesus preaches around in different cities and villages*	8:1–3 (likely a summary statement and preview of 8:4–9:50)	-	-
Christ's feet anointed*	7:36–50	-	-
Question from John**	7:18–35	11:2–19	-
Raising a widow's son at Nain*	7:11–17	-	-
Healing the centurion's servant**	7:1–10	8:5–13	-
Sermon on the plain*	6:17–49	-	-
The choosing of the twelve***	6:12–16	-	3:13–19

*unique in Luke

**Only in Luke and Matthew

***Only in Luke and Mark

Writing order identified: chronological

3.3.1.31 Announcement of a new spiritual kinship (8:19–21) (Thomas and Gundry, 1988:85)

Category: 3

Time: According to Matthew 12:46, this happens while Jesus is speaking to a crowd. Mark and Luke seem to agree with Matthew on this point. Mark seems to indicate in 3:28–31 that Jesus' mother and brothers arrive when Jesus is teaching. Luke records this incident after the parable of the soils and 8:19 mentions that Jesus' mother and brothers are not able to get near Jesus because he is surrounded by a crowd, who likely is hearing Jesus at that time. However, there is no specific information about the timing of this event in the synoptic gospels.

Observations: While Luke, Matthew and Mark have all recorded this account, Matthew and Mark differ from Luke and place this account before the parable of the soils.

Table 12. Comparison of the sequences of "parable of the soils" and "new spiritual kinship" in the synoptic gospels

	Parable of the soils	New spiritual kinship
Luke	8:4–18	8:19–21
Matthew	13:1–23	12:46–50
Mark	4:1–25	3:31–35

Matthew seems to indicate in 13:1 that this incident happens earlier on the same day on which Jesus delivers the parable of the soils. Mary and Jesus' brothers come to visit Jesus while he is teaching in a house (Matt 12:46), and after Jesus has commented on the new spiritual kinship (Matt 12:48–50), he comes out from the house "in that day" (Matt 13:1) and delivers the parables of the soils to the crowds (Matt 13:3–23). However, a study of the phrase "in that day" (Ἐν τῇ ἡμέρᾳ ἐκείνῃ) in Matthew 13:1 discovers that it can also mean "in those days" or "during that period of time."[77] As a result, we cannot be certain

---

77. Of the 182 usages of this phrase in the Septuaginta (Bible, 1935) and the *Novum Testamentum Graece* (Bible, 1993), it can mean "in those days/ during that period of time" in 62 usages (i.e., 34%). The 62 usages are as follows: (a) 2 usages in Deut 31:17–18

whether this incident happens on the day when Jesus delivers the parable of the soils, since this phrase can also imply that it happens at about the time when Jesus delivers the parable, but not necessarily on the same day. Furthermore, if the phrase "in that day" really means "in that particular day", then Matthew together with Mark would have portrayed an exceptionally long day for Jesus in Matthew 12:15–13:52 and Mark 3:20–4:41. Matthew 12:15–21 seems to say that when Jesus is on the road he heals many people. Then Jesus enters a house (Mark 3:20a) and heals a demon-oppressed man who is blind and mute (Matt 12:22–23). Because Jesus has to minister to the crowd, he cannot find time to eat (Mark 3:20b); Jesus likely gives up his lunch or both his breakfast and lunch that day, since it is unlikely that his family would come to seize him just because he does not have breakfast (Mark 3:21).

When the Pharisees learn of the people's reaction towards Jesus' healing of the man who is blind and mute (Matt 12:24), they accuse him of casting out demons by Beelzebul and Jesus debates with them (Matt 12:24–45, Mark 3:22–30). While Jesus is still speaking to the crowd (Matt 12:46), his mother and brothers come to see him, and Jesus talks about spiritual kinship (Matt 12:46–50, Mark 3:31–35).

---

refer to the times when the Israelites worship other gods and break their covenant with the Lord, not to a particular day; (b) 1 usage in 1 Sam 3:12 refers to the times (instead of a particular day) when the Lord fulfills against Eli all that he has spoken concerning Eli's house. God's prophecies against Eli's house are fulfilled at different times. For example, the deaths of Eli's two sons happen in 1 Sam 4:11 when Eli is still alive, but the prophecy about the termination of the priestly services of Eli's household is fulfilled much later in 1 Kings 2:27 during the time of King Solomon; (c) 1 usage in 1 Sam 8:18 refers to the times (instead of a particular day) when the Israelites feel oppressed by their kings and call upon the Lord; (d) 1 usage in 2 Kings 3:6 likely means 'in that period of time' instead of one single day, when King Jehoram is gathering an army to go to war with Moab; (e) 1 usage in Micah 2:4 refers to the times (instead of a particular day) when God exercises judgment on the Israelites and when they are mocked by others; (f) all the 23 usages in the book of Isaiah (2:11,17; 3:7,18; 5:30; 7:18,20,21,23; 11:10; 12:1,4; 17:4; 19:21; 22:12,20,25; 23:15; 27:12,13; 29:18; 30:25; 52:6), 3 in the book of Jeremiah (30:8; 39:17; 49:22), 6 in Ezekiel (29:21; 30:9; 38:10,14,18,19), 2 in Amos (8:13; 9:11); 1 in Micah (4:6); 1 in Joel (3:18); 1 in Zephaniah (3:11); 1 in Haggai (2:23); 17 usages in Zechariah (2:11; 9:16, 12:3,4,6,8,9,11; 13:1,2,4; 14:4,8,9,13,20,21), and 1 usage in the gospel of Luke (10:12) refer to the end times, or a time of judgment or the "day of the Lord," referring to a period of time rather than a specific day. Ryken *et al.* (1998:196) also comments that "(the d)ay of the Lord . . . refer(s) to any specific period of time (instead of a particular day) in which the God of Israel intervenes in human affairs to save and judge."

Then "in that particular day" (ἐν τῇ ἡμέρᾳ ἐκείνῃ—Matt 13:1) Jesus comes out of the house and goes to the lake, and goes on board a boat and preaches to the crowd (Matt 13:1–35, Mark 4:1–34). After he has finished preaching he leaves the crowd and goes back to the house to teach his disciples (Matt 13:36–52). "After evening came in that particular day" (ἐν ἐκείνῃ τῇ ἡμέρᾳ ὀψίας γενομένης—Mark 4:35), Jesus comes out from the house again, goes to the lake and sets sail for the land of the Gerasenes, where a storm suddenly arises and Jesus has to calm his disciples (4:35–41). It seems quite unlikely that all the above events occur in a single day:

Table 13. Estimated time of Jesus' activities in Matthew 12:15–13:52 and Mark 3:20–4:41

Activities	Estimated time
Heals many on the road	It may already have occupied the whole morning—at least two to three hours
Enters a house to minister to a crowd, heals a demon-oppressed man who is blind and mute, debates with the Pharisees, ministers at length in the house to a crowd to the point that he has no time to eat, teaches about spiritual kinship when his mother and brothers come to see him	At least another three to four hours
Walks to the lakeshore, waits for the crowd to gather and settle, preaches to them, dismisses the crowd when he has finished his sermon, and walks back to the house	Depending on the length of his sermon and the distance between the house and the lakeshore, may be at least two to three hours
Explains the meaning of a parable to his disciples	At least one hour
Walks to the lakeshore again and sets sail for Gerasenes	Another one to two hours
Total estimated time:	9 to 13 hours

If we take the median between the high and the low of the total estimated time, it will be eleven hours, almost all the daylight hours of a whole day according to John 11:9, not to mention that the Bible usually will only record selected activities but not all. For example, Matthew does not record the time Jesus needs to clean up and get ready before he can be on the road in the morning (it may be an hour or so), his devotional time, and all the short breaks and the possible meal break (if Jesus eventually has a late lunch) throughout the day. And even if Jesus could do all the above in one day, it is hard to believe that Jesus would have finished all these activities and sailed to the land of the Gerasenes in the evening which, according to Gould (1898:84), likely occurs between 3 and 6 pm.[78] Consequently, I think that the phrase "in that day" in Matthew 13:1 actually means "in those days" or "during that period of time." Moreover, we noticed that Matthew has a tendency to rearrange and relocate traditions for thematic purposes (see narrative account 3.3.1.14 above). Therefore, we cannot be certain when this account actually happened.

As compared to Matthew, Mark at first glance seems to be a more reliable source of information on the timing of the incident, as thus far, up to 3:19, Mark seems to record all events in chronological order. However, as noted by many biblical scholars, such as Hooker (2006:17), Edwards (2002:11–12) and France (2002:18–20), Mark frequently employs a writing technique called intercalation in which he sandwiches one narrative account within another in his gospel, the purpose being, as France (2002:19) says: "to maintain interest and to allow the reader/hearer to gain a wider perspective on the constituent elements of the story, placing one alongside another so that they become mutually illuminating." Each intercalated unit includes an A-B-A' sequence where A and A' belong to one narrative account and B belongs to another. The intercalated units in Mark include at least 3:20–35, 6:7–30, 11:12–21, 14:1–11, 14:17–31 and 14:53–72, where the new spiritual kinship in 3:31–35 is a part (A', while 3:20–21 is A and 3:22–30 is B) of the first intercalated unit identified. A study of all the intercalated units above reveals that Mark, when employing this writing technique, may sometimes relocate and rearrange traditions and not necessarily record the incidents in chronological order. For example, in the intercalated unit 6:7–30 between Jesus' sending of the twelve apostles (A, 6:7–13) and the apostles' returning to Jesus (A', 6:30), Mark inserts the reason for the death of John the Baptist (6:17–29), which is a flashback that

---

78. The opinion of Gould seems to match that of Danker (2000:n.5471): evening (ὀψία) is "the period between late afternoon and darkness."

obviously happened before 6:14–16 (Herod's belief that Jesus is John the Baptist raised from the dead).

Moreover, it seems that Mark has intentionally grouped parables which Jesus has spoken on different occasions in Mark 4:1–33. In Mark 4:1–20 Jesus delivers the parable of the soils and when Jesus is alone with the twelve and his disciples, he explains the meaning of the parable to them. Bock (2004:742) seems to think that Mark 4:21–25 follows 4:1–20 in time, as he believes that Mark 4:21–25 is a challenge from Jesus for his audience to respond to the word of God in Mark 4:14. Bock says "Jesus' teaching (i.e., the word of God in Mark 4:14) is light (Mark 4:21) . . . Hearing aright will lead to receiving more from God, but failure to hear will mean losing what one already has (Mark 4:25)."

If Bock is correct, then Mark has placed 4:1–20 and 4:21–25 in their correct time sequence. However, the parable of the seed's spontaneous growth in Mark 4:26–29 and the parable of the mustard tree in 4:30–32 seem to be of a different theme (the kingdom of God [Mark 4:26 and 4:30], while 4:1–25 is about the word of God) and they are likely traditions selected by Mark and placed here together with the parable of the soils to give additional illustrations of Jesus' teachings in parables. This observation is supported by Mark 4:33–34 where Mark explicitly says that Jesus teaches only in parables to the people and explains to his disciples everything in private. Mark 4:26–29 and 4:30–32 are parables without explanations; it is unlikely that Jesus would deliver them to his disciples. But, if these two parables are delivered to the crowd, it seems to contradict Mark 4:10 which apparently says that Jesus has already left the crowd and is alone at that time. It would be quite impossible that Jesus would go out again to teach parables to a crowd after he has left them just moments ago. One reasonable explanation, therefore, is that these two parables are taught by Jesus in different occasions but Mark groups them here with the parable of the soils. Based on the above observations, Mark may have a tendency deliberately to record the parable of the soils after the new spiritual kinship so as to: 1) form an intercalated unit in 3:20–35 to make his narrative accounts more illuminating, and 2) place all the parables in one section for easier reading of Jesus' teachings.

On the other hand, when Luke records the new spiritual kinship account in Luke 8:19–21, he uses the phrase "the word of God" (τὸν λόγον τοῦ θεοῦ) in 8:21 to describe those who hear "the word of God" and practice it as Jesus' spiritual mother and brothers. This phrase is exactly the same one Jesus uses when he explains to his disciples the parable of the soils (in 8:11 Luke uses "the word of God" for the seed the sower sows). Luke is the only one who uses "the word of God" in the new spiritual kinship account. Matthew and Mark use "the will of my Father in heaven" (τὸ θέλημα τοῦ πατρός μου τοῦ ἐν οὐρανοῖς in Matt 12:50) and "the will of God" (τὸ θέλημα τοῦ θεοῦ in Mark 3:35) respectively. This phrase, "the word of God," may be the actual words of Jesus when he comments on new spiritual kinship. If this is the case, the reason for using this phrase may be that Jesus wants to elaborate on the importance of hearing and practicing the word of God, which indeed is the "good soil" as described in Luke 8:15, a concept which he has taught the same crowd not long ago. Therefore, Luke may have actually recorded this account in the correct time sequence.

Writing order identified: possibly chronological.

3.3.1.32 Crossing the lake and calming the storm (8:22–25) (Thomas and Gundry, 1988:91)

Category: 2

Time: Luke 8:22 says this incident happens "in one of the days" (ἐν μιᾷ τῶν ἡμερῶν). According to the context it likely means that this incident happens at about the time when Jesus delivers the parable of the soils to the public (8:4–18) and comments on the new spiritual kinship (8:19–21). This understanding also matches Mark 4:35. Mark says that this incident happens either "in that day when evening came" or "after (one) evening came in those days" (ἐν ἐκείνῃ τῇ ἡμέρᾳ ὀψίας γενομένης—please see footnote 77 under narrative account 3.3.1.31 for the meaning of ἐν ἐκείνῃ τῇ ἡμέρᾳ). According to the observations in the narrative account 3.3.1.31, this phrase likely means this incident happens in one of the evenings during those days when Jesus delivers the parable of the soils to the public.

Observations: Matthew (8:18, 23–27)[79], Mark (4:35–41) and Luke all record this incident. Matthew places it after Jesus heals Peter's mother-in-law, casts out some evil spirits and heals oth-

---

79. In "crossing the lake and calming the storm" (8:18, 23–27), Matthew inserts "complete commitment required of followers" (8:19–22), an account which is recorded much later in Luke (9:57–62). Matthew likely has relocated this tradition here for thematic purposes (see narrative account 3.3.1.14).

ers who are sick (Matt 8:14–17); and Matthew seems to indicate that this incident happens on the same day, as he uses "after Jesus saw the crowd around him" (ἰδὼν δὲ ὁ Ἰησοῦς ὄχλον περὶ αὐτὸν) in Matthew 8:18. However, a detailed study of Matthew 8 to 9 reveals that very likely this is not the case. If we interpret Matthew chapters 8 to 9 by its surface meaning, it would seem that Jesus has done all the events therein consecutively without a break in a very short period of time, which is highly unlikely.

It would seem that after Jesus enters Capernaum, he heals the centurion's servant (8:5–13), then goes to Simon's home to heal his mother-in-law (8:14–15), and continues to heal many others that night (8:16–17). Later, when he sees a crowd around him he decides to go to the other side of the lake (8:18), and while he is on the way to the lake, he answers the requests from a scribe and one of the disciples (8:19–22), and when he is finally on the boat, a storm suddenly develops and Jesus has to calm the storm and use the occasion to teach his disciples to have faith in him (8:23–27). After he has arrived on the other side of the lake, he casts out the evil spirits from a demon-processed man (8:28–34), and so on. I have already argued in narrative account 3.3.1.14 that Matthew chapters 8–9 is probably written in topical instead of chronological order (i.e., the events probably do not happen consecutively) to reflect Matthew's thematic concerns. Therefore, it seems reasonable to focus on Mark and Luke when we try to determine the timing of this incident. And because both Mark[80] and Luke record this incident after the new spiritual kinship account, it seems reasonable to believe that this incident happens after the new spiritual kinship teaching and is recorded in chronological order.

Writing order identified: likely chronological.

3.3.1.33 Healing the Gerasene demoniacs and resultant opposition (8:26–39) (Thomas and Gundry, 1988:92–94)

Category: 1

Time: It happens after Jesus has calmed the storm (8:26–27)

---

80. Between "new spiritual kinship" (3:31–35) and "crossing the lake and calming the storm" (4:35–41), Mark inserts the parable of the soils and the other parables (4:1–34) which I have briefly discussed in narrative account 3.3.1.30 and 3.3.1.31.

Observations: Luke describes that this incident happens when Jesus and his disciples "sailed down into the country of the Gerasenes" (κατέπλευσαν εἰς τὴν χώραν τῶν Γερασηνῶν, 8:26) and "and after (Jesus) had disembarked on the land" (ἐξελθόντι δὲ αὐτῷ ἐπὶ τὴν γῆν, 8:27). 8:26–27 indicates that this incident happens after "crossing the lake and calming the storm" in 8:22–25.

This incident is also recorded in Matthew and Mark and, same as Luke, they place this account immediately after "crossing the lake and calming the storm." Therefore, it is reasonable to believe that this account is recorded chronologically in Luke.

Writing order identified: chronological.

3.3.1.34 Return to Galilee, healing of woman who touches Jesus' garment, and raising of Jairus' daughter (8:40–56) (Thomas and Gundry, 1988:94–96)

Category: 1

Time: It happens after Jesus has returned from the country of the Gerasenes (8:40)

Observations: Luke describes in 8:40 that the raising of Jairus' daughter happens "when Jesus returned" (ἐν ... τῷ ὑποστρέφειν τὸν Ἰησοῦν). According to the context, this very likely means when Jesus has returned from the country of the Gerasenes. And 8:42 and 8:45 describe the healing of the woman who touches Jesus' garment as happening when Jesus is on the way to raise Jairus' daughter and is surrounded by the crowd.

Matthew[81] and Mark also record these incidents (Matt 9:18–26 and Mark 5:21–43) and place them in the same order as Luke—that is, the raising of Jairus' daughter is placed after Jesus has returned from the land of the Gerasenes and the healing of the woman happens when Jesus is on the way to Jairus' home. Therefore, it is reasonable to believe that these incidents are recorded in chronological order in Luke.

Writing order identified: chronological.

---

81. Contrary to Luke and Mark's sequence, Matthew records the forgiving and healing of the paralytic (narrative account 3.3.1.19), the calling of Matthew and the discussion of fasting and the parable about old and new (narrative account 3.3.1.20) in 9:1–17. As discussed in narrative account 3.3.1.14, Matthew likely has relocated these two accounts here for thematic purposes.

3.3.1.35 Commissioning of the twelve
(9:1–6) (Thomas and Gundry, 1988:98–100)

Category: 2

Time: Probably after the healing of the woman who touched Jesus' garment, and the raising of Jairus' daughter.

Observations: Matthew and Mark also record this event. All three gospels record it as happening after Jesus' return to Galilee, the healing of the woman who touches Jesus' garment, and the raising of Jairus' daughter, which is the immediately preceding event in Luke.[82] It is therefore reasonable to believe that this incident is recorded chronologically in Luke.

Writing order identified: chronological.

3.3.1.36 Herod Antipas hears about Jesus (9:7–9)
(Thomas and Gundry, 1988:100–101)

Category: 2

Time: The time of Herod Antipas, between 4 B.C. and A.D. 39 (Schürer, 2007, vol.2:17), and after Jesus has commissioned the twelve (Mark 6:14).

Observations: Thomas and Gundry (1988:100) comment that the "multiplied outreach of Jesus' ministry through the Twelve was what brought him increased fame. Herod Antipas, whose domain included Galilee and Perea, was now forced to give him attention." In other words, Herod Antipas' attention to Jesus seems to be a result of Jesus' sending out the twelve in 9:1–6. If this is the case, then this account is chronologically recorded after the "commissioning of the twelve" in Luke. Mark 6:14 also seems to support this observation by saying "and King Herod

---

82. Between the "healing of woman who touches Jesus' garment, and raising of Jairus' daughter" (Matt 9:18–26) and "commissioning of the twelve" (Matt 10:1–11:1), Matthew records the miraculous healing of two blind men (9:27–31), the casting out of a demon from a man who has been mute (9:32–34), and Jesus' comment on the shortage of labor (9:35–38). These accounts are unique to Matthew and have no parallel in Luke and Mark. Between the "healing of the woman who touches Jesus' garment, and the raising of Jairus' daughter" (Mark 5:21–43) and the "commissioning of the twelve" (Mark 6:7–13), Mark records a visit of Jesus to Nazareth (6:1–6). Matthew has a parallel account in 13:54–58 but Luke does not. See comments in the footnote under narrative account 3.3.1.13.

heard" (καὶ ἤκουσεν ὁ βασιλεὺς Ἡρῴδης). Mark does not provide an object for this Greek phrase. A reasonable way to interpret it is to supply the object from the previous context, which is the evangelistic activities, the healing of the sick and the casting out of the demons by the twelve described in Mark 6:12–13. If this understanding is correct, the lack of the object in this Greek phrase implies that this event immediately follows the "commissioning of the twelve" in Mark.

Furthermore, Matthew, Mark and Luke[83] all place this account after the "commissioning of the twelve." It is therefore reasonable to believe that this account happens after the "commissioning of the twelve."[84]

---

83. Thomas and Gundry believe that Matthew and Mark also record this incident in Matt 14:1–2 and Mark 6:14–16. Herod's response in Luke is a bit different from that in Matthew and Mark: in Luke, Herod seems uncertain of who Jesus is (9:9), but both Matthew (14:2) and Mark (6:16) say that Herod believes Jesus is John the Baptist come back to life. However, the details of the accounts in all three gospels match: for example, public opinions about Jesus are the same in Mark (14b–15) and Luke (7b–8), and all three gospels indicate that what Jesus does has captured Herod's attention (Matt 14:1, Mark 6:14a, Luke 9:7a). I would agree with Thomas and Gundry that these passages are describing the same incident. The difference in Herod's response as portrayed by Luke as opposed to the other two synoptic gospels can be explained by Herod actually doing both—that is, at first Herod Antipas is perplexed, but later forms an opinion about Jesus.

84. Matthew inserts the following events between the "commissioning of the twelve" (10:1–11:1) and "Herod Antipas hears about Jesus" (14:1–2):

Table 14. Narrative accounts inserted between
Matthew 10:1–11:1 and 14:1–2

Matthew	Description	Narrative account #
11:2–19	Question from John the Baptist	3.3.1.27
11:20–30	Jesus' comments on the non-repentant towns and his thanksgiving prayer	3.3.2.3, 3.3.2.4
12:1–8	Controversy over disciples' picking grain on the Sabbath	3.3.1.21
12:9–14	Healing the man with a withered hand	3.3.1.22
12:15–21	Withdrawal to the Sea of Galilee with large crowds from many places	*
12:22–37	Blasphemous accusation by the teachers of the law and Pharisees	*
12:38–45	Request for a sign refused	**

Writing order identified: chronological.

3.3.1.37 Withdrawal to Bethsaida and feeding the five thousand (9:10–17) (Thomas and Gundry, 1988:103–105)

Category: 1

Time: After the apostles have returned from their mission (9:10) and very likely after Herod has heard of the mission (9:7)

Observations: Luke 9:10 describes the withdrawal to Bethsaida as happening after the apostles have completed their mission and returned to Jesus. If "all the things which were happening" (τὰ γινόμενα πάντα), heard by Herod the tetrarch in Luke 9:7, refers to the mission of the apostles which is in progress but not completed, it would indicate that this event likely happens

Matthew	Description	Narrative account #
12:46–50	New Spiritual kinship	3.3.1.31
13:1–23	The parable of the soils	3.3.1.30
13:24–30	The parable of the weeds	**
13:31–32	The parable of the mustard tree	*
13:33–35	The parable of the leavened loaf	*
13:36–43	The parable of the weeds explained	**
13:44	The parable of the hidden treasure	**
13:45–46	The parable of the valuable pearl	**
13:47–50	The parable of the net	**
13:51–53	The parable of the house owner	**
13:54–58	Jesus' final visit to unbelieving Narazeth	*

* : This narrative account is recorded in Matthew and Mark but not in Luke

**: This narrative account is recorded only in Matthew

Of the 18 narrative accounts in Matthew, only 6 have parallels in Luke. As discussed in narrative account 3.3.1.14 above, Matthew has a tendency to rearrange and relocate traditions for thematic purposes. Matthew may have grouped these narrative accounts together in 11:2–13:58 to demonstrate the doubts and opposition Jesus faces from all sectors at that time: John the Baptist (11:2), some cities (11:20) the Pharisees (12:2, 14, 24, 38), the teachers of law (12:38), his mother and brothers (12:46), and the people from his hometown of Nazareth (13:54, 57) and also to describe how Jesus continues his ministry in the midst of skepticism: he begins to preach in parables.

after "Herod Antipas hears about Jesus." Luke 9:11-12 says that "feeding the five thousand" happens after the withdrawal to Bethsaida, as Luke 9:11 says that after the crowds learn about Jesus' withdrawal they follow him and as a result Jesus preaches to them and feeds them when evening comes.

Moreover, Matthew, Mark and Luke all agree with each other in the sequencing of these incidents. It is therefore reasonable to believe that Luke has recorded these accounts in chronological order.

Table 15. Comparison of the sequences of "Herod Antipas hears about Jesus," "withdrawal to Bethsaida," and "feeding the five thousand" in the synoptic gospels

	Herod Antipas hears about Jesus	Withdrawal to Bethsaida	Feeding the five thousand
Luke	9:7-9	9:10-11	9:12-17
Matthew	14:1-2	14:13-14[29]	14:15-21
Mark	6:14-16	6:30-34[30]	6:35-44

Writing order identified: chronological.

3.3.1.38 Peter's identification of Jesus as Christ, Jesus' first explicit prediction of rejection, crucifixion, and resurrection, and Jesus' teaching about following him, his second coming, and judgment (9:18-27) (Thomas and Gundry, 1988:116-118)

Category: 2

Time: After Jesus has entered the region of Caesarea of Philippi (Matt 16:13, Mark 8:27).

Observations: This account has parallels in both Matthew and Mark. Both mention that this incident happens when Jesus comes to the region of Caesarea Philippi (Matt 16:13, Mark

---

85. Matthew inserts the reason for the death of John the Baptist, which is not described in Luke, in 14:3-12.

86. Mark inserts the reason for the death of John the Baptist, which is not described in Luke, in 6:17-29.

8:27) but do not state when it happens. Luke, Matthew and Mark[87] all place this event after "withdrawal to Bethsaida and the feeding of the five thousand." It is therefore reasonable to believe that it happens after the "withdrawal to Bethsaida and the feeding of the five thousand" and is recorded in chronological order in Luke.

Writing order identified: chronological.

3.3.1.39 Transfiguration of Jesus (9:28–36) (Thomas and Gundry, 1988:119–120)

Category: 1

Time: After Peter's confession that Jesus is Christ, Jesus' prediction of his own death and resurrection, and his teaching on following him (9:28).

87. Between the "withdrawal to Bethsaida and feeding the five thousand" (Matt 14:31–21; Mark 6:30–44) and "Peter's confession and Jesus' prediction of his upcoming ordeal and his teachings about his second coming and judgment" (Matt 16:13–28; Mark 8:27–9:1), Matthew and Mark insert a number of events which are not recorded in Luke. The sequence of these events matches each other in Matthew and Mark:

Table 16. Narrative accounts inserted by Matthew and Mark between Matthew 14:31–21/Mark 6:30–44 and Matthew 16:13–28/Mark 8:27–9:1

Description	Matthew	Mark
A premature attempt to make Jesus king blocked	14:22–23	6:45–46
Walking on the water during a storm on the lake	14:24–33	6:47–52
Healings at Gennesaret	14:34–36	6:53–56
Conflict over the tradition of ceremonial uncleanness	15:1–20	7:1–23
Ministry to a believing Greek woman in the region of Tyre and Sidon	15:21–28	7:24–30
Healings in Decapolis	15:29–31	7:31–37
Feeding the four thousand in Decapolis	15:32–38	8:1–9a
Return to Galilee and encounter with the Pharisees and Sadducees	15:39–16:4	8:9b-12
Warning about the error of the Pharisees, Sadducees, and Herodians	16:5–12	8:13–21
Healing a blind man at Bethsaida	-	8:22–26*

*recorded only in Mark

Observations: Luke 9:28 clearly says this incident happens *about* eight days after Jesus' prediction of his own death and resurrection and his teaching on following him in 9:18–27. This matches the descriptions of Matthew 17:1 and Mark 9:2, which say that this incident happens six days after Jesus' prediction of his own death and resurrection and his teaching on following him. Moreover, Matthew, Mark and Luke all place this incident immediately after Jesus' prediction and teaching above. It is therefore reasonable to believe that Luke has recorded this account in chronological order.

Writing order identified: chronological.

3.3.1.40 Healing of demoniac boy and unbelief rebuked (9:37–43a) (Thomas and Gundry, 1988:121)

Category: 1

Time: Luke 9:37 clearly states that this incident happens the day after Jesus' transfiguration.

Observations: Matthew, Mark[88] and Luke all place this account after Jesus' transfiguration, which supports the argument that Luke has recorded this incident in its proper sequence.

Writing order identified: chronological.

3.3.1.41 Jesus' second prediction of his death and resurrection (9:43b-45) (Thomas and Gundry, 1988:122–123)

Category: 1

Time: After Jesus' healing of the demoniac boy, while he and his disciples are in Galilee (Luke 9:43, Matt 17:22 and Mark 9:30)

Observations: At first glimpse 9:43b seems to indicate that this incident happens at the place where Jesus heals the demoniac boy after Jesus has performed the healing miracle. However, Matthew (17:22) and Mark (9:30) state that it happens after Jesus and his disciples have left that place and when they are in

---

88. Between "Jesus' transfiguration" (Matt 17:1–9; Mark 9:2–10) and "healing of demoniac boy and unbelief rebuked" (Matt 17:14–21; Mark 9:14–29), both Matthew (17:10–13) and Mark (9:11–13) insert Jesus' discussion about resurrection, Elijah, and John the Baptist, which is not recorded in Luke.

Galilee. Therefore, the incident likely happens when Jesus and his disciples are in Galilee, while the people are still marveling at all that Jesus has done (Luke 9:43).

Because all three synoptic gospels place this incident after the healing of the demoniac boy, it is reasonable to believe that Luke has recorded it chronologically.

Writing order identified: chronological.

3.3.1.42 Rivalry over greatness in the kingdom (9:46–48) (Thomas and Gundry, 1988:123–124)

Category: 2

Time: After Jesus' second prediction of his death and resurrection, while Jesus and his disciples are in Capernaum (Mark 9:33)

Observations: Luke does not mention the time when this incident happens. Mark 9:33 says that Jesus and his disciples are in Capernaum. It seems that at that time they are on a journey travelling from north to south: Peter confesses that Jesus is Christ in Caesarea Philippi (narrative account 3.3.1.38), Jesus gives his second prediction of death and resurrection as he and his disciples pass through Galilee (narrative account 3.3.1.41), and now they are in Capernaum (Matt 17:24, Mark 9:33). If this is so, then this account likely is recorded in chronological order.

Since Matthew[89], Mark and Luke all place this incident after Jesus' second prediction of his death and resurrection, it is reasonable to believe that Luke has recorded it chronologically in its right sequence.

Writing order identified: chronological.

3.3.1.43 Apostle John's question (9:49–50) (Thomas and Gundry, 1988:124–126)

Category: 1

---

89. Between "Jesus' second prediction" (17:22–23) and "rivalry over greatness in the kingdom" (18:1–5), Matthew inserts a narrative account about Jesus' payment of the temple tax (17:24–27), which is not recorded in both Luke and Mark.

Time: After Jesus finishes teaching on the "rivalry over greatness in the kingdom" account (9:49).

Observations: Luke 9:49 says "and, after he answered, John said" (ἀποκριθεὶς δὲ Ἰωάννης εἶπεν). If the antecedent of ἀποκριθεὶς is Jesus (which is feasible in the context) instead of the Apostle John, it indicates that John asks this question right after Jesus' teaching in 9:46–48. Moreover, since all three synoptic gospels (Matt: 18:6–14, Mark: 9:38–50) place this incident after the "rivalry over greatness in the kingdom," it is reasonable to believe that Luke has recorded this account in chronological order.

Writing order identified: chronological.

3.3.1.44 Summary of 1:5–9:50

An analysis of the narrative accounts in 1:5–9:50 is as follows.

Table 17. Analysis of the narrative accounts in Luke 1:5–9:50

Section[1] (no. of accounts therein)	Category[2] 1[3] (%)	2 (%)	3 (%)	% (Category 2+3)
1:5[4]–1:80 (4)	4 (100)	-	-	0
2:1–2:40 (3)	3 (100)	-	-	0
2:41–2:52 (1)	1 (100)	-	-	0
3:1–3:20 (1)	1 (100)	-	-	0
3:21–4:15 (2)[5]	2 (100)	-	-	0
4:16–4:44 (4)	4 (100)	-	-	0
5:1–8:3 (13)	7 (53.8)	5 (38.5)	1 (7.7)	46.2
8:4–9:52(a) (14)	8 (57.1)	5 (35.7)	1 (7.1)	42.8
Total no. of accounts (42)	30 (71.4)	10 (23.8)	2 (4.8)	28.6

[1] "Section" refers to the sections divided by overlapping summary statements identified in this chapter.

[2] For the definitions of the different categories, see 3.1.

[3] Number of narrative accounts in category 1. The order identified in all category 1 and 2 accounts from 1:5 to 9:52(a) is chronological.

[4] 1:1–4 is the preface of the gospel which does not belong to any section and is not evaluated here.

[5] 3:23b–38 is Jesus' genealogy. Since it is not related to my study of narrative sequence, it is not included in the analysis here.

We have three observations. First, out of the forty-two narrative accounts in 1:5–9:50, forty accounts (i.e., 95.2%) are classified as either category 1 or 2. This means that there are explicit or implicit indications in these accounts or in their parallel accounts in the other synoptic gospels to help us understand their written order. All the category 1 accounts therein are identified as being written in chronological order, and when the other accounts are compared with their parallels (if any) in Matthew and Mark, we find that 5 out of 5 accounts (100%) in section 5:1–8:3 and 5 out of 6 accounts (83.3%) in section 8:4–9:52(a) are recorded in chronological order. There are only two category 3 accounts (i.e., accounts with their written order unidentified due to lack of or insufficient information in the accounts and in their parallel accounts, if any.) The category 3 account in section 5:1–8:3 (narrative account 3.3.1.28) is unique to Luke and thus has no additional information from Matthew and Mark to help ascertain its order. The other category 3 account is in section 8:4–9:52(a) (narrative account 3.3.1.31). Its parallels in Matthew and Mark do not provide adequate information for us to ascertain its order due to the possible relocation of traditions in Matthew and Mark (see discussion in narrative account 3.3.1.31). However, from the two category 3 accounts above, we cannot find concrete evidence to prove that they are written in an order other than chronological. Consequently, it is very likely that these two category 3 accounts are also written in the same order (i.e., chronological) as Luke does for other accounts in 1:5–9:50.

Second, our study shows that Luke has apparently divided 1:5–9:50 into sections through the use of overlapping summary statements (1:80, 2:40, 2:52, 3:19–20, 4:14–15, 4:42–44, 8:1–3 and 9:51–52a) and has recorded them in overlapping chronological order. It means that the sections are recorded in chronological order and each section ends with an overlapping summary statement. The implied time frame of each summary statement overlaps and covers the time frame of its immediately following section (see narrative account 3.3.1.4, 3.3.1.7, 3.3.1.8, 3.3.1.9, 3.3.1.12, 3.3.1.16 and 3.3.1.29).

Third, it seems that there is a change in Luke's writing style from 5:1 onward. All the narrative accounts from 1:5 to 4:44 are classified as category 1 accounts, which means that Luke has provided adequate explicit or implicit indication of time/or writing order in these accounts to help us determine their order. Although many narrative accounts here are unique in Luke (e.g., the conception and birth accounts of John the Baptist and Jesus, Mary's visit to Elizabeth and her song, Jesus' Passover in Jerusalem as a child, etc.), it is not difficult to determine their order since Luke has used clear spatial and temporal information to indicate when and where an incident happens. For example: the pregnancies of Elizabeth and Mary happen in the days of Herod (1:5); Jesus is born in Bethlehem (2:4) during the reign of Caesar Augustus when Quirinius is the governor of Syria (2:1–2); John the Baptist begins his ministry in the regions around the Jordan River in the fifteenth year of the reign of Tiberius Caesar, when Pontius Pilate is the governor of Judea, Herod is the tetrarch of Galilee, his brother Philip tetrarch of Ituraea and Trachonitis, and Lysanias tetrarch of Abilene, and Annas and Caiaphas are the high priests (3:1–3); after Jesus has experienced the temptations in the wilderness, he returns from the Jordan River (4:1), first goes to Nazareth (4:16) and finally settles in Capernaum (4:44). Since it is relatively easy for the reader to examine the truthfulness of an event with clear spatial and temporal information, the inclusion of this information at the beginning of the gospel undoubtedly sets the stage for the reliability of Luke's accounts to his reader Theophilus (1:4), apparently with the purpose of convincing him of the certainty of the things he has been taught (1:4). However, the accounts in 5:1–9:52(a) have less spatial and temporal information as compared with the first four chapters and, as a result, the percentage of category 1 accounts in the sections in 5:1–9:52(a) stands at an average of only 55.45% (as compared with 100% in 1:5–4:44). There is no evidence from our study that indicates that the change of writing style would affect Luke's writing order.

Based on the above observations, we conclude that chronological order and overlapping chronology are reasonable possibilities in Luke 1:5–9:52(a).

3.3.2 Luke 9:51–19:44—Jesus' Last Trip to Jerusalem

This section (from 9:52b to 19:44, about nine and a half chapters) about Jesus' final trip to Jerusalem is quite different from the previous sections. It includes a lot of materials unique to Luke. In fact, according to Thomas and Gundry (1988: 127–159), other than 9:57–62 which is paralleled in Matthew 8:19–22, all narrative accounts from 9:52b to 18:14 have no parallel in Matthew and Mark. Moreover, Matthew and Mark have much shorter descriptions about Jesus' final trip to Jerusalem as compared to that of Luke: Matthew uses only two and a half chapters (Matt 19:1–21:9) to describe the trip while Mark uses only a bit more than one chapter (Mark 10:1–11:10) to do so. Other than the incidents which are unique and not found in Matthew and Mark, such as "Jesus' journey through Samaria" (9:51–56), "Jesus' visit with Mary and Martha" (10:38–42), "opposition from a synagogue ruler for healing a woman on the Sabbath" (13:10–21), "healing of a man with dropsy while eating with a prominent Pharisee on the Sabbath" (14:1–24) etcetera, Luke also records a number of teachings Jesus gives during the trip which are left out by the other two synoptic gospels (for example: 12:1–59; 14:1–24; 15:1–17:10 and 17:20–18:14.) Jesus' teachings cover various subjects from the cost of discipleship to the hypocrisy of the Pharisees, which are apparently targeted to prepare his followers for his upcoming ordeal and eventual glorification in Jerusalem. Some of Jesus' sayings (e.g., 12:1–3; 14:1–6; 15:1–31; 18:9–14) have inevitably increased the tension between him and the Jewish leaders. Since many events in this section are unique to Luke, it will be difficult to ascertain their order if Luke himself makes no clear indication of time or order in these accounts, as reference to Matthew and Mark cannot be made.

Scholars have divided opinions on how to interpret this lengthy section, and not many of them comment on the order in which it is written. I will present various scholarly opinions about the interpretation and order of this section. Then I will evaluate them and give my point of view on the interpretation and order. A study of thirty-one writings of thirty-three scholars finds that there are basically six categories of opinion regarding this section's interpretation.

First category: eight scholars conclude that this section is written for soteriological, ecclesiological (in particular about discipleship and mission) and/or Christological purposes. Green (1997:399) believes that this section "concerns the fulfillment of God's redemptive purpose together with the thematization of the formation of a people who will hear and obey the word of God" and it is soteriological in focus. Morris (1998:197) thinks that it is about Jesus' suffering according to God's will and equipping the disciples for future missions. Fitzmyer (2008:825-826) is of the opinion that it is "a literary compilation of sayings of Jesus" and "a piece of deliberate editorial work" to stress the Christological role in the gospel and is "a collection of teachings for the young missionary church." Stein (1992:297) basically agrees with Fitzmyer's view. To Garland (2012:409) this section "shows the movement of salvation from Galilee to Jerusalem" and is written for both Christological and ecclesiological purposes. Bock (1992:501) opines that the section is not recorded in a chronological manner and "the thrust of this section is that Jesus initiates a new way to follow God. Its theme is 'listen to him.'" Bock (2004, vol.2:959–961), while quoting Egelkraut, seems to agree with Egelkraut that the section lacks clear chronological and geographical indicators and concludes that "(o)ne need not insist . . . on strict chronology when Luke himself avoids it." Resseguie (1982:41) seems to support the view that this section is written for ecclesiological purposes through the presentation of "two conflicting ideological points of view—the view of Jesus, and the view opposed to his." According to Gill (1970:199, 221) this section is a theological-Christological entity and promotes themes of discipleship and Gentile mission.

Second category: six scholars believe that this section should be interpreted together with the relevant section in the Gospel of John. Thomas and Gundry (1988:128) believe that this section fits in nicely with John chapters 7–12. They believe that John chapters 7–12 indicate Jesus makes more than one trip to Jerusalem in the period of time described by Luke 9:51–19:44, and that John chapters 7–12 also explain the route Jesus takes between Luke 9:51 and 19:44. They (1988:127–174, as evident from their ordering of events for this section) also think that both this section and John chapters 7–12 are recorded in chronological order. Plummer (1896:260) thinks that the Gospel of John provides some important incidents in the period between Jesus' Galilean ministry and the Passion, though he is uncertain about how to fit them into Luke 9:51–19:44. Godet (1881:6–7) is of the opinion that this section should be read together with John chapter 7 and the chapters that follow, and he (1881:62) believes that this section is written in chronological order. To Lange (2008:161) this section is recorded chronologically; he holds that Luke 9:51 should be read in parallel with John 7:10, and that Jesus' trips to Jerusalem in John 7 (for the Feast of the Tabernacles) and John 10 (for the Feast of Dedication) should also be fitted into this section. Guthrie (2009:617) also seems to believe that Luke's section involves more than one visit by Jesus to Jerusalem and that these visits are supported by the gospel of John chapters 7–10.

Third category: five scholars opine that this section involves a chiastic structure. Blomberg (2009:336) seems to believe that this section is not written in chronological order, and he thinks that "Luke used a chiastically arranged parables source (either oral or written), around which he grouped topically related teachings of Jesus to create a thematically organized section." Nolland (1998:530) agrees with Blomberg that the parables in this section "can be convincingly paired. The five most obvious pairs (10:25–37 par. 18:9–14; 11:5–8 par. 18:1–8; 12:13–21 par. 16:19–31; 12:35–38 par. 16:1–13; 13:1–9 par. 15:1–32) in fact line up in chiastic order, and all belong to the travel-narrative materials distinctive to Luke, (and) 14:7–24 offers itself as a suitable center piece." Talbert (2002:117–118, 120) thinks that this section "is an editorial framework created by the evangelist" and "the arrangement of the journey to Jerusalem . . . (has) a chiastic pattern (which) determines the overall arrangement of the material." He believes that the content of this section can be divided into 20 chiastically arranged units. Similar to Talbert, Bailey (1983:79–85) also holds that the section can be divided into 19 chiastically arranged units with Luke 13:22–35 (which Bailey denotes as concerning Jesus' death and the eschatological day) as the center unit and the climax of this section. To Farrell (1986:34) this section "is structured chiastically . . . (and) develops seven basic themes or scenes which are then repeated in reverse order."

Fourth category: five scholars think that this section is somehow related to the Book of Deuteronomy. Moessner (1983:580, 582) thinks that "the analogy with Deuteronomy would appear to be the most promising of all the solutions (for the interpretation of this section) . . . Jesus, the 'prophet like Moses' of Deuteronomy 18:15–19, is essentially a teacher, now delivering a new Torah which in sequence and substance parallels the old (Deut 1–26)" and he thinks that this section is "the journey of the Prophet Jesus whose calling and fate both recapitulate and consummate the career of Moses in Deuteronomy." Woods (2001:60) believes that this section "emphasizes the importance of obeying 'the prophet like Moses' both in terms of salvation and discipleship, otherwise judgment is inevitable," and καθεξῆς in Luke 1:3 refers to a logical and persuasive account. According to Strauss (1995:277–278), "Jesus is indeed presented as a prophetic figure who, like the prophets before him, faces rejection and ultimately death at the hands of God's stubborn and resistant people. In addition, Moessner . . . has rightly pointed to the significant role of Moses in Luke-Acts." Pao and Schnabel (2007:314) are of the opinion that "the significance of Deuteronomy (in this section) can no longer be denied."

Fifth category: three scholars are of the opinion that this section has to be interpreted together with Luke's theology of the "way." Tiede (1988:196) believes that "Luke has used the schema of the journey as a device for pulling a variety of traditional stories within a narrative framework which is going somewhere . . . Luke has clearly organized this larger section into a three-phase journey (9:51–13:21; 13:22–17:10; 17:11–19:27). And the "way of the determined Messiah" provides a revelation of God's dominion and a catechesis in discipleship." Baban (2006:177, 179–180) agrees with Tiede that Luke "shapes the story line into three similarly built parts (9:51–13:21; 13:22–17:10; 17:11–19:27)" and "the various, different types of journey stories in Luke 9–19 ('journey within a journey' stories, . . . journey parables, etc.) . . . are evidence of a constant style and provide a fresh point of view for the assessment of Luke's theology of the Way." Robinson (1960:20) also holds that this section "was arranged by the final editor/author of Luke-Acts in accord with his view of Heilsgeschichte, which he seems to have conceived as a ὁδός 'way'/ and that the chief function of the account of the trip—as a stage along that way—is in connection with his concept of authenticated witness, on which he saw the life and ministry of the Christian church based."

Sixth category: six scholars' opinions do not fall into any of the above categories. Marshall (1978:401–402) is of the opinion that "it is probable that the journey motif was present in Luke's sources," and "the difficulty of tracing a logical progression through the section may well be due to the nature of the material as it reached Luke. He was governed by what he found in his sources." Leifeld (1984:932) thinks that "it is more reasonable and more consistent with the data to understand this section as showing that Jesus' ministry has entered a new phase and has taken on some new characteristics." To Craddock (1990:140, 142) this section is "an editorial structure created by Luke. That Luke found the travel motif helpful for telling the story of Jesus," and it is "Luke's presentation of Jesus' journey to Jerusalem into a pilgrimage with Jesus in an unfolding and deepening way, not only to the passion but into the kingdom of God." McComiskey (2004:202–203) believes that "possibly the multi-fold parallel cyclical structure of the Elijah-Elisha cycles (1 Kings 17:1–19:21), to which (Luke) refers so regularly throughout the Gospel, is his structural model" for this section. While Kistemaker does not give comment on the interpretation of this section, he (1982:34, 39) opines that this section is not necessarily written in chronological order

ANALYSIS OF NARRATIVE SEQUENCE IN LUKE'S GOSPEL 133

and "Luke's sequence seems to be dictated not by strict chronology but by emphases, themes, literary balance and design." Like Kistemaker, Bebb also does not give comment on the section's interpretation, but thinks that (1911-1912:171) "St. Luke in this section impresses upon us so often his uncertainty as to time and place, that a chronological sequence seems out of the question."

Regarding the interpretation of this section, I believe that, as suggested by the scholars in categories 1 and 5, it includes contents which are soteriological, ecclesiological and Christological in nature, as these are also the key themes throughout the gospel. Some contents in this section do seem to correspond to the themes in the Book of Deuteronomy. As Pao and Schnabel (2007:314) indicate: "four (Deuteronomic) themes are repeatedly emphasized by Luke: (1) like their ancestors, this generation is a faithless and rebellious generation (11:14-54; 12:54-13:9; 17:20-37); (2) God sent his prophet to reveal his will and to call his people to repent (10:1-16; 11:14-54; 12:54-13:9; 13:22-35; 14:15-24; 15; 17:22-37; 19:1-27); (3) but Israel rejects his prophets (9:52-58; 10:25-37; 11:37-54; 12:35-53; 13:22-35); and (4) as a result, Israel will be judged (11:31-32, 50-51; 12:57-59; 13:24-30, 35; 14:24; 17:26-30; 19:27, 41-44)." However, I have reservations about some opinions which seem to indicate that Jesus' journey is only a creation by Luke to promote his theological ideas (e.g. Talbert and Craddock), and I would disagree if they imply that the journey itself is a creation but is not real, because it would contradict Luke's commitment to investigate carefully the information he has collected from the eyewitnesses and to record truth and facts in his gospel (Luke 1:1-4). I also have reservations about the theory that Luke's ordering of events in this section resembles that in Deuteronomy chapters 1-26.[90] From the view that Theophilus, the reader of this gospel, is very likely only a God-fearer or a young Christian,[91] it is unlikely that Luke would structure the section this way, as Theophilus could hardly understand the meaning. Concerning the theory of chiasm, it seems that there is no consensus on which is the best pattern so far, and some suggestions seem forced. For example: Talbert (2002:117-118) concludes that 9:51-56 parallels with 19:11ff and shares the same theme: the rejection Jesus

---

90. This is a theory suggested by C. F. Evans, and discussed by Pao and Schnabel (2007:313).

91. Luke 1:4 seems to indicate that Theophilus is either a God-fearer or a young Christian, because Luke must write to him to let him know for certain the things he has been taught. This is supported by Luke 2:23, which indicates that Theophilus likely does not know the commonly known requirement among the Jews that every firstborn male is to be consecrated to the Lord, and Luke must explain this to him.

experienced. However, this theme seems to contradict 19:35–38 (part of 19:11ff) which is about Jesus' triumphant entry to Jerusalem. Moreover, the supporters of this theory have yet to prove whether the chiastic approach is a writing style commonly used by contemporary Greco-Roman historians. If not, Theophilus, who is likely a Gentile (see footnote 62), might not be able to understand this structure and it would be meaningless for Luke to write to him in this way.

The proposal that John chapters 7–12 should be read together with this section seems to be a feasible approach to explain Jesus' route to Jerusalem in this section. Luke records that Jesus takes a circular route (south→east→northwest→south) to go to Jerusalem. He first travels south to Samaria (9:52), then goes further south to Bethany where Martha and Mary live (10:38), which is only about a mile and half east of Jerusalem (Anon., 1988:284). He then likely goes east to Perea (13:31),[92] then northwest to the middle of Galilee and Samaria (17:11), south again to Jericho (18:35), then southwest to Bethphage and Bethany (19:29), then the Mount of Olives (19:39) and finally Jerusalem (19:45). From chapter 7 to 12 the apostle John records a similar circular route (south→east→west→north→south) that Jesus takes to Jerusalem. Jesus travels south from Galilee to Jerusalem (7:9–10) for the Feast of Tabernacles, which is around September/October (Anon., 1988:783). John mentions that Jesus is also in Jerusalem during the Feast of Dedication (10:22), which is around November/December (Anon., 1988:783). Jesus then travels east across the River Jordan to where John the Baptist has been baptizing at first (10:40), which is likely at Bethany[93] on the east side of the River Jordan (1:28.) Afterwards, Jesus goes west to the other Bethany[94] which is on the west side of the River Jordan, where Martha and Mary live (11:1, 6–7), to heal Lazarus. Jesus then leaves Judea and goes north to Ephraim in Samaria[95] (11:54), before finally going south

---

92. Luke 13:31 indicates that very likely Jesus is either in Perea or Galilee at that time, as Herod Antipas is the ruler of Perea and Galilee during Jesus' time. If my observation in narrative account 3.3.1.21 is true, that one of the reasons Jesus condemns the non-repentant towns in Luke 10:13–15 is that he does not intend to return to Galilee, then Jesus is mostly likely in Perea in Luke 13:31.

93. According to Anderson (2009:563), "considerable debate surrounds the identification of this site, though a strong possibility is the traditional location at the Wadi el-Kharar, some 6 mi. E of Jericho; at the nearby Qaṣr el Yehud."

94. Anderson (2009:563) describes that this Bethany is "a village less than 2 mi. SE of Jerusalem on the road to Jericho (Jn. 11:18). It was on the E side of the Mount of Olives."

95. Ewing and Hughes (1979–1988:119) describe that "it is generally identified with modern eṭ-Ṭaiyibeh, about 21 km (13 mi) NNE of Jerusalem and 6 1/2 km (4 mi) NE

again through Bethany (12:1) to Jerusalem (12:12) for his passion. If it is correct to read John chapters 7–12 with this section, it would mean that Jesus, during the period of time between the end of his Galilean ministry and his passion, has made a circular trip in Israel, beginning from Galilee and ending at Jerusalem, and that he has visited Jerusalem more than once in the above-mentioned time period. It would also explain why, after Jesus has begun his journey from Galilee in the north and has headed south to Jerusalem in 9:51, he is again in the north in the middle of Galilee and Samaria in 17:11, after visiting Bethany, which is close to Jerusalem in the south, in Luke 10:38.

With regard to the order of this section, while many of the scholars above do not discuss it, the ones who believe that this section is not written in chronological order do not always give reasons.[96] The only two reasons noted from above are as follows: (1) The section lacks clear chronological and geographical indicators, and this is an indication that Luke does not intend to write this section in chronological order (Bock, 2004, vol.2:959–961); and (2) Luke seems to be uncertain about time and place. Jesus seems to be wandering from place to place rather than heading directly to Jerusalem (Bebb, 1911–1912:171; Strauss, 1995:272.) However, Jesus' circular route to Jerusalem ("wandering from place to place") does not necessarily indicate that this section is not written in chronological order. Moreover, many scholars (Thomas and Gundry, 1988:127–174; Godet, 1881:62; and Lange, 2008:161) who suggest that this section should be read together with John chapters 7–12, which describes a circular route Jesus takes from Galilee to Jerusalem, believe that this section is written in chronological order. But, as suggested by Bock, does that lack of chronological and geographical indicators indicate that this section is not written in chronological order? We will evaluate the order of each narrative account therein and give a conclusion at the end of this section.

---

of Bethel. "Aphaerema," in the district of Samaria, may also refer to this city (1 Macc. 11:34; cf. Josephus, *Ant*. xiii.4.9)."

96. The same also happens to the recently published *Chronological Study Bible*—while stating that Luke 11:1–36 and 13:18–21 are not written in chronological order (Bible, 2014:1122–1129, 1132–1135, 1139–1141), it does not give reasons to support its claims.

3.3.2.1 Journey through Samaria (9:51–56)
(Thomas and Gundry, 1988:128–129)

Category: 1

Time: After Jesus has completed his Galilean ministries (9:51).

Observations: 9:51 clearly states that the reason Jesus sets out for Jerusalem is that the time has come for him to be taken up to heaven. It likely means that this trip to Jerusalem is going to be his last: logically it must happen after Jesus has completed his Galilean ministries. Therefore, this account must have been recorded chronologically after the apostle John's question, which apparently is raised when Jesus is still ministering in Capernaum, a city in Galilee (see narrative account 3.3.1.42 and 3.3.1.43).

Luke is the only one who has recorded this incident. 9:51–52a (v. 52a: "and he sent messengers before his presence" [καὶ ἀπέστειλεν ἀγγέλους πρὸ προσώπου αὐτοῦ]) seemingly is another overlapping summary statement Luke employs, following those in 1:80, 2:40, 2:52, 3:19–20, 4:14–15, 4:42–44 and 8:1–3. It likely gives a brief summary of Jesus' final trip to Jerusalem from 9:52b to 19:44, up to just before 19:45–48 where the next overlapping summary occurs. If this is so, its time frame probably overlaps 9:52b–19:44. After the training they have received in 9:1–10 and 9:40, the apostles and the disciples are now more capable of ministering independently and as a result, Jesus sends them before him on his trip to Jerusalem (see 9:52b; 10:1, 17 and 19:29). The women who have been financially supporting Jesus (8:2–3) also follow them to Jerusalem (see 23:49, 55; 24:1, 10). This section is a continuation of the previous section in 8:4–9:50 (see narrative account 3.3.1.29). Jesus' team is now ready and the time has come for them to proceed to Jerusalem, where Jesus will carry out his final mission, resulting in his death, resurrection and ascension.

Writing order identified: the narrative account is recorded chronologically, and overlapping chronology is noted in Luke 9:51–52a.

3.3.2.2. Complete commitment required of followers (9:57–62) (Thomas and Gundry, 1988:127–128)

Category: 1

Time: After the "journey through Samaria," while Jesus is on the way to a village (9:57).

Observations: Immediately after the end of the "journey through Samaria" account in 9:56, "and they went to another village" (καὶ ἐπορεύθησαν εἰς ἑτέραν κώμην), at the beginning of this narrative account in 9:57, Luke writes "and when they are going in the way" (καὶ πορευομένων αὐτῶν ἐν τῇ ὁδῷ . . .). If Luke does not intend to convey to his readers the idea that this event chronologically comes after the immediately preceding "journey through Samaria," then it would be hard to explain why Luke has to begin 9:57 with such a phrase, as he could have omitted this phrase while still conveying the message of this account. Therefore, it seems reasonable to believe that this event happens after the "journey through Samaria."

Mark does not have a parallel of this account. Matthew has a parallel but records it much earlier in Matthew 8:19–22. Matthew likely has relocated this narrative account for thematic purposes (see narrative account 3.3.1.14).

Writing order identified: chronological.

3.3.2.3 Commissioning of the seventy-two (10:1–16) (Thomas and Gundry, 1988:138)

Category: 1

Time: After the "complete commitment required of followers" account (10:1).

Observations: 10:1 says "and after these things . . . " (μετὰ δὲ ταῦτα . . .), indicating that this happens after the preceding event. Mark has no parallel of this narrative account. Matthew likely has combined this mission with the mission in the "commissioning of the twelve" account (i.e., narrative account 3.3.1.35. See narrative account 3.3.1.14 for explanation) as one mission.

Writing order identified: chronological.

3.3.2.4 Return of the seventy-two (10:17–24)
(Thomas and Gundry, 1988:138–139)

Category: 1

Time: After the "commissioning of the seventy-two" (10:17).

Observations: 10:17 says "and the seventy-two returned with joy" (ὑπέστρεψαν δὲ οἱ ἑβδομήκοντα μετὰ χαρᾶς), indicating that this happens after the immediately preceding event. Again, Mark has no parallel of this account and Matthew likely has combined the mission in this account with the mission in the "commissioning of the twelve" account (narrative account 3.3.1.35. See narrative account 3.3.1.14).

Writing order identified: chronological.

3.3.2.5 Story of the good Samaritan (10:25–37)
(Thomas and Gundry, 1988:139)

Category: 1

Time: Immediately after the "Return of the seventy-two" account in Luke 10:17–24 (10:25).

Observations: Luke 10:25 uses "and behold" (καὶ ἰδοὺ) at the beginning of this story account. The *Greek New Testament Novum Testamentum Graece* (NA27) indicates that the gospel of Luke and the book of Acts together have 34 usages of this phrase[97] and a study of all the usages finds that this phrase in 10:25 very likely means "shortly afterwards." If this is true, then this incident likely happens shortly after the "return of the seventy-two" in Luke 10:17–24 and is recorded in chronological order. This account is unique to Luke, having no parallel in Matthew and Mark.

Writing order identified: chronological.

---

97. The meaning of the other 33 usages of καὶ ἰδοὺ (besides 10:25; i.e., Luke 1:20, 31, 36; 2:25; 5:12, 18; 7:12, 37; 8:41; 9:30, 38, 39; 11:31, 32, 41; 13:11, 30; 14:2; 19:2; 23:50; 24:4, 13, 49; Acts 1:10; 5:28; 8:27; 10:30 11:11; 12:7; 16:1, 27:24, 23:14 and 15) likely falls into the first category of the meaning of καὶ ἰδοὺ in Matthew (see footnote 69 under narrative account 3.3.1.18,) indicating that the current event happens while the previous event is still happening (i.e., both events happen simultaneously), and the phrase can be translated as "at that time" or "and now." The καὶ ἰδοὺ in Luke 10:25 likely has the same meaning and, if this is true, it implies that the narrative account of 10:25–37 happens at the same time, when Jesus has finished talking to his disciples in Luke 10:23–24.

3.3.2.6 Jesus' visit with Mary and Martha (10:38-42)
(Thomas and Gundry, 1988:139-140)

Category: 3

Time: While Jesus and his disciples are on their last trip to Jerusalem (9:51, 10:38).

Observations: Luke does not mention the place or time when this event happens. He only says Jesus "comes into a certain village" (εἰσῆλθεν εἰς κώμην τινά.) From John 11:1 we know that Mary and Martha live in Bethany, a place less than two miles away from Jerusalem (John 11:18). Jesus and the disciples keep traveling south through Samaria (9:52) and now they have arrived in Bethany. As Luke is the only one who records this account, we do not have sufficient information to decide what writing order Luke employs to record it.

Writing order identified: cannot be ascertained.

3.3.2.7 Lesson on how to pray and parable of the bold friend
(11:1-13) (Thomas and Gundry, 1988:140)

Category: 3

Time: Not described.

Observations: Luke does not mention the account's time of occurrence. As in the previous account, "Jesus' visit with Mary and Martha," Luke is vague about the location where the incident happens. In 10:38 of the previous account Luke says Jesus "came into a certain village" (εἰσῆλθεν εἰς κώμην τινά) where he is welcomed by Martha. Now in 11:1 Luke says Jesus "was praying in a certain place" (ἐν τόπῳ τινὶ προσευχόμενον) when this incident happens. Luke also does not mention the name of the disciple asking Jesus to teach them to pray; he only uses "a certain one of his disciples" (τις τῶν μαθητῶν αὐτοῦ). Luke apparently believes that the exact time, location and name are not as important when compared with the message he is going to describe and he chooses not to mention them. This account is unique to Luke, having no parallel in Matthew and Mark.

At first glance it seems that Matthew 6:9-13, where Jesus gives a similar instruction about prayer, is describing the same incident. However, a study of the two accounts reveals that the settings do not match and they may be different instructions about prayer given on different occasions. Bock (2004, vol.2:1046) has a similar view on this matter: "since the setting and form of the two prayers differ. The Matthean prayer occurs in the Sermon on the Mount, a public setting in which Jesus simply prays the prayer ... in Luke (one of) the disciples ask(s) for instruction and Jesus responds with this shorter form. Luke's setting is a private one ... Luke's form of the prayer, though almost verbally the same as Matthew's prayer, lacks two lines of Matthew's version: the reference to God's will being done and the request to be delivered from evil ... It seems more likely that these are distinct prayers in distinct settings."

As Luke does not provide adequate information for the time when this event happens, and since this account is unique to Luke, we do not have sufficient information to decide the writing order of this narrative account.

Writing order identified: cannot be ascertained.

3.3.2.8 Blasphemous accusation and debate (11:14–36) (Thomas and Gundry, 1988:141–142)

Category: 3

Time: Not described.

Observations: Luke has not mentioned this event's time of occurrence. But does it have parallel(s) in other synoptic gospels? And, if there is (are), can we learn more about the timing of this incident from its parallel account(s)? Thomas and Gundry (1988:141) believe that though Matthew 12:22–30 and Mark 3:22–27 seem to describe the same incident, this event happens about one year later than Matthew 12:22–30 and Mark 3:22–27 indicate, and is unique to Luke based on the following reasons: (1) the incident in Luke likely happens in Judea but the one in Matthew and Mark happens in Galilee; (2) in Luke's account the man healed is dumb, but in Matthew and Mark's account he is both dumb and blind; and (3) the incident following Luke's account is different from the incidents which follow Matthew and Mark's account. Bock (2004, vol.2:1069) has a different view on this matter. He disagrees with Thomas and Gundry with the following arguments: (1) Jesus' journey to Jerusalem covers a lot of regions and Judea may not be where this incident takes place; (2) Luke may want to abbreviate the narrative, so chooses not to describe the blindness of the man healed; and (3) the possible topical arrangements of the gospels may lead to different narrative accounts recorded after this account. Bock (2004, vol.2:1069–1070) believes that Luke 11:14–23, Matthew 12:22–30 and Mark 3:22–27 are describing the same incident due to their strong verbal ties (compare Luke 11:15b with Mark 3:22b, 11:17b with Mark 3:24a, 11:18 with Mark 3:26, 11:17 with Matt 12:25, 11:18 with Matt 12:26, 11:19–20 with Matt 12:27–28, and 11:23 with Matt 12:30); and Matthew has likely recorded this incident in its proper sequence while Luke and Mark have relocated this account for thematic purposes: since Matthew uses a temporal note "then," (τότε), for the setting of the incident (Matt 12:22) while Luke (Luke 11:14) and Mark (Mark 3:22) only use "and" (καὶ), a connector that does not indicate time.

While I would agree with Bock that Luke's account, Matthew 12:22–30 and Mark 3:22–27 are describing the same incident due to their strong verbal ties, and that Jesus' last journey does cover quite a number of different regions (Bethany in 10:38 and 19:29, Samaria in 9:52 and 17:11, Galilee in 17:11, Jericho in 18:35 and 19:1, and Bethphage in 19:29) and, accordingly, that this incident does not necessarily happen in Judea, I have reservations about whether Matthew has recorded this incident in its proper sequence. Τότε is only a loose temporal connector which does not inevitably indicate time. For example, in Matthew 11:20 Matthew uses τότε in the setting of Jesus' condemnation of Chorazin and Bethsaida for their failure to repent (Matt 11:20–30); however, it does not mean that this event necessarily comes immediately after the previous event (Jesus' comment about John the Baptist's relationship to the kingdom in Matt 11:2–19) in time. As discussed in narrative accounts 3.3.1.14 and 3.3.1.21 above, Matthew apparently has combined two to three different missions into one and put it in 9:36–11:1 for thematic purposes. If this is the case, then Matthew 11:20–30 likely happens at a much later time, when Jesus is on the way to Jerusalem after he has completed his Galilean ministries (see Luke 10:1–24 and narrative account 3.3.1.21) and not after Jesus' comment about John the Baptist. Consequently, it seems that we cannot rely on Matthew's τότε to determine the timing of this narrative account.

Matthew and Mark both record this incident before the spiritual kinship narrative account, which is different from Luke, who records this incident before Jesus dines with a Pharisee (11:37). However, as already discussed in narrative account 3.3.1.31 above, both Matthew and Mark may have the tendency to relocate traditions here: Matthew may relocate them for thematic purposes and Mark may relocate them for the construction of his intercalated unit in 3:20–35. Since all the synoptic gospels do not have specific information about the timing of this incident, its writing order cannot be ascertained.

Writing order identified: cannot be ascertained.

3.3.2.9 Woes against the Pharisees and teachers of law while eating with a Pharisee (11:37–54) (Thomas and Gundry, 1988:142)

Category: 1

Time: Immediately after the "blasphemous accusation and debate" account in 11:14–36 (11:37).

Observations: Luke 11:37 says "and when (Jesus) was speaking, a Pharisee asked him in order that he might eat a meal with him" (ἐν δὲ τῷ λαλῆσαι ἐρωτᾷ αὐτὸν Φαρισαῖος ὅπως ἀριστήσῃ παρ' αὐτῷ). It likely indicates that a Pharisee asks Jesus to dine with him when Jesus is about to finish his teaching in the "blasphemous accusation and debate" account. And, if this is the case, this account is recorded chronologically by Luke. This account is unique to Luke.

Writing order identified: chronological.

3.3.2.10 Warning the disciples about hypocrisy (12:1–12) (Thomas and Gundry, 1988:143)

Category: 1

Time: Immediately after the "woes against the Pharisees and teachers of law while eating with a Pharisee" account (12:1).

Observations: Luke 12:1 uses ἐν οἷς.[98] It means "during which things, meanwhile" (Zerwick and Grosvenor, 1996:228) and

---

98. This phrase, according to Bibleworks version 9, appears 18 times in the New Testament. 16 times it is used in the middle of a sentence and likely means "by which," "in which," "among which," etc. For example, Acts 11:14 reads "who will speak a message to you, *by which* you and all your household will be saved" (ὃς λαλήσει ῥήματα

"under which circumstances" (Bauer, 2000:727.) If the translation is accurate, this account most likely happens after Jesus has finished his meal with a Pharisee, and when the scribes and the Pharisees begin to press him severely, trying to provoke him to say something inappropriate (Luke 11:53). Therefore, this account likely appears in chronological order. Again this account is unique to Luke, having no parallel in Matthew and Mark.

According to Bock (2004, vol.2:1129) some scholars such as Fitzmyer and Schneider believe that in 12:1-12 "Luke brought together a diverse group of teachings based on thematic considerations," the major reason being that many materials in this narrative account find parallels in different narrative accounts of Matthew and Mark. It seems that Luke 12:1 = Matthew 16:5-6 = Mark 8:14-15, Luke 12:2-9 = Matthew 10:26-33, Luke 12:10 = Matthew 12:31-32 = Mark 3:28-30, and Luke 12:11-12 = Matthew 10:19-20 = Mark 13:11. If the discourse contents in this account are originally delivered by Jesus on various occasions but Luke has relocated them here for thematic purposes, it is possible that the materials in this narrative are not recorded in chronological order. But how convincing is this argument? As discussed in narrative account 3.3.1.24, it is likely that Jesus as an itinerant preacher and teacher would repeat his messages on different occasions. A study of the context of Luke 12:2-9 and Matthew 10:26-33 reveals that though the contents look similar, the reasons for delivering the contents are different. In Luke Jesus intends to exhort his disciples to avoid hypocrisy by speaking the truth, but in Matthew Jesus wants the disciples not to keep the gospel to themselves but to proclaim the gospel bravely to the public. Moreover, while Luke 12:11-12 is similar to Matthew 10:19-20 and Mark 13:11, Luke records a similar message of Jesus in Luke 21:14-15 which supports the argument that Jesus sometimes does repeat certain messages on different occasions. Therefore, it is quite possible that 12:1-12 is part of a sermon (according to the context the complete sermon should be from 12:1 to 13:9) Jesus gives at that particular time. Furthermore,

---

πρὸς σὲ ἐν οἷς σωθήσῃ σὺ καὶ πᾶς ὁ οἶκός σου), and Acts 17:34 reads "and some men, after they cleaved to him they believed, and *among which* Dionysius the Areopagite and . . . " (τινὲς δὲ ἄνδρες κολληθέντες αὐτῷ ἐπίστευσαν, ἐν οἷς καὶ Διονύσιος ὁ Ἀρεοπαγίτης καὶ . . .) It is used only twice at the beginning of a sentence (Luke 12:1 and Acts 26:12) to mean "during that time" or "meanwhile." For example, Acts 26:12 reads "*During that time* while going to Damascus with authority and the commission of the chief priests" (Ἐν οἷς πορευόμενος εἰς τὴν Δαμασκὸν μετ᾽ ἐξουσίας καὶ ἐπιτροπῆς τῆς τῶν ἀρχιερέων,) ἐν οἷς here indicates that Paul experiences a vision from God *while* he is on the way to Damascus.

from the context Luke seems to portray this as a single sermon Jesus delivers alternately to his disciples and to the crowd hearing him at that time, rather than a collection of Jesus' sayings on different occasions. According to 12:1, although there is a large crowd listening to Jesus, he speaks first to the disciples; in 12:13 someone from the crowd asks Jesus a question and Jesus uses a parable (12:16-21) to respond; Jesus speaks to the disciples again in 12:22 and in 12:32. In 12:41 Peter seems to be confused as to whether Jesus' earlier teaching is for the disciples or for the crowd, and so he clarifies this with Jesus; finally, in 13:1, a person, likely from the crowd, informs Jesus of the tragic deaths of some Galileans, triggering his comment on the matter.

Writing order identified: chronological.

3.3.2.11 Warning about greed and trust in wealth, the coming of the Son of Man, and the coming division (12:13-59) (Thomas and Gundry, 1988:143-145)

Category: 1

Time: Immediately after the "Warning the disciples about hypocrisy" account.

Observations: According to Thomas and Gundry, the whole chapter of Luke 12 is unique, having no parallel in the other gospels. Luke 12 is portrayed as a single teaching on various subjects Jesus gives to his disciples and the crowd at that time. Luke 12:13 says "and someone from the crowd said to him" (εἶπεν δέ τις ἐκ τοῦ ὄχλου αὐτῷ). This phrase most likely correlates with 12:1, which describes a gigantic crowd of many thousands gathered to listen to Jesus. According to the context this phrase in 12:13 likely implies that this incident happens in the middle of Jesus' teaching in Luke 12 and comes after the immediately preceding account of 12:1-12. If this is true, this account is recorded in chronological order.

Writing order identified: chronological.

3.3.2.12 Two alternatives: repent or perish (13:1-9) (Thomas and Gundry, 1988:146)

Category: 1

Time: Immediately after the "warning about greed and trust in wealth, the coming of the Son of Man, and the coming division" account (13:1).

Observations: Luke 13:1 says "and some were arriving in the same time" (παρῆσαν δέ τινες ἐν αὐτῷ τῷ καιρῷ), indicating that this account happens at the same time after Jesus has finished his teaching in Luke 12 and is recorded in chronological order.

Writing order identified: chronological.

3.3.2.13 Opposition from a synagogue ruler for healing a woman on the Sabbath (13:10–21) (Thomas and Gundry, 1988:146–147)

Category: 3

Time: On a Sabbath day (13:10).

Observations: As Luke does not mention the exact time or order of this account, and because this account is unique to Luke, having no parallel in the other gospels, there is insufficient information to determine its writing order.

Writing order identified: cannot be ascertained.

3.3.2.14 Question about salvation and entering the kingdom (13:22–30) (Thomas and Gundry, 1988:149)

Category: 3

Time: While Jesus is on his way to Jerusalem (13:22).

Observations: Luke 13:22 says, "and he was journeying through cities and villages while he was teaching and making a way for himself to Jerusalem" (καὶ διεπορεύετο κατὰ πόλεις καὶ κώμας διδάσκων καὶ πορείαν ποιούμενος εἰς Ἱεροσόλυμα). It indicates that this incident happens while Jesus is travelling to Jerusalem. However, because no concrete time or writing order is described, and because this account is unique to Luke, with no parallel in the other gospels, there is insufficient information to determine its writing order.

Writing order identified: cannot be ascertained.

3.3.2.15 Anticipation of Jesus' coming death and his sorrow over Jerusalem (13:31-35) (Thomas and Gundry, 1988:149-150)

Category: 1

Time: Immediately after the "Question about salvation and entering the kingdom" account.

Observations: Luke 13:31 says "in the same hour" (ἐν αὐτῇ τῇ ὥρᾳ), indicating that this happens when Jesus finishes his teaching on salvation and entering the kingdom in 13:22-30. Therefore, this account very likely is recorded in chronological order.

Writing order identified: chronological.

3.3.2.16 Healing of a man with dropsy while Jesus is eating with a prominent Pharisee on the Sabbath, and three parables suggested by the occasion (14:1-24) (Thomas and Gundry, 1988:150-151)

Category: 3

Time: On a Sabbath day (14:1).

Observations: Luke does not describe the time or the order of this incident. Luke 14:1 says only that it happens on a Sabbath day. As this account is unique to Luke, with no parallel in the other gospels, there is insufficient information to determine its writing order.

Writing order identified: cannot be ascertained.

3.3.2.17 Cost of discipleship (14:25-35) (Thomas and Gundry, 1988:151)

Category: 3

Time: While a great multitude is traveling with Jesus on the way to Jerusalem (14:25).

Observations: Luke does not describe the exact time when this incident happens. At first glance Luke 14:26-27 and Matthew 10:37-38 look similar. However, the settings of the two passages are different. In Matthew Jesus teaches his twelve apostles (see Matt 10:1) various truths including the cost of discipleship, while he is commissioning them to evangelize in Galilee. In Luke Jesus teaches a great crowd following him as he is traveling towards Jerusalem. Moreover, according to Bock (2004, vol.2:1281) the vocabularies in these two passages seldom overlap. Based on the above observations, I think that Luke 14:26-27 and Matthew 10:37-38 are two distinct teachings on a similar subject which Jesus gives on different occasions. Because this account is unique to Luke, with no parallel in the other gospels, there is insufficient information to determine its writing order.

Writing order identified: cannot be ascertained.

3.3.2.18 Parables in defense of association with sinners (15:1–32) (Thomas and Gundry, 1988:152–153)

Category: 3

Time: Not described.

Observations: Luke does not describe the exact time this incident happens. Luke 15:4-7 looks similar to Matthew 18:12-13: in both passages Jesus uses the example of a lost sheep to illustrate God's concern for sinners. However, the settings of the two passages are different. In Matthew Jesus is teaching his disciples in Galilee (Matt 17:22, 24; 18:1) but in Luke Jesus is talking to the tax-collectors, sinners, Pharisees and scribes (Luke 15:1-2) while he is on the way to Jerusalem. I think that they are different teachings on a similar subject which Jesus gives at different times. Luke 15:1-32 is unique to Luke and there is insufficient information to decide its writing order.

Writing order identified: cannot be ascertained.

3.3.2.19 Parable teaching the proper use of money (16:1–13) (Thomas and Gundry, 1988:153)

Category: 1

Time: Immediately after Jesus' parables in defense of association with sinners in 15:1–32 (16:1).

Observations: Luke 16:1 says, "and he was also saying to the disciples" (ἔλεγεν δὲ καὶ πρὸς τοὺς μαθητάς). Luke uses the imperfect tense "he was saying" (ἔλεγεν) and "also" (καὶ) together, which likely implies that the parable is part of the teaching which begins at 15:1 and follows 15:1–32 in time. Other than 16:1 Luke also uses the phrase "and he was also saying" (ἔλεγεν δὲ καὶ) in 5:36, 12:54 and 14:12. When Thomas and Gundry divide the Gospel of Luke into individual narrative accounts they regard 5:33–39 (1988:64–65) and 14:1–24 (1988:150–151) as individual events. They seemingly conclude that the contents after 5:36 and 14:12 naturally follow those of 5:33–35 and 14:1–11; thus they place 12:54–59 and 16:1–13 immediately after 12:49–53 (1988:145) and 15:1–32 (1988:152–153), respectively. Apparently they agree that the events following ἔλεγεν δὲ καὶ come immediately after its preceding narrative accounts in time. They agree that this account is recorded chronologically. This account is unique to Luke.

Writing order identified: chronological.

3.3.2.20 Story teaching the danger of wealth (16:14–31) (Thomas and Gundry, 1988:154)

Category: 1

Time: Immediately after Jesus' parable teaching the proper use of money in Luke 16:1–13 (16:14).

Observations: Luke 16:14 ("and, being fond of money, the Pharisees were hearing all these (things)" [ἤκουον δὲ ταῦτα πάντα οἱ Φαρισαῖοι φιλάργυροι]) indicates that this happens immediately after Jesus' parable teaching the proper use of money in Luke 16:1–13.

Luke 16:16–17 looks similar to Matthew 11:12–13 and 5:18, and Luke 16:18 seems parallel with Matthew 5:32, 19:9 and Mark 10:11–12. However, the settings of the passages of Matthew 5:18, 32 and 11:12–13 are different from Luke 16:16–18. Luke 16:16–18 is a part of Jesus' teachings to his disciples on the way to Jerusalem, while Matthew 5:18, 5:32 and 11:12–13 are messages Jesus gives in Galilee: 5:18 and 5:32 are parts of Jesus' Sermon on the Mount, and 11:12–13 is Jesus' comment about John the Baptist to his disciples while Jesus is in Galilee, after he has answered the question raised by the disciples of John the Baptist. Moreover, sometimes even the subjects of the discussion are different. For example, Luke 16:16 (Bible, 1971) says "the law and the prophets were until John; since then the good news of the kingdom of God is preached, and every one enters it violently." Apparently it means that those who want to enter the kingdom of God have to make an exceptional effort; but Matthew 11:12 (Bible, 1971) says "from the days of John the Baptist until now the kingdom of heaven has suffered violence, and (people) of violence take it by force," which seemingly means that the kingdom of heaven has suffered a lot of assaults or attacks since John the Baptist. Luke 16:16 is about an effort which has to be made to enter the kingdom of God, but Matthew 11:12 is apparently about the attacks the kingdom of God has suffered from its enemies, which are two different subjects. Consequently, they are likely different teachings on a similar subject which Jesus gives on different occasions. As in Luke 16:18, Jesus gives the messages in Matthew 19:9 and Mark 10:11–12 after he has left Galilee and is probably on his way to Jerusalem (see Matt 19:1 and Mark 10:1). Matthew 19:9 and Mark 10:11–12 are describing the same incident, as they are answers Jesus gives to the same question raised by the Pharisees (i.e., is it lawful to divorce one's wife, see Matt 19:3 and Mark 10:2.) Luke does not record this question as raised by the Pharisees, while Matthew 19:3 and Mark 10:2 do, and his message is not exactly the same as that of Mark. Luke 16:18b (Bible, 1971) says "and he who marries a woman divorced from her husband commits adultery," meaning the man who marries the divorced woman commits adultery, but Mark 10:12 (Bible, 1971) says "and if she divorces her husband and marries another, she commits adultery," meaning the divorced woman who remarries commits adultery.

Therefore, though there is a possibility that Luke 16:18, Matthew 19:9 and Mark 10:11–12 are describing the same incident, we cannot be certain in view of the differences among them as discussed above. Even if Luke 16:18, Matthew 19:9 and Mark 10:11–12 are describing the same incident, Luke 16:18, Matthew 19:9 and Mark 10:11–12 all happen after Jesus has begun his trip to Jerusalem but before the "example of little children in relation to the kingdom" account (i.e., Matt 19:13–15, Luke 18:15–17 and Mark 10:13–16, see narrative account 3.3.2.25). If this is the case, Luke still most likely records 16:18 in chronological order, as the sequence of events (Jesus begins his journey to Jerusalem → Jesus teaches about divorce → "Example of little children in relation to the kingdom" account) match in all the synoptic gospels.

Writing order identified: chronological.

3.3.2.21 Four lessons on discipleship (17:1–10)
(Thomas and Gundry, 1988:155)

Category: 1

Time: Probably after 16:14–31, after the story teaching the danger of wealth.

Observations: Although Luke has not explicitly described the time or the order of this incident, it likely occurs after 16:14–31 because according to the context this seems to be the last part of a single teaching of Jesus from 15:1 to 17:10. At first glance some sections seem to parallel certain passages in Matthew and Mark, namely:

a. Luke 17:1–3a seems parallel with Matthew 18:6–7 and Mark 9:42;

b. Luke 17:3b-4 with Matthew 18:15; and

c. Luke 17:5–6 with Matthew 17:19–21 and Mark 9:28–29

However, Luke 17 likely happens while Jesus is on the way to Jerusalem, but Matthew 17 to 18 and Mark 9 describe the events that occur while Jesus is still ministering in Galilee (Matt 17:22, 24; Mark 9:30, 33), around the time of his transfiguration (Matt 17:1–3, Mark 9:2–4). Moreover, though the messages given by Jesus in Luke are similar to those in Matthew and Mark, the contents and the use of words are quite different. For example, both Matthew and Mark mention that if one's hand, foot or eye causes one to stumble, one should cut it off to prevent this from happening (Matt 18:8–9, Mark 9:43–47), but Luke lacks this saying. Luke 17:4 describes Jesus teaching his disciples to forgive their brothers or sisters even if they sin against them seven times a day, but in Matthew Jesus only says that his disciples should go and resolve the issue when they are alone with those who sinned against them. Jesus uses "a mulberry tree" (συκάμινος) in Luke 7:6 in his teaching about faith but uses "a mountain" (ὄρος) in Matthew 19:20 to convey a similar message. Therefore, it is likely that Luke's account is different from that in Matthew and Mark and happens at a different time. This account seems to be unique to Luke.

Writing order identified: chronological.

3.3.2.22 Jesus' healing of ten lepers while passing between Samaria and Galilee (17:11–21) (Thomas and Gundry, 1988:158)

Category: 3

Time: While Jesus is on the way to Jerusalem, travelling along the border between Samaria and Galilee (17:11).

Observations: Luke does not describe the time or the order of this incident. Since this account is unique to Luke, having no parallel in the other gospels, there is insufficient information to determine whether this account is recorded chronologically.

Luke 17:11 says "and it happened when he was going to Jerusalem and he was passing through the middle of Samaria and Galilee" (καὶ ἐγένετο ἐν τῷ πορεύεσθαι εἰς Ἰερουσαλὴμ καὶ αὐτὸς διήρχετο διὰ μέσον Σαμαρείας καὶ Γαλιλαίας). Apparently this account indicates that Jesus does not travel in a straight line from Galilee to Jerusalem. After Jesus has begun his journey to Jerusalem in 9:51, he travels south but is refused the passage through a Samarian village (9:52). He likely continues south by another route and reaches Bethany, where Mary and Martha live (10:38), about two miles from Jerusalem. In Luke 13:31 Jesus probably has already traveled a bit back to the north and reaches either Perea or Galilee,[99] and now in 17:11 he is travelling along the border of Galilee and Samaria. From the above passages it seems that after Jesus has left Galilee in 9:51, he travels around Israel (Samaria, Judea, Galilee or Perea and now in between Samaria and Galilee) before he goes to Jerusalem, preaching and teaching in the areas he passes through.

Writing order identified: cannot be ascertained.

3.3.2.23 Instructions regarding the Son of Man's coming (17:22–37) (Thomas and Gundry, 1988:158–159)

Category: 1

Time: Probably after Jesus answers the question raised by the Pharisees in 17:20–21.

---

99. Luke 13:31 says that some Pharisees urge Jesus to leave the area as Herod Antipas wants to kill him. But what area? According to Schürer (2007, vol.2:17–18), Herod Antipas is the ruler of Galilee and Perea (which is south of Galilee on the other side of the River Jordan) during Jesus' time, so Jesus is probably in either Galilee or Perea.

Observations: According to the context this event likely follows the immediately preceding event. The Pharisees in 17:20–21 ask about the coming of the kingdom of God, which they seem to believe will be inaugurated in the future. After answering their question, Jesus touches on another topic which will happen in the future: his departure to heaven and his second-coming.

At first glance this account seems to parallel some passages in Matthew 24 (in particular vv.17–18, 23, 26–27 and 37–39) and Mark 13 (in particular vv.5–6, 14–16 and 19–23), but the settings are different. Both Matthew 24 and Mark 13 mention that Jesus has already arrived in Jerusalem at that time and he is on the Mount of Olives when giving his teaching (Matt 24:3, Mark 13:3). However, according to Luke 17:11, Jesus most likely is still on the way to Jerusalem, between Samaria and Galilee while he gives this teaching. Moreover, the content of Jesus' teaching on the Mount of Olives in Matthew and Mark is very different from the content in Luke 17:22–37. For example, other than the verses listed above, the rest of Matthew 24 and Mark 13 are not mentioned in Luke 17:22–37. There are also noticeable differences between the above-listed verses in Matthew/Mark and Luke. For example, in Luke Jesus mentions that he will suffer and be rejected by this generation (17:25), and the day will come just like the days of Lot (17:28–29); but these are not mentioned in either Matthew 24 or Mark 13. Therefore, I think that this account in Luke is a different account happening at a different time and is unique to Luke.

Writing order identified: chronological.

3.3.2.24 Parables on prayer: the persistent widow, and the Pharisee and the tax collector (18:1–14) (Thomas and Gundry, 1988:159)

Category: 1

Time: Likely after Jesus has given instructions about the Son of Man's coming in 17:22–37 (18:1).

Observations: Luke 18:1 says, "and he said a parable to them" (ἔλεγεν δὲ παραβολὴν αὐτοῖς). "To them" (αὐτοῖς) likely refers to "the disciples" (τοὺς μαθητάς) in Luke 17:22. If this is the case, it suggests that Jesus' audience in the narrative accounts 17:22–37 and 18:1–14 is the same—the disciples. This event likely follows 17:22–37 in time. This parable is unique to Luke.

Writing order identified: likely chronological.

3.3.2.25 Example of little children in relation to the kingdom (18:15–17) (Thomas and Gundry, 1988:161)

Category: 1

Time: When Jesus is in the region of Judea beyond the Jordan River (Matt 19:1 and Mark 10:1).

Observations: Luke does not specify the time or the order of this event. Thomas and Gundry believe that Matthew 19:13–15 and Mark 10:13–16 are describing the same incident. I would agree with them, as the key elements of the accounts in Luke, Matthew and Mark match each other: (1) Matthew and Mark tell us that at that time Jesus leaves Galilee and enters the region of Judea beyond the Jordan (Matt 19:1, Mark 10:1) and is likely on his way to Jerusalem (Matt 20:17; Mark 10:32). This matches Luke's statement that at that time Jesus is on his way to Jerusalem; (2) in all three gospels children/ babies are brought to Jesus for him to touch (Matt 19:13, Mark 10:13, Luke 18:15); (3) the reaction of the disciples is the same: they rebuke the people (Matt 19:13, Mark 10:13, Luke 18:15); and (4) Jesus' responses are the same: he tells the disciples to let the little children/babies come to him, and says that the kingdom of God belongs to people such as these (Matt 19:14, Mark 10:14–15, Luke 18:16). In Luke 17:11 Jesus appears to be between Samaria and Galilee when he gives the messages from 17:20–18:14. Matthew 19:1 and Mark 10:1 indicate Jesus is in Judea beyond the Jordan River when this incident happens. Since Jesus is on the way to Jerusalem at that time and Judea is closer to Jerusalem than Samaria and Galilee, this incident seemingly happens in Judea after Luke 17:20–18:14.

Writing order identified: chronological.

3.3.2.26 Riches and the kingdom (18:18–30) (Thomas and Gundry, 1988:161–163)

Category: 2

Time: Likely immediately after the "Example of little children in relation to the kingdom" account in Luke 18:15–17.

Observations: Luke does not specify the precise time or the order. Thomas and Gundry believe that Matthew 19:16–30 and Mark 10:17–31 describe the same incident. This seems plausible because all the key elements match in Luke, Matthew and Mark: (1) in all three gospels a man/a certain ruler comes up to Jesus and asks the same question: what must he do to inherit eternal life; (2) Jesus' response and his challenge to the man are the same: God is the only one who is good; he has to follow the commandments, sell everything he has and follow him; (3) the young man's answer and his response to Jesus are the same: he has kept the commandments, but he is unwilling to sell his possessions and he sadly goes away; (4) the contents of Jesus' subsequent conversation with his disciples are the same: it is easier for a camel to go through the eye of a needle than for a rich man to enter the kingdom of God, those who have sacrificed to follow him will receive much more as their reward.

Matthew 19:16 uses "and behold" (καὶ ἰδοὺ) at the beginning of this account to connect it with its immediate preceding account. According to our study of καὶ ἰδοὺ (see note 69 under narrative account 3.3.1.18), καὶ ἰδοὺ here likely means "shortly afterwards." Hence, this account very likely happens after the previous account in Matthew 19:13–15/Mark10:13–16/Luke 18:15–17. Moreover, Matthew, Mark and Luke all place this account after the "Example of little children in relation to the kingdom" account, it is therefore reasonable to believe that Luke has recorded this account chronologically.

Writing order identified: chronological.

3.3.2.27 Third prediction of Jesus' death and resurrection (18:31–34) (Thomas and Gundry, 1988:164)

Category: 2

Time: While Jesus is on the way up to Jerusalem (Luke 18:31, Matt 20:17, Mark 10:32), likely after the "Riches and the kingdom" account in Luke 18:18–30.

Observations: Luke does not give us the time or the order of this event. Thomas and Gundry believe that Matthew 20:17–19 and Mark 10:32–34 describe the same incident. I would agree, as all the key elements match in Luke, Matthew and Mark: (1) it happens when Jesus is on the way to Jerusalem and is recorded after the "Riches and the kingdom" account in all three gospels; (2) the audience of Jesus' message is the twelve apostles; (3) the content of what Jesus says is very much the same: he will be handed over to the Gentiles, they will mock him and kill him, and three days later he will rise again.

As Matthew,[100] Mark and Luke all record this incident after the "Riches and the kingdom" account, it is reasonable to believe that Luke has recorded this account chronologically after the "Riches and the kingdom" account.

Writing order identified: chronological.

3.3.2.28 Healing of blind Bartimaeus and his companion (18:35-43) (Thomas and Gundry, 1988:165-166)

Category: 2

Time: When Jesus is near Jericho (Luke 18:35, Matt 20:29, Mark 10:46), likely after the "Third prediction of Jesus' death and resurrection" account in Luke 18:32-34.

Observations: Luke does not specify the time or the order of this incident, but his reference to the city of Jericho in 18:35 indicates that Jesus is now near Jerusalem. As noted by Alden (1988:1119), the city is only 14 miles from Jerusalem. Jesus is now close to the end of his long journey to Jerusalem. Thomas and Gundry believe that Matthew 20:29-34 and Mark 10:46-52 describe the same incident Luke describes here. This is reasonable, as the key elements of the accounts in Luke, Matthew and Mark seem to match each other:

1. It happens when Jesus is near Jericho. Matthew 20:29 describes it as happening when Jesus is *leaving* Jericho, Mark 10:46 also says that Jesus comes to Jericho and is *leaving* the town when it happens, but Luke 18:35 says that it happens when Jesus *approaches* Jericho. It seems that if the gospels are describing the same incident, then Luke contradicts Matthew and Mark as to when this incident happens. Alden (1988:1119) concludes that there is no contradiction as there were two Jericho cities at that time, and he believes

---

100. Between "Riches and the kingdom" (19:16-30) and "Third prediction of Jesus' death and resurrection" (20:17-19), Matthew records the parable of the landowner's sovereignty (20:1-16). According to Thomas and Gundry (1988:163-164) this account is unique to Matthew, with no parallel in Luke and Mark.

that Jesus is leaving the old city (as described in Matthew and Mark) and heading towards the new city (as described in Luke) when this incident happens:

> ... it must be understood that the Jericho of NT times was built by Herod more than a mile to the south of the OT site, at the mouth of the Wadi Qilt. It is possible to sort out the healing of the blind men episodes in the synoptic Gospels by understanding that Jesus was passing from the site of ancient Jericho (Matt 20:29; Mark 10:46) and approaching Herodian Jericho (Luke 18:35).

Plummer (1896:429) and Bock (2004:1503) have reservations about this explanation, as they believe that old Jericho may not have been actively inhabited at Jesus' time. If so, it seems difficult to explain why Jesus would pass through old Jericho. However, whether old Jericho was inhabited or not at that time may not necessarily have affected Jesus' decision to pass through it. For example, it may be a shorter route. Therefore, Alden's explanation is still possible and gives a reasonable explanation for the apparent contradiction.

2. A blind man sits by the roadside begging. A seeming contradiction is the number of beggar(s) mentioned in the three synoptic gospels: Matthew 20:30 says that there are two blind men, but Mark 10:46 and Luke 18:35 mention only one. One possible explanation is that Luke and Mark may have deliberately described the one who is more desperate and vocal in seeking Jesus while Matthew describes the actual number of beggars seeking Jesus. Another apparent contradiction is that Matthew and Mark mention that Jesus and his disciples meet the blind man as they are leaving the city (Matt 20:29, Mark 10:46), while Luke says that Jesus meets the blind man when he approaches Jericho (18:35); Thomas and Gundry (1988:165) suggest a possible solution, that Jesus encounters the blind man when he approaches the city, but performs the miracle when he leaves the city.

3. The other details match: the blind beggar shouts to Jesus for mercy after knowing that he is passing by, and, though being rebuked, he shouts even louder to get Jesus' attention; Jesus stops and orders him to be brought to him; Jesus asks him what he wants and the beggar replies that he wants to see; and Jesus heals him.

As Matthew,[101] Mark[102] and Luke all record this incident after the "Third prediction of Jesus' death and resurrection" account, it is reasonable to conclude that Luke has recorded the event chronologically, after the "Third prediction of Jesus' death and resurrection" account.

Writing order identified: chronological.

3.3.2.29 Salvation of Zaccheus (19:1–10) (Thomas and Gundry, 1988:166–167)

Category: 1

Time: When Jesus enters and is passing through Jericho (19:1).

Observations: In the immediately preceding account Luke describes Jesus approaching Jericho (18:35), and now Jesus has entered and is passing through the city (19:1). Therefore, it is very likely that this incident happens after its immediately preceding account and is recorded in chronological order. This account is unique to Luke.

Writing order identified: chronological.

3.3.2.30 Parable to teach responsibility while the kingdom is delayed (19:11–28) (Thomas and Gundry, 1988:167)

Category: 1

Time: Very likely after the "Salvation of Zaccheus" account (19:11).

Observations: Luke 19:11 describes this event happening " . . . while they were hearing these [things]" (ἀκουόντων . . . αὐτῶν ταῦτα), indicating that it happens immediately after the preceding account. This account looks similar to that in Matthew 25:14–30, but the details of the two accounts are very different despite their messages being much alike. For example, (1) the

---

101. Matthew and Mark have inserted the "Warning against ambitious pride" account (Matt 20:20–28, Mark 10:35–45) between the "Third prediction of Jesus' death and resurrection" account (Matt 20:17–19, Mark 10:32–34) and the "Healing of the blind man" account (Matt 20:29–34, Mark 10:46–52), which is not recorded by Luke.

102. Refer to footnote 101.

settings of the two accounts are different: in Luke this happens while Jesus is still on his way to Jerusalem (19:11), but in Matthew's account it happens after Jesus has arrived in Jerusalem (Matt 24:1) and is teaching on the Mount of Olives (Matt 24:3); (2) in Luke there are ten servants while Matthew mentions only three; (3) in Luke the master seems to give an equal amount of money to each servant, but in Matthew the amount given to each is different; (4) in Luke the unproductive servant puts the money in a piece of cloth, in Matthew he digs a hole in the ground and hides the money. In view of the many differences, these two accounts are likely similar messages Jesus gives on different occasions. Again, this account is unique to Luke.

Writing order identified: chronological.

3.3.2.31 Triumphal entry into Jerusalem (19:29–44) (Thomas and Gundry, 1988:169–173)

Category: 1

Time: After Jesus gives the "Parable to teach responsibility while the kingdom is delayed" in Jericho (19:29).

Observations: 19:29 says that Jesus is near Bethphage and Bethany, which are respectively a "village on the Mount of Olives adjacent to Jerusalem" (Anon., 1988:291) and a "village on the eastern slope of the Mount of Olives about a mile and a half east of Jerusalem" (Anon., 1988:284). As these two villages are much closer to Jerusalem than Jericho (about 14 miles away from Jerusalem, see narrative account 3.3.2.28) to Jerusalem, and because Jesus at that time is on the way to Jerusalem, it is very likely that this incident happens immediately after the previous account in 19:11–28, which most likely happens in Jericho (19:1).

Thomas and Gundry believe that this account has parallels in Matthew 21:1–11, 14–17 and Mark 11:1–11. This is plausible as the settings in all these accounts match: Jesus is on his way to Jerusalem and has arrived at Bethphage and Bethany, and the disciples follow Jesus' instruction to find a colt for Jesus to ride to Jerusalem. In all three synoptic gospels this account is recorded after the "Healing of blind Bartimaeus and his companion" event. Both Matthew and Mark place this account immediately after the "Healing of blind Bartimaeus and his companion" event, which supports the idea that this account is recorded chronologically after the "Healing of blind Bartimaeus and his companion" account.

Table 18. Comparison of the sequences of "healing of the blind man" and "triumphal entry into Jerusalem" in the synoptic gospels

	Healing of the blind man	Triumphal entry into Jerusalem
Luke	18:35–43	19:29–44[47]
Matthew	20:29–34	21:1–11, 14–17[48]
Mark	10:46–52	11:1–11

Writing order identified: chronological.

3.3.2.32 Cleansing of the temple (19:45–48) (Thomas and Gundry, 1988:173–174)

Category: 1

Time: Likely the day after Jesus has arrived in Jerusalem (Mark 11:11–12, 15).

Observations: This event comes after Jesus' triumphant entry into Jerusalem in Luke 19:29–44 as now Jesus is cleansing the temple there. According to Mark 11:12 this incident happens on the day after Jesus has arrived in Jerusalem.

19:45–48 apparently is another overlapping summary statement Luke has employed, following the ones in 1:80, 2:40, 2:52, 3:19–20, 4:14–15, 4:42–44, 8:1–3 and 9:51–52a. In addition to Jesus' various teachings against the Jewish leaders while he is on the way to Jerusalem (see 11:14–12:3, 14:1–24, 15:1–32, 16:13–15 and 18:9–14) which have already increased the tension between him and the Jewish leaders, 19:45–46 describes another event

---

103. The two narrative accounts 3.3.2.29 and 3.3.2.30 between 18:43 and 19:29 are unique to Luke.

104. Thomas and Gundry believe that Matthew 21:12–13 happens later and is parallel with Mark 11:15–18 and Luke 19:45–48 (i.e., narrative account 3.3.2.32). It is very likely that Matthew has combined here the events happening during Jesus' two visits to the temple in the first two days after he has arrived in Jerusalem (the first visit is recorded in Mark 11:11 and the second in Mark 11:15–18), taking into consideration that Matthew seems to have a history of combining traditions (see narrative account 3.3.1.14).

which further intensifies the conflict: the cleansing of the temple apparently is a serious challenge to the financial system of the Jews in Jerusalem at that time and causes great embarrassment to the Jewish leaders who allow it. All of the above lead to the introduction to the next section in 19:47–48: the chief priests, the scribes and the principal leaders of the people now actively seek to destroy Jesus. This summary statement apparently covers the narrative accounts from 20:1 up to 21:36, before the next summary statement in 21:37–22:2. Again the time frame of 19:47–48 seemingly overlaps that of the narrative accounts between 20:1 to 21:36. This section is a continuation of the previous section 9:52b–19:44: in the previous section Jesus is travelling to Jerusalem for his predestined ordeal and now he has arrived in Jerusalem and the curtain of the final scene of his life has been raised. The common theme of 9:52b-19:44 and 20:1–36 seems to be Jesus, the Messiah, getting closer and closer to his destiny of suffering and death, and the fulfillment of his life goal: salvation for all.

Writing order identified: the narrative account is recorded chronologically, and overlapping chronology is noted in Luke 19:47–48.

3.3.2.33 Summary of 9:51–19:48

An analysis of the narrative accounts in this section from 9:52(b) to 19:48 is conducted and the results are compared with those of the earlier sections from 1:5 to 9:52(a):

Table 19. Analysis of the narrative accounts in Luke 1:5–19:48

Section[1] (no. of accounts therein)	Category[2]			%
	1[3] (%)	2 (%)	3 (%)	(Category 2+3)
1:5[4]–1:80 (4)	4 (100)	-	-	0
2:1–2:40 (3)	3 (100)	-	-	0
2:41–2:52 (1)	1 (100)	-	-	0
3:1–3:20 (1)	1 (100)	-	-	0
3:21–4:15 (2)[5]	2 (100)	-	-	0
4:16–4:44 (4)	4 (100)	-	-	0
5:1–8:3 (13)	7 (53.8)	5 (38.5)	1 (7.7)	46.2
8:4–9:52(a) (14)	8 (57.1)	5 (35.7)	1 (7.1)	42.8
9:52(b)–19:48 (32)	20 (62.5)	3 (9.4)	9 (28.1)	37.5

[1] Section refers to the sections divided by overlapping summary statements identified in this chapter.

[2] For the definitions of the different categories, see 3.1.

[3] Number of narrative accounts in category 1. The order identified in all categories 1 and 2 accounts from 1:5 to 19:48 is chronological.

[4] 1:1–4 is the preface of the gospel, which does not belong to any section and is not evaluated here.

[5] 3:23b-38 is Jesus' genealogy. Since it is not related to my study of narrative sequence, it is not included in the analysis here.

The three sections between chapters 5 and 19 (which include the second and the final phrase of Jesus' ministry before he heads towards Jerusalem, and his trip to Jerusalem) have less spatial and temporal information as compared with the first four chapters. While Luke may be less concerned to show his reader Theophilus the "when's" and the "where's" of the events in these chapters, this does not necessarily mean that he does not record the events in chronological order, which is what he does in the first four chapters. In these three sections the percentages of the accounts which are classified as category 2 and 3 are similar. This means that Luke does not give adequate explicit or implicit information about the time of occurrence or writing order for 46.2% (for the sections from 5:1 to 8:3), 42.8% (8:4–9:52(a)) and 37.5% (9:52(b)-19:48) of the narrative accounts. Nonetheless, as mentioned in the summary of 1:5–9:50 (3.3.1.44), it is very likely that the first two sections (5:1–8:3 and 8:4–9:52[a]) are written in chronological order. In section 9:52(b)-19:48 the percentage of category 1 accounts (62.5%) is slightly higher than in the two previous sections 5:1–8:3 (53.8%) and 8:4–9:52(a) (57.1%). This indicates that though Luke has reduced his use of chronological and geographical indicators from 5:1 onwards, he has not deliberately reduced the use of them in 9:52(b)-19:48 as compared with that of 5:1–8:3 and 8:4–9:52(a). The main difference between 9:52(b)-19:48 and the two previous sections is that the percentage of category 3 accounts (28.1%) in 9:52(b)-19:48 is much higher than in 5:1–8:3 (7.7%) and 8:4–9:52(a) (7.1%). This is due to the fact that in 9:52(b)-19:48 Luke has included the largest number of accounts which are not only unique but which also have no clear geographical and temporal information.

This leads to the difficulty in assessing their writing order, as there is inadequate information in both Luke and the other synoptic gospels to do so. In short, the above analysis shows that Luke seems to have adopted a different writing style for 5:1 to 19:48 from the one he has used for chapters 1 to 4 and has reduced his use of chronological and geographical indicators.

Nevertheless, the writing order for 5:1 to 19:48 as a whole may be helpful for evaluation rather than just to assess the writing order of 9:52(b)-19:48 since they likely share the same writing order. If they do, the writing order of 5:1–8:3 and 8:4–9:52(a) very likely can serve as an indicator for the writing order of 9:52(b)-19:48. The analysis of 5:1–8:3 and 8:4–9:52(a) in 3.3.1.44 finds that, though these two sections have quite a number of accounts for which Luke has not provided adequate information for the determination of their writing order, comparisons with their parallels in Matthew and Mark reveal that these accounts are very likely written in chronological order. Consequently, it is also reasonable to believe that those accounts in 9:52(b)-19:48 for which Luke does not give sufficient spatial and temporal information are also written in the same order (i.e., chronological) which Luke has employed for 5:1–8:3 and 8:4–9:52(a), unless there is evidence to indicate otherwise. Moreover, if the suggestion by scholars such as Thomas and Gundry (see 3.3.2) is correct, that the circular route taken by Jesus to Jerusalem in this section can be compared and explained by the circular route he takes in John chapters 7–12, and that John chapters 7–12 is written in chronological order, then this section is probably also written in chronological order. Therefore, it seems that Luke does not necessarily, as Bock believes, employ fewer chronological and geographical indicators particularly for this section to avoid strict chronology. But why, then, does Luke change his writing style and reduce his use of chronological and geographical indicators for chapters 5–19? Chapter 5 describes Jesus beginning his ministry as an itinerant preacher after he has found a base in Capernaum (see 4:43–44); and chapter 19 shows him reaching Jerusalem (see 19:45–48), marking the end of his ministry as an itinerant preacher. Luke likely employs a different writing style for Luke chapters 5–19 because of the nature of Jesus' ministry as an itinerant preacher described in these chapters. Jesus, as an itinerant preacher, very likely has to travel frequently to a lot of places in a very short period of time and gives similar teachings. And, apparently, what is important to Luke is not how many places Jesus has visited, or how many times he has visited the same place, or when he makes all these trips, but what are Jesus' key teachings and the essential miracles he performs in this period. If this is true, Luke seemingly chooses to use this writing style with limited chronological and geographical indicators to avoid duplication and meaningless descriptions.

For example, the itinerary of Jesus for any two consecutive days may be as follows: on day one, Jesus travels to village A in the morning and preaches a sermon on discipleship, after lunch he goes to city B to preach the same sermon, and afterwards he goes back to village A and spends the night there. The next morning, on day two, Jesus visits village C, and in the afternoon he comes back to city B to solidify the believers, then going to village D to preach the same sermon on discipleship. Instead of recording the full itinerary of Jesus on these two days, Luke probably would choose to record only the key messages of Jesus' sermon on discipleship, and he likely would not mention in detail where and when Jesus gives this sermon, since Jesus has given this sermon a few times in different cities and villages in that two-day period. At first glance the lack of geographical and chronological indicators in 9:51–19:44 appear to compliment Luke's referral in 9:51 that Jesus "set his face to go to Jerusalem" (αὐτὸς τὸ πρόσωπον ἐστήρισεν τοῦ πορεύεσθαι εἰς Ἰερουσαλήμ), seemingly an indication that the Messiah who appears so attractive to the crowd (see Luke 9:43) would now be less attractive because he would become the "crucified" Messiah. However, it does not seem to be the case because Luke employs the writing style of limited geographical and chronological indicators for 5:1–19:44 and not only for 9:51–19:44. Although Luke has employed many materials in this section which are unique, there is no indication that Luke's usage of a source of materials different from that of Matthew and Mark would affect his writing order.

In view of the above analysis, I would conclude that the narrative accounts in this section are very likely recorded in chronological order.

3.3.3 Luke 20:1–24:53—Jesus' Last Days in Jerusalem, His Passion and Resurrection

This section describes the last days of Jesus after he has arrived at Jerusalem: his passion, his suffering and death, his resurrection and his ascension.

3.3.3.1 Questioning of Jesus' authority by the chief priests, teachers of the law and elders (20:1-8) (Thomas and Gundry, 1988:176-177)

Category: 1

Time: After Jesus has cleansed the temple in Jerusalem (Matt 21:17-18, 23; Mark 11:19-20, 27).

Observations: Luke 20:1 says "and it happened in one of the days when he was teaching the people in the temple and preaching the good news" (καὶ ἐγένετο ἐν μιᾷ τῶν ἡμερῶν διδάσκοντος αὐτοῦ τὸν λαὸν ἐν τῷ ἱερῷ καὶ εὐαγγελιζομένου.) At first glance it seems that Luke does not describe the exact time and order of this incident; however, it very likely comes after the "cleansing of the temple" as logically Jesus would have cleansed the temple before he begins teaching there.

Thomas and Gundry believe that Matthew 21:23-27 and Mark 11:27-33 are describing the same incident. I agree with them as the details of the accounts in the gospels match each other: (1) it happens after Jesus has arrived at Jerusalem and is preaching in the temple, (2) the chief priests and the elders come to challenge Jesus with the same question: with what authority does Jesus do those things; (3) Jesus' response is the same in all three gospels: he asks them whether John the Baptist's baptism comes from heaven or from humans, and (4) when they refuse to give a clear answer, Jesus also refuses to answer their question about his authority. According to Mark 11:12 and 11:15 Jesus cleanses the temple on the day after his arrival at Jerusalem, and Mark 11:19-20 and 11:27 apparently indicate that this incident happens after the cleansing of the temple. It likely happens on Jesus' third day in Jerusalem (Mark 11:11—day one, 11:12-19—day two, 11:20ff—day three). Matthew's account also seems to match that of Mark: 21:17-18 indicates that Jesus leaves Jerusalem for Bethany to spend the night after he has cleansed the temple (Matt 21:12-13), and in the early morning (Matt 21:18) he goes back to Jerusalem and the temple (Matt 21:23), where the chief priests and elders question his authority. Since both Matthew[105]

---

105. Between the "cleansing of the temple" account (21:12-13) and "questioning Jesus' authority" account (21:23-27), Matthew inserts a description which has no parallel in Luke or Mark: Jesus heals the blind and lame at the temple and the children shout "hosanna to the Son of David" in the temple area in Matt 21:14-17. Matt 21:18-22 is about Jesus' cursing of a fig tree. It is paralleled in Mark 11:12-14 and 11:19-26. Matthew seems to have condensed the fig tree incident into one single incident. According to Mark, it happens in two separate occasions in a period of two days. The cursing of

and Mark[106] seem to indicate that this incident happens after Jesus' cleansing of the temple, it is reasonable to believe that this account in Luke is recorded in chronological order.

Writing order identified: chronological.

3.3.3.2 Jesus' parable of the bad tenants of a vineyard (20:9-19) (Thomas and Gundry, 1988:177-180)

Category: 1

Time: Immediately right after Jesus' authority is questioned (Luke 20:9, Matt 21:33, Mark 12:1).

Observations: Luke 20:9 says "and he began to speak to the people..." (ἤρξατο δὲ πρὸς τὸν λαὸν λέγειν...) Luke uses ἤρξατο δὲ ("and he began") only twice in his gospel. Other than 20:9 he uses it in 4:21 where ἤρξατο δὲ connects what Jesus says in 4:21 with what he has said in 4:18-20, with 4:21 obviously coming after 4:18-20 in time. According to the context of 20:1-19, it is very likely that Luke again uses ἤρξατο δὲ to connect 20:1-8 and 20:9-19, where 20:9-19 follows immediately after 20:1-8 in time.

Thomas and Gundry believe that Matthew 21:33-46 and Mark 12:1-12 are parallels of Luke 20:9-19. Although there are differences among the accounts (for example, Luke mentions only three servants who are sent to the tenants, but in Matthew and Mark there are more; moreover, in Luke the tenants beat the servants or wound them but do not kill any of them, while in Matthew and Mark some are killed), I would agree with Thomas and Gundry as the key elements of the accounts match: (1) the setting is the same. In all three gospels the parable appears immediately after the questioning of Jesus' authority and in all three Jesus speaks against the chief priests and other Jewish leaders (Matt 21:45- the Pharisees, Mark 11:18 and Luke 20:19- the scribes); (2) the contents of the parables are almost the same: the owner of the vineyard sends servants to collect his rent but is denied; at the end he sends his son, who is killed by

---

the fig tree is available only in Matthew and Mark but not in Luke.

106. Between the "cleansing of the temple" account (11:15-18) and "questioning Jesus' authority" account (11:27-33), Mark inserts the second part of the "cursing of the fig tree" account (i.e., 11:19-26, the first part being in 11:12-14), which is not recorded in Luke.

the tenants, and Jesus says the owner will punish the tenants for their evil-doings; (3) the same verse, Psalm 118:22, is quoted in all the gospels, and (4) the reactions of the Jewish leaders are the same: they understand that Jesus is speaking against them and want to arrest him, but they are afraid of the people. Matthew 21:33 says "Hear another parable" (ἄλλην παραβολὴν ἀκούσατε): ἀκούσατε ("hear") is in the second person plural with its antecedent borrowed from "the chief priests and the elders of the people" in the questioning of Jesus' authority in Matthew 21:23. Similarly Mark 12:1 says "and he began to speak to them in parables" (καὶ ἤρξατο αὐτοῖς ἐν παραβολαῖς λαλεῖν), αὐτοῖς ("to them") is a personal pronoun in the masculine plural with its antecedent, "the chief priests, the teachers of the law and the elders," borrowed from the questioning of Jesus' authority account in Mark 11:27. Therefore, grammatically speaking, both Matthew and Mark indicate that this incident happens right after the questioning of Jesus' authority, as both antecedents are borrowed from that account, which means that after Jesus' response to the chief priests and elders regarding his authority, he continues his conversation with them in the event under discussion.

Moreover, Matthew[107], Mark and Luke all record this account after the questioning of Jesus authority account, it is very likely that this account is recorded in chronological order, after the questioning of Jesus' authority.

Writing order identified: chronological.

3.3.3.3 Attempts by Pharisees and Herodians to trap Jesus with a question about paying taxes to Caesar (20:20–26) (Thomas and Gundry, 1988:180–181)

Category: 1

Time: After the parable of the bad vineyard tenants (20:20).

Observations: It seems that Luke has not explicitly given the time and the order of this event.

---

107. Between "Questioning Jesus' authority" (Matt 21:23–27) and "Parable of the bad tenants" (Matt 21:33–46), Matthew inserts a unique parable which is not recorded in Mark or Luke: Matt 21:28–32 is a parable about a man and his two sons which deals with contrasting responses to God's commands.

Thomas and Gundry believe that Matthew 22:15-22 and Mark 12:13-17 are parallels of Luke 20:20-26. I would concur, given that the key elements of the accounts in the three gospels match: (1) the settings are the same: all the gospels record this event right after Jesus' parable of the bad vineyard tenants and with the Jewish leaders (Luke 20:19- chief priests and the scribes, Mark 11:27- chief priests, the scribes and the elders, Matt 22:15- the Pharisees) plotting against Jesus; (2) the contents of what the spies say are similar: in all three gospels Jesus is praised first as a man of integrity or one who speaks and teaches what is right and does not show partiality, after which the spies ask the same question—is it right to pay taxes to Caesar; (3) Jesus' response in all three gospels is the same: give Caesar what belongs to him and give God what belongs to God, and (4) the reaction of those who question Jesus is the same: after hearing Jesus' answer they are amazed or astonished.

It seems that like Luke, Matthew and Mark have not specified the time or the order of this event. However, ἀποστέλλουσιν (they sent—in the present tense) in "and they sent to him (i.e., Jesus)" (καὶ ἀποστέλλουσιν πρὸς αὐτόν) in Mark 12:13 takes its antecedent from Mark 11:27, which means that "they" in the phrase "they sent" represents the chief priests and the scribes and the elders to whom Jesus has spoken the parable of the bad tenants. Similar to Matthew, ἀπέστειλαν (they sent—in aorist tense form) in "and after they watched closely they sent spies" (καὶ παρατηρήσαντες ἀπέστειλαν ἐγκαθέτους) in Luke 20:20 takes its antecedent from Luke 20:19. "They" represents "the scribes and the chief priests" who have heard the parable of the vineyard in the previous account. Therefore, the antecedent of ἀποστέλλουσιν in Mark 12:13 and the antecedent of ἀπέστειλαν in Luke 20:20 likely indicate that this event happens after Jesus has given the parable of the bad vineyard tenants.

Furthermore, since Matthew[108], Mark and Luke all place this event after Jesus' parable of the bad vineyard tenants, it is therefore very likely that it is recorded chronologically, after the parable.

Writing order identified: chronological.

---

108. Between the "parable of the bad tenants" (21:33-46) and the "Pharisees and Herodians wanting to trap Jesus" (22:15-22), Matthew inserts a unique account not recorded in Luke and Mark. Matt 22:1-14 is a parable of Jesus about a king who is preparing a wedding banquet for his son.

3.3.3.4 Sadducees' puzzling question about the resurrection (20:27–40) (Thomas and Gundry, 1988:181)

Category: 2

Time: Likely after the attempts by the Pharisees and the Herodians to trap Jesus with a question about paying taxes to Caesar (20:39).

Observations: At first glance it seems that Luke does not mention the time or the order of this event. However, Luke 20:39 says that some scribes praise Jesus for his well-spoken comment about the resurrection. These are not the Sadducees who have asked the question, but likely the scribes who are still around, as described in the previous account in 20:19–26 (in particular see 20:19), though this cannot be certain. If so, then this account most likely comes after 20:20–26 in time.

Thomas and Gundry believe that Matthew 22:23–33 and Mark 12:18–27 are describing the same incident here. But even if they are, it seems that they do not mention the time or order of this incident either. Matthew 22:23 says that it happens ἐν ἐκείνῃ τῇ ἡμέρᾳ. But according to narrative account 3.3.1.31 above, the phrase can either mean "in that particular day" or "in those days/during that period of time" and both meanings are feasible here. Even if the phrase means "in that particular day," the context in Matthew still does not give a clear indication as to whether this incident happens after the immediately preceding incident.

However, since Matthew, Mark and Luke all record this incident after the account of the Pharisees and Herodians trying to trap Jesus, it is reasonable to believe that it does happen after that event.

Writing order identified: chronological.

3.3.3.5 Christ's relationship to David as Son and Lord (20:41–44) (Thomas and Gundry, 1988:183)

Category: 1

Time: While Jesus is teaching in the temple courts (Mark 12:35) and after the Sadducees' question about the resurrection (Matt 22:41).

Observations: It seems that Luke is describing in 20:27–47 one conversation Jesus has in the temple courts (Mark 12:35). This event apparently follows the immediately preceding event of 20:27–40. The αὐτούς ("them") in "and he said to them" (εἶπεν δὲ πρὸς αὐτούς) from 20:41 takes its antecedent from τινες τῶν γραμματέων ("some of the scribes") in 20:39 of the immediately preceding account. Thus, very likely Jesus continues his conversation with the scribes after the Sadducees' question regarding the resurrection.

Thomas and Gundry believe that Matthew 22:41–46 and Mark 12:35–37 are describing the same incident here. This is reasonable because the question from Jesus (how is it that they say Christ is the Son of David?) and Jesus' quotation from Psalm 110:1 are almost the same in all three synoptic gospels. Matthew seems to agree with Luke and indicates that this account comes after the Sadducees' question about the resurrection. Matthew 22:34 says "and after the Pharisees heard that he (Jesus) put to silence the Sadducees, they gathered together in one place" (οἱ δὲ Φαρισαῖοι ἀκούσαντες ὅτι ἐφίμωσεν τοὺς Σαδδουκαίους συνήχθησαν ἐπὶ τὸ αὐτό). According to the context, the gathering together of the Pharisees happens after Jesus has silenced the Sadducees regarding their question about the resurrection. Then Matthew 22:41 says "and while the Pharisees were gathering together, Jesus asked them (the question about Christ's relationship to David)" (συνηγμένων δὲ τῶν Φαρισαίων ἐπηρώτησεν αὐτοὺς ὁ Ἰησοῦς). According to the context, "and while the Pharisees were gathering together" naturally refers to the occasion in Matthew 22:34. If so, then Matthew is indicating that this incident happens after Jesus has silenced the Sadducees. Moreover, Matthew[109], Mark[110] and Luke all record this incident after the Sadducees' question about the resurrection, which is the immediately preceding account in Luke. It is therefore reasonable to believe that this account is recorded chronologically.

Writing order identified: chronological.

---

109. Between the "Sadducees' question about resurrection" (22:23–33) and the "Christ's relationship to David" (22:41–46), Matthew inserts a Pharisee's question about the greatest commandment in the Law. According to Thomas and Gundry (1988: 182–183), it has a parallel in Mark 12:28–34, but Luke does not record it.

110. Between the "Sadducees' question about resurrection" (12:18–27) and the "Christ's relationship to David" (12:35–37), Mark inserts another account. See footnote 109.

3.3.3.6 Beware of the teachers of the Law (20:45–47)
(Thomas and Gundry, 1988:184–185)

Category: 1

Time: Likely after the "Christ's relationship to David as Son and Lord" account (20:45).

Observations: Luke 20:45 says "and while all the people were listening, he said to (his) disciples" (ἀκούοντος δὲ παντὸς τοῦ λαοῦ εἶπεν τοῖς μαθηταῖς [αὐτοῦ]). If "all the people" refers to "the people" (τοῦ λαοῦ) in 20:26, then very likely 20:19-47 is part of a teaching session Jesus gives in 20:1-47 to the same crowd, with 20:45-47 being the latter part of this teaching which follows the first part in 20:41-44. Thomas and Gundry believe that Matthew 23:1-7 and Mark 12:38-40 are parallels of this account. I concur, as the contents of Matthew 23:5b-7, Mark 12:38b-40 and Luke 20:46b-47 closely match each other. If this is true, the fact that Matthew, Mark and Luke all place this incident after the "Christ's relationship to David" event makes it reasonable to believe that it comes after that event chronologically.

Writing order identified: chronological.

3.3.3.7 A poor widow's gift of all she had (21:1–4)
(Thomas and Gundry, 1988:186)

Category: 1

Time: Likely after the "beware of the teachers of the Law" account (21:3, Mark 12:43).

Observations: Thomas and Gundry believe that Luke's account has a parallel in Mark 12:41-44 (Matthew does not record this). I agree with them, as the contents resemble each other. Luke does not mention the time or the order of this event. However, "to you" (ὑμῖν) in "truly I say to you" (ἀληθῶς λέγω ὑμῖν) in 21:3, according to Mark 12:43, probably refers to the disciples in 20:45. If so, this account likely follows the previous event of 20:45-47. Moreover, as both Mark and Luke record this event right after the "beware of the teachers of the Law" account, it is reasonable to believe that it occurs after the "beware of the teachers of the Law" event.

Writing order identified: chronological.

3.3.3.8 The Olivet discourse about the temple and Jesus' second coming (21:5–36) (Thomas and Gundry, 1988:187–194)

Category: 2

Time: After Jesus has finished his lengthy teaching (20:1–21:4) and left the temple (Matt 24:1, Mark 13:1), and while he is sitting on the Mount of Olives (Matt 24:3, Mark 13:3).

Observations: Luke does not mention the time or the order of this event. Thomas and Gundry believe that Matthew 24:1–25:46 (in particular 24:1–44) and Mark 13:1–37 are describing the same incident. I would agree with them because: (1) in all three gospels the long discourse is triggered by Jesus' disciple(s) admiring the temple (Matt 24:1, Mark 13:1 and Luke 21:5), and (2) the contents in all three accounts are very similar. For example, compare Matthew 24:2,4, Mark 13:2,4 and Luke 21:6–7; Matthew 24:4–10, Mark 13:5–9 and Luke 21:8–13, etc. Matthew 24:1 says this incident happens "after Jesus came out from the temple" (. . . ἐξελθὼν ὁ Ἰησοῦς ἀπὸ τοῦ ἱεροῦ). This phrase seems to correlate with "and after he (Jesus) entered into the temple" (καὶ ἐλθόντος αὐτοῦ εἰς τὸ ἱερὸν) in Matthew 21:23 and indicates that the whole of Matthew 21:23 to 23:39 is a lengthy teaching given by Jesus on a single occasion when he is in the temple, and this discourse happens afterwards. Mark also seems to agree with Matthew on this point as Mark 13:1 also seems to correlate with Mark 11:27 in a similar way, indicating that Jesus' conversations in between are a single teaching in the temple and the discourse under discussion happens after the "poor widow's gift" account (the last part of Jesus' lengthy teaching in the temple in Mark) after Jesus has left the temple. Luke's context also seems to fit this view. Based on the above observation, this discourse (21:5–36) mostly likely happens after Jesus has left the temple and after the immediately previous event ("a poor widow's gift").

Table 20. Comparison of the sequences of "a small gift of all she had" and "the Olivet discourse about the temple and Jesus' second coming" in Luke and Mark

	A small gift of all she had	The Olivet discourse about the temple and Jesus' second coming
Luke	21:1–4	21:5–36
Mark	12:41–44	13:1–37

Note: Matthew does not have the "poor widow's gift" account; the Olivet discourse, according to Thomas and Gundry (1988:187-194), is also recorded in Matt 24:1-25:30.

Writing order identified: chronological.

3.3.3.9 Jesus' last days in Jerusalem and the plot by the Sanhedrin to arrest and kill him (21:37-22:2) (Thomas and Gundry, 1988:195)

Category: 1

Time: After Jesus' Olivet discourse in 21:5-36 (Matt 26:1-3).

Observations: Thomas and Gundry believe that this account, in particular 22:1-2, has parallels in Matthew 26:1-5 and Mark 14:1-2. I concur, as the content of all three passages is very similar: (1) all three gospels mention that Passover is near—Matthew and Mark say that it is two days away (Matt 26:2, Mark 14:1) and Luke says that Passover is approaching (22:1); (2) all three gospels describe the chief priests and the teachers of law as looking for a way to get rid of Jesus (Matt 26:3, Mark 14:1, Luke 22:2), and (3) being afraid of the people (Matt 26:5, Mark 14:2, Luke 22:2). If this is true, this event very likely happens after Jesus has given his Olivet discourse in 21:5-36. Matthew 26:1-3 clearly indicates that the Sanhedrin is trying to find a way to arrest and kill Jesus around the time after Jesus has finished his Olivet discourse. Matthew 26:1 says "and it happened when Jesus finished all these words" (καὶ ἐγένετο ὅτε ἐτέλεσεν ὁ Ἰησοῦς πάντας τοὺς λόγους τούτους). "All these words" (πάντας τοὺς λόγους τούτους) seemingly refers to Jesus' Olivet discourse in Matthew 24:1-25:46. Moreover, Matthew, Mark and Luke all record the plot by the Sanhedrin to arrest and kill Jesus after Jesus' Olivet discourse. It is therefore reasonable to believe that this incident happens after Jesus' Olivet discourse.

Writing order identified: chronological.

3.3.3.10 Judas' agreement to betray Jesus (22:3-6) (Thomas and Gundry, 1988:196-197)

Category: 1

Time: After the "plot by the Sanhedrin to arrest and kill Jesus" (22:1, vv.4-5).

Observations: In the previous account, 22:1–2, the Sanhedrin is trying to find a way to arrest and kill Jesus, and in 22:3–6 the solution appears: Judas Iscariot, one of the Twelve, is willing to betray him for money. Therefore, logically 22:3–6 occurs after 22:1–2.

Thomas and Gundry believe that Matthew 26:14–16[111] and Mark 14:10–11[112] are describing the same incident. This appears reasonable, as all key elements in the three gospels are the same: (1) Judas goes to see the chief priests to betray Jesus; (2) the chief priests agree to give Judas money; and (3) Judas then watches for an opportunity to hand Jesus over to them. All the synoptic gospels place this after the "plot by the Sanhedrin to arrest and kill Jesus" which immediately precedes this event in Luke. It is therefore reasonable to believe that 22:3–6 comes after 22:1–2.

21:37–22:6 (i.e., narrative accounts 3.3.3.9 and 3.3.3.10 together) seem to be another overlapping summary following 1:80, 2:40, 2:52, 3:19–20, 4:14–15, 4:42–44, 8:1–3, 9:51–52a and 19:45–48. 21:37–38 seems to be a summary statement for the section 20:1–21:36 which describes Jesus' actions during his last days in Jerusalem. Apparently 22:1–6 is a brief preview of the next section, 22:7–53, which describes how Judas betrays Jesus and the plot of the Sanhedrin to arrest and kill Jesus. As in the other summary statements, the time frame of the preview of the next section (i.e., 22:1–6) seemingly overlaps the events of 22:7 to 22:53. The common thread between sections 20:1–21:36 and 22:7–22:53 likely is the Jewish leaders' long-desired arrest of Jesus (see 19:47, 20:19–20, 22:1–6), which is a key part of God's sovereign plan for the Messiah finally accomplished.

Writing order identified: the narrative account is recorded chronologically, with overlapping chronology noted in Luke 22:1–6.

---

111. Between the "Sanhedrin's plot to arrest and kill Jesus" account (26:1–5) and "Judas' agreement to betray Jesus" (26:14–16), Matthew inserts an account of Mary's anointing of Jesus for his burial (Matt 26:6–13). It has a parallel in Mark 14:3–9 but not in Luke.

112. Between the "Sanhedrin's plot" (14:1–2) and "Judas' agreement" (14:10–11), Mark also inserts an account of Mary's anointing of Jesus for his burial. See footnote 111 for its parallel in Matthew.

3.3.3.11 Preparation for the Passover meal (22:7–13) (Thomas and Gundry, 1988:197)

Category: 2

Time: On the day of Unleavened Bread, on which the Passover lamb is sacrificed (22:7), very likely after "Judas' agreement to betray Jesus," which apparently happens as the Passover draws near (22:1).

Observations: Although Luke mentions that this incident happens on the day of Unleavened Bread (22:7), he does not indicate whether it happens before or after Judas' agreement to betray Jesus. Thomas and Gundry believe that Matthew 26:17–19 and Mark 14:12–16 are describing the same incident. I concur, as all three gospels describe the preparation of Jesus' last Passover dinner. As all the synoptic gospels record this incident immediately after Judas' agreement to betray Jesus, it seems that Luke does record this incident chronologically.

Writing order identified: chronological.

3.3.3.12 The Passover meal (22:14–38)[113] (Thomas and Gundry, 1988:198–204)

Category: see category of individual events in the table below.

Time: Logically, after the preparation of the Passover meal.

Observations: A number of events happen during the Passover meal and before Jesus reaches Gethsemane:

---

113. Thomas and Gundry divide the Passover meal (22:14–38) into four different accounts: the beginning of the Passover meal and discussion among the disciples over greatness, identification of the betrayer, prediction of Peter's denial and conclusion of the meal and the Lord's Supper instituted. As all four accounts describe the Passover meal, I combine them into one account for easier reading. The seeming contradictions noted between Luke and Matthew/Mark will be addressed here.

Table 21. Events during the Passover meal and
before Jesus reaches Gethsemane

	Events during the Passover meal and before Jesus' prayer at Gethsemane	Luke	Matthew	Mark	Category[1]
1	Beginning of the Passover meal	22:14–16	26:20	14:17	1
2	First comment about the betrayer	-	26:21–25	14:18–21	-
3	Lord's Supper instituted	22:17–20	26:26–29	14:22–25	1
4	Second comment about betrayer	22:21–23	-	-	1
5	Discussion among the disciples over greatness	22:24–30	-	-	1
6	First prediction of Peter's denial	22:31–38	-	-	1
7	Second prediction of Peter's denial	-	26:30–35	14:26–31	-

[1] Category assigned for Luke's accounts only, with the assessment based on the discussions of events #4, 5 and 6 below.

Regarding events #2 and #4 in the table, Thomas and Gundry (1988:199-201) believe that Jesus' comment about his betrayer in Luke 22:21-23 parallels Matthew 26:21-25 and Mark 14:18-21. If so, Luke's sequence seemingly contradicts those of Matthew and Mark, as Luke places Jesus' comment about his betrayer after the institution of the Lord's Supper, while Matthew and Mark record these two events in reverse order. With regard to this apparent contradiction Bock (2004, vol.2:1734) opines that Luke has likely rearranged the events while Matthew and Mark have recorded the actual sequence. Although Bock may be right, it is also possible that Jesus has given more than one comment about the betrayer that night. The Apostle John seems to support this proposal, as he has recorded three comments Jesus gives about the betrayer at different times that night during the Passover meal and before Jesus reaches Gethsemane. Jesus gives his first comment about the betrayer in John 13:10-11 during the meal (see 13:2) while he is washing his disciples' feet, telling Peter that not every one of the twelve disciples is clean. John explains that Jesus gives this comment because he knows that one of his disciples will betray him. Jesus then gives the second comment in John 13:18-26 after he finishes washing his disciples' feet, puts on his garment and resumes his place at the table (see

13:12). He quotes Psalm 41:9, saying that one of the disciples who eats his bread has lifted his heel against him, and then goes on to explain that one of them is going to betray him. Jesus later indicates to John that Judas is that betrayer. Jesus' third comment about the betrayer is in John 17:12, after Jesus has finished the last supper and is on the way to Gethsemane (see John 14:30 and 18:1). He says none of the disciples will be lost other than the betrayer, Judas. Therefore, according to John, Jesus has given more than one comment about the betrayer that night and Luke has likely recorded a comment which is different from those in Matthew and Mark. This is probable because the wording of Jesus' comment in Luke is quite different as compared to those in Matthew and Mark (e.g., compare Luke 22:21 with Matt 26:23 and Mark 14:20, and Luke does not have a parallel for Matt 26:24b and Mark 14:21b).

Concerning events #6 and #7, Thomas and Gundry (1988:202, note b) believe that Jesus has made at least two predictions regarding Peter's denial, and the prediction in Matthew 26:30–35 and Mark 14:26–31 is different from that in Luke 22:31–38 and is an event Luke does not mention in his gospel. I would agree, because the timing of the two is different. The prediction in Luke happens before Jesus and his disciples leave for the Mount of Olives (Luke 22:39), but the prediction in Matthew and Mark happen while they are on the way to Gethsemane (see Matt 26:30, v36 and Mark 14:26, v32). Moreover, the contents of the two are different. For example, both Matthew and Mark quote Zechariah 13:7 and mention that Jesus will go ahead of his apostles into Galilee after his resurrection, but Luke does not mention this. Luke records that Satan has demanded to have them and to sift them like wheat but Jesus has prayed for Peter so that his faith may not fail, but this is also not mentioned in Matthew and Mark.

With regard to events #4, #5 and #6, if the observations above are correct, then Luke contains three unique accounts in a row, describing events not mentioned in Matthew and Mark: the second comment about the betrayer, the discussion among the disciples over greatness, and the first prediction of Peter's denial. So, in what order has Luke recorded the five events listed in the above table? The beginning of the Passover meal obviously comes after the preparation of the Passover meal and is recorded in chronological order. The institution of the Lord's Supper logically comes after the beginning of the Passover meal and happens during the meal. It is supported by 22:20 where Luke says "and likewise the cup after they have eaten" (καὶ τὸ ποτήριον ὡσαύτως μετὰ τὸ δειπνῆσαι), indicating that Jesus has likely instituted the Lord's Supper at the end of the meal. And if "but behold" (πλὴν ἰδοὺ, which appears only once in the NT) in 22:21 has a meaning similar to "and behold" (καὶ ἰδοὺ) (see footnotes 69 and 97 above)—which is very likely—then it probably means "at that time" or "now." If this is true, then Jesus' second comment about the betrayer would come after the institution of the Lord's Supper. Regarding the discussion among the disciples over greatness, though it seems to parallel Matthew 20:24–28 and Mark 10:41–45, they are likely different events, as their backgrounds are very different. In Matthew and Mark the event happens while Jesus and his disciples are on the way to Jerusalem (Matt 20:17, Mark 10:32), where James and John, encouraged by their mother (Matt 20:20–21), come to Jesus to request places of honor in his kingdom. In Luke the event happens during the Passover meal, according to 22:27 apparently after Jesus has washed the disciples' feet (see John 13:1–20 which includes it during the Passover meal) but before they set out for Gethsemane (22:39).

Consequently, I think that Luke's account is of a different event from that of Matthew and Mark: the dispute over greatness among the disciples is likely a recurring one and has already lasted for some time. This dispute starts with "and now also" (ἐγένετο δὲ καὶ) in 22:24. Luke uses ἐγένετο δὲ 17 times in his gospel[114]; a detailed study of all 17 occurrences seems to indicate that the function of this phrase is only to draw the reader's attention to the time when the event about to be described happens, meaning that it can be translated as "and now."

For example, in Luke 1:8 ἐγένετο δὲ comes before "while he was serving as a priest" (ἐν τῷ ἱερατεύειν αὐτὸν). It can be translated as "and now," used for emphasis, to draw the readers' attention to the time when Zechariah was serving as a priest at the temple of the Lord, during which something happens as described in the following section. Although ἐγένετο δὲ alone in 22:24 does not define the precise time of the event, together with the καὶ ("also") which comes after it, it seems to indicate that it happens at about the time of the previous event (Jesus' second comment about the betrayer). Therefore, I agree with Reiling and Swellengrebel (1993:690) that this phrase "marks the transition to a new event in the same situation." If this is the case, then Luke very likely records this event in its actual sequence, as there seems to be no reason why he would not, especially considering the

---

114. The 17 occurrences in Luke's gospel are in 1:8; 2:1, 6; 3:21; 5:1; 6:1, 6, 12; 8:22, 9:28, 37, 51; 11:14, 27; 16:22; 18:35; and 22:24.

order Luke has used so far. Jesus' first prediction of Peter's denial seems to be part of the conversation Jesus has in 22:24–38; if so, it most likely follows the disciples' dispute over greatness. It is also hard to imagine that this part of the conversation would happen before the dispute, as the disciples most likely would not discuss this subject if Jesus has already told them that he will be numbered with transgressors (22:37) and that they need to buy a sword for the dangerous upcoming events (22:36). Consequently, all five events placed by Luke during the Passover meal are likely recorded in chronological order.

Writing order identified: chronological.

3.3.3.13 Jesus' three agonized prayers in Gethsemane (22:39–46) (Thomas and Gundry, 1988:210–211)

Category: 1

Time: According to Luke 22:39–40, after the Passover meal, and after Jesus and his disciples have reached the Mount of Olives.

Observations: Thomas and Gundry believe that Matthew 26:36–46 and Mark 14:32–42 are describing the same incident. As Matthew, Mark and Luke all record Jesus' three prayers in Gethsemane after the meal, it is reasonable to believe that this account is recorded chronologically.

Writing order identified: chronological.

3.3.3.14 Jesus betrayed, arrested and forsaken (22:47–53) (Thomas and Gundry, 1988:212–214)

Category: 1

Time: According to Luke 22:47, after Jesus' agonized prayers in Gethsemane.

Observations: Luke 22:47 says "while he was still speaking" (ἔτι αὐτοῦ λαλοῦντος). This phase indicates that this happens right after Jesus' three prayers, when he is speaking to his disciples. Thomas and Gundry believe that Matthew 26:47–56 and Mark 14:43–52 are describing the same incident. If Matthew, Mark and Luke all record this event after Jesus' prayers, it very likely is recorded in chronological order.

Contrary to what he has done so far in his gospel, Luke does not design another summary statement here giving a brief summary of the previous section (22:7–53) and a preview of the next. However, he does give a final summary of Jesus' final message to his disciples in 24:44–49, which includes a brief summary of what happened from 22:54 to 24:43 and a preview of what he will describe in the Book of Acts. Please refer to narrative account 3.3.3.26 for detailed discussion.

Writing order identified: chronological.

3.3.3.15 Jesus' trial (22:54–23:25)
(Thomas and Gundry, 1988:217–226)

Category: see category of individual events in the table below.

Time: According to Luke 22:54, after Jesus is arrested, likely between A.D. 18 and A.D. 36 (see footnote 115 below). A number of events happen during Jesus' trial; the timing of each event is discussed below.

Observations: See the table and the discussions below.

Table 22. Events during Jesus' trial

	Events happen during Jesus' trial	Luke	Matthew	Mark	Category[1]
1	Jesus' trial—first Jewish phase (before Annas)[59]	-	-	-	-
2	Peter's denials	22:54b-62	26:58, 69–75	14:54, 66–72	1

---

115. This event appears only in John 18:13–14, not in any of the synoptic gospels. John 18:13 says Jesus is first brought to Annas, the father-in-law of Caiaphas. According to Schürer, who quotes from Josephus (2007, vol.3:199), Annas is appointed high priest by Quirinus and holds the office from A.D. 6 to A.D. 15, while Caiaphas is appointed high priest by Valerius Gratus somewhere from A.D. 18 to A.D. 36. If Schürer is correct, then most likely Caiaphas is officially the high priest at the time of Jesus' trial, meaning Jesus' trial happened between A.D. 18 and A.D. 36. However, John 18:13–14,19, 22, 24 and Acts 4:6 all seem to indicate that Annas serves as a high priest together with Caiaphas at that time. Luke 3:2 also describes both Annas and Caiaphas serving in the highpriesthood during the time when John the Baptist begins to minister. Carson (1991:580–581) explains that as Annas was once the high priest and no fewer than five of his sons and his son-in-law Caiaphas have held this office at one time or another, Annas is therefore regarded as the patriarch of the highpriestly family and as the "real" high priest by the Jews at that time. I agree with Carson that this fact probably contributes to the sayings about Annas as the high priest in John and Luke.

Events happen during Jesus' trial	Luke	Matthew	Mark	Category[1]
3 Jesus' trial—second Jewish phase (before Caiaphas and Sanhedrin)	22:54a, 63–65	26:57, 59–68	14:53, 55–65	1
4 Jesus' trial—third Jewish phase (before the Sanhedrin)	22:66–71	27:1	15:1a	1
5 Death of Judas Iscariot	-	27:3–10	-	-
6 Jesus' trial—first Roman phase (before Pilate)	23:1–5	27:2, 11–26	15:1b-15	1
7 Jesus' trial—second Roman phase (before Herod Antipas)	23:6–12			1
8 Jesus' trial—third Roman phase (before Pilate)	23:13–25			1

[1] Category assigned for Luke's accounts only, assessment based on the findings in the respective discussions below.

Regarding event #2 in the table, according to Luke 22:54, Peter's denials happen after Jesus is betrayed, arrested and brought into the high priest's house. Luke records this event before the second Jewish phase of Jesus' trial, while Matthew and Mark record it the other way round. Is there a contradiction between Luke and Matthew/Mark regarding the sequence of this event? And when does this event actually happen: before or after the second Jewish phase of Jesus' trial? According to John, Peter's denials apparently happen over a period of time covering the first Jewish phase and at least part of the second Jewish phase of Jesus' trial; John records Peter's first denial while Jesus is with Annas during the first Jewish trial (see John 18:12–23), and it is only after Jesus is bought to Caiaphas (the second Jewish phase) that John records Peter's second and third denials (see John 18:24–27). Luke seems to agree with John that Peter's denials happen over a period of time, as Luke 22:59 indicates that the denials last for at least one hour. Luke says that after Peter's second denial, "and after about one hour passed away" (καὶ διαστάσης ὡσεὶ ὥρας μιᾶς), Peter is again challenged and gives his third denial. Matthew and Mark also seem to support this view, describing many false witnesses coming forward to accuse Jesus (Matt 26:60, Mark 14:56), seemingly a lengthy process. If this is correct, then likely both Luke and Matthew/Mark have recorded this event in its proper sequence. In short, Peter's denials seemingly happen over a lengthy period of time. Luke apparently chooses to show Peter's denials happening at an earlier point, based on the time when Peter gives his first denial (before the second Jewish phase of the trial); while Matthew/Mark choose to record the denials at a later time in the same period, after the second Jewish phase of Jesus' trial, since the second and the third denials very likely happen during the second Jewish phase of the trial. Therefore, there is no contradiction between Luke and Matthew/Mark in how they sequence these denials.

Concerning event #3, according to John 18:24, Annas sends Jesus bound to Caiaphas after he has questioned him (John 18:19-23). This event, therefore, should come after Jesus' trial before Annas. John does not indicate that Annas has come to a conclusion of how to deal with Jesus, and this may be the reason why Annas sends Jesus to Caiaphas. Luke gives only a brief description of Jesus being mocked, beaten and insulted, while Matthew and Mark give more detailed accounts of this: the chief priests and the whole Sanhedrin look for false evidence to put Jesus to death and even find false witnesses to testify that Jesus has claimed he can destroy the temple and rebuild it in three days. The judgment of condemning Jesus to death is reached after Caiaphas has specifically asked Jesus whether he is the Son of God and Jesus answers that he is (Mark 14:61-64).

With regard to event #4, Luke 22:66 describes the third Jewish phase of Jesus' trial as beginning when day comes. Jesus' arrest and the first two phases of his trial before the Jews seem to happen during the previous night (see 21:17 and 22:39). Luke, Matthew and Mark all record the third Jewish phase of the trial after the second phase and Peter's denials. This time Luke gives more specifics, while Matthew and Mark describe it only briefly. Matthew and Mark only say early in the morning the chief priests and the elders of the people (Mark includes the teachers of the Law and the whole Sanhedrin) have reached a decision about how to deal with Jesus (Matt 27:1 says they have decided to put Jesus to death). Luke, on the other hand, gives a more lengthy description: the council of the elders and the teachers of the Law meet and ask Jesus whether he is the Christ and the Son of God, finally reaching their decision to get rid of him. Marshall (1978:847) notes debates supporting one long trial carrying on throughout the night until daybreak versus two sessions held separately one at night and one in the morning, and concerning the time of the final decision of the Sanhedrin—at night or the next morning. As these debates do not seem to affect our decision as to whether the third Jewish phase of the trial comes after the second Jewish phase, no further work on these debates is conducted.

As to event #5, the death of Judas is unique to Matthew, not recorded in Mark and Luke.

Regarding events #6, #7 and #8, Luke 23:1 says "and after the whole company of them arose" (καὶ ἀναστὰν ἅπαν τὸ πλῆθος αὐτῶν). The antecedent of "the whole company of them" is "the assembly of the elders of the people, both chief priests and scribes" (τὸ πρεσβυτέριον τοῦ λαοῦ, ἀρχιερεῖς τε καὶ γραμματεῖς) mentioned in 22:66 (the third Jewish phase of Jesus' trial). Seemingly, this phrase indicates that this event happens after the third Jewish phase of Jesus' trial. Both Matthew and Mark seem to support this observation: Matthew 27:1-2 and Mark 15:1 state that in the morning the chief priests and the elders of the people make plans to have Jesus executed, and so deliver him to Pilate. John 18:31 says that they do this because they do not have the authority to carry out capital punishment. Therefore, it seems reasonable to believe that after the chief priests and elders have reached a consensus to execute Jesus, they deliver him to Pilate. Thus, this event likely happens after the third Jewish phase of Jesus' trial and is recorded in chronological order.

Only Luke has divided Jesus' trial before the Romans into three phases, inserting the event where Jesus is questioned before Herod Antipas (23:7-11, the second Roman phase of Jesus' trial). Matthew and Mark have not recorded the second Roman phase, instead combining the first and third Roman phases before Pilate into one. Luke mentions that during the first Roman phase, when Pilate discovers that Jesus is a Galilean, he sends him to Herod, who is in Jerusalem at that time, because Galilee and its inhabitants are under Herod's jurisdiction (23:6-7). Luke describes that because Jesus does not answer any of Herod's questions and the chief priests and the teachers are vehemently accusing him, Herod despises him and sends him back to Pilate (23:9-11), where the third Roman phase begins. According to Luke's descriptions above, he has recorded all three phases in chronological order.

Writing order identified: chronological.

3.3.3.16 Journey to Golgotha (23:26-33a)
(Thomas and Gundry, 1988:227-228)

Category: 1

Time: According to Luke 23:25 this happens after Pilate has handed Jesus over to the Jewish people to crucify him according to their will. Therefore, it happens after Jesus' trial before Pilate (the third Roman phase) and is recorded in chronological order.

Observations: Thomas and Gundry believe that Matthew 27:31-34 and Mark 15:20-23 are describing the same incident. Matthew[116], Mark[117] and Luke all record this incident after Jesus' trial before Pilate.

Writing order identified: chronological.

3.3.3.17 First three hours of crucifixion (23:33b-43)
(Thomas and Gundry, 1988:229-231)

Category: 1

Time: According to Luke 23:33, the crucifixion happens after Jesus' journey to Golgotha and is recorded in chronological order. Mark 15:25 says that it is the third hour when Jesus is crucified, and Luke 23:44 says darkness comes over the whole land from the sixth hour until the ninth hour. That is, up to Luke 22:43 three hours have already passed since Jesus' crucifixion began.

Observations: Thomas and Gundry believe that Matthew 27:35-44 and Mark 15:24-32 are describing the same incident. Matthew, Mark and Luke all record this account after Jesus' journey to Golgotha.

Writing order identified: chronological.

---

116. Between the "Jesus' trial before Pilate" account (Matt 27:2, 11-26; Mark 15:1b-15) and the "Journey to Golgotha" account (Matt 27:31-34; Mark 15:20-23), Matt 27:27-30 and Mark 15:16-19 include Jesus being mocked by the Roman soldiers after the trial but before he is on the way to Golgotha. It is not mentioned in Luke.

117. See footnote 116 above.

3.3.3.18 Last three hours of crucifixion (23:44-46)
(Thomas and Gundry, 1988:232)

Category: 1

Time: According to Luke 23:44 it is now the sixth hour. Therefore this account is recorded in chronological order.

Observations: Thomas and Gundry believe that Matthew 27:45-51 and Mark 15:33-38 describe the same incident. Matthew, Mark and Luke all record the last three hours of the crucifixion after the events of first three hours. I have included the description of the temple curtain tearing into half (Luke 23:45b) in the latter account. Thomas and Gundry have excluded this description from this account, instead including it in the next account, "Witnesses of Jesus' death," probably because both Matthew and Mark record this description (Matt 27:51, Mark 15:38) right after Jesus' death (Matt 27:50, Mark 15:37), while Luke describes it (Luke 23:45b) just before Jesus' death (Luke 23:46). The event of the temple curtain very likely happens simultaneously with Jesus' death; both Matthew/Mark and Luke are correct in their sequence. This is evident from Matthew 27:51 where "and behold" (καὶ ἰδοὺ) is used, which likely means "at that time" or "and now," according to the context (see footnote 69 under narrative account 3.3.1.18 for a detailed discussion of καὶ ἰδοὺ).

Writing order identified: chronological.

3.3.3.19 Witnesses of Jesus' death (23:47-49)
(Thomas and Gundry, 1988:233)

Category: 1

Time: Soon after Jesus has died (23:47).

Observations: 23:47 says "and after the centurion saw what had happened" (ἰδὼν δὲ ὁ ἑκατοντάρχης τὸ γενόμενον). According to the context, "what had happened" refers to the unexpected darkness which had fallen over the entire land and lasted for three hours (23:44-45a), and the manner in which Jesus died (23:46). Therefore, this event seemingly comes after Jesus' crucifixion. Thomas and Gundry believe that Matthew 27:52-56 and Mark 15:39-41 are describing the same incident. Matthew, Mark and Luke all place this account after the last three hours of Jesus' crucifixion.

Writing order identified: chronological.

3.3.3.20 Procurement of Jesus' body (23:50–52) (Thomas and Gundry, 1988:234–235)

Category: 1

Time: After the "Witnesses of Jesus' death" account (24:52).

Observations: Since it seems that the centurion gives his comments about Jesus almost immediately after Jesus' death in the "Witnesses of Jesus' death" account, now the news of Jesus' death has reached Pilate (24:52), apparently some time after Jesus' death. Therefore, it is very probable that this event comes after the "Witnesses of Jesus' death" account.

Thomas and Gundry believe that Matthew 27:57–58 and Mark 15:42–45 describe the same incident. Matthew, Mark and Luke all place this account after the "Witnesses of Jesus' death" account.

Writing order identified: chronological.

3.3.3.21 Jesus' body placed in a tomb (23:53–54) (Thomas and Gundry, 1988:235–236)

Category: 1

Time: After the "Procurement of Jesus' body" account (23:53).

Observations: Luke 23:53 indicates that Joseph has already obtained approval from Pilate to take Jesus' body down from the cross and bury it. The burial logically comes after the procurement of the body. Thomas and Gundry believe that Matthew 27:59–60 and Mark 15:46 are describing the same incident. Matthew, Mark and Luke all place this account after the "Procurement of Jesus' body" account.

Writing order identified: chronological.

3.3.3.22 The tomb watched by the women and guarded by soldiers (23:55–56) (Thomas and Gundry, 1988:236)

Category: 1

Time: Event occurs after Jesus' body is placed in a tomb (23:55).

Observations: Luke 23:56 says that the women, after they have seen Jesus' body laid in the tomb, go home to prepare spices and perfumes. Logically it happens after Jesus' body is placed in a tomb. Thomas and Gundry believe that Matthew 27:61–66 and Mark 15:47 are describing the same incident. Thus this event comes after Jesus' body is placed in the tomb in all three synoptic gospels.

Writing order identified: chronological.

3.3.3.23 The tomb found empty by the women (24:1–8) (Thomas and Gundry, 1988:237–238)

Category: 1

Time: After "the tomb watched by the women and guarded by the soldiers" account (24:1).

Observations: According to Luke 24:1 this happens on the first day of the week after Jesus' death and burial and, therefore, after the previous account and in chronological order.

Thomas and Gundry believe that Matthew 28:1, 5–8 and Mark 16:1–8 describe the same incident[118]. Matthew[119], Mark and Luke all record this account after "the tomb watched by the women and guarded by the soldiers" account.

Writing order identified: chronological.

3.3.3.24 The tomb found empty by Peter and John (24:9–12) (Thomas and Gundry, 1988:238–239)

Category: 1

Time: After "the tomb found empty by the women" account (24:9–12, John 20:2–3).

Observations: Thomas and Gundry believe that this account has its parallel in John 20:2–10 but is not mentioned in Matthew

---

118. Thomas and Gundry separate Matthew 28:1 and Mark 16:1 into a different account, "The tomb visited by the women", but as the contents are related to this account, I combine them here.

119. In the "tomb found to be empty by the women" account (Matt 28:1, 5–8), Matthew inserts 28:2–4 which describes an angel coming down from heaven and rolling back the stone. This is unique to Matthew, not mentioned in either Mark or Luke.

and Mark. John 20:2–3 clearly states that after Peter and John have heard from Mary Magdalene, they start for the tomb. This description matches that of Luke 24:9–12 which describes Peter going to the tomb after receiving a report from the women, who have already been there. Therefore, this event likely occurs after the women find the tomb empty and is recorded in chronological order. Luke 24:10 names these women as "Mary Magdalene and Joanna and Mary the mother of James" and others who are with them. From 8:1–3 we know that Mary Magdalene and Joanna have been following Jesus and supporting him financially since they were in Galilee. This verse indicates that they have followed Jesus all the way to Jerusalem and have witnessed his death and resurrection (also see 23:49, 55).

Writing order identified: chronological.

3.3.3.25 Jesus appears to the two disciples traveling to Emmaus (24:13–35)[120] (Thomas and Gundry, 1988:240–241)

Category: 1

Time: After the tomb is found empty by the women and Peter and John (24:22–24).

Observations: Luke 24:13 says this event happens "in the same day" (ἐν αὐτῇ τῇ ἡμέρᾳ) when the women and Peter and John visit Jesus' tomb. The description of Jesus' tomb found empty by the companions of Cleopas in 24:22–24 indicates that this event likely happens after the above-mentioned visits to Jesus' tomb. Thomas and Gundry believe that Mark 16:12–13 is also describing this appearance, but there is no parallel in Matthew. Both Mark[121] and Luke place this account after "the tomb found to be empty by the women" account.

Writing order identified: chronological.

---

120. Thomas and Gundry have divided 24:13–35 into two accounts, with 24:33–35 as the "report of the two disciples (travelled to Emmaus) to the rest." I combine the two for easier reading, as they are basically one event.

121. Between the "tomb found empty by the women" account (Mark 16:1–8) and the "appearance to the two disciples traveling to Emmaus" account (Mark 16:12–13), Mark 16:9–11 is Jesus' appearance to Mary Magdalene which is not mentioned in Luke, and Luke 24:9–12 describes Jesus' tomb being found empty by Peter, a description only in Luke and John but not in the other synoptic gospels.

3.3.3.26 Jesus appears to the assembled disciples in Jerusalem (24:36–49)[122] (Thomas and Gundry, 1988:242–243)

Category: 1

Time: After Jesus' appearance to the two disciples travelling to Emmaus (24:36).

Observations: Luke 24:36 says, "and when they are speaking these (things)" (Ταῦτα δὲ αὐτῶν λαλούντων), which indicates that this event happens while the two disciples are describing to the eleven apostles and the others what has happened on the way to Emmaus (24:35). We may conclude that it happens after the events on the way to Emmaus.

Following 1:80; 2:40, 2:52; 3:19–20; 4:14–15, 4:42–44; 8:1–3; 9:51–52a; 19:45–48 and 21:37–22:6, Luke 24:44–49 appears to be another summary statement (and the final one) Luke uses in his gospel. In 24:44 Luke explains that what has happened to Jesus is a fulfillment of everything written about him in the Law of Moses, the Prophets and the Psalms, that "the Christ should suffer and rise from dead on the third day, and repentance into remission of sins is to be preached in his name to all the nations" (παθεῖν τὸν χριστὸν καὶ ἀναστῆναι ἐκ νεκρῶν τῇ τρίτῃ ἡμέρᾳ, καὶ κηρυχθῆναι ἐπὶ τῷ ὀνόματι αὐτοῦ μετάνοιαν εἰς ἄφεσιν ἁμαρτιῶν εἰς πάντα τὰ ἔθνη) (24:46–47).

While 24:46 seems to be a summary of what happened between 22:54 and 24:43, 24:47 gives a preview of what will be recounted in the Book of Acts. Luke 24:48 continues the description of the apostles and the disciples as the witnesses of these things. In fact, in the Book of Acts these people, in particular apostles such as Peter, John, and James, will become the main characters through whom the Holy Spirit will witness God's redemptive power to others. Also, 24:49 specifies that Jesus tells his apostles and disciples to wait in Jerusalem for the promise of the Father, in order to accomplish what is described in 24:47. As discussed in chapter 2, "the promise of the Father" is precisely the main theme of the Book of Acts. The ending of Luke's gospel sets up the stage for the events of the Book of Acts.

Seemingly the preface in the Book of Acts (1:1–5), the sequel to the Gospel of Luke, is another overlapping summary statement. As discussed in chapter 2, Acts 1:1–2 apparently gives a summary for the whole gospel of Luke, while 1:3–5 gives a preview to what

---

122. Thomas and Gundry divide this account into two: Luke 24:36–43 and 44–49, but as it seems they are describing the same incident, I combine the two here.

is about to happen in the Book of Acts. If this is true, the content of the gospel should be "all things . . . of which Jesus began to do and also to teach, until the day in which he was taken up, after commanding to the apostles through the Holy Spirit whom he had chosen" (περὶ πάντων . . . ὧν ἤρξατο ὁ Ἰησοῦς ποιεῖν τε καὶ διδάσκειν, ἄχρι ἧς ἡμέρας ἐντειλάμενος τοῖς ἀποστόλοις διὰ πνεύματος ἁγίου οὓς ἐξελέξατο ἀνελήμφθη) (Acts 1:1–2).

What is the theme of the gospel? At first glance it seems that Luke does not explicitly mention the theme of the gospel. As the preface describes only the objective (1:4—that Theophilus may have certainty about the things he has been taught) but not the theme. Also, it seems nowhere in the gospel Luke has explicitly mentioned its theme. Furthermore, a study of the beginning section and the ending section of each book in Josephus' *Jewish War* (has a total of 7 books) and Herodotus' *The Persian War* (9 books) finds that the Greco-Roman historians likely only mention objectives in their histories (usually it is to give a truthful account of the events), and do not mention themes. If this is the case, does Luke's Gospel have a theme? Since Luke's gospel apparently belongs to the category of biography in the Greco-Roman histories, study of a biography, Philostratus' *The Life of Apollonius of Tyana* (8 books), is conducted. It is found that though Philostratus does not explicitly mention the theme of his work, he repeatedly implies that Apollonius is a deity both at the beginning of his first book (e.g., 1:4—in a dream a deity tells Apollonius' mother that Apollonius is Proteus, an Egyptian god; 1:6—the people of Tyana say that Apollonius is the son of Zeus) and in the last section of his last book (e.g., 8:31—"Apollonius had then departed from humanity, but his transfiguration caused amazement and nobody ventured to deny that he was immortal"). It seems quite clear that Philostratus' main theme is to promote Apollonius as a deity. Moreover, though Philostratus's work has eight books, this appears to be the only theme. If Luke has followed the writing methodologies of the Greco-Roman historians to write his gospel, it is likely that there is only one theme for his gospel and Acts, instead of a different theme for each of them. Also, even though Luke does not explicitly mention the theme, it would likely be implied in the prefaces or the ending sections of his two books. A study of the prefaces and the last sections of Luke's gospel and Acts indicates that the theme most likely is Luke 24:46–47 ("the Christ should suffer and rise from the dead on the third day, and repentance into remission of sins should be preached in his name to all the nations"). As Luke tries to convey the message that Jesus is Christ throughout the whole gospel (e.g., through his miraculous birth, the extraordinary messages he gives, the miracles he performs, his predestined death and resurrection), and these two verses cover the key messages in both his gospel and Acts ([1] Jesus is Christ, he has suffered, died and resurrected, and [2] the gospel has to be preached to all nations), these are likely the things with which Luke wants Theophilus to have certainty (1:4).

Writing order identified: events are recorded chronologically, and overlapping chronology is noted in Luke 24:46.

3.3.3.27 Christ's parting blessing and departure (24:50–53) (Thomas and Gundry, 1988:246–247)

Category: 1

Time: After Jesus' appearance to the assembled disciples in Jerusalem.

Observations: Luke seems to purposefully employ Jesus' ascension account as the end for his gospel. Luke elaborates on Jesus' ascension in much greater detail in Acts 1:6–11 (right after the preface, 1:1–5 in the Book of Acts), which includes Jesus' last conversation with his apostles (1:6b-8), a part not recorded in Luke 24:50-53. In particular, 1:8 (Bible, 1971) "but you shall receive power when the Holy Spirit has come upon you; and you shall be my witnesses in Jerusalem and in all Judea and Samaria and to the end of the earth" is an elaboration of what "the promise of the Father" actually is in Luke 24:49a and Acts 1:4. It also outlines the Book of Acts (please refer to section 3 of chapter 2 for a detailed discussion on this subject). Therefore, the ending of the gospel (24:47–53) does form a preview of what is to be said in Acts, exhibiting the overlapping writing technique consistently used by Luke throughout his gospel.

Writing order identified: chronological.

3.3.3.28 Summary of 20:1–24:53

Out of the 36 accounts in 20:1–24:53, 34 accounts (94.4%) are categorized as 1 and 2 accounts (5.6%) are categorized as 2 (see table 23 in 3.4). There is no category 3 account. It means that Luke has provided adequate indications of time and/or sequence for almost all the accounts for his readers to determine their writing order except two; and for these two accounts, with the information provided in their parallel accounts from other synoptic gospels, their writing order can also be determined. All category 1 and 2 accounts are identified to be written in chronological order. The writing style of 20:1–24:53 seems different from that of the three sections between chapters 5 and 19, in which Luke has not provided adequate information for quite a number of accounts for us to determine their writing order. Its writing style resembles that which Luke has used for his chapters 1 to 4, in which adequate information of time and/or sequence is provided for all the accounts. The reason for using such a writing style very likely is to prove the reliability of the information therein to his reader Theophilus (see 3.3.1.44 for more details) so that he can be certain of the things he has been taught (see Luke 1:4).

3.4 CONCLUSION

This chapter has sought to ascertain the type of writing order of the Gospel of Luke through a study of its apparent event sequencing. The study shows that Luke has divided his gospel into twelve sections by means of summary account statements (1:80; 2:40, 2:52; 3:19–20; 4:14–15, 4:42–44; 8:1–3; 9:51–52a; 19:45–48; 21:37–22:6 and 24:44–49) and has recorded them in overlapping chronological order.[123] Luke seems to have structured these sections so that each section has a common subject(s) of discussion with the section immediately before and after it. At the end of each section there is a summary account statement, which serves as a brief summary ending that section, and most of the time also giving a preview of the next section. Its implied time frame also overlaps the time frame of the immediately following section. Luke's writing technique for these sections seems to be the technique suggested by Lucian, a contemporary of Luke, for writing of histories: when a historian "has finished the first topic he will introduce the second, fastened to it and linked with it like a chain, . . . the first and second topics must not merely be neighbors but have common matter and overlap" (Lucian, 1999:67).

As for the individual narrative accounts, the results of this study are documented in the following table.

---

123. See narrative accounts 3.3.1.4, 3.3.1.7, 3.3.1.8, 3.3.1.9, 3.3.1.12, 3.3.1.16, 3.3.1.29, 3.3.2.1, 3.3.2.32, 3.3.3.10 and 3.3.3.26

Table 23. Analysis of the narrative accounts in Luke 1:5–24:53

Section[1] (no. of accounts therein)	Category 1[2] (%)	Category 2[2] (%)	Category 3 (%)	% (Category 2+3)
1:5[3]–1:80 (4)	4 (100)	-	-	0
2:1–2:40 (3)	3 (100)	-	-	0
2:41–2:52 (1)	1 (100)	-	-	0
3:1–3:20 (1)	1 (100)	-	-	0
3:21–4:15 (2)[4]	2 (100)	-	-	0
4:16–4:44 (4)	4 (100)	-	-	0
5:1–8:3 (13)	7 (53.8)	5 (38.5)	1 (7.7)	46.2
8:4–9:52(a) (14)	8 (57.1)	5 (35.7)	1 (7.1)	42.8
9:52(b)–19:48 (32)	20 (62.5)	3 (9.4)	9 (28.1)	37.5
20:1–22:6 (10)	8 (80)	2 (20)	-	20.0
22:7–22:53 (8)[5]	8 (100)	-	-	0
22:54–24:53 (18)[6]	18 (100)	-	-	0
Total no. of accounts (110)	**84 (76.4)**	**15 (13.6)**	**11 (10)**	**23.6**

[1.] This refers to the sections divided by Lucian summary statements identified in this chapter.

[2.] Number of narrative accounts in category 1. The writing order identified in all category 1 and 2 accounts is chronological.

[3.] 1:1–4 is the preface of the gospel, which does not belong to any section and is not evaluated here. A thorough analysis of this preface is conducted in chapter 2 of this thesis.

[4.] Narrative account 3.3.1.11 is Jesus' genealogy, which is not assigned to a category. As a result, there are only two accounts in this section.

[5.] The Passover meal (narrative account 3.3.3.12) includes five events and is treated as five accounts here.

[6.] Jesus' trial (narrative account 3.3.3.15) includes six events and is treated as six accounts.

The results reveal that out of 110 accounts, 84 are categorized as 1 (i.e. 76.4%) and 15 are categorized as 2 (13.6%). Category 1 accounts have explicit or implicit indications of time and/or sequence which help us determine the type of writing order of the account. Category 2 accounts have no explicit or implicit indication of time and/or sequence, but do have explicit or implicit indications of time and/or sequence in parallel accounts in other synoptic gospels which help us determine the type of writing order. The above results mean that 99 out of 110 accounts (90%) have explicit or implicit indications of time and/or sequence either in Luke's narrative (76.4%) or in other synoptic gospels (13.6%), to facilitate the determination of their writing order. Moreover, the writing order of all 99 accounts is determined to be chronological.

The remaining 11 accounts (10%) are classified as category 3, for which a writing order cannot be ascertained. There is one category 3 account in each of sections 5:1–8:3 and 8:4–9:52(a), the other nine category 3 accounts being from section 9:52(b)-19:48, which describes Jesus' final journey to Jerusalem. The high percentage of category 3 accounts in section 9:52(b)-19:48 is due to the fact that Luke has included many unique accounts which have no parallel in other synoptic gospels and which also have no clear locational or temporal information. Because of the difficulty in ascertaining the writing order, a chronological order for this section is questioned by many scholars. For example, Bock, Strauss and Bebb all have reservations about a chronological order (see 3.3.2). However, the findings of this study suggest that the events of 9:52(b)-19:48 are probably recorded in chronological order: Luke has likely employed the same writing style for three consecutive sections 5:1–8:3, 8:4–9:52(a) and 9:52(b)-19:48. Luke has utilized fewer temporal and/or locational indicators in these sections as compared with other sections.

The average percentage of category 1 accounts in the three sections in 5:1–19:48 stands at only 57.8%, whereas 100% of the narrative accounts in 1:5–4:44 and 22:7–24:53 are category 1 accounts, and 80% of the narrative accounts in 20:1–22:6 are category 1. The relative lack of temporal and/or locational indicators in 5:1–19:48 is apparently due to the nature of Jesus' ministry as an itinerant preacher described in these sections. Luke likely employs this style to avoid duplication and meaningless descriptions (see 3.3.2.33). If Luke does employ a consistent style in 5:1–19:48, it is very likely that the ordering of sections 5:1–8:3 and 8:4–9:52(a) would indicate the ordering in 9:52(b)-19:48. As it is found that the order of the accounts in 5:1–8:3 and 8:4–9:52(a) is very likely chronological, logically the order of the accounts in 9:52(b)-19:48 is also chronological (see 3.3.1.44). Moreover, the chronological order of 9:52(b)-19:48 seems to be supported by John chapters 7–12, which is believed by scholars such as Thomas and Gundry to be in chronological order, the route Jesus takes to Jerusalem therein seeming to match that described in 9:52(b)-19:48 (see 3.3.2).

The narrative accounts from 1:5 to 4:44 and from 22:7 to 24:53 (i.e., the supernatural birth accounts of Jesus and his forerunner John the Baptist, Jesus' Spirit-filled baptism, the beginning stage of his Spirit-empowered ministry, his predestined suffering and death and his miraculous resurrection) are classified as category 1 accounts, though quite a number of them are unique to Luke, having no parallel in the other synoptics. This is because Luke gives clear locational and temporal information for these events, apparently to emphasize to his reader Theophilus their truthfulness. If so, it is likely that Luke intentionally places greater emphasis on these accounts to prove to Theophilus that Jesus is the Son of God in whom he should put his faith.

Based on the above findings, we obtain a better understanding of καθεξῆς (1:3). In chapter 2 it is discovered that the word: (1) has a meaning "next down to the end," (2) refers to a sequence, and the "next" in "next down to the end" refers to the neighbor closest to the predecessor in the unit of measure explicitly mentioned or implied in the context, and shares the same subject under discussion with the predecessor, and (3) based on the biblical context in Luke 1:3, likely refers to chronological order. This study of narrative sequence not only supports the idea that καθεξῆς very likely indicates chronological order, but also indicates that there are possibly two different meanings of "next" in (1) and (2) above. First, "next" may refer to each section divided by overlapping summary statement(s) from an adjoining section, and recorded in chronological order, and second, "next" may also mean each individual account, also likely recorded in chronological order.

I have already discussed the significance of identifying the writing order of the gospel of Luke at the beginning of chapter 2. As the type of writing order will affect our approach to understanding the gospel, it seems important to ascertain Luke's writing order. If Luke's gospel is written in chronological order, then a study of its chronology may be important for understanding the gospel as a whole, and when we study a particular event, attention may have to be paid also to the previous accounts, as these accounts may provide additional background information, particularly regarding timing, for the event under study. Furthermore, based on the study in this chapter, we find that if the gospel of Luke is written in chronological order, it will help identify the order of events as recorded in other synoptic gospels. Consequently, the chronological writing order of Luke may help us understand more about the arrangements of the narrative accounts in other gospels and the purposes for these arrangements. Lastly, the chronological arrangement of events in the gospel is to enable its reader Theophilus (as well as the readers nowadays) to have certainty of things which have been taught to him (Luke 1:4).

CHAPTER 4

A Study of Overlapping Summary Statements in Greco-Roman Historian Writings

4.0 INTRODUCTION

ONE OF THE MAJOR findings in my analysis of narrative sequence in Luke's gospel (chapter 3) is Luke's employment of overlapping summary statements to divide his gospel into different sections. This writing technique seems to be the technique suggested by Lucian, a contemporary of Luke, for writing of histories: when a historian "has finished the first topic he will introduce the second, fastened to it and linked with it like a chain, . . . the first and second topics must not merely be neighbors but have common matter and overlap" (Lucian, 1999:67). As discussed in 3.3.1.44 and 3.4, I find that Luke has divided his gospel into twelve sections by means of eleven overlapping summary statements (1:80; 2:40, 2:52; 3:19–20; 4:14–15; 4:42–44; 8:1–3; 9:51–52a; 19:45–48; 21:37–22:6 and 24:44–49). Each overlapping summary statement usually has four characteristics. First, it serves as a final note to end the previous section, and sometimes it includes a brief summary of the events described in the previous section. Second, the statement usually gives a preview of the next section. Third, the time frame involved in the statement overlaps that of its immediately following section (i.e., the narrative accounts in the immediately following section seem to happen during the time frame implied in the overlapping summary statement), though the events it describes may not be those mentioned in the following section but an expansion of the narratives in the current section. Fourth, if the statement includes a summary of events of the preceding section, then the time frame involved in the summary overlaps that of the events described in the preceding section. Our objective of this chapter is to check when Greco-Roman historians separate their writings into sections, whether they will adopt any overlapping summary statements in their section summaries as Luke does; that is, whether Luke's overlapping summary statements is a commonly adopted writing technique by other Greco-Roman historians.

4.1 METHODOLOGY

From my studies in chapters 2 and 3 I find that Luke's gospel is very likely written in chronological order. I will select for this exercise those writings of the Greco-Roman historians in 2.3.3 which are identified to be written in chronological order.[124] Because the ending of a book at the same time indicates the ending of a section, I will check the ending of each book of the writings selected to see whether Luke's writing technique of overlapping summary statement is employed (the beginnings of the books of the selected writings will also be checked, in case that the summary statements are placed at the beginnings of the next books instead of at the ends of the current books).[125] To facilitate the checking process I will select those writings which have more than one book in size.[126] The writings selected for this exercise are as follows.

1. Thucydides—*The Peloponnesian War* (8 books) (4.3.1)
2. Xenophon—*Anabasis* (7 books) (4.3.2)
3. Polybius—*Histories* (only the first 5 books, because the others are fragments and therefore are not studied) (4.3.3)

124. That is, only writings recommended by classicist Dr Catherine Kroger which are found to be written in chronological order are included in this exercise (see 2.3.3).

125. The contents in the middle of each book are not checked, in view that the checking of the ending and the beginning of each book in the selected writings seems to be a more effective way to achieve my objective, which is to verify whether Lucian's suggested writing technique of overlapping summary statements is a commonly adopted writing technique by other Greco-Roman historians (see 4.0), no matter whether it is employed in the middle or at the end/beginning of a book.

126. A writing which only has one book, while there may be a final note at the end of the book, it will not have an overlapping summary statement which would likely include a preview of the next book, as the next book is not available in this case.

4. Pausanias—*Description of Greece* (this writing is divided by the names of the cities described, not by book number) (4.3.4)
5. Philostratus—*The Life of Apollonius of Tyana* (8 books) (4.3.5)
6. Josephus—*The Jewish War* (7 books) (4.3.6)
7. Eusebius—*The Ecclesiastical History* (Books 2 to10, Book 1 is not selected because it is written in a logical order instead of chronological order—see 2.3.3.10) (4.3.7)

4.2 OTHER SCHOLARS' OPINIONS ON THE WRITING TECHNIQUE OF SUMMARY STATEMENTS

Quite a number of scholars share the view that summary statements are commonly used writing technique among the ancient writers as well as writers in the Greco-Roman times. David Aune (1987:54) believes that the writing technique of a summary statement is a "common literary technique in Hellenistic prose narrative writing." He opines that summaries function (a) as independent summary reports, (b) to generalize introductions; (c) to generalize conclusions; or (d) to generalize transitions. Lawson Younger (1990:252) also thinks that "it is quite natural to have a summary statement in ancient near Eastern royal inscriptions," and "the use of summary statements in a historical account should not lead modern interpreters to necessarily conclude that such statements are the product of redactional work as biblical scholars have often envisioned it." Aune (1987:99, 106, 130–31, 145) observes that summary is a common writing technique among the ancient Jewish and Christian writers: "The narrative of 1–2 Kings is regularly punctuated with regnal summaries which introduce (1 Kings 14:21–24; 2 Kings 14:1–4) or conclude a reign (1 Kings 21:41–44; 2 Kings 13:8–9)"; the author of 2 Maccabees usually uses summary reports to conclude a section (e.g., 4:50, 5:27), sometimes as a transition or to provide background information; Luke in his Book of Acts includes quite a number of summaries (e.g., 1:14, 2:43–47, 4:32–35; 5:11–16) to generalize incidents or as transitions to introduce or conclude episodes; and *Acts of Peter* contains three summaries similar to those in canonical Acts (e.g., *Acts Pet.* 29: "From that same hour they venerated him [Peter] as a god, and laid at his feet such sick people as they had at home, so that he might heal them.") Mark Brighton (2009:82) also notices that Josephus gives summary statements from time to time in his *Jewish War*. For example, in the middle of Book 2 (2.647) Josephus uses a summary statement to give a brief summary of what was previously described and a preview of what is to be described ("and thus were the disturbances of Galilee quieted, when, upon their ceasing to prosecute their civil dissensions, they betook themselves to make preparations for the war with the Romans.")

Martin Dibelius (quoted by Douglas Hume, 2011:7) thinks that Luke uses "general summaries" to "thread together various surrounding scenes, offering 'links' and 'elaborations' to tie together pre-existing source materials in Acts 1–5," and Dibelius "lists Acts 1:13–14, 2:43–47, 4:32–35 and 5:12–16" in the first five chapters of the Book of Acts as narrative summaries. Hume (2011:7) also mentions that there is another proposal around the time of Dibelius which claims that the Book of Acts is divided by summaries into six panels, which are 1:1–6:7, 6:8–9:31, 9:32–12:24, 12:25–16:5, 16:6–19:20 and 19:21–28:31. Hume (2011:8) also discusses Henry Cadbury's proposal that the summaries in the Book of Acts are "sometimes summarizing or expanding the conclusion of preceding stories, but often prefacing others;" and he (2011:9) mentions Ulrich Wendel's view that "Luke uses summary reports as carriers of important theological themes that demonstrates God's activity with the congregation and the world . . . summaries are best understood as presenting a kind of ecclesial model" which is still relevant to us today. A quick scan of the first five chapters of the Book of Acts finds that seemingly Dibelius and Cadbury are correct that Luke also employs the same technique of overlapping summary statement in his Book of Acts (see 2:43–47, 4:32–35, 5:12–16, 5:41–42 which are likely overlapping summary statements). Apparently Luke has adopted a similar writing style for both his Gospel and the Book of Acts.

In general scholars (e.g., Aune and Cadbury) believe that summary functions to conclude or introduce a section, some (e.g. Aune and Dibelius) believe that it may also function as transition, and some (e.g., Wendel) believe that it carries important theological themes. The summary statements discussed by the above scholars seem to be the overlapping summary statements investigated in this chapter, because apparently the summary statements possess the same characteristics mentioned in 4.0: they often function to conclude sections and/or give previews to introduce new sections, and when they conclude or introduce sections, sometimes they include summaries of the events described in previous sections or previews of the events in the next sections, and if this is the case, the time frames involved in the statements overlap those in the previous or the next sections.

4.3 A STUDY OF THE GRECO-ROMAN HISTORIAN WRITINGS

4.3.1 Thucydides—*The Peloponnesian War* (8 books)

Thucydides (460 B.C. to 395 B.C.) is an Athenian historian and general. In his *Peloponnesian War* he records the fifth century B.C. war between Sparta and Athens.[127]

At the end of Book 1 (1:146) Thucydides gives a final note and writes:

> These were the grounds of complaint and the causes of disagreement on both sides before the war, and they began to appear immediately after the affair of Epidamnus and Corcyra. Nevertheless the two parties continued to have intercourse with one another during these recriminations and visited each other without heralds, though not without suspicion; for the events which were taking place constituted an actual annulment of the treaty and furnished an occasion for war.

Apparently this final note is not an overlapping summary statement as its implied time frame does not overlap the time frame of Book 2; because in the final note above Thucydides says "the two parties continued to have intercourse . . . without heralds", however, at the beginning of Book 2 (2:1) Thucydides writes "At this point . . . they ceased having communication with one another except through heralds . . . " These are obviously two stages of events and do not overlap each other.

At the end of Book 2 (2:103) Thucydides uses another final note to describe Phromio and the Athenians leaving Acarnania and returning to Athens:

> The Athenians and Phormio set out from Acarnania and arrived at Naupactus, and later, at the beginning of spring, sailed back to Athens, bringing with them the captured ships and also the prisoners of free birth whom they had taken in the sea-fights. These were exchanged man for man. And this winter ended, concluding the third year of this war of which Thucydides wrote the history.

---

127. From Logos Bible Software Factbook.

However, Book 3 (3:1) begins with a totally different event from that mentioned at the end of Book 2: it is about the invasion of Attica by the Peloponnesians and their allies which happens in the summer immediately following the winter mentioned at the end of Book 2. The final note at the end of Book 2 is not an overlapping summary statement as its implied time frame does not overlap the time frame of the events of the next book. The endings from Books 3 to 7 are found to be the same: Thucydides uses a final note to end each book but it is not an overlapping summary statement: its implied time frame does not overlap the events of the next book. It seems that Thucydides does not use the writing technique of overlapping summary statement in his *Peloponnesian War*.

4.3.2 Xenophon—*Anabasis* (7 books)

Pinker (2006:3–4) describes that Xenophon (427 B.C. to 355 B.C.) is an Athenian, a Greek historian, soldier, mercenary, and a student of Socrates. He participates in the failed campaign of Cyrus the Younger to claim the Persian throne and writes about it and the ultimate return of Cyrus' ten thousand Greek mercenary soldiers to western Asia Minor in his *Anabasis*.

Although there is no overlapping summary statement at the end of Book 1, there is one at the beginning of Book 2 which includes a summary of the events in Book 1, the events and the time period it describes overlap those in Book 1 (2:1):

> The preceding narrative has described how a Greek force was collected for Cyrus at the time when he was planning an expedition against his brother Artaxerxes, what events took place during the upward march, how the battle was fought, how Cyrus met his death, and how the Greeks returned to their camp and lay down to rest, supposing that they were victorious at all points and that Cyrus was alive.

Again, a similar situation is noted in Book 2: there is no summary statement at the end of the book but there is a brief description of the preceding narratives at the beginning of Book 3 overlapping the events of Books 1 and 2 (as a result the time period involved also overlaps that of the preceding books) (3:1):

> The preceding narrative has described all that the Greeks did in the course of the upward march with Cyrus until the time of the battle, and all that took place after the death of Cyrus while the Greeks were on the way back with Tissaphernes during the period of the truce.

The ending of Book 3 and the beginning of Book 4 are similar to those of the previous books, while there is no summary statement at the end of Book 3, there is a summary at the beginning of Book 4 to describe the preceding events from Books 1 to 3 (4:1–3); the time period involved and the events described in 4:1–3 overlap those in Books 1 to 3. Following 4:1–3 there is also a brief preview of the events of Book 4 in 4:4:

> (4:1–3) The preceding narrative has described all that took place on the upward march until the time of the battle (i.e., events described in Book 1), all that happened after the battle during the truce concluded by the King and the Greeks who had made the upward march in company with Cyrus (i.e., events described in Book 2), and likewise the whole course of the warfare carried on against the Greeks after the King and Tissaphernes had broken the truce, when the Persian army was hanging upon the Greek rear (i.e., events described in Book 3). When the Greeks finally reached a point where the Tigris River was quite impassable by reason of its depth and width, and where there was no passage alongside the river, since the Carduchian Mountains hung sheer and close above it, the generals were forced to the conclusion that they must make their way through the mountains. For they heard from the prisoners who were taken that once they had passed through the Carduchian mountains and reached Armenia, they could there cross the headwaters of the Tigris river, if they so desired, or, if they preferred, could go round them. They were also informed that the headwaters of the Euphrates were not far from those of the Tigris—and such is indeed the case (i.e., events described in 3.4). (4.4) Now they conducted their invasion of the country of the Carduchians in the following way, since they were seeking not only to escape observation, but

at the same time to reach the heights before the enemy could take possession of them.

Overlapping summary statements are noted at the beginning of Books 2, 3, 4, 5 and 7. Book 6 begins with (6.1): "After this . . . " The beginning of Book 6 seems to be a continuation of the story of Book 5, and apparently it is going to describe what happens after the last event mentioned in Book 5. Although the implied time frame of the word "this" seems to overlap that of the last event in Book 5, it is not considered an overlapping summary statement because it is only one word and does not give a description of its preceding event(s). Seemingly, Xenophon adopts the writing technique of overlapping summary statement at the beginning instead of at the end of each book (except Books 1 and 6 where there is no summary statement at the beginnings and at the ends of the books), where the time period involved and the events described in the overlapping summary statements overlap those of their preceding books, and occasionally (e.g., 4.4) the statement also gives a preview of what is to be described next, where the time period involved and the events described overlap those of the upcoming narratives.

4.3.3 Polybius—*The Histories* (5 books)

Edwards (1922: vii) describes that "Polybius was born about 208 B.C. at Megalopolis in Arcadia," and his original scheme of *Histories* (1922: x) "was to record the raise of Rome to supremacy over the Mediterranean states in the years 220 -168 B.C., *i.e.* from the beginning of the Second Punic War to the end of the Third Macedonian War. He subsequently extended this scheme in order to include an account of events from the first expedition of the Romans outside Italy (*i.e.* from the beginning of the First Punic War, in 264 B.C., . . .) and to continue the record to the year (146 B.C.) which witnessed the destruction of Carthage and of Corinth."

There is no summary statement at the end of Book 1 but there is an overlapping summary statement at the beginning of Book 2 (2.1.1–4). It briefly describes what has happened in Book 1 (thus in 2.1.1 the events described and the time period involved overlap those in Book 1) and it gives a preview of the upcoming events in Book 2 (2.1.2–4):

In the preceding book I stated in the first place at what date the Romans having subjected Italy began to concern themselves in enterprises outside the peninsula; next I narrated how they crossed to Sicily and what were their reasons for undertaking the war with Carthage for the possession of that island. After relating when and how they first built naval forces, I pursued the history of the war on both sides until its end, at which the Carthaginians evacuated all Sicily, and the Romans acquired the whole island except the parts which were Hiero's dominions. In the next place I set myself to describe how the mercenaries mutinied against Carthage and set ablaze the so-called Libyan war; I described all the terrible atrocities committed in this war, all its dramatic surprises, and their issues, until it ended in the final triumph of Carthage. I will now attempt to give a summary view,[128] according to my original project, of the events immediately following.

A final note is noted at the end of Book 2 (2.71.6–10), giving a summary of the events which have happened in Book 2:

> . . . I have thus completed this introduction or preliminary part of my History. In it I have shown in the first place when, how, and why the Romans first entered on enterprises outside Italy and disputed the command of the sea with the Carthaginians, and next I have dealt with the state of Greece and Macedonia and with that of Carthage. So having, as was my original purpose, reached the date at which the Greeks were on the eve of the Social War, the Romans on the eve of the Hannibalic War, and the kings of Asia about to enter on the war for Coele-Syria, I must now bring this Book to its close, which coincides with the final events

---

128. "Summary view . . . of the events," according to the context, most likely refers to a summary of the key points of the events. Walbank (1957:171) also agrees with this view and quotes 1.13.7–8 to support his claim, where Polybius writes: "for it is not my purpose to write their history (i.e., events described in Books 1 and 2) but to mention them summarily as introductory to the events which are my real theme. I shall therefore attempt by such summary treatment of them in their proper order to fit in the end of the Introduction to the beginning of the actual History." Apparently "summary view" here does not relate to overlapping summary statement studied in this exercise.

preceding these wars and the death of the three kings who had up to now directed affairs.

Overlapping summary statements are noted at both the beginning and the ending of Book 3. At the beginning of Book 3 Polybius refers to what he has explained and discussed in Books 1 and 2 (with the explanation and discussion described overlap those in these two books) and he gives a preview of the upcoming events in Book 3 (3.1.1–3):

> In my first Book, the third, that is, from this counting backwards, I explained that I fixed as the starting-points of my work, the Social war, the Hannibalic war, and the war for Coele-Syria. I likewise set forth in the same place the reasons why I wrote the two preceding Books dealing with events of an earlier date. I will now attempt to give a well attested account of the above wars, their first causes and the reasons why they attained such magnitude; but in the first place I have a few words to say regarding my work as a whole . . .

At the end of Book 3, similar with that of Book 2, Polybius gives an overlapping summary statement with a summary of what he has discussed in Book 3, and a preview of the events in Book 4 (the events described and time period involved overlap those in Book 4) (3.118.10–12):

> I therefore end this Book at this point, having now described the events in Spain and Italy that occurred in the 140th Olympiad. When I have brought down the history of Greece in the same Olympiad to the same date, I shall pause to premise to the rest of the history a separate account of the Roman constitution; for I think that a description of it is not only germane to the whole scheme of my work, but will be of great service to students and practical statesmen for forming or reforming other constitutions.

Similar to Books 2 and 3, overlapping summary statements are noted both at the beginning and at the end of Book 4. The statement at the beginning of Book 4 gives a summary of the previous events (with the events described and the time period involved overlap those of the previous book) and a preview of what he is about to describe next (4.1.1–9):

> In the preceding Book after pointing out the causes of the second war between Rome and Carthage, I described the invasion of Italy by Hannibal, and the engagements which took place between the belligerents up to the battle on the river Aufidus at the town of Cannae. I shall now give an account of the contemporary events in Greece from the 140th Olympiad onwards (220–216 B.C.), after briefly recalling to the minds of my readers the sketch I gave in my second Book of Greek affairs and especially of the growth of the Achaean League, the progress of that state having been surprisingly rapid in my own time and earlier . . . Summarizing, next, the occurrences dealt with in my introductory sketch up to the deaths of Antigonus Doson, Seleucus Ceraunus, and Ptolemy Euergetes, which all took place about the same time, I announced that I would enter on my main history with the events immediately following the above period.

At the end of Book 4 there is a final note with a preview of the events described in Book 5 (with the events described and the time period involved overlapping those of the following book) (4.87.12–13):

> As to how and by what means this happened, I shall defer speaking for the present and bring this Book to a close; but in subsequent ones I shall try to give a clear account of the whole matter, Philip, after making the arrangements I mentioned, returned to Argos and there spent the remainder of the winter with his friends, dismissing his troops to Macedonia.

There is no overlapping summary statement at the beginning of Book 5. It describes a totally different event (the retirement of Aratus) from the last event in Book 4 (Philip returning to Argos) and there seems to be no connection between them. However, there is an overlapping summary statement at the end of Book 5 which gives a brief summary of the events described previously, and again gives a preview of what is to be in the next book (with the events described and the time period involved overlapping those of the next book) (5.111.7b-10):

Such was the state of affairs in Greece and Asia. The greater part of Italy, as I mentioned in the last Book, went over to the Carthaginians after the battle of Cannae. I choose this date for interrupting my narrative, having now described what took place in Asia and Greece during the 140th Olympiad. In the following Book, after a brief recapitulation of my introductory narrative, I will proceed according to my promise to treat of the Roman Constitution.

Based on the above observations, it seems that Polybius employs overlapping summary statements in almost every book of his *Histories*, besides Book 1, and most of the times both at the beginning and at the end of a book. The overlapping summary at the beginning of a book includes a summary of the preceding book (with the time period involved and the events described overlap those of the preceding book) and a preview of the upcoming book (with the time period involved and the events described overlapping those of the upcoming book); and the overlapping summary at the end of a book sometimes includes a summary of that book and a preview of the next book (e.g., Books 3 and 5), but sometimes it either has a summary of that book (e.g., Book 2), or a preview of the next book (e.g., Book 4).

4.3.4 Pausanias—*Description of Greece*

Long (1870, vol.3:161) describes that Pausanias was a Greek traveler and geographer of the second century A.D., who lived in the times of Antoninus Pius and Marcus Antoninus. His *Description of Greece* describes ancient Greece from firsthand observations. Long (1870, vol.3:161) opines that "his account is minute; but it mainly refers to objects of antiquity, and works of art, such as buildings, temples, statues, and pictures. He also mentions mountains, rivers, and fountains, and the mythological stories connected with them, which indeed are his chief inducements to speak of them." In 2.3.3.5 I find that whenever Pausanias describes the history of an important family or the history of a city he writes in chronological order.

Overlapping summary statement does not seem to be a helpful writing technique for the beginnings and the endings of the books in Pausanias' *Description of Greece*, because basically this work is not a narrative but it describes distinct geographical and social phenomena of different cities, one after another. The descriptions of different cities therein do not seem to have any obvious link between them which facilitates the application of this writing technique. Out of all the beginnings and the endings of the descriptions of cities (Attica, Corinth, Laconia, Messenia, Elis, Achaia, Boeotia, Phocis and Ozolian Locri), the only time Pausanias seems to apply this writing technique is when he describes Elis: his description of Elis is divided into two books, and at the beginning of the second book for Elis there is an overlapping summary statement describing what he has already described for Elis in his first book and what he is going to write next (*Elis* 2.1): "After my description of the votive offerings I must now go on to mention the statues of racehorses and those of men, whether athletes or ordinary folk." In conclusion, Pausanias uses the writing technique of overlapping summary statement in only 1 out of 9 of his descriptions of cities in his *Description of Greece*, likely because the writing is not a narrative but geographical and social descriptions of different cities, where this writing technique can hardly be applied. The only overlapping summary statement at the beginning of the second book about Elis has both a summary of the preceding book (where the events described overlap those of the preceding book) and a preview of what is about to be described next (where the events described overlap those of the upcoming book).

4.3.5 Philostratus—*The Life of Apollonius of Tyana* (8 books)

Gunn (1870, vol.3:323) describes that Philostratus' (later second century A.D.—middle of third century A.D.) *Life of Apollonius of Tyana* tells the story of Apollonius, a philosopher and teacher.

There is no overlapping summary statement at the end of Books 1, 2, 5, 6 and 7. There is a final note at the end of Book 3 which gives a preview of the events at the beginning of the next Book (its time frame overlaps that of the events at the beginning of the upcoming book) (3.58.31): "Thence he sailed to Ionia, where he was much admired and highly esteemed by devotees of wisdom." Apparently the beginning of Book 4 (4.1.1) is an elaboration of 3.58.31 and confirms our understanding that the final note in 3.58.31 is an overlapping summary statement:

> When they saw the Master as he entered Ephesus in Ionia, not even workmen stayed at their crafts, but followed him in admiration of his wisdom, his

> appearance, his diet, his dress, or all at once. Pronouncements about him circulated, for example from the oracle at Colophon praising the Master as a sharer in its own knowledge, perfectly wise, and so on, and also from Didyma and the sanctuary outside Pergamum. There the god advised many of those seeking health to visit Apollonius, that being the god's own wish and the will of the Fates . . .

Moreover, at the end of Book 4 Philostratus gives a preview of where Apollonius will go next (Gadeira) in Book 5, and it seems to be an overlapping summary statement because it overlaps the description at the beginning of Book 5 (4.47):

> Nero was departing for Greece, and had issued a general edict that no one was to teach philosophy in Rome. Apollonius therefore turned his thoughts towards the western part of the world, of which they say the Pillars are the limit. He planned to see the Ocean tides and Gadeira, and he had also heard something about the love of wisdom of the people there and their high degree of sanctity. All his pupils followed him, praising the expedition as well as the Master.

The beginning of Book 5 describes that Apollonius goes to Gadeira (5.1):

> About the Pillars which Heracles is said to have set up as boundary markers for the world, I pass over the fanciful stories, preferring to point out those worth hearing and telling. The promontories of Europe and Africa are divided by a strait sixty stades wide, through which they admit the Ocean into the inner waters . . . The European promontory, called Calpis, is on the right of the strait, with a length of six hundred stades, ending at Old Gadeira ...

At the end of Book 6 Philostratus gives a final note but it does not include a preview of the next Book, nor does its time frame overlaps that of the events in Book 7 (6.43.3): "These are the Master's deeds on behalf of sanctuaries and cities, with regard to populaces and on their behalf, and on behalf of the dead and the sick, and with regard to the wise, the ignorant, and those emperors who made him their adviser on the subject of virtue."

At the beginning of Book 7 there is a preview of what is to be written in the book, but there is no summary of events of the preceding book, and the preview's time frame does not overlap that of the events of the preceding book (7.1):

> I know that tyranny is the surest test of true philosophers, and I am prepared to ask in what respect any one philosopher has proved more or less heroic than another. The point of my remark is this. At the time of Domitian's tyranny, the Master was beset by accusations and indictments, and I will discuss later how they began, from what quarter, and their terms. But I am bound to record the words he spoke and the impression that he made, which brought it about that he left the court after condemning the tyrant rather than being condemned. I think, therefore, that before all this I must recount such noteworthy deeds as I have been able to find performed by truly wise men against tyrants, and compare them with those of Apollonius, because this is surely how we must arrive at the truth.

Based on the above observations, it seems that Philostratus uses the writing technique of overlapping summary statement from time to time, but not always (only in Books 3 and 4, i.e., 2 out of 8 books), in *The Life of Apollonus of Tyana*. Overlapping summary statements are only noted at the end of Books 3 and 4, where they give previews of the upcoming events in Books 4 and 5 (with the time period involved and the events described overlap those of the upcoming narratives) respectively.

4.3.6 Josephus—*The Jewish War* (7 books)

According to McLaren (2010:838), *Jewish War* is "the first of the extant works written by the first-century historian Flavius Josephus (A.D. 37 to 100), ... (it) provides a vivid account of the conflict (between the Romans and the Jews) that resulted in the destruction of Jerusalem and its Temple in A.D. 70."

There are no overlapping summary statements at the end of Books 1 to 6. However there is an elaboration of an event which is mentioned at the end of Book 4 at the beginning of

Book 5. The end of Book 4 (4.663) mentions that Titus comes to "Caesarea, having taken a resolution to gather all his other forces together at that place." The beginning of Book 5 again describes this event (5.1): "when therefore Titus had marched over that desert which lies between Egypt and Syria, in the manner forementioned, he came to Cesarea, having resolved to set his forces in order at that place, before he began the war." This elaboration in Book 5 overlaps the same event described at the end of Book 4.

4.3.7 Eusebius—*The Ecclesiastical History* (Books 2 to 10)

Kirsopp (1926–1932:ix-xi) comments that Eusebius is probably born around A.D. 260. He is the Bishop of Caesarea and the chief theological adviser of Emperor Constantine. Eusebius' *The Ecclesiastical History* is about the approximately first three hundred years of church history. According to Kirsopp (1926–1932:xxxiii-xxxiv) the writing is organized in chronological order: "The chronology adopted is that of the Roman Emperors, and the events are arranged reign by reign . . . The object of the whole book was to present the Christian 'Succession,' which did not merely mean, though it certainly included, the apostolic succession of the bishops . . . but rather the whole intellectual, spiritual, and institutional life of the Church."

There is no overlapping summary statement at the end of Books 3, 5, 6, 7, 8 and 9. There is a preface at the beginning of Book 2 which includes a description of what is written in Book 1 and what will be written in Book 2:

> All that needed stating by way of preface in the history of the Church—the proof of the divinity of the saving Logos, the ancient history of our teaching, and the antiquity of the dogmas of the Christian life according to the Gospel, particularly all the points concerning his recently fulfilled advent, the events before his Passion, and the story of the choice of the Apostles—all this we traced in the preceding book, summarizing the demonstration. Let us now consider in the present book what followed his Ascension, noting some things from the divine writings, and adding what is taken from

other sources from treatises which we will quote from time to time.

The time frame of this preface does not overlap that of Book 1, because Book 1 is not a narrative but a book of discussions of theological matters; the concept of time frame does not apply to Book 1.

At the end of Book 2 Eusebius describes the deaths of Peter and Paul (2.25.5–8):

> In this way then was he (Nero) the first to be heralded as above all a fighter against God, and raised up to slaughter against the Apostles. It is related that in his time Paul was beheaded in Rome itself, and that Peter likewise was crucified, and the title of "Peter and Paul," which is still given to the cemeteries there, confirms the story . . . And that they both were martyred at the same time Dionysius, bishop of Corinth, affirms in this passage of his correspondence with the Romans: "By so great an admonition you bound together the foundations of the Romans and Corinthians by Peter and Paul, for both of them taught together in our Corinth and were our founders, and together also taught in Italy in the same place and were martyred at the same time." And this may serve to confirm still further the facts narrated.

Eusebius elaborates further the deaths of Peter and Paul at the beginning of Book 3 (3.1):

> Such was the condition of things among the Jews, but the holy Apostles and disciples of our Saviour were scattered throughout the whole world . . . but Peter seems to have preached to the Jews of the Dispersion in Pontus and Galatia and Bithynia, Cappadocia, and Asia, and at the end he came to Rome and was crucified head downwards, for so he had demanded to suffer. What need be said of Paul, who fulfilled the gospel of Christ from Jerusalem to Illyria and afterward was martyred in Rome under Nero? This is stated exactly by Origen in the third volume of his commentary on Genesis.

Regarding the deaths of Peter and Paul, Eusebius seems to give a brief description of this account close to the end of Book 2 and indicates that this incident will be elaborated further later ("And this may serve to confirm still further the facts narrated.") This description seemingly is an overlapping summary statement with its time period described overlapping Eusebius' elaboration on the same matter in Book 3.

At the end of Book 4, there is a brief comment of bishop Soter (4.30.3): "At this time Soter, bishop of Rome, died." At the beginning of Book 5 (5.1.) Eusebius gives a short elaboration of bishop Soter: "Soter, the bishop of the church of Rome, ended his life in the eighth year of his rule." Although the comment of bishop Soter at the end of Book 4 is relatively short and seemingly not a summary of any preceding event in Book 4, the time frame involved in this brief comment overlaps Eusebius' description of bishop Soter at the beginning of Book 5. The writing technique of overlapping summary statement seems to be applied here.

In the preface at the beginning of Book 8, Eusebius again seems to adopt the writing technique of overlapping summary statement. Eusebius gives a brief summary of the contents of the first seven books (i.e., the succession from the apostles, the time frame involved and the event described overlap those of its seven preceding books), and a preview of what will be written next (the time period involved overlaps that of the upcoming narratives in Book 8):

> Having concluded the succession from the apostles in seven entire books, in this eighth treatise we regard it as one of our most urgent duties to hand down, for the knowledge of those that come after us, the events of our own day, which are worthy of no casual record; and from this point our account will take its beginning.

Based on the observations above I conclude that Eusebius adopts the writing technique of overlapping summary statement from time to time (at the beginnings of Books 2, 3, 5 and at the end of Book 8, i.e., 4 out of 9 books) in his *Ecclesiastical History*. When Eusebius employs the writing technique of overlapping summary statements, sometimes he gives both a summary of the events of the preceding book and a preview of the events of the upcoming book, where the events described and the time frame involved in the summary and the preview overlap those of the preceding book and the upcoming book (e.g., the overlapping summary statement at the end of Book 8); but sometimes at the beginning of a book he only gives an elaboration of a certain event which is mentioned at the end of the preceding book (e.g., the overlapping summary statement about the deaths of Peter and Paul at the beginning of Book 3, and the statement about the death of Bishop Soter at the beginning of Book 5), where the time frame of that particular event overlaps that of the same event in the preceding book.

4.4 CONCLUSION

I have studied the endings and the beginnings of each book of the selected writings of seven Greco-Roman historians. My findings are summarized in Table 24. I find that two of them (Xenophon and Polybius) use the writing technique of overlapping summary statements frequently (5 out of 7 books in Xenophon's *Anabasis* and 4 out of 5 books in Polybius' *Histories*) in their writings, four of them (Pausanias, Philostratus, Josephus and Eusebius) use this technique from time to time or occasionally in their writings (1 out of 9 occasions in Pausanias' *Description of Greece*, 2 books out of 8 in Philostratus' *The Life of Apollonius of Tyana*, 1 out of 7 books in Josephus' *Jewish War*, and 4 out of 9 books in Eusebius' *The Ecclesiastical History*). One of them (Thucydides) does not seem to use the technique at all in his work.

Table 24. An overview of the study of overlapping statements in Greco-Roman historian writings

Author / Writing (no. of books studied)	Beginning of a book which has overlapping statement (S = Summary, P = preview, E = elaboration)	Ending of a book which has overlapping statement	What is overlapped?
Thucydides *The Peloponnesian War* (8 books)	None	None	–
Xenophon *Anabasis* (7 books)	2(S)[129], 3(S), 4(S,P[130]), 5(S), 7(S)	None	The events described and the time frame involved in each S overlap those in *all* the preceding books (e.g., 3S events and time frames overlap those in Books 1 & 2); the events described in a P overlap the events in the upcoming book (e.g., 4P events and the time frame involved overlap those in Book 4).
Polybius *The Histories* (5 books)	2(S,P), 3(S,P), 4(S,P)	2(S), 3(S,P), 4(P), 5(S,P)	The events described and the time frame involved in each S overlap those in the immediate preceding book; and the events described and the time frame involved in a P overlap those in the upcoming book.
Pausanias *Description of Greece*[131]	Elis vol.2[132] (S,P)	None	The events described in S overlap those in the previous book, and the P describes what will be written in the upcoming book
Philostratus *The Life of Apollonius of Tyana* (8 books)	None	3(P), 4(P)	The events described and the time frame involved in each P overlap those in the upcoming narratives.

129. 2(S) = In Book 2 there is a Summary of the events described in the preceding book.

130. 4(P) = In Book 4 there is a Preview of the events to be described in the upcoming book.

131. Description of Greece is divided by the names of the cities described, *not by book number*.

132. The description of the city Elis is divided into 2 volumes.

A STUDY OF OVERLAPPING SUMMARY STATEMENTS   215

Author / Writing (no. of books studied)	Beginning of a book which has overlapping statement (S = Summary, P = preview, E = elaboration)	Ending of a book which has overlapping statement	What is overlapped?
Josephus *The Jewish War* (7 books)	5(E)	None	There is an E at the beginning of Book 5 for an event mentioned at the end of Book 4 (Titus goes to Cesarea).
Eusebius *The Ecclesiastical History* (Books 2–10)[133]	2(S), 3(E), 5(E)	8(S,P)	The beginning of Book 2 gives a S of what is described in Book 1, and the contents of the S overlap those of Book 1.[134] At the beginnings of Books 3 and 5, there are Es of events described in preceding books and the time frame involved in the Es overlap their respective descriptions in preceding books.[135]

The table illustrates that it is not uncommon for Greco-Roman historians to employ the writing technique of overlapping summary statements at the end of a book to thread together sections. These summary statements, same as what I have found in Luke's summary statements, usually include the following characteristics, also mentioned in 4.0: (a) they serve as final notes of the sections, and sometimes include summaries for the events described in the previous sections; (b) the statements frequently include previews of the next immediate sections; (c) if the statements are used as summaries for the events of the preceding sections, the time frames involved in the statements overlap the time frames of the events described in their preceding sections (or the time frames of the statements overlap those of the events described in their upcoming sections when the statements are used as or include a

---

133. Book 1 is not selected because it is written in a logical order instead of chronological order—see 2.3.3.10.

134. Book 1 is not a narrative but merely discussions of theological matters; the concept of time frame does not apply here (i.e., there is no overlapping of time frame here).

135. At the beginning of Book 3 the elaboration is about the deaths of Apostles Peter and Paul, which is mentioned at the end of Book 2; and at the beginning of Book 5 the elaboration is about the death of Bishop Soter, which is described at the end of Book 4.

preview of the upcoming sections). Apparently there is no rigid rule regarding when to use this technique. Thucydides does not use it at the ends of his books in *Pelponnessian War*, but Polybius employs it at the end of almost every book in the first five books of his *Histories*. Out of the eight books of *The Life of Apollonius of Tyana* Philostratus only uses this technique at the end of Books 4 and 5 but not the others; and similarly Eusebius only uses this technique at the end of Book 8 of *The Ecclesiastical History*. Moreover, historians are also different in the extent of coverage in their overlapping summary statements. Xenophon prefers a summary to cover the contents of all the preceding books of that summary, while Polybius' summaries only cover the contents of their immediate preceding books; and Philostratus's previews, same as Eusebius' two summaries at the end of Books 2 and 4 , only cover a particular event in their immediate upcoming books.[136] My findings agree with other scholarly observations (e.g., Aune [1987:54], Cadbury [quoted by Hume, 2011:8] and Dibelius [quoted by Hume, 2011:7]) in 4.2 that summaries are frequently used by historians in the past to conclude or introduce sections, or as transitions. However, in my study I do not find that overlapping summary statements of Greco-Roman historians carry important theological themes (as believed by Wendel [quoted by Hume, 2011:9]). A study of the eleven overlapping summary statements in Luke's Gospel (see 4.0) finds that all of them except three (i.e., 27.2%) are descriptive and do not carry theological themes. All the above three statements involve Jesus' sayings. 4:42–44 includes v. 43b: "I must preach the good news of the kingdom of God to the other towns as well; for I was sent for this purpose" which spells out Jesus' ministry objective; 19:45–48 includes v. 46b: "My house shall be a house of prayer,' but you have made it a den of robbers" which indicates what is the real purpose of the temple; and 24:44–49 includes vv. 46b-47: "the Christ should suffer and on the third day rise from the dead, and that repentance and forgiveness of sins should be proclaimed in his name to all nations, beginning from Jerusalem" which explains the main theme of Luke-Acts. In conclusion Luke does sometimes structure his overlapping summary statements to carry important theological themes.

---

136. Philostratus' previews at the end of Books 3 and 4 only cover a part of the events (not all) in their immediate upcoming books. The preview at the end of Book 3 describes that Apollonius goes to Ephesus in Ionia, but in Book 4 Apollonius also goes to other cities after Ephesus (e.g., in 4.11.1 Apollonius goes to Greece). Similarly, the preview at the end of Book 4 mentions that Apollonius visits Gadeira, but Apollonius also visits other places after he leaves Gadeira (e.g. 5.11.1 mentions that Apollonius goes to Africa and Etruria).

Seemingly, Greco-Roman historians will employ more elaborate summaries or previews (i.e., summaries or previews which will at least cover all the events in its immediate preceding or upcoming books) when they want to conclude or introduce major sections, and apparently only give brief summary statements (i.e., a brief elaboration of a particular event at the end of the preceding book, e.g., the two elaborations at the beginnings of Books 3 and 5 in Eusebius' *The Ecclesiastical History*) to facilitate transition in the narratives. Although some of Luke's overlapping summary statements in his gospel are more elaborate and each includes a summary of the events in the previous section and a preview of the events in the upcoming section (e.g., 21:37–22:6 and 24:44–49), some are quite brief (e.g., 1:80, 2:40, 2:52, 3:19–20). Instead of just elaborations of previously mentioned events, these brief summaries tend to be expansions of the current narratives, and include new information not discussed both in the current and the upcoming sections, and its time frame involved overlapping the events in the upcoming section. This special feature of narrative expansion is not found in this study of Greco-Roman historian writings, and may be unique to Luke. While Luke only employs the technique of overlapping summary statement at the end of each section in his gospel, I find that Greco-Roman historians employ this technique at the end or at the beginning of a section or both.

In view that six out of seven historians (85.7%) whom I studied adopt this writing technique in their writings, I conclude that the overlapping summary statement technique employed by Luke in his Gospel is a commonly used writing technique adopted by the Greco-Roman historians in their writings which are written in chronological order.

Chapter 5

Conclusion

5.0 SUMMARY OF FINDINGS

Although Luke has mentioned in the preface of his gospel that he is writing the Gospel in "an orderly account" (καθεξῆς—1:3), scholars have been uncertain about the meaning of the word and have no consensus on the writing order of Luke's gospel. The aim of this research is to ascertain Luke's writing order for his gospel through the following objectives (1.1.2): (1) to analyze and evaluate the different suggestions of "orderly" account by various scholars; (2) to conduct textual, grammatical and semantic studies of Luke's two prefaces; (3) to conduct a thorough word study for καθεξῆς; (4) to analyze the narrative sequence in Luke's gospel; and (5) to analyze and evaluate the writing methodologies of Greco-Roman and Jewish historians as compared and contrasted with Luke's gospel. The above five objectives are addressed in the corresponding chapters described below. Due to restrictions of the length of this thesis, I have limited my study to the gospel of Luke and have not conducted a thorough investigation of the narrative sequence in the book of Acts. However, I have referred to the book of Acts when pertinent.

Chapter 2 addressed objectives 1, 2, and 3 and investigated different scholars' opinions about Luke's writing order. It also investigated the textual, grammatical and semantic aspects of Luke's two prefaces and compared Luke's prefaces with those of Greco-Roman and Jewish historians, and conducted a word study for καθεξῆς. Some scholars (e.g., Lockwood [1995:101–104] and Easton [1926:2]), based on the study of the meaning of the word καθεξῆς, believe that Luke's writing order is strictly chronological. However, most scholars have reservations about the Gospel's order being strictly chronological; because when the content of the Gospel is compared with those of Matthew and Mark's, unresolved problems about chronology lead them to believe that καθεξῆς may not actually mean chronological order, but refers to some other order or no particular order at all.

However, I concluded, after study of Luke's two prefaces and those of Greco-Roman and Jewish historians, that Luke very likely writes in chronological order. Luke has adopted the common approaches of Greco-Roman and Jewish historians in writing his gospel and the book of Acts. The preface of the Gospel includes the four elements commonly adopted by Greco-Roman and Jewish historians: (a) what the historian will write (content—1:3), why the historian writes this narrative (reason—1:1), how the narrative will be written (methodology—1:2–3) and what the historian expect from the reader (expected result—1:4). The preface of Acts also seems to follow the commonly adopted approach of Greco-Roman and Jewish historians and addresses only the element that will be changed (i.e., the content) as compared with that of the first book (i.e., the Gospel) and does not address other elements in the preface of the first book which will remain the same in the sequel (i.e., the book of Acts). This likely indicates that the writing order of Acts, an element not addressed in the preface of Acts, is the same as that of Luke's Gospel. As a result, if we could ascertain the writing order of Acts or the Gospel, we may declare that the other book is also written in the same order.

The study of καθεξῆς reveals that its root components are κατά and ἑξῆς, giving a possible meaning "next down to the end." Further study of contemporary Greek usages of καθεξῆς indicates that καθεξῆς does not refer to just any logical order but to a sequence, and in its definition, "next down to the end," "next" refers to the neighbor closest to its predecessor in the unit of measure explicitly mentioned or implied in the context, and shares the same subject under discussion with the predecessor. Καθεξῆς in Luke 1:3, therefore, likely refers to a sequence which means "next down to the end," with "next" referring to the next act or teaching closest in time (the unit of measure) to the preceding act or teaching conducted by Jesus (subject under discussion). Consequently, based on the biblical usages of καθεξῆς and ἑξῆς, καθεξῆς in Luke 1:3 most likely refers to chronological order; which is contrary to the scholarly opinions that καθεξῆς refers to some literary order appropriate to the Gospel of Luke (e.g., Talbert [2002:22]) , or refers to a logical order (e.g., Morris [1995:73–74]), or indicates no order at all (e.g., Brown [1978:107]).

Moreover, I discovered that if Greco-Roman and Jewish historians do not mention in their prefaces what order they are going to write, they will write in chronological order, which gives further confirmation that Luke's writing order is chronological. Therefore, the findings from chapter 2 lead to the conclusion that Luke likely writes both his gospel and the book of Acts in chronological order.

Chapter 3 addressed objective 4 and investigated the narrative sequence of Luke's gospel. I have divided the Gospel into separate narrative accounts; studied, compared them with their parallel accounts in the gospels of Matthew and Mark (if there is any) and categorized them. The investigation shows that Luke has separated his gospel into twelve sections by means of eleven summary account statements (1:80; 2:40, 2:52; 3:19–20; 4:14–15, 4:42–44; 8:1–3; 9:51–52a; 19:45–48; 21:37–22:6 and 24:44–49) and has recorded them in overlapping chronological order. That is, Luke seems to have structured these sections so that each section has a common subject(s) of discussion with the section immediately before and after it. At the end of each section there is a summary account statement, which serves as a brief summary ending that section, and most of the time also giving a preview of the next section. Its implied time frame overlaps the time frame of the immediately following section. Luke's writing technique of overlapping chronology at the end of each section seems to be the technique suggested by Lucian, a contemporary of Luke, for writing of histories: when a historian "has finished the first topic he will introduce the second, fastened to it and linked with it like a chain, . . . the first and second topics must not merely be neighbors but have common matter and overlap" (Lucian, 1999:67).

Furthermore, out of the 110 narrative accounts identified in the Gospel, 99 of them (90%) I have observed to be chronological. The writing order for the remaining 11 accounts (10%) cannot be ascertained because: (1) Luke has not provided adequate temporal and locational indicators to facilitate the determination of the writing order and (2) there is no parallel account in Matthew and Mark or the information in the parallel account is not adequate for determining the writing order. However, there is no indication that these 11 accounts are not recorded in chronological order. I also notice that 9 out of the above 11 accounts are from section 9:52(b)-19:48, which describes Jesus' final journey to Jerusalem, due to the fact that Luke has included many unique accounts which have no parallel in other synoptic gospels and which also have no clear locational or temporal information. Because of the difficulty in ascertaining the writing order, a chronological order for this section is questioned by many scholars. For example, Bock (2004, vol.2:959–961), Strauss (1995:272) and Bebb (1911–1912:171) all have reservations about a chronological order. However, the findings in chapter 3 suggest that the events of 9:52(b)-19:48 are probably recorded in chronological order. I notice that Luke has utilized fewer temporal and/or locational indicators in three consecutive sections 5:1–8:3, 8:4–9:52(a) and 9:52(b)-19:48, and has likely employed the same writing style for these sections. As my findings indicate that sections 5:1–8:3 and 8:4–9:52(a) are very likely written in chronological order, as a result it is reasonable to believe that section 9:52(b)-19:48 is also written in that same order. Moreover, the chronological order of 9:52(b)-19:48 seems to be supported by John chapters 7–12, which is believed by scholars such as Thomas and Gundry to be in chronological order (1988:127–174, as evident from their ordering of events for this section), the route Jesus takes to Jerusalem therein seemingly to match that described in 9:52(b)-19:48.

The findings of chapter 3 enrich those in chapter 2 in the sense that they do not only support the argument that the Gospel is written in chronological order, but further indicate that καθεξῆς very likely means the twelve sections identified in the Gospel are written in chronological order, or all the 110 narrative accounts identified are written in chronological order, or both.

Chapter 4 addressed objective 5 and investigated whether the writing technique of overlapping summary statement, which is frequently employed by Luke in his gospel, is also commonly used by Greco-Roman and Jewish historians. The results of this study indicate that Greco-Roman and Jewish historians frequently use this technique to thread together sections. The results agree with other scholarly observations that summaries are frequently used by historians in the past to conclude or introduce sections, or as transitions (e.g., Aune [1987:54], Dibelius [quoted by Hume {2011:7}]). The overlapping summary statements found in the Greco-Roman and Jewish historian writings share similar characteristics with those of Luke in his gospel: (a) they serve as final notes of the sections, and sometimes include summaries for the events described in the previous sections; (b) the statements frequently include previews of the next immediate sections; (c) if the statements are used as summaries for the events of the preceding sections, the time frames involved in the statements overlap the time frames of the events described in their preceding sections (or the time frames of the statements overlap those of the events described in their upcoming sections when the statements are used as or include a preview of the upcoming sections). Besides the above common features, Luke's overlapping summary statements are found to be unique in the following two ways: (a) sometimes they include Jesus' sayings which carry important theological themes (see Luke 4:43, 19:46 and 24:46–47), and (b) sometimes they tend to be expansions of the current narratives, and include new information not discussed both in the current and the upcoming sections, and its time frame involved overlapping the events in the upcoming section. The findings in this chapter support the fact that Luke writes as a historian and adopts the writing techniques and methodologies of Greco-Roman and Jewish historians when writing his gospel. These findings further support the argument in chapter 2 that even if the results of the study of the word καθεξῆς in Luke 1:3 are somehow incorrect and do not indicate any particular writing order, Luke still would have followed the writing methodology of Greco-Roman and Jewish historians and write his gospel in chronological order.

5.1 THEOLOGICAL REFLECTION

As I have mentioned at the beginning of chapter 1 and at the ends of chapters 2 and 3, the type of writing order will affect our approach to understanding Luke's gospel. If the Gospel is written in chronological order, a study of the chronology may be important to understand the Gospel as a whole, and when we study a particular event, attention may have to be paid also to the previous narrative accounts, as these accounts may provide additional background information, particularly regarding timing, for the event under study. But if the Gospel is written in a logical order, a study of the logic Luke uses for the book may be the key to understand the Gospel as a whole, and to study a particular narrative account we may have to study the reason why Luke places that account in that particular position in his Gospel and what relevance that account has to Luke's overall logic.

The evidences in this thesis show that Luke's gospel is very likely written in chronological order. When we want to study a particular subject, a study of chronology related to the subject in the Gospel may give us insights for that subject. For example, if we want to know more about the steps Christian missionaries should consider initially when they arrive at a society foreign to them, we may refer to the Gospel's first five sections: 1:1–3:20, 3:21–4:15, 4:16–4:44, 5:1–8:3 and 8:4–9:52(a). The first section (1:1–3:20) conveys the importance of contextualization: to present the Gospel in culturally relevant ways. One of the reasons why Jesus has to be born as a human being is to communicate to us human beings in the ways we can understand. The second section describes the importance of the power of the Holy Spirit, which every Christian missionary should acquire for effective ministries, and this, together with total submission to God's words (4:4, 8 and 12), is the way to overcome temptations. The following three sections seem to describe the three phases of Jesus' ministry in Galilee, the first of the many places where God's good news has to be penetrated: in phase one (4:16–4:44) Jesus ministers alone while at the same time trying to find a base; in phase two (5:1–8:3) after Jesus has found a base in Capernaum, he begins to build a core ministry team and train them while continuing his ministry; and phase three (8:4-9:52[a]) seems to describe that Jesus' core team (the twelve apostles in 8:1) and extended support team (a group of women in 8:2-3) have already been well established, and Jesus continues to train his team while he ministers, up to the point when they are ready to minister independently (9:1-6, 9:10). Consequently, the mission model in Luke 1:1-9:52(a) seems to be: contextualization => acquire the power of the Holy Spirit => find a base => build a core team => train the core team to minister independently. Thus, the chronological sequence in Luke's gospel is a helpful guide for chronological sequence in ministry today.

Based on my observation in 3.3.3.26 the overall theme of Luke's gospel and Acts very likely is Luke 24:46-47 ("the Christ should suffer and rise from the dead on the third day, and repentance into remission of sins should be preached in his name to all the nations"). Luke has described the key elements of the theme in his gospel and Acts according to their sequence in Luke 24:46-47 (which are also in chronological order): Luke conveys the message that Jesus is Christ throughout his gospel (e.g., through his miraculous birth, the extraordinary messages he gives, the miracles he performs), then Luke describes Jesus' suffering during the trial in Jerusalem and on the cross, his death and resurrection, and in the book of Acts the gospel is preached to all nations. Seemingly Luke's chronological arrangement of the key elements in the theme is to enable the reader of his gospel, Theophilus, to have certainty of the things he has been taught (Luke 1:4).

The chronological writing order of the Gospel may also shed light on the writing orders of other synoptic gospels. It may help us understand more about the arrangements of the narrative accounts in other gospels and the purposes for these arrangements. For example, evidence shows that Matthew seems to have a tendency to relocate and combine traditions while apparently Mark records almost all of the events, besides a few episodes (e.g., Mark 4:1-33), according to their actual sequence. If this is the case, why does Matthew have to relocate and combine tradition and what is the purpose behind it? Does Matthew do this solely to emphasize certain themes? If so, what are these themes and why are they so important? And what is the overall theme of Matthew's gospel? Regarding Mark's gospel, why does he rearrange some of the events but not the others; what is the logic behind Mark's overall arrangement of his gospel? Luke's chronology also shed light on the sequencing of events in the Gospel of John and the book of Acts, which, if given more careful thought, would likely give us new insights in understanding these two books.

Another point worthy of our attention is Luke's attitude of giving his best when composing his Gospel. Evidences show that Luke has carefully adopted the writing methodologies of the most renowned Greco-Roman and Jewish historians in his time when he writes his gospel. He writes as a historian and uses the best writing methodologies he knows to convey carefully the information which he has closely followed for some time to his reader Theophilus, so that he may have the certainty of the things he has been taught (Luke 1:4). His zeal and passion and his great effort to pass on the most accurate information he knows in the best way he could should not be ignored by today's readers.

Annexure 2.1

Sentence Flow and Translation of Luke 1:1–4

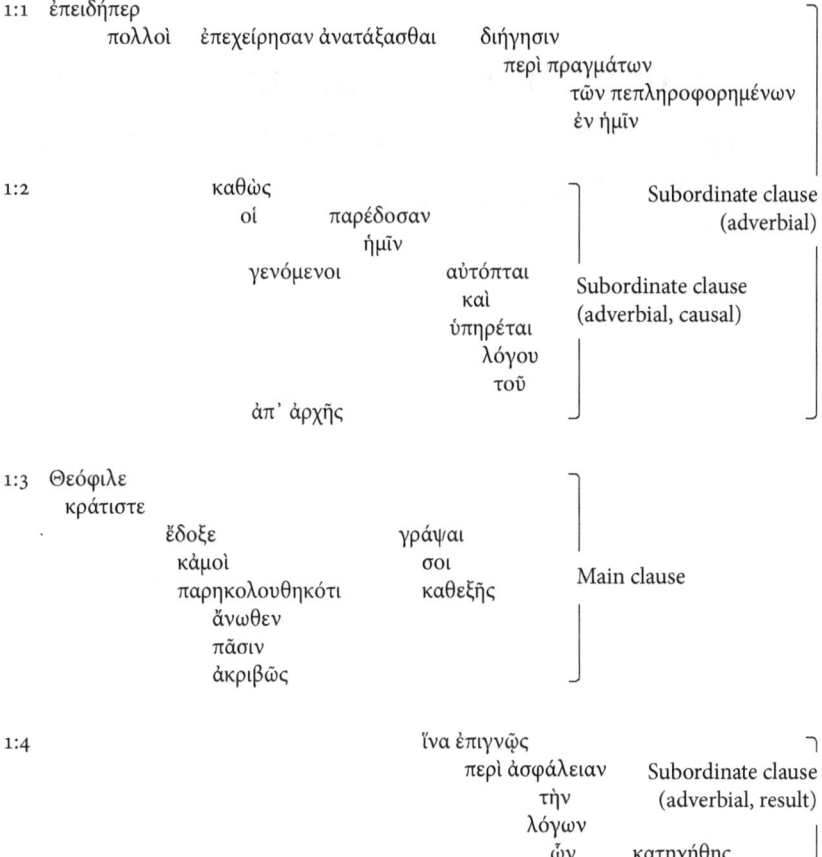

My translation: "Inasmuch as many have attempted to compile a narrative concerning the things having been accomplished among us, just as those who are from the beginning eyewitnesses and servants of the Word have delivered to us, it seemed best also to me, after having followed from the beginning in all things carefully, to write to you in an orderly account, most excellent Theophilus, in order that you may know exactly about the certainty of the words of which you have been informed."

Annexure 2.2

Analysis of the Components Used by Greco-Roman Historians in the Prefaces of their First Books

ANNEXURE 2.2: ANALYSIS OF THE COMPONENTS USED   227

Components in the Preface of the Historian's First Book

Historian (Writing)	Description of Content (1)	Description of Reason for Writing (2)	Description of Methodology of Writing (3)	Description of Expected Results (4)	Order of components (Subordinate Clause or Independent Clause comes first?)
Herodotus (*The Persian War*)	The long explanation in 1:1–5 serves as an explanation of what Herodotus will write and as background information on the war between the Greeks and the Persians. (1:1 - "The Persian learned men say that the Phoenicians were the cause of the feud …")	*Pers. wars* 1.1: "in order that the memory of the past may not be blotted out from among men by time, and that great and marvelous deeds done by Greeks and foreigners and especially the reason why they warred against each other may not lack renown."	*Pers. wars* 1.1: "What Herodotus the Halicarnassian has learnt by inquiry is here set forth …" (methodology for collecting information) *Pers. wars* 1.5: "I should proceed at once to point out the person who first within my knowledge inflicted injury on the Greeks, after which I shall go forward with my history, describing equally the greater and the lesser cities of men." (the writing order)	None	3-2-1-3 (subordinate)

Annexure 2.2: Analysis of the Components Used

Components in the Preface of the Historian's First Book

Historian (Writing)	Description of Content (1)	Description of Reason for Writing (2)	Description of Methodology of Writing (3)	Description of Expected Results (4)	Order of components (Subordinate Clause or Independent Clause comes first?)
Thucydides (*History of the Peloponnesian War*)	*Pel. war* 1.1: "Thucydides, an Athenian, wrote the history of the war waged by the Peloponnesians and the Athenians against one another"	*Pel. war* 1.1: "in the belief that it would be great and noteworthy above all the wars that had gone before . . . For this was the greatest movement that had ever stirred the Hellenes, extending also to some of the barbarians, one might say even to a very large part of mankind."	*Pel. war* 1.1: "He began the task at the very outset of the war (from the very beginning) . . . . . . but from the evidence which, on pushing my inquiries to the furthest point" (methodology for collecting information)	None	1–3–2–3 (independent)

ANNEXURE 2.2: ANALYSIS OF THE COMPONENTS USED   229

Components in the Preface of the Historian's First Book

Historian (Writing)	Description of Content (1)	Description of Reason for Writing (2)	Description of Methodology of Writing (3)	Description of Expected Results (4)	Order of components (Subordinate Clause or Independent Clause comes first?)
Polybius (*The Histories*)	*Hist.* 1.1: "... under what system of polity the Romans in less than fifty-three years have succeeded in subjecting nearly the whole inhabited world to their sole government- a thing unique in history"	Extracts from *Hist.* 1.1-2: "But all historians ... have impressed on us that the soundest education and training for a life of active politics is the study of history, and that the surest and indeed the only method of learning how to bear bravely the vicissitudes of fortune, is to recall the calamities of others." *Hist.* 1.4. – no one has ever tried to write a general history before.	*Hist.* 1.3: "The date from which I propose to begin is the 140th Olympiad, and the events are the following ..."(the writing order) *Hist.* 1.5: "I shall adopt as the starting-point of this book the first occasion on which the Romans crossed the sea from Italy. This follows immediately on the close of Timaeus' History and took place in the 129th Olympiad. Thus we must first state how and when the Romans established their position in Italy, and what prompted them afterwards to cross to Sicily, the first country outside Italy where they set foot ..." (the writing order)	*Hist.* 1.1: "For the very element of unexpectedness in the events I have chosen as my theme will be sufficient to challenge and incite everyone, young and old alike, to peruse my systematic history."	2-4-1-2-3-2-3 (subordinate)

Components in the Preface of the Historian's First Book

Historian (Writing)	Description of Content (1)	Description of Reason for Writing (2)	Description of Methodology of Writing (3)	Description of Expected Results (4)	Order of components (Subordinate Clause or Independent Clause comes first?
Philostratus (*The Life of Apollonius of Tyana*)	*Life Apoll.* 1.2: Philostratus is going to write about Apollonius *Life Apoll.* 1.2: "but write a true account of the man, detailing the exact times at which he said or did this or that, as also the habits and temper of wisdom by means of which he succeeded in being considered a supernatural and divine being."	*Life Apoll.* 1.2: "It seems to me then that I ought not to condone or acquiesce in the general ignorance, but write a true account of the man"	*Life Apoll.* 1.2–3: "And I have gathered my information partly from the many cities where he was loved, and partly from the temples whose long-neglected and decayed rites he restored, and partly from the accounts left of him by others and partly from his own letters…There was a man, Damis, by no means stupid, who formerly dwelt in the ancient city of Nineveh. He resorted to Apollonius in order to study wisdom, and having shared, by his own account, his wanderings abroad, wrote an account of them. And he records his opinions and discourses and all his prophecies . . . ." (the source materials used)	*Life Apoll.* 1.3: "but let my work, I pray, rebound to the honor of the man who is the subject of my compilation, and also be of use to those who love learning. For assuredly, they will here learn things of which as yet they were ignorant."	1–2–1–3–4 (subordinate)

ANNEXURE 2.2: ANALYSIS OF THE COMPONENTS USED   231

Components in the Preface of the Historian's First Book

Historian (Writing)	Description of Content (1)	Description of Reason for Writing (2)	Description of Methodology of Writing (3)	Description of Expected Results (4)	Order of components (Subordinate Clause or Independent Clause comes first?)
Josephus (*Jewish Antiquities*)	In *Ant.* 1.2.6 he says he will describe the origin of the Jews and their history.	*Ant.* 1.1: "... others again have been constrained by the mere stress of events in which they themselves took part to set these out in a comprehensive narrative; while many have been induced by prevailing ignorance of importance affairs of general utility to publish a history of them for the public benefit. Of the aforesaid motives the two last apply to myself..."	*Ant.* 1.3: "I have promised to follow throughout this work (the Hebrew and the Greek Scriptures), neither adding nor omitting anything..." (faithful to the Scripture – attitude of writing) In *Ant.* 1.4 Josephus then continues to describe in what order he will write: he will speak about Moses, etc. (the writing order).	*Ant.* 1.3: "the main lesson to be learnt from this history ... is that men who conform to the will of God, and do not venture to transgress laws that have been excellently laid down, prosper in all things beyond belief, and for their reward are offered by God felicity"	2-1-4-3 (independent)

232 ANNEXURE 2.2: ANALYSIS OF THE COMPONENTS USED

Components in the Preface of the Historian's First Book

Historian (Writing)	Description of Content (1)	Description of Reason for Writing (2)	Description of Methodology of Writing (3)	Description of Expected Results (4)	Order of components (Subordinate Clause or Independent Clause comes first?)
Josephus (*The Jewish War*)	J.W. 1.1.1: He will write about the Jewish war with the Romans.	J.W. 1.1.3: "to provide the subjects of the Roman Empire with a narrative of facts, by translating into Greek the account which I previously composed in my vernacular tongue and sent to the barbarians in the interior."	J.W. 1.1.3: He writes as a participant at the beginning and subsequently an onlooker (indicate the methodology of collecting information). J.W. 1.7–12: describes the writing order of all 7 books: from how Antiochus took over Jerusalem and was later expelled by the Hasmonaeans; then how the Hasmonaeans were overthrown by Herod; then how the war began after Herod's death, then how the Jews fortified their towns, then how the Roman General Vespasian and his son Titus penetrated into Galilee, then how the Romans advanced against Jerusalem and how Jerusalem eventually fell. (the writing order)	None	1-3-2-3 (subordinate)

ANNEXURE 2.2: ANALYSIS OF THE COMPONENTS USED   233

Components in the Preface of the Historian's First Book

Historian (Writing)	Description of Content (1)	Description of Reason for Writing (2)	Description of Methodology of Writing (3)	Description of Expected Results (4)	Order of components (Subordinate Clause or Independent Clause comes first?)
Josephus (*Against Apion*)	*Ag. Ap.* 1.1.3: "I consider it my duty to devote a brief treatise to all these points...."	*Ag. Ap.* 1.1.2–3: "I observe that a considerable number of persons, influenced by the malicious calumnies of certain individuals, discredit the statements in my history concerning our antiquity, and adduce as proof of the comparative modernity of our race the fact that it has not been thought worthy of mention by the best known Greek historians, I consider it my duty to devote a brief treatise to all these parties; in order at once to convict our detractors of malignity and deliberate falsehood, to correct the ignorance of others, and to instruct all who desire to know the truth concerning the antiquity of our race."	*Ag. Ap.* 1.1.3: "As witnesses to my statement I propose to call the writers who, in the estimation of the Greeks, are the most trustworthy authorities on antiquity on a whole. The authors of scurrilous and mendacious statements about us will be shown to be confuted by themselves. I shall further endeavour to set out the various reasons which explain why our nation is mentioned by a few only of the Greek historians; at the same time I shall bring those authors who have not neglected our history to the notice of any who either are, or feign to be, ignorant of them." (the writing order)	None	2–1–3 (independent)

Annexure 2.3

Textual Analysis for the Preface of the Book of Acts

The objective of this annexure is to study the textual variation units in the preface of the book of Acts and to establish the original Greek text. There is only one variant mentioned by UBS4, which is an insertion found in some manuscripts in verse 2. The first variant ἡμέρας . . . ἀνελήμφθη ("the day . . . he was taken up") (used by USB4) as text is supported by P74^{vid}, ℵ, A, B, C^{vid}, E, Ψ, 33, 36, 81, 181, 307, 453, 610, 614, 945, 1175, 1409, 1678, 1739, 1891, 2344, the majority of Byzantine witnesses, the majority of the lectionaries, it$^{c, dem, e, p, ph, ro, w}$, vulgate, syr^h, arm, eth, geo, slav, and church fathers Basil, Chrysostom, Severian and Nestorius. The second variant ἡμέρας ἀνελήμφθη . . . καὶ ἐκέλευσεν κηρύσσειν τὸ εὐαγγέλιον ("the day he was taken up . . . and he ordered to preach the gospel") is supported by D, it$^{(ar), d, (gig), (t)}$, (vg^{mss}), syr^{hmg}, (cop$^{sa, meg}$), and church fathers Augustine and Varimadum. The manuscripts which support the first variant have a much wider variety of text types, which means that they are probably composed and used in different areas of the ancient world. Just to name a few: p74, ℵ, A, B, C, 33 and 1739 are of the highest quality Alexandrian text type, while 614 is of Western text type and E is of Byzantine text type. On the contrary, the second variant has mainly Western text types which are inferior in quality as compared with the Alexandrian text type and are substantially composed and used in limited areas of the world (mostly Gaul, Italy and North Africa) in the past. Moreover, ℵ and B, which support the first variant, are the earliest witnesses (4th century). Since the first variant is derived from manuscripts which are of higher quality and are composed at earlier dates, and the manuscripts were composed and circulated in a much wider region in the ancient world, I prefer the first variant to the second variant. As Western text types are known for their free addition to and omission from the original text (see Metzger and Ehrman, 2005:277), the insertion is probably a free addition by the scribes to emphasize the importance of evangelism.

Other than the variant mentioned above, NA27 also mentions seven more variants in the preface. In verse 1 witnesses B and D omit the article ὁ ("the") before Ἰησοῦς ("Jesus") while other witnesses such as p56, ℵ, A, E, Ψ, 33, 81, 323, 614, 945, 1175, 1241, 1505, 1739 all have the article ὁ. B (4th century) is an Alexandrian text type and D (5th) is a Western text type, while among the witnesses supporting the variant with the article ℵ is one of the earliest witnesses (4th century) and is an Alexandrian text type. Moreover, the witnesses supporting the variant with the article are more numerous and have a wider variety of text types: Alexandrian (p56, ℵ, A, 33, 81, 1175, 1739), Byzantine (E, Ψ), Caesarean (323, 945, 1505), and Western (614, 1421). Therefore, the variant with the article is preferred. According to Metzger (1994:236), B and D "were probably impressed by . . . the circumstance that this is the first instance of Ἰησοῦς in the book of Acts, . . . according to Attic Greek standards, would not call for the use of the article."

In verse 4, there are three variation units. In the first unit, the first variant συναλιζόμενος ("after gathering together") is supported by NA27 and the majority of witnesses including p56, p74, ℵ (4th), A, B (4th), C, 33, 81, 1175 which are Alexandrian text types, E, Ψ which are Byzantine text types, and 945, 1505 which are Caesarean text types. The second variant is supported by D* (Western, 5th) which reads συναλισκομενος ("after taking captive"). The third variant is supported by 1739 (Alexandrian, 11th), two Western texts (614, 1241) and a Caesarean text (323) and reads συναυλιζομενος ("after spending the night with"). As compared with the second and the third variants, the first variant has the support of the earliest Alexandrian texts (ℵ and B) and the support from more witnesses with different text types; therefore it is preferable. The second variant probably is a copying error while the third variant is probably a free adjustment towards the original text by a scribe in the Western part of the Roman Empire. In the second variation unit in verse 4, the first variant is supported by NA27 and by almost all witnesses and it omits μετ' αὐτῶν ("with them"), while variant two is supported by Western text types D, *it* and *sy* and has an insertion μετ' αὐτῶν after συναλιζόμενος. The first variant is preferred because the witnesses supporting it are earlier (ℵ and B are both from the 4th century), have higher quality and have more text types; μετ' αὐτῶν in variant two is probably a free addition. In the third variation unit in verse 4, the first variant is supported by NA27 and the majority of witnesses which omits φησὶν διὰ τοῦ στόματός μου ("he said through my mouth"); while the second variant is supported by D and some Vulgate witnesses which are Western text types and it reads φησὶν διὰ τοῦ στόματός μου. The first variant is preferred because the witnesses supporting it are earlier, have higher quality and have more text types, while the second variant is probably a free adjustment to the original text by a scribe in the West.

In verse 5 there are three variation units. In the first unit the first variant is supported by NA27 and Alexandrian text type witnesses such as ℵ (4th), B (4th) and 81, and reads ἐν πνεύματι βαπτισθήσεσθε ἁγίῳ ("in the Holy Spirit you will be baptized"). The second variant is supported by Alexandrian text type witnesses such as ρ74, A (5th), C (5th), 33, 1739, and Byzantine text type witnesses such as E, Ψ, and Western text type witnesses such as the Vulgate, and church fathers Origen and Cyril of Alexandria, and reads βαπτισθήσεσθε ἐν πνεύματι ἁγίῳ ("you will be baptized in the Holy Spirit"); the third variant is supported by two Western texts, D and *it*, and reads ἐν πνεύματι ἁγίῳ βαπτισθήσεσθε ("in the Holy Spirit you will be baptized"). It is difficult to choose between variants one and two because of the high quality of the witnesses supporting them while the third variant obviously has much inferior text quality. The first variant is preferred because the two earliest Alexandrian texts support it. In the second variation unit the first variant is supported by NA27 and most witnesses, and reads ἐν πνεύματι βαπτισθήσεσθε ἁγίῳ ('in the Holy Spirit you will be baptized'), while the second variant is supported by Western text type witness D and Augustine, and adds καὶ ὃ μέλλετε λαμβάνειν ("also what you are about to receive") after ἐν πνεύματι βαπτισθήσεσθε ἁγίῳ. The first variant is preferred because the witnesses supporting it are earlier, have higher quality and have more variety of text types; and the second variant is probably a free addition by a Western scribe to smooth syntax. In the third variation unit in verse 5 the first variant is supported by NA27 and most witnesses, and reads οὐ μετὰ πολλὰς ταύτας ἡμέρας ("not after many these days"), while the second variant is supported by a few witnesses including Western text type D* and it adds ἕως τῆς πεντηκοστῆς ("until the Pentecost") after the above phrase. The first variant is preferred because its supporting witnesses are earlier and have higher quality and more text types. The second variant is probably a free addition by a Western scribe.

In conclusion, the texts in USB4 and NA27 are preferred as the original text for Acts 1:1–5.

Annexure 2.4

Sentence Flow and Translation of Acts 1:1–5

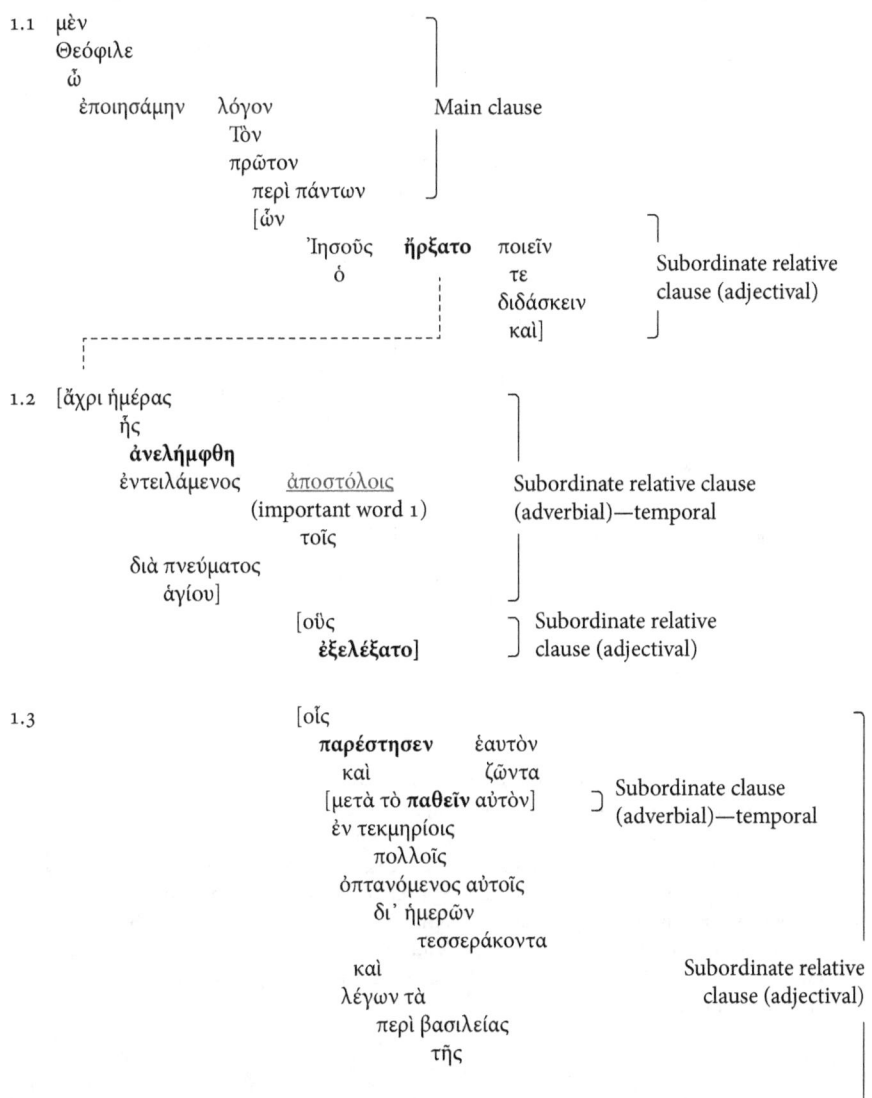

238 ANNEXURE 2.4: SENTENCE FLOW AND TRANSLATION

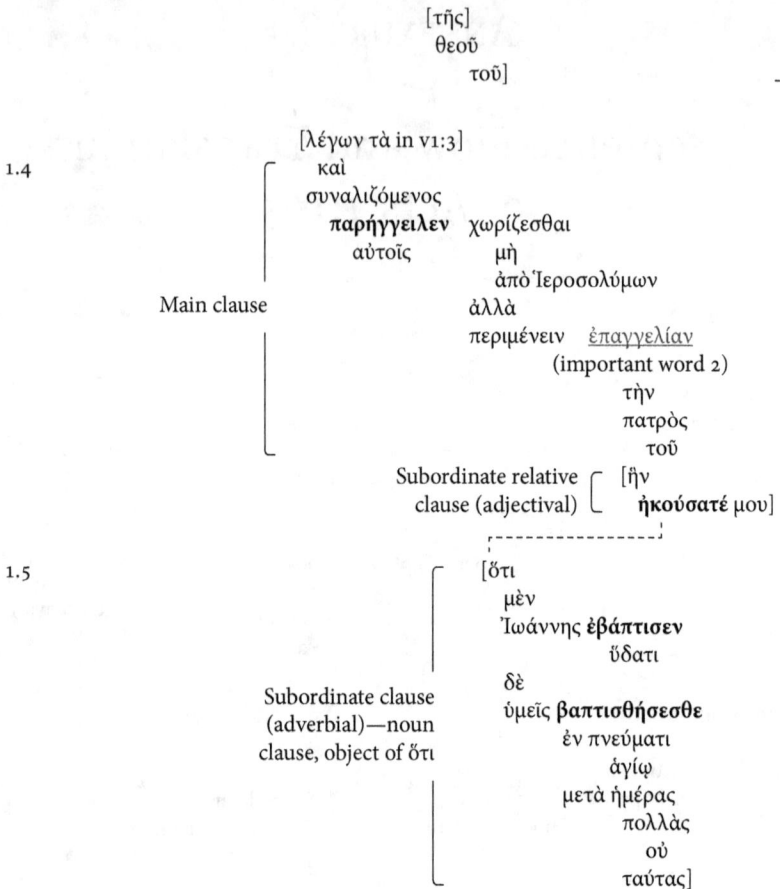

My translation: "Indeed I have produced the first book about all things, O Theophilus, of which Jesus began to do and also to teach, until the day in which he was taken up, after commanding to the apostles through the Holy Spirit whom he had chosen, to whom also he presented himself living after he had suffered by many proofs, through forty days while appearing to them and speaking the things about the kingdom of God; and while being assembled he commanded them 'not to depart from Jerusalem but to wait for the promise of the Father which, (he said), you have heard me, that on one hand John baptized with water, on the other hand you in the Holy Spirit will be baptized not after many these days.'"

ANNEXURE 2.5

Comparison of Acts 1:1–5 with the Gospel of Luke

Annexure 2.5: Comparison with the Gospel of Luke

Acts 1:1–5 (in Greek and RSV)	Corresponding passages in Luke (in Greek and RSV)	Observations
Acts 1:1–2— Τὸν μὲν πρῶτον λόγον ἐποιησάμην περὶ πάντων, ὦ Θεόφιλε, ὧν ἤρξατο ὁ Ἰησοῦς ποιεῖν τε καὶ διδάσκειν, 2 ἄχρι ἧς ἡμέρας ἐντειλάμενος τοῖς ἀποστόλοις διὰ πνεύματος ἁγίου οὓς ἐξελέξατο ἀνελήμφθη.	Luke 1–24—the whole Gospel.	1. Acts 1:1–2 is a brief summary of what Luke has mentioned in his Gospel.
Acts 1:1–2— In the first book, O Theophilus, I have dealt with all that Jesus began to do and teach, 2 until the day when he was taken up, after he had given commandment through the Holy Spirit to the apostles whom he had chosen.		
Acts 1:3— οἷς καὶ παρέστησεν ἑαυτὸν ζῶντα μετὰ τὸ παθεῖν αὐτὸν ἐν πολλοῖς τεκμηρίοις, δι' ἡμερῶν τεσσεράκοντα ὀπτανόμενος αὐτοῖς καὶ λέγων τὰ περὶ τῆς βασιλείας τοῦ θεοῦ	Luke 24—the last chapter of the Gospel.	1. Acts 1:3 is a summary of the various accounts of the resurrected Jesus appearing to the apostles and believers and his message about the kingdom of God in Luke 24.
Acts 1:3— To them he presented himself alive after his passion by many proofs, appearing to them during forty days, and speaking of the kingdom of God		2. The only information Acts has which is not mentioned by the gospel is that Jesus appeared to his apostles for forty days after his resurrection

ANNEXURE 2.5: COMPARISON WITH THE GOSPEL OF LUKE

Acts 1:1–5 (in Greek and RSV)	Corresponding passages in Luke (in Greek and RSV)	Observations
Acts 1:4–5—καὶ συναλιζόμενος παρήγγειλεν αὐτοῖς ἀπὸ Ἱεροσολύμων μὴ χωρίζεσθαι ἀλλὰ περιμένειν τὴν ἐπαγγελίαν τοῦ πατρὸς ἣν ἠκούσατέ μου, 5 ὅτι Ἰωάννης μὲν ἐβάπτισεν ὕδατι, ὑμεῖς δὲ ἐν πνεύματι βαπτισθήσεσθε ἁγίῳ οὐ μετὰ πολλὰς ταύτας ἡμέρας. Acts 1:4–5—And while staying with them he charged them not to depart from Jerusalem, but to wait for the promise of the Father, which, he said, "you heard from me, 5 for John baptized with water, but before many days you shall be baptized with the Holy Spirit."	Luke 24:49—the last verse before the last account in the Gospel: Jesus' ascension καὶ [ἰδοὺ] ἐγὼ ἀποστέλλω τὴν ἐπαγγελίαν τοῦ πατρός μου ἐφ᾽ ὑμᾶς· ὑμεῖς δὲ καθίσατε ἐν τῇ πόλει ἕως οὗ ἐνδύσησθε ἐξ ὕψους δύναμιν. 'And behold, I send the promise of my Father upon you; but stay in the city, until you are clothed with power from on high.'	1. Acts 1:4 and Luke 24:49 are the only two verses in the N.T. which mention τὴν ἐπαγγελίαν τοῦ πατρός ("the promise of the Father"). In Acts 1:4 Jesus says τὴν ἐπαγγελίαν τοῦ πατρὸς ἣν ἠκούσατέ μου ("the promise of the Father which you heard from me"). This indicates that Jesus must have mentioned τὴν ἐπαγγελίαν τοῦ πατρὸς more than once to his apostles. This must be an important message from Jesus. He gives it repeatedly in the limited time he has with the apostles, and Luke mentions it both at the end of his gospel and in the beginning of Acts. 2. Most of Acts 1:4 is Luke's paraphrase of Jesus' saying in Luke 24:49. 3. Jesus' direct discourse starts from ἣν ἠκούσατέ μου in Acts 1:4; this, together with the rest of Jesus' discourse in Acts 1:5, elaborates on ἐνδύσησθε ἐξ ὕψους δύναμιν in Luke 24:49: "Clothed with power from on high" (Luke 24:49) can now be understand as being "baptized with the Holy Spirit" (Acts 1:5). 4. What Jesus says in Acts 1:5 is very similar to what John the Baptist says in Luke 3:16. Jesus may be paraphrasing what John said in Luke 3:16: ἀπεκρίνατο λέγων πᾶσιν ὁ Ἰωάννης· ἐγὼ μὲν ὕδατι βαπτίζω ὑμᾶς· ἔρχεται δὲ ὁ ἰσχυρότερός μου, οὗ οὐκ εἰμὶ ἱκανὸς λῦσαι τὸν ἱμάντα τῶν ὑποδημάτων αὐτοῦ· αὐτὸς ὑμᾶς βαπτίσει ἐν πνεύματι ἁγίῳ καὶ πυρί "John answered them all, 'I baptize you with water; but he who is mightier than I is coming . . . he will baptize you with the Holy Spirit and with fire.'"

Annexure 2.6

Categorization of the Meanings of Καθεξῆς Found in the N.T., the Septuagint, and Contemporary Usages

Biblical/Other Reference	Meaning of καθεξῆς	Category (usage to describe...)
Luke 8:1	Following (days)—describes the time frame in which the event in 8:1 happened - in the period of time immediately after the event of 7:36–50.	Sequence—time
Acts 3:24	Following (prophets)—describes the prophets who come after Samuel in order of their appearance in history, probably refers to chronological order.	Sequence—time
Acts 11:4	Chronological order - Paul explains the events in the order in which they happened.	Sequence—time

Annexure 2.6: Categorization of the Meanings of Καθεξῆς

Biblical/Other Reference	Meaning of καθεξῆς	Category (usage to describe...)
Cynegetica 3.59	Chronological order of the number of cubs born in each pregnancy—describes the number of cubs, which is decreasing from five to four, four to three, three to two and two to one.	Sequence—time
Historical Miscellany 8:7	Successive (days)—describes how the five days of a large wedding are organized: they are successive, in a row. It refers to chronological order.	Sequence—time
Fragmenta	The meaning of καθεξῆς is unclear in the text, but if it refers to the sequence the context has described earlier, it probably means chronological order.	Sequence—time
ApcMos 8	The 72 different body parts of Adam upon which God's punishments will fall. Likely in a chronological manner.	Sequence—time
MarPol 22:3	Sequel of a book—describes the next book the author will write.	Sequence—spatial
Acts 18:23	Increasing numerical order of spatial distance—in an order of cities with increasing geographical distance from Antioch.	Sequence—spatial
Moralia 2.615b	Sequential order of the people sitting on the same couch: from the first person on a couch to the second one on the same couch to the third one and so on until the last person on the couch is reached.	Sequence—spatial
Vita Aesopi Westermanniana	The appropriate locations for the subjects to be placed. Some kind of spatial order.	Sequence - spatial
Geodaesia	In sequential order—the size of land which can be sown with respect to the increasing number of litres used.	Sequence—spatial

ANNEXURE 2.6: CATEGORIZATION OF THE MEANINGS OF Καθεξῆς

Biblical/Other Reference	Meaning of καθεξῆς	Category (usage to describe...)
Testjud 25:1	In sequence order of importance in God's view - the order of the twelve patriarchs according to how blessed (by God) they are; the most blessed comes first, down to the least blessed.	Sequence—hierarchy of significance
1 Clement 37:3	In decreasing number of soldiers commanded—in an order beginning with those who command more soldiers down to those who command fewer.	Sequence—hierarchy of significance
IGR IV 1432,9	In sequential order—the order of winners of contests: champion, first runner-up, second-runner up, etc.	Sequence—hierarchy of significance
Strategicus	A logical sequence describing the method of interviewing people. The sequence is likely one of hierarchy of significance.	Sequence—hierarchy of significance

Annexure 2.7

Categorization of the Meanings of Ἑξῆς Found in the N.T. and the Septuagint

Biblical Reference	Meaning of ἑξῆς	Usage to describe...
Luke 7:11	Next (time) or soon afterwards—describes when the event in 7:11 happened—soon after the event described in 7:1-10 (Jesus healing the servant of a centurion).	Time
Luke 9:37	Next (day)—describes the time when the event in 9:37 happened—on the next day of 9:28-36 (Jesus' transfiguration)	Time
Acts 21:1b	Next (day)—describes the itinerary of one of Paul's missionary trips	Time
Acts 25:17	Next (day)—Governor Festus says that he has dealt with Paul's case promptly, on the next day after he receives a complaint from the Jewish leaders.	Time

Annexure 2.7: Categorization of the Meanings of Ἑξῆς

Biblical Reference	Meaning of ἑξῆς	Usage to describe...
Acts 27:18	Next (day)—the people on the boat begin to throw the cargo overboard on the *next day* after they encounter a storm	Time
Exod 10:1	Next (plagues)—describes the remaining three plagues the Egyptians will face in a time sequence	Time
2 Macc 7:8	Next (death)—describes the death of the seven brothers killed by King Antiochus in a time sequence	Time
Deut 2:34	(City) in succession—describes the spatial sequence for the cities which are destroyed by the Israelites	Spatial
Deut 3:6	(City) in succession—same as above	Spatial
Judg 20:48	(City) in succession—same as above	Spatial
3 Macc 1:9	Next (acts)—describes the hierarchy of significance of the acts performed by Ptolemy	Hierarchy of significance

ANNEXURE 3.1

Harmony of the Narrative Accounts in the Synoptic Gospels

ANNEXURE 3.1: NARRATIVE ACCOUNTS IN THE SYNOPTIC GOSPELS

	Narrative Description	Luke[1]	Category[2]	Writing Order[2]	Time[2]	Matthew	Mark[3]
1	The birth of John the Baptist foretold to Zechariah	1:5–25	1	C[4]	Between 37 to 4 B.C.	—	—
2	Jesus' birth foretold to Mary	1:26–38	1	C	In the sixth month of Elizabeth's pregnancy	—	—
3	Mary's visit to Elizabeth, Elizabeth and Mary's songs	1:39–56	1	C	After the "Jesus' birth foretold to Mary" account	—	—
4	Birth of John the Baptist	1:57–80	1	C (Overlapping chronology is used in 1:80)	When Elizabeth's baby is born	—	—
5	Circumstances of Jesus' birth explained to Joseph	—	—	—	—	1:18–25	—
6	Jesus' birth and the shepherds' encounter with the angels	2:1–20	1	C	Between 30 B.C. to 19th August A.D. 14	—	—
7	Jesus' circumcision	2:21	1	C	On the eighth day after Jesus is born	—	—

ANNEXURE 3.1: NARRATIVE ACCOUNTS IN THE SYNOPTIC GOSPELS

	Narrative Description	Luke[1]	Category[2]	Writing Order[2]	Time[2]	Matthew	Mark[3]
8	Jesus is presented in the temple and receives the homage of Simeon and Anna, and the family returns to Nazareth	2:22–40	1	C (overlapping chronology is used in 2:40)	About 33 days after Jesus' circumcision	—	—
9	Visit of the magi from the East, the escape of Joseph's family to Egypt, Herod's killing of the boys in Bethlehem and in its vicinity, and the return of Joseph's family to Israel after Herod's death	—	—		—	2:1–23	—
10	Jesus' Passover in Jerusalem as a child	2:41–52	1	C (overlapping chronology is used in 2:52)	When Jesus is twelve years old	—	—
11	The public ministry of John the Baptist	3:1–20	1	C (overlapping chronology is used in 3:19–20)	A.D. 28–29	3:1–12	1:2–8

250 ANNEXURE 3.1: NARRATIVE ACCOUNTS IN THE SYNOPTIC GOSPELS

	Narrative Description	Luke[1]	Category[2]	Writing Order[2]	Time[2]	Matthew	Mark[3]
12	Jesus' baptism	3:21–23a	1	C	When Jesus is about thirty years old	3:13–17	1:9–11
13	Jesus' ministry begins	3:23b–38	N/A[5]	T	N/A[5]	1:1–17	—
14	Jesus' temptation in the desert	4:1–15	1	C (overlapping chronology is used in 4:15)	After Jesus' baptism	4:1–11	1:12–13
15	Ministry and rejection at Nazareth in Galilee	4:16–30	1	C	After Jesus' temptation in the desert	4:12–17	1:14–15
16	Jesus calls four disciples	—	—	—	—	4:18–22	1:16–20
17	Teaching in the synagogue of Capernaum	4:31–37	1	C	After Jesus' ministry at Nazareth	—	1:21–28
18	Healing of Peter's mother-in-law	4:38–39	1	C	After Jesus' teaching at the Capernaum's synagogue	8:14–15	1:29–31
19	Others healed	4:40–44	1	C (overlapping chronology is used in 4:44)	When the sun is setting, probably on the same day that Jesus has healed Peter's mother-in-law	8:16–17, 4:23–25	1:32–39

ANNEXURE 3.1: NARRATIVE ACCOUNTS IN THE SYNOPTIC GOSPELS 251

	Narrative Description	Luke[1]	Category[2]	Writing Order[2]	Time[2]	Matthew	Mark[3]
20	Calling of Peter	5:1–11	1	C	After Jesus has become famous	—	—
21	Sermon on the mount	—	—	—	—	5:1–7:28	—
22	Cleansing a leper	5:12–16	2	C	Shortly after the Sermon on the Mount	8:1–4	1:40–45
23	Forgiving and healing of a paralytic	5:17–26	2	C	Some days after Jesus has cleansed the leper	9:1–8	2:1–12
24	The calling of Matthew, the discussion of fasting and the parables about the old and the new	5:27–39	1	C	After healing the paralytic	9:9–17	2:13–22
25	Controversy over disciples' picking grain on Sabbath	6:1–5	2	C	On a Sabbath day, at about the time when Jesus carries out a mission in Galilee	12:1–8	2:23–28
26	Healing the man with a withered hand	6:6–11	2	C	On another Sabbath day	12:9–14	3:1–6
27	Withdrawal to the Sea of Galilee with large crowds from many places	—	—	—	—	12:15–21	3:7–12

ANNEXURE 3.1: NARRATIVE ACCOUNTS IN THE SYNOPTIC GOSPELS

	Narrative Description	Luke[1]	Category[2]	Writing Order[2]	Time[2]	Matthew	Mark[3]
28	The choosing of the twelve	6:12–16	2	C	At about the time when Jesus heals the man with a withered hand	—	3:13–19
29	Sermon on the plain	6:17–49	1	C	After Jesus has chosen the twelve apostles and after Jesus comes down from a mountain	—	—
30	Healing the centurion's servant	7:1–10	1	C	After the Sermon on the Plain and when Jesus is in Capernaum	8:5–13	—
31	Raising a widow's son at Nain of Galilee	7:11–17	1	C	After healing the centurion's servant	—	—
32	Question from John the Baptist	7:18–35	1	C	After Jesus has raised the widow's son at Nain	11:2–19	—
33	Christ's feet anointed	7:36–50	3	U	Before Jesus travels around to preach the gospel in Galilee with the twelve apostles and with the women who financially provide for Jesus	—	—

ANNEXURE 3.1: NARRATIVE ACCOUNTS IN THE SYNOPTIC GOSPELS 253

	Narrative Description	Luke[1]	Category[2]	Writing Order[2]	Time[2]	Matthew	Mark[3]
34	Jesus preaches in various cities and villages	8:1–3	1	C (overlapping chronology is used in 8:1–3)	After Christ's feet are anointed	—	—
35	Blasphemous accusation by the teachers of the law and Pharisees	—	—	—	—	12:22–37	3:20–30
36	The parable of the soils	8:4–18	1	C	After Christ's feet is anointed when Jesus preaches in various cities and villages	13:1–23	4:1–25
37	Announcement of a new spiritual kinship	8:19–21	3	U	When Jesus is speaking to a crowd	12:46–50	3:31–35
38	The parable of the seed's spontaneous growth	—	—	—	—	—	4:26–29
39	The parable of the weeds	—	—	—	—	13:24–30	—
40	The parable of the mustard tree and the leavened loaf	—	—	—	—	13:31–35	4:30–34

ANNEXURE 3.1: NARRATIVE ACCOUNTS IN THE SYNOPTIC GOSPELS

	Narrative Description	Luke[1]	Category[2]	Writing Order[2]	Time[2]	Matthew	Mark[3]
41	The parable of the weeds explained, the parable of the hidden treasure, the parable of the valuable pearl, the parable of the net and the parable of the house owner	—	—	—	—	13:36–53	—
42	Crossing the lake and calming the storm	8:22–25	2	C	On one of the evenings at about the time when Jesus delivers the parable of the soils to the public	8:18, 23–27	4:35–41
43	Healing the Gerasene demoniacs and resultant opposition	8:26–39	1	C	After Jesus has calmed the storm	8:28–34	5:1–20
44	Return to Galilee, healing of woman who touches Jesus' garment, and raising of Jairus' daughter	8:40–56	1	C	After Jesus has returned from the country of the Gerasenes	9:18–26	5:21–43
45	Three miracles of healing and another blasphemous accusation	—	—	—	—	9:27–34	—
46	Final visit to unbelieving Nazareth	—	—	—	—	13:54–58	6:1–6a

ANNEXURE 3.1: NARRATIVE ACCOUNTS IN THE SYNOPTIC GOSPELS   255

	Narrative Description	Luke[1]	Category[2]	Writing Order[2]	Time[2]	Matthew	Mark[3]
47	Shortage of workers	—	—	—	—	9:35–38	6:6b
48	Commissioning of the twelve	9:1–6	2	C	After the healing of the woman who touched Jesus' garment, and raising of Jairus' daughter	10:1–11:1	6:7–13
49	Herod Antipas hears about Jesus	9:7–9	2	C	Between 4 B. C. and A. D. 39, after Jesus has commissioned the twelve	14:1–2	6:14–16
50	Earlier imprisonment and beheading of John the Baptist	—	—	—	—	14:3–12	6:17–29
51	Withdrawal to Bethsaida and feeding the five thousand	9:10–17	1	C	After the apostles have returned from their mission and very likely after Herod has heard of their mission	14:13–21	6:30–44
52	A premature attempt to make Jesus king blocked	—	—	—	—	14:22–23	6:45–46
53	Walking on the water during a storm on the lake	—	—	—	—	14:24–33	6:47–52
54	Healings at Gennesaret	—	—	—	—	14:34–36	6:53–56

Annexure 3.1: Narrative Accounts in the Synoptic Gospels

	Narrative Description	Luke[1]	Category[2]	Writing Order[2]	Time[2]	Matthew	Mark[3]
55	Conflict over the tradition of ceremonial uncleanness	—	—	—	—	15:1–20	7:1–23
56	Ministry to a believing Greek woman in the region of Tyre and Sidon	—	—	—	—	15:21–28	7:24–30
57	Healings in Decapolis	—	—	—	—	15:29–31	7:31–37
58	Feeding the four thousand in Decapolis	—	—	—	—	15:32–38	8:1–9a
59	Return to Galilee and encounter with the Pharisees and Sadducees	—	—	—	—	15:39–16:4	8:9b–12
60	Warning about the error of the Pharisees, Sadducees, and Herodians	—	—	—	—	16:5–12	8:13–21
61	Healing a blind man at Bethsaida	—	—	—	—	—	8:22–26
62	Peter's identification of Jesus as Christ, Jesus' first explicit prediction of rejection, crucifixion, and resurrection, and Jesus' teaching about following him, his second coming, and judgment	9:18–27	2	C	After Jesus has entered the region of Caesarea Philippi	16:13–28	8:27–9:1

ANNEXURE 3.1: NARRATIVE ACCOUNTS IN THE SYNOPTIC GOSPELS 257

	Narrative Description	Luke[1]	Category[2]	Writing Order[2]	Time[2]	Matthew	Mark[3]
63	Transfiguration of Jesus	9:28–36	1	C	After Peter's confession that Jesus is Christ and Jesus' prediction of his own death and resurrection, and his teaching on following him	17:1–9	9:2–10
64	Discussion of resurrection, Elijah, and John the Baptist	—	—	—	—	17:10–13	9:11–13
65	Healing of demoniac boy and unbelief rebuked	9:37–43a	1	C	The day after Jesus' transfiguration	17:14–21	9:14–29
66	Jesus' second prediction of his death and resurrection	9:43b–45	1	C	After Jesus' healing of the demoniac boy and when he and his disciples are in Galilee	17:22–23	9:30–32
67	Payment of temple tax	—	—	—	—	17:24–27	—
68	Rivalry over greatness in the kingdom	9:46–48	2	C	After Jesus' second prediction of his death and resurrection and when Jesus and his disciples are in Capernaum	18:1–5	9:33–37
69	Apostle John's question	9:49–50	1	C	Just after Jesus finishes teaching on the "rivalry over greatness in the kingdom"	18:6–14	9:38–50

ANNEXURE 3.1: NARRATIVE ACCOUNTS IN THE SYNOPTIC GOSPELS

	Narrative Description	Luke[1]	Category[2]	Writing Order[2]	Time[2]	Matthew	Mark[3]
70	Treatment and forgiveness of a sinning brother	—	—	—	—	18:15–35	—
71	Journey through Samaria	9:51–56	1	C (overlapping chronology is used in 9:51–52(a))	After Jesus has completed his Galilean ministries	—	—
72	Complete commitment required of followers	9:57–62	1	C	After the "journey through Samaria" event, when Jesus is on the way to a village	8:19–22	—
73	Commissioning of the seventy-two	10:1–16	1	C	After the "complete commitment required of followers" event	11:20–24	—
74	Return of the seventy-two	10:17–24	1	C	After the "commissioning of the seventy-two" event	11:25–30	—
75	Story of the good Samaritan	10:25–37	1	C	After the "return of the seventy-two" event	—	—
76	Jesus' visit with Mary and Martha	10:38–42	3	U	When Jesus and his disciples are on their last trip to Jerusalem	—	—
77	Lesson on how to pray and parable of the bold friend	11:1–13	3	U	Not described	—	—

ANNEXURE 3.1: NARRATIVE ACCOUNTS IN THE SYNOPTIC GOSPELS   259

	Narrative Description	Luke[1]	Category[2]	Writing Order[2]	Time[2]	Matthew	Mark[3]
78	Blasphemous accusation and debate	11:14–36	3	U	Not described	12:38–45	—
79	Woes against the Pharisees and teachers of law while eating with a Pharisee	11:37–54	1	C	After the "blasphemous accusation and debate" account	—	—
80	Warning the disciples about hypocrisy	12:1–12	1	C	After the "woes against the Pharisees and teachers of law while eating with a Pharisee" account	—	—
81	Warning about greed and trust in wealth, the coming of the Son of Man, and the coming division	12:13–59	1	C	Just after the "warning the disciples about hypocrisy" event	—	—
82	Two alternatives: repent or perish	13:1–9	1	C	Just after the "warning about greed and trust in wealth, the coming of the Son of Man, and the coming division" event	—	—
83	Opposition from a synagogue ruler for healing a woman on the Sabbath	13:10–21	3	U	On a Sabbath day	—	—
84	Question about salvation and entering the kingdom	13:22–30	3	U	When Jesus is on the way to Jerusalem	—	—

ANNEXURE 3.1: NARRATIVE ACCOUNTS IN THE SYNOPTIC GOSPELS

	Narrative Description	Luke[1]	Category[2]	Writing Order[2]	Time[2]	Matthew	Mark[3]
85	Anticipation of Jesus' coming death and his sorrow over Jerusalem	13:31–35	1	C	Just after the "question about salvation and entering the kingdom" event	—	—
86	Healing of a man with dropsy while Jesus is eating with a prominent Pharisee on the Sabbath, and three parables suggested by the occasion	14:1–24	3	U	On a Sabbath day	—	—
87	Cost of discipleship	14:25–35	3	U	When a great multitude is traveling with Jesus on the way to Jerusalem	—	—
88	Parables in defense of association with sinners	15:1–32	3	U	Not described	—	—
89	Parables teaching the proper use of money	16:1–13	1	C	Just after Jesus' parables in defense of association with sinners	—	—
90	Story teaching the danger of wealth	16:14–31	1	C	Just after Jesus' parables teaching the proper use of money	—	—
91	Four lessons on discipleship	17:1–10	1	C	Likely after the story teaching the danger of wealth	—	—

ANNEXURE 3.1: NARRATIVE ACCOUNTS IN THE SYNOPTIC GOSPELS   261

	Narrative Description	Luke[1]	Category[2]	Writing Order[2]	Time[2]	Matthew	Mark[3]
92	Jesus' healing of ten lepers while passing between Samaria and Galilee	17:11–21	3	U	When Jesus is on the way to Jerusalem traveling along the border between Samaria and Galilee	—	—
93	Instructions regarding the Son of Man's coming	17:22–37	1	C	Likely after Jesus answers the question raised by the Pharisees in Luke 17:20–21	—	—
94	Parables on prayer: the persistent widow, and the Pharisee and the tax collector	18:1–14	1	C	Likely after Jesus has given instructions about the Son of Man's coming	—	—
95	Conflict with Pharisaic teaching on divorce	—	—	—	—	19:1–12	10:1–12
96	Example of little children in relation to the kingdom	18:15–17	1	C	When Jesus is in the region of Judea beyond the Jordan River	19:13–15	10:13–16
97	Riches and the kingdom	18:18–30	2	C	Likely just after the "example of little children in relation to the kingdom" account	19:16–30	10:17–31
98	Parable of the landowner's sovereignty	—	—	—	—	20:1–16	—

ANNEXURE 3.1: NARRATIVE ACCOUNTS IN THE SYNOPTIC GOSPELS

	Narrative Description	Luke[1]	Category[2]	Writing Order[2]	Time[2]	Matthew	Mark[3]
99	Third prediction of Jesus' death and resurrection	18:31–34	2	C	When Jesus is on the way going up to Jerusalem	20:17–19	10:32–34
100	Warning against ambitious pride	—	—	—	—	20:20–28	10:35–45
101	Healing of blind Bartimaeus and his companion	18:35–43	2	C	When Jesus is near Jericho, likely after the "third prediction of Jesus' death and resurrection" event	20:29–34	10:46–52
102	Salvation of Zaccheus	19:1–10	1	C	When Jesus is passing through Jericho	—	—
103	Parable to teach responsibility while the kingdom is delayed	19:11–28	1	C	Very likely after the "salvation of Zaccheus" event	—	—
104	Triumphal entry into Jerusalem	19:29–44	1	C	After Jesus gives the "parable to teach responsibility while the kingdom is delayed" in Jericho	21:1–11, 14–17	11:1–11
105	Cursing of the fig tree having leaves but no figs	—	—	—	—	21:18–19a	11:12–14

ANNEXURE 3.1: NARRATIVE ACCOUNTS IN THE SYNOPTIC GOSPELS

	Narrative Description	Luke[1]	Category[2]	Writing Order[2]	Time[2]	Matthew	Mark[3]
106	Cleansing of the temple	19:45–48	1	C (overlapping chronology is used in 19:47–48)	On the day after Jesus has arrived in Jerusalem	21:12–13	11:15–18
107	Withered fig tree and the lesson on faith	—	—	—	—	21:19b–22	11:19–26
108	Questioning of Jesus' authority by the chief priests, teachers of the law and elders	20:1–8	1	C	After Jesus has cleansed the temple in Jerusalem	21:23–27	11:27–33
109	Parable about a man and his two sons	—	—	—	—	21:28–32	—
110	Jesus' parable of the bad tenants of a vineyard	20:9–19	1	C	After Jesus' authority is questioned	21:33–46	12:1–12
111	Parable about a king who prepares a wedding banquet for his son	—	—	—	—	22:1–14	—
112	Attempts by Pharisees and Herodians to trap Jesus with a question about paying taxes to Caesar	20:20–26	1	C	After the parable of the bad vineyard tenants	22:15–22	12:13–17

ANNEXURE 3.1: NARRATIVE ACCOUNTS IN THE SYNOPTIC GOSPELS

	Narrative Description	Luke[1]	Category[2]	Writing Order[2]	Time[2]	Matthew	Mark[3]
113	Sadducees' puzzling question about the resurrection	20:27–40	2	C	Likely after the attempts by the Pharisees and the Herodians to trap Jesus with a question about paying taxes to Caesar	22:23–33	12:18–27
114	A Pharisee's legal question	—	—	—	—	22:34–40	12:28–34
115	Christ's relationship to David as Son and Lord	20:41–44	1	C	When Jesus is teaching in the temple courts and after the Sadducees' question about resurrection	22:41–46	12:35–37
116	Beware of the teachers of the law	20:45–47	1	C	Likely after the "Christ's relationship to David as Son and Lord" event	23:1–7	12:38–40
117	The seven woes against the teachers of the law and Pharisees	—	—	—	—	23:8–36	—
118	Jesus' sorrow over Jerusalem	—	—	—	—	23:37–39	—
119	A poor widow's gift of all she had	21:1–4	1	C	Likely after the "beware of the teachers of law" account	—	12:41–44

ANNEXURE 3.1: NARRATIVE ACCOUNTS IN THE SYNOPTIC GOSPELS   265

	Narrative Description	Luke[1]	Category[2]	Writing Order[2]	Time[2]	Matthew	Mark[3]
120	The Olivet discourse about the temple and Jesus' second coming	21:5–36	2	C	After Jesus finishes his lengthy teaching and leaves the temple, when he is sitting on the Mount of Olives	24:1–25:30	13:1–37
121	Judgment at the Son of Man's coming	—	—	—	—	25:31–46	—
122	Jesus' last days in Jerusalem and the plot by the Sanhedrin to arrest and kill him	21:37–22:2	1	C (overlapping chronology is used in 22:1–6)	After Jesus' Olivet discourse	26:1–5	14:1–2
123	Mary's anointing of Jesus for burial	—	—	—	—	26:6–13	14:3–9
124	Judas' agreement to betray Jesus	22:3–6	1	C (overlapping chronology is used in 22:1–6)	After the "plot by Sanhedrin to arrest and kill Jesus" account	26:14–16	14:10–11

ANNEXURE 3.1: NARRATIVE ACCOUNTS IN THE SYNOPTIC GOSPELS

	Narrative Description	Luke[1]	Category[2]	Writing Order[2]	Time[2]	Matthew	Mark[3]
125	Preparation for the Passover meal	22:7–13	2	C	On the day of Unleavened Bread, on which the Passover lamb is sacrificed, very likely after "Judas' agreement to betray Jesus" event, apparently as the Passover draws near	26:17–19	14:12–16
126	The Passover meal – the beginning of the meal	22:14–16	1	C	After the preparation for the Passover meal	26:20	14:17
127	The Passover meal – first comment about betrayer	—	—	—	—	26:21–25	14:18–21
128	The Passover meal – Lord's Supper instituted	22:17–20	1	C	Likely at the end of the meal	26:26–29	14:22–25
129	The Passover meal – second comment about betrayer	22:21–23	1	C	After the institution of the Lord's Supper	—	—
130	The Passover meal – discussion among the disciples over greatness	22:24–30	1	C	After the second comment about betrayer	—	—
131	The Passover meal – first prediction of Peter's denial	22:31–38	1	C	Follows the discussion among the disciples over greatness	—	—

ANNEXURE 3.1: NARRATIVE ACCOUNTS IN THE SYNOPTIC GOSPELS 267

	Narrative Description	Luke[1]	Category[2]	Writing Order[2]	Time[2]	Matthew	Mark[3]
132	The Passover meal – second prediction of Peter's denial	—	—	—	—	26:30–35	14:26–31
133	Jesus' three agonized prayers in Gethsemane	22:39–46	1	C	After the Passover meal after Jesus and his disciples have reached the Mount of Olives	26:36–46	14:32–42
134	Jesus betrayed, arrested and forsaken	22:47–53	1	C	After Jesus' prayers in Gethsemane	26:47–56	14:43–52
135	Jesus' trial – Peter's denials	22:54b-62	1	C	After Jesus is betrayed, arrested and forsaken, during the second Jewish phase of Jesus' trial	26:58, 69–75	14:54, 66–72
136	Jesus' trial – second Jewish phase (before Caiaphas and Sanhedrin)[6]	22:54a, 63–65	1	C	Likely in the time period when Peter gives his denials	26:57, 59–68	14:53, 55–65
137	Jesus' trial – third Jewish phase (before the Sanhedrin)	22:66–71	1	C	After the second Jewish phase of Jesus' trial when the day comes	27:1	15:1a
138	Death of Judas Iscariot	—	—	—	—	27:3–10	—

ANNEXURE 3.1: NARRATIVE ACCOUNTS IN THE SYNOPTIC GOSPELS

	Narrative Description	Luke[1]	Category[2]	Writing Order[2]	Time[2]	Matthew	Mark[3]
139	Jesus' trial – first Roman phase (before Pilate)	23:1–5	1	C	After the third Jewish phase of Jesus' trial	27:2, 11–26	15:1b–15
140	Jesus' trial – second Roman phase (before Herod Antipas)	23:6–12	1	C	After the first Roman phase, Pilate sends Jesus to Herod Antipas		
141	Jesus' trial – third Roman phase (before Pilate)	23:13–25	1	C	After the second Roman phase, Herod Antipas sends Jesus back to Pilate		
142	Mockery by the Roman soldiers	—	—	—	—	27:27–30	15:16–19
143	Journey to Golgotha	23:26–33a	1	C	After Pilate has handed Jesus over to the Jewish people to crucify him, after Jesus' trial before Pilate (the third Roman phase)	27:31–34	15:20–23
144	First three hours of crucifixion	23:33b–43	1	C	After Jesus' journey to Golgotha	27:35–44	15:24–32
145	Last three hours of crucifixion	23:44–46	1	C	After the first three hours of crucifixion	27:45–50	15:33–37
146	Witnesses of Jesus' death	23:47–49	1	C	Soon after Jesus has died	27:51–56	15:38–41

ANNEXURE 3.1: NARRATIVE ACCOUNTS IN THE SYNOPTIC GOSPELS

	Narrative Description	Luke[1]	Category[2]	Writing Order[2]	Time[2]	Matthew	Mark[3]
147	Procurement of Jesus' body	23:50–52	1	C	After the "witnesses of Jesus' death" account	27:57–58	15:42–45
148	Jesus' body placed in a tomb	23:53–54	1	C	After the "procurement of Jesus' body" event	27:59–60	15:46
149	The tomb watched by the women and guarded by soldiers	23:55–56	1	C	After Jesus' body is placed in a tomb	27:61–66	15:47
150	The stone rolled away	—	—	—	—	28:2–4	—
151	The tomb found empty by the women	24:1–8	1	C	After the "tomb watched by the women and guarded by the soldiers" event	28:1, 5–8	16:1–8
152	The tomb found empty by Peter and John	24:9–12	1	C	After the "tomb found to be empty by the women" event	—	—
153	Jesus appears to the other women	—	—	—	—	28:9–10	—
154	Report of the soldiers to the Jewish authorities	—	—	—	—	28:11–15	—
155	Jesus appears to the two disciples traveling to Emmaus	24:13–35	1	C	After the tomb is found empty by the women and Peter and John	—	—

Annexure 3.1: Narrative Accounts in the Synoptic Gospels

	Narrative Description	Luke[1]	Category[2]	Writing Order[2]	Time[2]	Matthew	Mark[3]
156	Jesus appears to the assembled disciples in Jerusalem	24:36–49	1	C (overlapping chronology is used in 24:46)	After Jesus' appearance to the two disciples travelling to Emmaus	28:16–20	—
157	Christ's parting blessing and departure	24:50–53	1	C	After Jesus' appearance to the assembled disciples	—	—

1. Luke 1:1–4 is the preface of the book and is not a narrative account, therefore it is not included in this harmony.
2. Refer 3.0 for the meanings of categories 1, 2 and 3. Only Luke's accounts are assessed. Refer to detailed discussion of the time of each account in chapter 3.
3. Mark 1:1 "the beginning of the gospel of Jesus Christ [the son of God]" (Ἀρχὴ τοῦ εὐαγγελίου Ἰησοῦ Χριστοῦ [υἱοῦ θεοῦ]) likely serves as a heading or an introductory note to the Gospel. Since it is not a narrative phrase, it is not included in this harmony.
4. C = Chronological, T = Thematic, U = Unknown
5. N/A = not applicable. The section is about Jesus' genealogy, since it is not a narrative account it is not categorized.
6. The first Jewish phase of Jesus' trial (before Annas) is recorded in John 18:13–14 but not in any of the synoptic gospels. It most likely happens after the "Jesus betrayed, arrested and forsaken" event and before the "Peter's denials" event.

Bibliography

AELIAN. 1997. Historical miscellany. Translated from the Greek by N. G. Wilson. Cambridge, MA: Harvard University Press.

ALAND, K. 2001. Synopsis of the four gospels. Stuttgart, Germany: Deutsche Bibelgesellschaft. Available: Logos Bible Software, v. 5.

ALDEN, R.L. 1988. Jericho. (*In* Baker Encyclopedia of the Bible, p. 1118–1120. Available: Logos Bible Software, v. 5.)

ANDERSON, H.G. 2009. Bethany. (*In* Zondervan Encyclopedia of the Bible, 1:562–563. Available: Logos Bible Software, v. 6.)

ANON. 1988. Bethany. (*In* Baker Encyclopedia of the Bible, p. 284–285. Available: Logos Bible Software, v. 5.)

ANON. 1988. Bethphage. (*In* Baker Encyclopedia of the Bible, p. 291. Available: Logos Bible Software, v. 5.)

ANON. 1988. Feasts and Festivals of Israel. (*In* Baker Encyclopedia of the Bible, p. 783–788. Available: Logos Bible Software, v. 5.)

ARISTOTLE, LONGINUS & DEMETRIUS. 1995. Aristotle: the poetics; Longinus: on the sublime; Demetrius: on style. Translated from the Greek by S. Halliwell, W.H. Fyfe & D.C. Innes. Cambridge, MA: Harvard University Press.

AUNE, D.E. 1987. The New Testament in its literary environment. Philadelphia, PA: The Westminster Press.

BABAN, O. 2006. On the road encounters in Luke-Acts: Hellenistic mimesis and Luke's theology of the way. Milton Keynes, UK: Paternoster. Available: Logos Bible Software, v. 6.

BAILEY, K.E. 1983. Poet & peasant and through peasant eyes: a literary-cultural approach to the parables in Luke. Combined ed. Grand Rapids, MI: Eerdmans. Available: Logos Bible Software, v. 6.

BARRETT, C.K. 2004. A critical and exegetical commentary on the acts of the apostles. Edinburgh, UK: T&T Clark. Available: Logos Bible Software, v. 6.

BAUER, W. 2000. A Greek-English lexicon of the New Testament and other early Christian literature. 3rd ed. (BDAG). Danker, F., ed. Chicago, IL: University of Chicago Press. Available: Logos Bible Software, v. 6.

BEBB, L.J.M. 1911-1912. Luke, gospel of. (*In* Hastings, J. et al., *eds.* A dictionary of the Bible: dealing with its language, literature, and contents including the biblical theology. Edinburgh, UK: T & T Clark. 3:162-173. Available: Logos Bible Software, v. 6.)

BIBLE. 1935. Septuaginta. Stuttgart, Germany: Deutsche Bibelgesellschaft. Available: Bibleworks, v. 9.

BIBLE. 1971. Revised standard version of the Bible (RSV). United States of America: Eerdmans and Zondervan. Available: Bibleworks, v. 9.

BIBLE. 1989. New revised standard version of the Bible (NRSV), United States of America: Division of Christian Education of the National Council of the Churches of Christ. Available: Bibleworks, v. 10.

BIBLE. 1989. Revised English Bible (REB). UK: Oxford and Cambridge Universities Presses. Available: Bibleworks, v. 7.

BIBLE. 1993. Novum testamentum graece. 27th ed. Stuttgart, Germany: Deutsche Bibelgesellschaft. Available: Bibleworks, v. 9.

BIBLE. 1994. The Greek new testament. 4th rev. ed. Stuttgart, Germany: United Bible Societies.

BIBLE. 1996-2006. New English translation of the Bible (NET). United States of America: Biblical Studies Press. Available: Bibleworks, v. 9.

BIBLE. 2011. English standard version of the Bible (ESV). Wheaton, IL: Crossway Bibles. Available: Bibleworks, v. 9.

BIBLE. 2011. New international version of the Bible (NIV). Grand Rapids, MI: Zondervan. Available: Bibleworks, v. 9.

BIBLE. 2014. Chronological study Bible: New International version. Nashville, TN: Thomas Nelson.

BLASS, F., DEBRUNNER, A. & FUNK, R.W. 1961. A Greek grammar of the New Testament and other early Christian literature. (BDF). Chicago, IL: University of Chicago Press.

BLIGHT, R.C. 2008. An exegetical summary of Luke 1-11. Dallas, TX: SIL International. Available: Logos Bible Software, v. 5.

BLOMBERG, C.L. 1992. Gospels: historical reliability. (*In* Dictionary of Jesus and the Gospels, p. 292-297. Available: Logos Bible Software, v. 6.)

BLOMBERG, C.L. 1992. Matthew. Nashville, TN: Broadman & Holman. Available: Logos Bible Software, v. 6.

BLOMBERG, C.L. 2009. Jesus and the gospels: an introduction and survey. 2nd ed. Nashville, TN: B&H Academic. Available: Logos Bible Software, v. 6.

BOCK, D.L. 1991. Understanding Luke's task: carefully building on precedent (Luke 1:1-4). *Criswell Theological Review* 5:183-201, Spring.

BOCK, D.L. 1992. Luke, gospel of. (*In* Dictionary of Jesus and the Gospels, p. 495-510. Available: Logos Bible Software, v. 6.)

BOCK, D.L. 1996. Luke. Grand Rapids, MI: Zondervan. Available: Logos Bible Software, v. 6.

BOCK, D.L. 2004. Luke. 2 vols. Grand Rapids, MI: Baker Academic. Available: Logos Bible Software, v. 5.

BOCK, D.L. 2007. Acts. Grand Rapids, MI: Baker Academic. Available: Logos Bible Software, v. 6.
BOVON, F. 2002. Luke. Vol. 1. Minneapolis, MN: Augsburg Fortress.
BRENTON, L.C.L. 1998-1999. The English translation of the Septuagint version of the Old Testament. London: Samuel Bagster and Sons. Available: Bibleworks, v. 9.
BRIGHTON, M.A. 2009. The sicarii in Josephus's Judean war: rhetorical analysis and historical observations. Atlanta, GA: Society of Biblical Literature.
BROWN, S. 1978. The role of the prologues in determining the purpose of Luke-Acts. (*In* Talbert, C.H., *ed.* Perspectives on Luke-Acts. Edinburgh, UK: T. & T. Clark. p. 99–111).
BRUCE, F.F. 1988. The book of the Acts. Grand Rapids, MI: Eerdmans. Available: Logos Bible Software, v. 6.
BULTMANN, R. 1962. The Study of the synoptic gospels. (*In* Form criticism: two essays on New Testament research. Translated from German by Frederick Grant. New York, NY: Harper & Brothers. p. 11–75.)
CADBURY, H.J. 1999. The making of Luke-Acts. Peabody, MA: Hendrickson.
CARROLL, J.T. 2012. Luke. Grand Rapids, MI: Zondervan. Available: Logos Bible Software, v. 7.
CARSON, D.A. 1984. Matthew. (*In* Gæbelein, F., *ed.* Matthew, Mark, Luke. Grand Rapids, MI: Zondervan. p. 1–600. Available: Logos Bible Software, v. 5.)
CARSON, D.A. 1991. The gospel according to John. Grand Rapids, MI: Eerdmans. Available: Logos Bible Software, v. 5.
CCD (Collins Cobuild Advanced Learner's English Dictionary). 2003. "Etymology". [CD].
CHARLES, R.H. 1913. The apocrypha and pseudepigrapha of the Old Testament in English. 2 vols. Oxford, UK: Clarendon Press. Available: Bibleworks, v. 7.
CHARLES, R.H. 1966. The Greek Versions of the Testaments of the Twelve Patriarchs. Hildesheim, Germany: Oxford University Press.
CRADDOCK, F.B. 1990. Luke. Louisville, KY: John Knox Press. Available: Logos Bible Software, v. 6.
CREED, J.M. 1960. The gospel according to St. Luke: the Greek text with introduction, notes, and indices. London, UK: Macmillan & Co Ltd.
DAVIES, W.D. & ALLISON D.C. 1988. A critical and exegetical commentary on the Gospel according to Saint Matthew. London, UK: T&T Clark International. Available: Logos Bible Software, v. 5.
DEISSMANN, A. 1995. Light from the ancient East: the New Testament illustrated by recently discovered texts of the Graeco-Roman world. Peabody, MA: Hendrickson.
DIBELIUS, M. 2004. The book of Acts: form, style, and theology. Minneapolis, MN: Fortress Press. Available: Logos Bible Software, v. 6.
EASTON, B.S. 1926. The gospel according to St. Luke: a critical and exegetical commentary. Edinburgh, UK: T & T Clark.
EDWARDS, H.J. 1922. Introduction. (*In* Polybius' the histories. Translated from Greek by W. R. Paton, p. vii-xvi. New York, NY: G. P. Putnam's Sons. Available: Logos Bible Software, v. 6.)
EDWARDS, J.R. 2002. The gospel according to Mark. Grand Rapids, MI: Eerdmans. Available: Logos Bible Software, v. 5.
ELLIS, E.E. 1974. The gospel of Luke. Greenwood, SC: Attic Press.

EUSEBIUS. 1965. The ecclesiastical history. Translated from the Greek by Kirsopp Lake. 2 vols. Cambridge, MA: Harvard University Press. (Loeb Classical Library.)

EUSEBIUS. 1983. The history of the church from Christ to Constantine. Translated from the Greek by G. A. Williamson. Middlesex, UK: Dorset Press.

EUSEBIUS. 2007. The church history. Translated from the Greek by P. L. Maier. Grand Rapids, MI: Kregel.

EVANS, C.A. 1990. Luke. Peabody, MA: Hendrickson.

EWING, W. & HUGHS, R.J. 1979-1988. Ephraim. (*In* The International Standard Bible Encyclopedia, Rev. ed. 2: 119. Available: Logos Bible Software, v. 6.)

FAITHLIFE CORPORATION. 2016. Thucydides. (*In* Logos Bible Software Factbook. Available: https://ref.ly/logos4/Factbook;ref=bio.thucydides.)

FARRELL, H.K. 1986. The structure and theology of Luke's central section. *Trinity Journal*, 7(2):33-54, Fall.

FEE, D. G. 2002. New Testament exegesis. Louisville, KY: Westminster John Knox Press, 2002.

FELIX, P.W. 1997. Literary dependence and Luke's prologue. *Master's Seminary Journal* 8(1):61-82, Spring.

FINLEY, M.I. 1971. The portable Greek historians: the essence of Herodotus, Thucydides, Xenophon, PolyBius. New York, NY: The Viking Press.

FITZMYER, J.A. 2008. The acts of the apostles: a new translation with introduction and commentary. New Haven, CT: Yale University Press. Available: Logos Bible Software, v. 6.

FITZMYER, J.A. 2008. The gospel according to Luke I-IX: introduction, translation, and notes. New Haven, CT: Yale University Press. Available: Logos Bible Software, v. 6.

FRANCE, R.T. 2002. The gospel of Mark: a commentary on the Greek text. Grand Rapids, MI: Eerdmans. Available: Logos Bible Software, v. 5.

FRANCE, R.T. 2007. The gospel of Matthew. Grand Rapids, MI: Eerdmans. Available: Logos Bible Software, v. 5.

GARLAND, D.E. 2011. Luke. Grand Rapids, MI: Zondervan. Available: Logos Bible Software, v. 6.

GEISLER, N.L. 1999. Baker encyclopedia of Christian apologetics. Grand Rapids, MI: Baker Books. Available: Logos Bible Software, v. 6.

GELDENHUYS, N. 1975. Commentary on the Gospel of Luke. Grand Rapids, MI: Eerdmans. Available: Logos Bible Software, v. 6.

GILL, D.H. 1970. Observations on the Lukan travel narrative and some related passages. *Harvard Theological Review*, 63(2):199-221, April.

GODET, F.L. 1881. A commentary on the gospel of St. Luke. New York, NY: I. K. Funk & Co. Available: Logos Bible Software, v. 6.

GOULD, E.P. 1896. A critical and exegetical commentary on the gospel according to St. Mark. Edinburgh, UK: T & T Clark. Available: Logos Bible Software, v. 5.

GREEN, J.B. 1997. The gospel of Luke. Grand Rapids, MI: Eerdmans. Available: Logos Bible Software, v. 6.

GRENFELL, B. & HUNT, A., eds. 1898-1994. Oxyrhynchus papyri. 18 vols. London, UK: Egypt Exploration.

GUNN, W.M. 1870. Philostratus (Φιλόστρατος). (*In* Smith, W., ed. Dictionary of Greek and Roman biography and mythology, 3:323-328. Available: Logos Bible Software, v. 7.)

GUTHRIE, D. 1996. New testament introduction. Downers Grove, IL: InterVarsity Press. Available: Logos Bible Software, v. 6.
GUTHRIE, D. 2009. Jesus Christ. (*In* Zondervan Encyclopedia of the Bible, 3:567–661. Available: Logos Bible Software, v. 6.)
HAGNER, D.A. 1998. Matthew 1–13. Dallas: Word. Available: Logos Bible Software, v. 6.
HAGNER, D.A. 2009. Pharisee. (*In* The Zondervan Encyclopedia of the Bible, 4:842–852. Available: Logos Bible Software, v. 6.)
HATCH, E. & REDPATH, H.A. 1998. A concordance to the Septuagint and other Greek versions of the Old Testament (including the apocryphal books). Grand Rapids, MI: Baker Books.
HENDRIKSEN, W. 1978. Luke. Grand Rapids, MI: Baker Book House.
HERNÁDEZ, J.J. 2013. Textual criticism. (*In* Green, J. B. et al., *eds*. Dictionary of Jesus and the Gospels. 2nd ed. Downers Grove, IL: InterVarsity Press. p. 959–963. Available: Logos Bible Software, v. 6.)
HERODOTUS. 1946. The Persian wars. Translated from the Greek by A.D. Godley. 4 vols. Cambridge, MA: Harvard University Press. (Loeb Classical Library.)
HOLMES, M.W. 1999. Apostolic fathers: Greek texts and English translations. Grand Rapids, MI: Baker Books.
HOOKER, M.D. 2006. The gospel according to St Mark. London, UK: Continuum. Available: Logos Bible Software, v. 5.
HORSELY, G.H.R., ed. 1981–1989. New documents illustrating early Christianity: a review of the Greek inscriptions and papyri. North Ryde, Australia: Ancient History Qumran Documentary Research Centre, Macquarie University.
HUME, D.A. 2011. The early Christian community: a narrative analysis of Acts 2:41–47 and 4:32–35. Tübingen, Germany: Laupp & Göbel.
JOSEPHUS. 1926. Works. Translated from the Greek by H.J. Thackeray and R. Marcus. 13 vols. Cambridge, MA: Harvard University Press. (Loeb Classical Library.)
JOSEPHUS. 1987. The works of Josephus: complete and unabridged. Translated from the Greek by W. Whiston. Peabody, MA: Hendrickson. Available: Logos Bible Software, v. 6.
KAISER, W.C., DAVIDS, P.H., BRUCE, F.F. & BRAUCH, M.T. 1996. Hard sayings of the Bible. Downers Grove, IL: InterVarsity. Available: Logos Bible Software, v. 5.
KEENER, C.S. 2012. Acts. Vol. 1: introduction and 1:1–2:47. Grand Rapids, MI: Baker Academic.
KIRSOPP, L. 1926–1932. Introduction. (*In* Page, T. E. et al., *eds*. The Ecclesiastical History. Translated from Greek by L. Kirsopp, 2 vols, p.v–xxxiv. Cambridge, MA: Harvard University Press. Available: Logos Bible Software, v. 6.)
KISTEMAKER, S. 1982. The structure of Luke's gospel. *Journal of the Evangelical Theological Society*, 25(1):33–39, March.
KOHLENBERGER III, J.R., GOODRICK, E.W. & SWANSON, J.A. 1995. The exhaustive concordance to the Greek New Testament. Grand Rapids, MI: Zondervan.
KOHLENBERGER III, J.R., GOODRICK, E.W. & SWANSON, J.A. 1997. The Greek-English concordance to the New Testament with the New International Version (GECNT). Grand Rapids, MI: Zondervan.
KÖSTENBERGER, A.J. 2004. John. Grand Rapids, MI: Baker Academic. Available: Logos Bible Software, v. 5.

LAFAYE, G., ed. 1927. Inscriptiones Graecae ad res Romanas pertinentes – inscriptiones Asiae II. Chicago, IL: Ares Publishers.

LAKE, K., ed. 1912-13. The Apostolic fathers. 2 vols. London, UK: Heinemann; Macmillan. Available: Bibleworks, v. 9.

LANGE, J.P. & VAN OOSTERZEE, J.J. 2008. A commentary on the holy scriptures: Luke. Bellingham, WA: Logos Bible Software. Available: Logos Bible Software, v. 6.

LEIFELD, W.L. 1984. Luke. (*In* Gæbelein, F., *ed*. Matthew, Mark, Luke. Grand Rapids, MI: Zondervan. p. 795–1059. Available: Logos Bible Software, v. 6.)

LIDDELL, H.G. & and SCOTT, R. 1996. A Greek-English lexicon. (LSJ). Oxford, UK: Clarendon Press. Available: Logos Bible Software, v. 6.

LOCKWOOD, G. J. 1995. The reference to order in Luke's preface. *Concordia Theological Quarterly*, 59 (1–2):101–104.

LONG, F.J. 2005. Kairos: a beginning Greek grammar. Mishawaka, IN: Available: Logos Bible Software, v. 7.

LONG, G. 1870. Pausanias (Παυσανίας). (*In* Smith, W., ed. Dictionary of Greek and Roman biography and mythology, 3:161–162. Available: Logos Bible Software, v. 7.)

LUCIAN. 1999. Lucian. Translated from the Greek by K. Kilburn. Vol. VI. Cambridge, MA: Harvard University Press.

LUZ, U. 2007. Matthew 1–7. Minneapolis, MN: Fortress Press. Available: Logos Bible Software, v. 6.

MARSHALL, H.I. 1978. The gospel of Luke: a commentary on the Greek text. Exeter, UK: Paternoster Press. Available: Logos Bible Software, v. 6.

MARSHALL, H.I. 1980. Acts: an introduction and commentary. Downers Grove, IL: InterVarsity Press. Available: Logos Bible Software, v. 6.

MARSHALL, H.I. 1988. Luke: historian and theologian. Downers Grove, IL: InterVarsity Press.

MATTHEWSON, D. 2007. Exegesis of Matthew: class lectures at Gordon-Conwell Theological Seminary. Hamilton, Massachusetts.

MCCOMISKEY, D.S. 2004. Lukan Theology in the light of the gospel's literary structure. Milton Keynes, UK: Paternoster. Available: Logos Bible Software, v. 6.

MCKNIGHT, S. 1992. Matthew, gospel of. (*In* Dictionary of Jesus and the gospels, p. 526–541. Available: Logos Bible Software, v. 5.)

MCLAREN, J.S. 2010. Josephus, Jewish War. (*In* Collins J. J. & Harlow D.C., *eds*. The Eerdmans dictionary of Early Judaism, p. 838–841. Available: Logos Bible Software, v. 6.)

METZGER, B.M. 1994. A textual commentary on the Greek New Testament. Stuttgart, Germany: Deutsche Bibelgesellschaft/German Bible Society. Available: Logos Bible Software, v. 6.

METZGER, B.M. & EHRMAN, B.D. 2005. The text of the New Testament. New York, NY: Oxford University Press.

MOESSNER, D.P. 1983. Luke 9:1–50: Luke's preview of the journey of the prophet like Moses of Deuteronomy. *Journal of Biblical Literature*, 102(4):575–606, December.

MOESSNER, D.P. 1999. The appeal and power of poetics (Luke 1:1–4): Luke's superior credentials (παρηκολουθηκότι), narrative sequence (καθεξῆς), and firmness of understanding (ἀσφάλειαν) for the reader. (*In* Moessner D.P., *ed*. Jesus and the heritage of Israel. Harrisburg, PA: Trinity. p. 84–123).

MORRIS, L. 1988. Luke: an introduction and commentary. Downers Grove, IL: InterVarsity Press. Available: Logos Bible Software, v. 6.
MORRIS, L. 1992. The gospel according to Matthew. Grand Rapids, MI: Eerdmans. Available: Logos Bible Software, v. 6.
MORRIS, L. 1995. Luke. Grand Rapids, MI: Eerdmans. Available: Logos Bible Software, v. 6.
MOULTON, J.H. & MILLIGIAN, G. 1930. The vocabulary of the Greek Testament. London, UK: Hodder & Stoughton. Available: Logos Bible Software, v. 6.
NOLLAND, J. 1989-1993. Luke. 3 vols. Dallas, TX: Word Books. Available: Logos Bible Software, v. 6.
NOLLAND, J. 2005. A gospel of Matthew. Grand Rapids, MI: Eerdmans. Available: Logos Bible Software, v. 5.
OPPIANUS. 1928. Oppian. Colluthus. Tryphiodorus. Translated from the Greek by A. W. Mair. New York, NY: G.P. Putnam's Sons.
PAO, D.W. & SCHNABEL, E.J. 2007. Luke. (*In* Commentary on the New Testament use of the Old Testament, p. 251-414. Available: Logos Bible Software, v. 6.)
PAUSANIAS. 1992. Description of Greece. Translated from the Greek by W. H. S. Jones. 4 vols. Cambridge, MA: Harvard University Press. (Loeb Classical Library.)
PETERSON, D.G. 2009. The Acts of the Apostles. Grand Rapids, MI: Eerdmans. Available: Logos Bible Software, v. 6.
PHILOSTRATUS. 1989. The Life of Apollonius of Tyana. Translated from the Greek by F. C. Conybeare. 2 vols. Cambridge, MA: Harvard University Press. (Loeb Classical Library.)
PINKER, A. 2006. Nahum and the Greek Tradition on Nineveh's Fall. *The Journal of Hebrew Scriptures*, 6(8): 3-4.
PLESSIS, D.I.I. 1974. Once more: the purpose of Luke's prologue (Lk 1:1-4). *Novum Testamentum*, 16:259-271, October.
PLUMMER, A. 1922. A critical and exegetical commentary on the gospel according to S. Luke. Edinburgh, UK: T & T Clark. Available: Logos Bible Software, v. 6.
PLUTARCH. 1969. Moralia. Translated from the Greek by Paul A. Clement. 15 vols. Cambridge, MA: Harvard University Press. (Loeb Classical Library.)
POLYBIUS. 1979. The Histories. Translated from the Greek by W. R. Paton. 6 vols. Cambridge, MA: Harvard University Press. (Loeb Classical Library.)
PORTER, S.E. 1999. Idioms of the Greek New Testament. London, UK: Continuum. Available: Logos Bible Software, v. 6.
REILING, J. & SWELLENGREBEL, J.L. 1993. A handbook on the Gospel of Luke. New York, NY: United Bible Societies. Available: Logos Bible Software, v. 5.
RESSEGUIE, J.L. 1982. Point of view in the central section of Luke (9:51-19:44). *Journal of the Evangelical Theological Society*, 25(1):41-47, March.
ROBERTS, A. & DONALDSON, J., eds. 1885-96. The ante-Nicene fathers. Buffalo, NY: The Christian Literature Publishing Company. Available: Bibleworks, v. 9.
ROBERTSON, A. T. 1920. Luke the historian in the light of research. Grand Rapids, MI: Baker.
ROBERTSON, A. T. 1930-1933. Word pictures in the New Testament. 6 vols. Nashville, TN: Broadman Press. Available: Logos Bible Software, v. 6.
ROBERTSON, A. T. 1934. A grammar of the Greek New Testament in the light of historical research. Nashville, TN: Broadman Press. Available : Logos Bible Software, v. 6.

ROBINSON, W.C. 1960. The theological context for interpreting Luke's travel narrative (9:51ff). *Journal of Biblical Literature*, 79(1):20-31, March.

RYKEN, L., WILHOIT J.C. & LONGMAN III, T., eds. 1998. Dictionary of Biblical Imagery. Downers Grove, IL: InterVarsity Press. Available: Logos Bible Software, v. 5.

SCHAFF, P., ed. 1997. The Nicene and post-Nicene fathers of the Christian church. 14 vols. Grand Rapids, MI: T&T Clark. Available: Logos Bible Software, v. 6.

SCHNABEL, E.J. 2012. Acts. Expanded digital edition. Grand Rapids, MI: Zondervan. Available: Logos Bible Software, v. 6.

SCHÜRER, E. 2007 (electronic edition from edition originally published by T & T Clark in 1890). The history of the Jewish people in the age of Jesus Christ. 5 vols. Edinburgh, UK. Available: Logos Bible Software, v. 5.

SILVA, M. 1983. Biblical words and their meanings: an introduction to lexical semantics. Grand Rapids, MI: Zondervan.

SNEEN, D.J. 1971. Exegesis of Luke 1:1-4 with special regard to Luke's purpose as a historian. *Expository Times*, 83: 40-43, November.

SPENCER, A.B. 1998. Paul's literary style. Lanham, MD: University Press of America.

SPENCER, A.B. 2007. Exegesis of the gospel of Luke: lecture cassette tape 3B. (Given at Gordon-Conwell Theological Seminary).

SPENCER, W.D. 2016. Written communication with the author. Hamilton, Massachusetts.

SPENCER, W.D. & SPENCER, A.B. 2001. How to write a New Testament exegesis paper. (Teaching manual for the New Testament interpretation course at Gordon-Conwell Theological Seminary in 2001). MA. (Unpublished.)

STEIN, R.H. 1992. Luke. Nashville, TN: Broadman & Holman Publishers. Available: Logos Bible Software, v. 6.

STRAUSS, M. 1995. The Davidic Messiah in Luke-Acts: the promise and its fulfillment in Lukan Christology. Sheffield, UK: Sheffield Academic Press. Available: Logos Bible Software, v. 6.

STRAUSS, M. 2002. Luke. (*In* Zondervan Illustrated Bible Backgrounds Commentary, 1:318-516. Available: Logos Bible Software, v. 5.)

TALBERT, C.H. 2002. Reading Luke: a literary and theological commentary on the third gospel. Rev. ed. Macon, GA: Symth & Helwys. Available: Logos Bible Software, v. 6.

TANNEHILL, R.C. 1986. The narrative unity of Luke-Acts: a literary interpretation. Philadelphia, PA: Fortress Press. Available: Logos Bible Software, v. 6.

THAYER, J.H. 1930. A Greek-English lexicon for the New Testament. London, UK: T & T Clark. Available: Bibleworks, v. 9.

THOMAS, R.L. & GUNDRY, S.N. 1988. The NIV harmony of the gospels. New York, NY: HarperCollins.

THOMPSON, G.H.P. 1972. The gospel according to Luke. Oxford, UK: Clarendon Press.

THUCYDIDES. 1934. The complete writings of Thucydides: the Peloponnesian war. Translated from the Greek by Joseph Gavorse. New York, NY: Randon House.

THUCYDIDES. 1996. History of the Peloponnesian war. Translated from the Greek by C. F. Smith. 4 vols. Cambridge, MA: Harvard University Press. (Loeb Classical Library.)

TIEDE, D.L. 1988. Luke. Minneapolis, MN: Augsburg Publishing House. Available: Logos Bible Software, v. 6.

TISCHENDORF, K.V., ed. 1866. Apocalypses apocryphae Mosis, Esdrae, Pauli, Iohannis: item Mariae dormitio, additis Evangeliorum et actuum Apocryphorum supplementis. Georg Olms Verlagsbughhandlung, Hildesheim: Reprografischer Nachdruck der Ausgabe Leipzig.

TURNER, D.L. 2008. Matthew. Grand Rapids, MI: Baker Academic. Available: Logos Bible Software, v. 6.

WALBANK, F.W. 1957. A historical commentary on Polybius vol. 1: commentary on books I-VI. Oxford, UK: Clarendon Press. https://www.scribd.com/doc/276712121/ Frank-W-Walbank-a-Historical-Commentary-on-Polybius-Vol-1-Commentary-on-Books-1-6-1957 Date of access: 22 June 2016.

WARMINGTON, E.H., ed. 1973. Aristotle: the poetics; Longinus: on the sublime; Demetrius: on style. Translated from the Greek by S. Halliwell, D.A. Russell & D.C. Innes. Cambridge, MA: Harvard University Press. (Loeb Classical Library.)

WILKINS, M.J. 2004. Matthew. Grand Rapids, MI: Zondervan. Available: Logos Bible Software, v. 5.

WOODS, E.J. 2001. The "finger of God" and pneumatology in Luke-Acts. Sheffield, UK: Sheffield Academic Press. Available: Logos Bible Software, v. 6.

XENOPHON. 1968. Anabasis. Translated from the Greek by Carleton L. Brownson. Cambridge, MA: Harvard University Press. (Loeb Classical Library.)

YOUNGER, K.L. 1990. Ancient conquest accounts: a study in Ancient Near Eastern and biblical history writing. Sheffield, UK: JSOT Press.

ZERWICK, M.S.J. & GROSVENOR, M. 1996. A grammatical analysis of the Greek New Testament. Rome, Italy: Biblical Institute Press. Available: Logos Bible Software, v. 5.

Index

Note: Greek terms are sorted by their English transliterations (e.g. παρακολουθέω is sorted at the 'p' section). Entries under certain headings are arranged in biblical rather than alphabetical order (e.g. Mark, chronological writing order, etc.)

Acts of Peter, 197
Acts preface
  compared to Greco-Roman historical texts, 36–40
  grammatical analysis, 43–47
  literary analysis, 36, 40–43
  overlapping summary statement in Luke, 188, 190
  overlapping summary statements in preface and book, 188–89, 198
  textual analysis, 35
Aelian, 59
Against Apion (Josephus), 21, 28–29, 40, 46
ἀκριβῶς (carefully), 21, 32
Aland, K., 107
Alden, R. L., 155–56
Allison, D. C., 97
Anabasis (Xenophon), 25–26, 200–202
ἀνατάξαςθαι (to compile), 23
Anderson, H. G., 134nn93–94

Anna and Simeon, 74
Annas, 179n115, 181
ἄνωθεν (from the beginning/from above), 21, 31–32
Antiochus Astrol., 62–63
Antiquities (Josephus), 21, 29, 40, 73n59
Apocalypsis Moses, 61
ἀποϲτόλοις (apostles), 43–44
Aune, David, 197

Baban, O., 132
Bailey, K. E., 131
baptism, of Jesus, 79–80
Bartimaeus, 155–57
BDAG, 20n12, 23–24n15, 48, 49n38, 52, 53, 56, 57, 58
BDF (Blass, Debrunner, Funk), 19n11, 43
Bebb, L. J. M., 133, 221
Blomberg, Craig, 4, 131

INDEX

Bock, Darrell L., 12n8, 14, 19–20n11, 23, 43, 74, 81n63, 82, 86n64, 88, 92–93, 95, 107–8, 115, 130, 135, 140–41, 143, 147, 156, 175, 221
Bovon, François, 12n8, 13, 14, 15, 82
Brenton, L. C. L., 54
Brighton, Mark, 197
broad chronological order, 13–14
Brown, S., 15
Bultmann, Rudolph, 3

Cadbury, Henry, 13, 198
Caiaphas, 179n115, 181
Carson, D. A., 85, 88, 101, 104–5, 179n115
CCD (Collins Cobuild Advanced Learner's English Dictionary), 51
census, 73
centurion's servant, healing of, 105
Charles, R. H., 60
chiastic writing structure, 131, 133–34
Christology, 129–30, 133
Chronological Study Bible, 135n96
chronological writing order
   in Greco-Roman historical texts, 24–30, 38–40
   scholarship on Luke's, 1n2, 12–15, 69–70
   birth of John the Baptist foretold to Zechariah (1:5–25), 70–71
   Jesus' birth foretold to Mary (1:26–38), 71
   Mary's visit to Elizabeth (1:39–56), 71–72
   birth of John the Baptist (1:57–80), 72–73
   Jesus' birth and shepherds' encounter with angels (2:1–20), 73
   Jesus' circumcision (2:21), 73
   Jesus presented in temple and return to Nazareth (2:22–40), 74–77
   Jesus' Passover in Jerusalem as child (2:41–52), 77–78
   public ministry of John the Baptist (3:1–20), 78–79
   Jesus' baptism (3:21–23a), 79–80
   temptation in desert (4:1–15), 81–85
   ministry and rejection at Nazareth (4:16–30), 86–87
   teaching in Capernaum synagogue (4:31–37), 87–90
   healing of Peter's mother-in-law (4:38–39), 88, 90–91
   healing of others (4:40–44), 91–94
   calling of Peter (5:1–11), 94–95
   healing of leper (5:12–16), 96–97
   healing of paralytic (5:17–26), 97–98
   calling of Matthew (5:27–39), 98–99
   work on Sabbath (6:1–5), 99–102
   healing of man with withered hand (6:6–11), 103
   choosing the twelve (6:12–16), 103–4
   Sermon on the Plain (6:17–49), 104–5
   healing centurion's servant (7:1–10), 105
   raising widow's son (7:11–17), 105–6
   question from John the Baptist (7:18–35), 106
   preaching in various cities and villages (8:1–3), 108–9
   parable of the soils (8:4–18), 109–11
   announcement of new spiritual kinship (8:19–21), 111–16
   crossing lake and calming storm (8:22–25), 116–17
   healing Gerasene demoniacs (8:26–39), 117–18
   return to Galilee (8:40–56), 118
   commissioning the twelve (9:1–6), 119
   Herod Antipas hears about Jesus (9:7–9), 119–21
   withdrawal to Bethsaida and feeding five thousand (9:10–17), 121–22
   Jesus' first prediction of death and resurrection (9:18–27), 122–23
   Transfiguration of Jesus (9:28–36), 123–24
   healing of demoniac boy (9:37–43a), 124

Jesus' second prediction of death
 and resurrection (9:43b–45),
 124–25
rivalry over greatness in the
 kingdom (9:46–48), 125
Apostle John's question (9:49–50),
 125–26
journey through Samaria (9:51–56),
 136
complete commitment required of
 followers (9:57–62), 137
commissioning of the seventy-two
 (10:1–16), 137
return of the seventy-two (10:17–
 24), 138
story of good Samaritan (10:25–37),
 138
woes against Pharisees and teachers
 of law (11:37–54), 142
warning disciples about hypocrisy
 (12:1–12), 142–44
warning about greed and trust in
 wealth (12:13–59), 144
repent or perish (13:1–9), 144–45
anticipation of Jesus' coming death
 (13:31–35), 146
parable on proper use of money
 (16:1–13), 147–48
story on danger of wealth (16:14–
 31), 148–49
four lessons on discipleship (17:1–
 10), 150
instructions regarding Son of Man's
 coming (17:22–37), 151–52
parables on prayer (18:1–14),
 152–53
example of little children in relation
 to kingdom (18:15–17), 153
riches and the kingdom (18:18–30),
 153–54
third prediction of Jesus' death and
 resurrection (18:31–34), 154–55
healing of blind Bartimaeus and
 companion (18:35–43), 155–57
salvation of Zaccheus (19:1–10), 157
parable to teach responsibility while
 kingdom is delayed (19:11–28),
 157–58

triumphal entry into Jerusalem
 (19:29–44), 158–59
cleansing of temple (19:45–48),
 159–60
questioning of Jesus' authority
 (20:1–8), 164–65
parable of bad vineyard tenants
 (20:9–19), 165–66
attempts by Pharisees and
 Herodians to trap Jesus with
 question (20:20–26), 166–67
Sadduccees' puzzling question on
 resurrection (20:27–40), 168
Christ's relationship to David
 (20:41–44), 168–69
beware of teachers of the Law
 (20:45–47), 170
poor widow's gift (21:1–4), 170, 171
Olivet discourse (21:5–36), 171–72
Jesus' last days in Jerusalem (21:37–
 22:2), 172
Judas' agreement to betray Jesus
 (22:3–6), 172–73
preparation for Passover meal
 (22:7–13), 174
Passover meal (22:14–38), 174–78
Jesus' three agonized prayers in
 Gethsemane (22:39–46), 178
Jesus betrayed, arrested and
 forsaken (22:47–53), 178–79
Jesus' trial (22:54–23:25), 179–82
journey to Golgotha (23:26–33a),
 183
first three hours of crucifixion
 (23:33b–43), 183
last three hours of crucifixion
 (23:44–46), 184
witnesses of Jesus' death (23:47–49),
 184–85
procurement of Jesus' body (23:50–
 52), 185
Jesus' body placed in tomb (23:53–
 54), 185
tomb watched and guarded (23:55–
 56), 185–86
tomb found empty by the women
 (24:1–8), 186

284 INDEX

chronological writing order *(continued)*
    tomb found empty by Peter and
        John (24:9–12), 186–87
    Jesus appears to two disciples
        traveling to Emmaus (24:13–35),
        187
    Jesus appears to assembled disciples
        in Jerusalem (24:36–49), 188–90
    Christ's parting blessing and
        departure (24:50–53), 190
circumcision, of Jesus, 73, 74
Clement, Paul A., 58
1 Clement, 61–62
cognates, 55–57
Craddock, F. B., 74, 132, 133
Creed, J. M., 14
crucifixion, of Jesus, 183–84
Cynegetica (Oppianus Apamensis
    Epicus), 60

Danker, F., 114n78
David, Christ's relationship to, 168–69
Davies, W. D., 97
Demetrius, 22n14
Description of Greece (Pausanias),
    27–28, 206–7
Deuteronomy, 54, 131–32, 133
Dibelius, Martin, 3, 198
disciples and discipleship
    calling of, 85, 94–95, 98–99
    choosing the twelve, 103–4
    commissioning and return of the
        seventy-two, 137–38
    commissioning the twelve, 119
    cost of, 146–47
    four lessons on, 150
    Jesus' appearance to, 188–90
    warnings to, 142–45
Donaldson, J., 61

Easton, B. S., 12, 69–70
ecclesiology, 129–30, 133
ἔχω, 51, 52
ἔδοξε (it seemed), 20
Edwards, H. J., 202
Edwards, J. R., 114
ἐγένετο δὲ (and now), 177
Elizabeth, 70–72

Ellis, E. E., 13
ἐν ἐκείνῳ τῷ καιρῷ (at that time),
    99–100
ἐν οἷς (during which time), 142–43n98
ἐν τῇ ἡμέρᾳ ἐκείνῃ (in those days),
    111–12
ἐπαγγελίαν (promise), 44
ἐπειδήπερ (inasmuch as), 20, 23
ἤρξατο δὲ (and he began), 165
Eusebius, 3n3, 29–30, 210–13, 216
Evans, C. F., 133n90
Ewing, W., 134–35n95
ἑξῆς, 51, 52–55
Exodus, 54

Farrell, H. K., 131
Felix, P. W., 14
Finley, M. I., 39
Fitzmyer, J. A., 74, 82, 95, 130, 143
five thousand, feeding of, 121–22
Fragmenta (Antiochus Astrol.), 62–63
France, R. T., 97, 114

Garland, D. E., 4, 74, 105, 130
GECNT (*Greek-English Concordance to
    the New Testament*), 56
Geisler, Norman, 3
Geldenhuys, N., 13
genealogy, 80–81
Geodaesia (Heron), 63–64
geographical order, 14–15, 82, 135,
    161–63, 206–7
Gerasene demoniacs, 117–18
Gill, D. H., 130
Godet, F. L., 130
good Samaritan, 138
Gospels, and textual criticism, 3–4
Gould, E. P., 114n78
grammatical structure
    of Acts preface, 43–47
    of Luke preface, 19–24
γράψαι (to write), 23
Greco-Roman historical texts
    and Lucian on overlapping
        summary statements, 27, 72, 76,
        93, 195, 220
    objectives *vs.* themes, 189

overlapping summary statements, 199–213
overview of overlapping summary statement usage, 213–17
preface structure, 21, 36–37
terminology usage, 31–33
writing order, 24–30, 38–40
Green, J. B., 13, 23, 74, 129–30
Gundry, S. N., 75, 78, 79n61, 84, 85, 86n64, 93, 95, 96, 97, 104, 108n74, 119, 120n83, 129, 130, 140, 144, 148, 153, 154, 155, 158, 159n104, 164, 165, 167, 168, 169, 170, 171, 172, 173, 174, 175, 176, 178, 183, 184, 185, 186, 187, 188n122
Gunn, W. M., 207
Guthrie, Donald, 4, 23, 130–31

Hagner, D. A., 108n73
Hebrews (book), 19n11
Hendriksen, W., 14
Herod Antipas, 119–20, 182
Herodotus, 25, 36–37, 189
Heron, 63–64
Historical Miscellany (Aelian), 59
The Histories (Polybius), 21, 26–27, 36, 39, 202–6, 216
The History of the Church (Eusebius), 29–30, 210–13, 216
Hofmann, Johann Christian Konrad von, 3
Holmes, M. W., 61
Hooker, M. D., 114
Hughes, R. J., 134–35n95
Hume, Douglas A., 198

Inscriptiones Graecae ad res Romanas Pertinentes, 59–60
intercalation, 114
itinerant preaching, 143, 162–63

Jairus, 118
Jewish Antiquities (Josephus), 21, 29, 40, 73n59
Jewish historical texts, *see* Greco-Roman historical texts

The Jewish War (Josephus), 37, 189, 197–98, 209–10
John the Baptist, 70–73, 78–80, 84–85, 106, 120
John (Apostle), 125–26
John (Gospel)
  interpreted together with Luke, 130–31, 134–35
  imprisonment of John the Baptist (3:24), 79, 85
  Jesus anointed (12:1–8), 107–8
  Judas (13:10–11, 18–26; 17;12), 175–76
  Jesus' trial (18:13–14, 19–23), 179n115
  tomb found empty by Peter and John (20:2–10), 186–87
Josephus
  mention of census, 73n59
  objectives in writings of, 189
  order in writings of, 28–29
  overlapping summary statements in writings of, 197–98, 209–10
  preface structure in writings of, 21, 37, 40, 46
  terminology usage, 31–33
journey stories, 132, 133
Judas, 172–73, 175–76
Judges, 54

καὶ ἐγένετο ὅτε (and it was when), 101–2
καὶ ἰδοὺ (and behold), 96n69, 138, 177
Kaiser, W. C., 90
κατά, 51–52
καθεξῆς (in an orderly account)
  biblical usage, 48–50
  contemporary usage, 57–64
  etymology, 50–55
  and grammatical structure of Luke preface, 19–24
  related words, 55–57
  scholarship on, 1n2, 12–15
  and textual analysis of Luke preface, 17–19
καθώς (just as), 20
Keener, C. S., 17n9
1–2 Kings, 197

Kirsopp, L., 210
Kistemaker, S., 132–33
Kohlenberger III, J. R., 51
Köstenberger, A. J., 108n74

Lake, Kirsopp, 30
Lange, J. P., 130
Leifeld, W. L., 132
leper healings, 91, 96–97, 151
The Life (Josephus), 28
The Life of Apollonius of Tyana
    (Philostratus), 28, 37, 189,
    207–9, 216
literary order, 12–13
Lockwood, G. J., 12, 69–70
logical order, 15
Long, F. J., 55–56, 206
LSJ, 49n38, 51–52, 53, 56, 57, 58
Lucian, 27, 72, 76, 93, 195, 220
Luke narrative sequence
    broad analysis, 191–94
    theme, 189–90, 216, 223
    theological reflection, 222–24
    1:5–9:50 analysis, 126–28
    9:51–19:44, scholarship on, 129–35
    9:51–19:48 analysis, 160–63
    20:1–24:53 analysis, 190–91
    see also chronological writing
        order; entries at writing order;
        overlapping chronology and
        summary statements
Luke preface
    compared to Greco-Roman
        historical texts, 24–30
    grammatical and literary analysis,
        19–24
    textual analysis, 17–19
    word studies, 31–33

2 Maccabees, 54, 197
3 Maccabees, 54–55
Mair, A. W., 60
manuscript tradition and variants,
    17–18, 92
Marcus, R., 40
Mark
    distinctions in narrative sequence
        and content, 84–85, 104n71,
        111–16, 119n82, 123n87,
        124n88, 143, 148–50, 152,
        157n101, 164–65nn105–106,
        169nn109–10, 173nn111–12,
        183n116, 187n121
    ministries outside Galilee, 92–93
    ministry of John the Baptist (1:2–8),
        78
    Jesus' baptism (1:9–11), 80
    Jesus' temptation in desert (1:12–
        13), 81
    calling of four disciples (1:16–20),
        85, 95
    healing of Peter's mother-in-law
        (1:29–31), 88, 91
    healing of others (1:32–29), 91
    healing of leper (1:40–45), 91, 96–97
    healing of paralytic (2:1–12), 97–98
    work on Sabbath (2:23–28), 99, 102
    healing of man with withered hand
        (3:1–6), 103
    choosing the twelve (3:13–19),
        103–4
    blasphemous accusation and debate
        (3:22–27), 140–42
    announcement of new spiritual
        kinship (3:31–35), 111
    parable of the soils (4:1–25), 109,
        111
    crossing lake and calming storm
        (4:35–41), 116–17
    healing Gerasene demoniacs (5:1–
        20), 118
    return to Galilee (5:21–43), 118
    ministry in Nazareth (6:1–6a),
        86n64, 119n82
    commissioning the twelve (6:7–13),
        119
    Herod Antipas hears about Jesus
        (6:14–16), 120
    withdrawal to Bethsaida and feeding
        five thousand (6:30–44), 121–22
    Jesus' first prediction of death and
        resurrection (8:27–9:1), 122–23
    Transfiguration of Jesus (9:2–10),
        124
    healing of demoniac boy (9:14–29),
        124

Jesus' second prediction of death
and resurrection (9:30–32),
124–25
rivalry over greatness in the
kingdom (9:33–37), 125
Apostle John's question (9:38–50),
125–26
example of little children in relation
to kingdom (10:13–16), 153
riches and the kingdom (10:17–31),
154
third prediction of Jesus' death and
resurrection (10:32–34), 154–55
healing of blind Bartimaeus and
companion (10:46–52), 155–57,
158–59
triumphal entry into Jerusalem
(11:1–11), 158–59
cleansing of temple (11:15–18),
159–60
questioning of Jesus' authority
(11:27–33), 164–65
parable of bad vineyard tenants
(12:1–12), 165–66
attempts by Pharisees and
Herodians to trap Jesus with
question (12:13–17), 167
Sadducees' puzzling question on
resurrection (12:18–27), 168
Christ's relationship to David
(12:35–37), 168–69
beware of teachers of the Law
(12:38–40), 170
poor widow's gift (12:41–44), 170,
171
Olivet discourse (13:1–37), 171–72
Jesus' last days in Jerusalem (14:1–
2), 172
Jesus anointed (14:3–9), 107–8
Judas' agreement to betray Jesus
(14:10–11), 173
preparation for Passover meal
(14:12–16), 174
Passover meal (14:17–31), 175–77
Jesus' three agonized prayers in
Gethsemane (14:32–42), 178
Jesus betrayed, arrested and
forsaken (14:43–52), 178

Jesus' trial (14:53–15:15), 179–82
journey to Golgotha (15:20–23), 183
first three hours of crucifixion
(15:24–32), 183
last three hours of crucifixion
(15:33–37), 184
witnesses of Jesus' death (15:38–41),
184
procurement of Jesus' body (15:42–
45), 185
Jesus' body placed in tomb (15:46),
185
tomb watched and guarded (15:47),
186
tomb found empty by the women
(16:1–8), 186
Jesus appears to two disciples
traveling to Emmaus (16:12–13),
187
Marshall, H. I., 14, 23, 42n31, 75, 81n63,
82, 95, 132
Martyrdom of Polycarp, 61
Mary (mother of Jesus), 71
Mary Magdalene, 187
Mary and Martha, 139
Matthew (Apostle), 98–99
Matthew (Gospel)
distinctions in narrative sequence
and content, 84–85, 88–90,
102n70, 111–16, 119n82, 120–
21n84, 123n87, 124n88, 125n89,
143, 146–50, 152, 155n100,
157–58, 164–65n105, 166n107,
167n108, 169n109, 173n111,
183n116, 186n119
ministries outside Galilee, 92–93
genealogy of Jesus (1:1–17), 80–81
Jesus in Egypt and Nazareth (2:1–
23), 74–76
ministry of John the Baptist (3:1–
12), 78
Jesus' baptism (3:13–17), 80
Jesus' temptation in desert (4:1–11),
81–84
ministry and rejection at Nazareth
(4:12–17), 87
calling of four disciples (4:18–22),
85, 95

288   INDEX

Matthew (Gospel) *(continued)*
   Sermon on the Mount (5–7), 104–5
   lesson on prayer (6:9–13), 139–40
   healing of leper (8:1–4), 91, 96–97
   healing centurion's servant (8:5–13), 88, 105
   healing of Peter's mother-in-law (8:14–15), 91
   healing of others (8:16–17), 91
   crossing lake and calming storm (8:18, 23–27), 116–17
   complete commitment required of followers (8:19–22), 137
   healing Gerasene demoniacs (8:28–34), 118
   healing of paralytic (9:1–8), 97–98
   return to Galilee (9:18–26), 102n70, 118
   commissioning the twelve (10:1–11:1), 102n70, 119, 137
   question from John the Baptist (11:2–19), 102n70, 106, 120n84
   commissioning of the seventy-two (11:20–24), 102n70, 120n84, 137
   return of the seventy-two (11:25–30), 138
   work on Sabbath (12:1–8), 99–102, 120n84
   healing of man with withered hand (12:9–14), 103, 120n84
   blasphemous accusation and debate (12:22–37), 120n84, 140–42
   announcement of new spiritual kinship (12:46–50), 111, 121n84
   parable of the soils (13:1–23), 109, 111, 121n84
   ministry in Nazareth (13:54–58), 86n64, 119n82, 121n84
   Herod Antipas hears about Jesus (14:1–2), 120, 122
   withdrawal to Bethsaida and feeding five thousand (14:13–21), 121–22
   Jesus' first prediction of death and resurrection (16:13–28), 122–23
   Transfiguration of Jesus (17:1–9), 124
   healing of demoniac boy (17:14–21), 124
   Jesus' second prediction of death and resurrection (17:22–23), 124–25
   rivalry over greatness in the kingdom (18:1–5), 125
   Apostle John's question (18:6–14), 125–26
   example of little children in relation to kingdom (19:13–15), 153
   riches and the kingdom (19:16–30), 154
   third prediction of Jesus' death and resurrection (20:17–19), 154–55
   healing of blind Bartimaeus and companion (20:29–34), 155–57, 158–59
   triumphal entry into Jerusalem (21:1–11, 14–17), 158–59
   cleansing of temple (21:12–13), 159–60
   questioning of Jesus' authority (21:23–27), 164–65
   parable of bad vineyard tenants (21:33–46), 165–66
   attempts by Pharisees and Herodians to trap Jesus with question (22:15–22), 167
   Sadduccees' puzzling question on resurrection (22:23–33), 168
   Christ's relationship to David (22:41–46), 168–69
   beware of teachers of the Law (23:1–7), 170
   Olivet discourse (24:1–25:30), 171–72
   Jesus' last days in Jerusalem (26:1–5), 172
   Jesus anointed (26:6–13), 107–8
   Judas' agreement to betray Jesus (26:14–16), 173
   preparation for Passover meal (26:17–19), 174
   Passover meal (26:20–35), 175–77
   Jesus' three agonized prayers in Gethsemane (26:36–46), 178
   Jesus betrayed, arrested and forsaken (26:47–56), 178

Jesus' trial (26:57–27:26), 179–82
journey to Golgotha (27:31–34), 183
first three hours of crucifixion
    (27:35–44), 183
last three hours of crucifixion
    (27:45–50), 184
witnesses of Jesus' death (27:51–56),
    184
procurement of Jesus' body (27:57–
    58), 185
Jesus' body placed in tomb (27:59–
    60), 185
tomb watched and guarded (27:61–
    66), 186
tomb found empty by the women
    (28:1, 5–8), 186
Matthewson, David, 83
McComiskey, D. S., 132
McKnight, S., 89–90
McLaren, J. S., 209
Metzger, B. M., 17–18
Middle Liddell lexicon, 57
Moessner, D. P., 13, 131
Moralia (Plutarch), 58–59, 64
Morris, L., 15, 85, 130

narrative sequence, *see* chronological
    writing order; *entries at writing
    order*
Nolland, J., 4–5, 13, 74, 82, 97, 131

Onasander Tact., 63
Oppianus Apamensis Epicus, 60
overlapping chronology and summary
    statements
    as concept, 27, 72, 195–96, 220
    scholarship on, 197–98
    in Acts, 188–89, 198
    in Greco-Roman historical texts,
        199–213
    overview of Greco-Roman usage,
        213–17
    early life of John the Baptist (1:80),
        72–73
    early life of Jesus (2:40), 76–77
    growth of Jesus (2:52), 77–78
    imprisonment of John the Baptist
        (3:19–20), 79, 84–85
    Jesus' ministry (4:15), 84–85

    preaching in Judea (4:44), 92–94
    preaching in disciples (8:1–3),
        108–9
    sending messengers (9:51–52a), 136
    conflict with Jewish leaders (19:47–
        48), 159–60
    plot against Jesus (22:1–6), 173
    Jesus' suffering and resurrection
        (24:46), 188
    outline of Acts (24:47–53), 190

Page, T. E., 38
Pao, D. W., 131–32, 133
parables, 109–11, 121n84, 138, 139–40,
    147–48, 152–53, 157–58,
    165–66
παρακολουθέω/παρηκολουθηκότι (to
    investigate), 17n9, 22, 23, 32–33
paralytic healing, 97–98
Passover, 77–78, 174–77
Paton, W. R., 26
Pausanias, 27–28, 206–7
The Peloponnesian War (Thucydides),
    25, 37, 38–39, 199–200, 216
πεπληροφορημένων (the things having
    been accomplished), 22, 23
periodic style, 19–20n11, 43
The Persian Wars (Herodotus), 25, 37,
    189
Peter
    calling of, 94–95
    denials of, 174n113, 176, 178,
        180–81
    finds empty tomb, 186–87
Peterson, D. G., 42n31
Philo, 31–33
Philostratus, 28, 37, 189, 207–9, 216
Pilate, 182
Pinker, A., 200
Plessis, D. I. I., 15
Plummer, A., 14, 23, 74–75, 77, 82,
    92–93, 105, 130, 156
Plutarch, 58–59, 64
Polybius, 21, 26–27, 36, 39, 202–6, 216
Porter, S. E., 23
prefaces
    grammatical analysis of Acts, 43–47
    grammatical and literary analysis of
        Luke, 19–24

prefaces *(continued)*
    in Greco-Roman historical texts, 24–30, 38–40
    literary analysis of Acts, 36, 40–43
    structure, 21, 36–37
    terminology usage, 31–33
    textual analysis of Acts, 35
    textual analysis of Luke, 17–19
    see also καθεξῆς

redaction critics, 3
Reiling, J., 74, 177
Resseguie, J. L., 130
Roberts, A., 61
Robertson, A. T., 14, 22, 52, 74–75, 95
Robinson, W. C., 132

Sabbath, work on, 99–102, 120n84
salvation-historical order, 14–15
Schanbel, E. J., 42n31, 131–32, 133
Schürer, E., 73n59, 151n99, 179n115
sentence flow, as concept, 19n10
Septuagint, 54–55
Sermon on the Mount, 104–5
Sermon on the Plain, 104–5
Silva, M., 50–51
Simeon and Anna, 74
Sneen, D. J., 15
soteriology, 129–30, 133
Spencer, A. B., 22
Spencer, William David, 83
Stein, R. H., 4–5, 15, 75, 130
Strategicus (Onasander Tact.), 63
Strauss, M., 87n65, 91, 221
summary statements, *see* overlapping chronology and summary statements; prefaces
Swellengrebel, J. L., 74, 177

Talbert, C. H., 13, 131, 133–34
Tannehill, R. C., 15
temptation, of Jesus, 79, 81–85
Testament of Judah, 60
Thackeray, H. J., 28, 29
Thayer, J. H., 51
thematic writing order, 80–81, 88–89, 102n70, 117, 131, 223–24
theology, impacted by writing order, 222–24

theology of the way, 132, 133
Theophilus, 5, 80–81, 133, 191
Thomas, R. L., 75, 78, 79n61, 84, 85, 86n64, 93, 95, 96, 97, 104, 108n74, 119, 120n83, 129, 130, 140, 144, 148, 153, 154, 155, 158, 159n104, 164, 165, 167, 168, 169, 170, 171, 172, 173, 174, 175, 176, 178, 183, 184, 185, 186, 187, 188n122
Thompson, G. H. P., 13
Thucydides, 25, 37, 38–39, 199–200, 216
Tiede, D. L., 132
TLG (Thesaurus Linguae Graecae), 62
tomb, 185–87
τότε (then), 141
Transfiguration of Jesus, 123–24
transparency, 50–51

Vita Aesopi Westermanniana, 63

Walbank, F. W., 203n128
Wendel, Ulrich, 198
widow's son, raising of, 105–6
Wilkins, M. J., 97
Wilson, N. G., 59
Woods, E. J., 131
writing order
    scholarship on Luke's, 1n2, 12–15, 69–70
    theological impact, 222–24
    see also chronological writing order; overlapping chronology and summary statements; prefaces; καθεξῆς
writing order, category 1
    explained, 69
    birth of John the Baptist foretold to Zechariah (1:5–25), 70–71
    Jesus' birth foretold to Mary (1:26–38), 71
    Mary's visit to Elizabeth (1:39–56), 71–72
    birth of John the Baptist (1:57–80), 72–73
    Jesus' birth and shepherds' encounter with angels (2:1–20), 73
    Jesus' circumcision (2:21), 73

Jesus presented in temple and return to Nazareth (2:22–40), 74–77
Jesus' Passover in Jerusalem as child (2:41–52), 77–78
public ministry of John the Baptist (3:1–20), 78–79
Jesus' baptism (3:21–23a), 79–80
temptation in desert (4:1–15), 81–85
ministry and rejection at Nazareth (4:16–30), 86–87
teaching in Capernaum synagogue (4:31–37), 87–90
healing of Peter's mother-in-law (4:38–39), 88, 90–91
healing of others (4:40–44), 91–94
calling of Peter (5:1–11), 94–95
calling of Matthew (5:27–39), 98–99
Sermon on the Plain (6:17–49), 104–5
healing centurion's servant (7:1–10), 105
raising widow's son (7:11–17), 105–6
question from John the Baptist (7:18–35), 106
preaching in various cities and villages (8:1–3), 108–9
parable of the soils (8:4–18), 109–11
healing Gerasene demoniacs (8:26–39), 117–18
return to Galilee (8:40–56), 118
withdrawal to Bethsaida and feeding five thousand (9:10–17), 121–22
Transfiguration of Jesus (9:28–36), 123–24
healing of demoniac boy (9:37–43a), 124
Jesus' second prediction of death and resurrection (9:43b–45), 124–25
Apostle John's question (9:49–50), 125–26
journey through Samaria (9:51–56), 136
complete commitment required of followers (9:57–62), 137
commissioning of the seventy-two (10:1–16), 137

return of the seventy-two (10:17–24), 138
story of good Samaritan (10:25–37), 138
woes against Pharisees and teachers of law (11:37–54), 142
warning disciples about hypocrisy (12:1–12), 142–44
warning about greed and trust in wealth (12:13–59), 144
repent or perish (13:1–9), 144–45
anticipation of Jesus' coming death (13:31–35), 146
parable on proper use of money (16:1–13), 147–48
story on danger of wealth (16:14–31), 148–49
four lessons on discipleship (17:1–10), 150
instructions regarding Son of Man's coming (17:22–37), 151–52
parables on prayer (18:1–14), 152–53
example of little children in relation to kingdom (18:15–17), 153
salvation of Zaccheus (19:1–10), 157
parable to teach responsibility while kingdom is delayed (19:11–28), 157–58
triumphal entry into Jerusalem (19:29–44), 158–59
cleansing of temple (19:45–48), 159–60
questioning of Jesus' authority (20:1–8), 164–65
parable of bad vineyard tenants (20:9–19), 165–66
attempts by Pharisees and Herodians to trap Jesus with question (20:20–26), 166–67
Christ's relationship to David (20:41–44), 168–69
beware of teachers of the Law (20:45–47), 170
poor widow's gift (21:1–4), 170, 171
Jesus' last days in Jerusalem (21:37–22:2), 172
Judas' agreement to betray Jesus (22:3–6), 172–73

writing order, category 1 *(continued)*
  Passover meal (22:14-38), 174-78
  Jesus' three agonized prayers in Gethsemane (22:39-46), 178
  Jesus betrayed, arrested and forsaken (22:47-53), 178-79
  Jesus' trial (22:54-23:25), 179-82
  journey to Golgotha (23:26-33a), 183
  first three hours of crucifixion (23:33b-43), 183
  last three hours of crucifixion (23:44-46), 184
  witnesses of Jesus' death (23:47-49), 184-85
  procurement of Jesus' body (23:50-52), 185
  Jesus' body placed in tomb (23:53-54), 185
  tomb watched and guarded (23:55-56), 185-86
  tomb found empty by the women (24:1-8), 186
  tomb found empty by Peter and John (24:9-12), 186-87
  Jesus appears to two disciples traveling to Emmaus (24:13-35), 187
  Jesus appears to assembled disciples in Jerusalem (24:36-49), 188-90
  Christ's parting blessing and departure (24:50-53), 190
writing order, category 2
  explained, 69
  healing of leper (5:12-16), 96-97
  healing of paralytic (5:17-26), 97-98
  work on Sabbath (6:1-5), 99-102
  healing of man with withered hand (6:6-11), 103
  choosing the twelve (6:12-16), 103-4
  crossing lake and calming storm (8:22-25), 116-17
  commissioning the twelve (9:1-6), 119
  Herod Antipas hears about Jesus (9:7-9), 119-21
  Jesus' first prediction of death and resurrection (9:18-27), 122-23
  rivalry over greatness in the kingdom (9:46-48), 125
  riches and the kingdom (18:18-30), 153-54
  third prediction of Jesus' death and resurrection (18:31-34), 154-55
  healing of blind Bartimaeus and companion (18:35-43), 155-57
  Sadduccees' puzzling question on resurrection (20:27-40), 168
  Olivet discourse (21:5-36), 171-72
  preparation for Passover meal (22:7-13), 174
writing order, category 3
  explained, 69
  Jesus' feet anointed (7:36-50), 107-8
  announcement of new spiritual kinship (8:19-21), 111-16
  visit with Mary and Martha (10:38-42), 139
  lesson on prayer and parable of bold friend (11:1-13), 139-40
  blasphemous accusation and debate (11:14-36), 140-42
  opposition from synagogue ruler (13:10-21), 145
  question about salvation and entering the kingdom (13:22-30), 145
  healing of man with dropsy (14:1-24), 146
  cost of discipleship (14:25-35), 146-47
  parables in defense of association with sinners (15:1-32), 147
  healing of ten lepers (17:11-21), 151
writing order, uncategorized
  genealogy of Jesus (3:23b-38), 80-81

Xenophon, 25-26, 200-202

Younger, Lawson, 197

Zaccheus, 157
Zechariah, 70-71

www.ingramcontent.com/pod-product-compliance
Lightning Source LLC
Chambersburg PA
CBHW071232230426
43668CB00011B/1407